P9-CNE-599

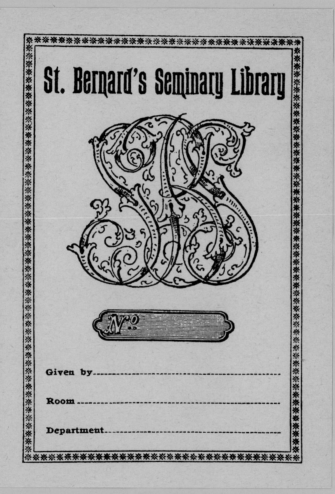

St. Bernard's Seminary Library

Nº

Given by_____

Room _____

Department_____

A LITERARY
HISTORY OF THE BIBLE

Books by Geddes MacGregor

A Literary History of the Bible

The Sense of Absence

God Beyond Doubt

The Hemlock and the Cross

The Coming Reformation

Introduction to Religious Philosophy

The Bible in the Making

Corpus Christi

The Thundering Scot

The Vatican Revolution

The Tichborne Impostor

From a Christian Ghetto

Les Frontières de la morale et de la religion

Christian Doubt

Aesthetic Experience in Religion

A LITERARY HISTORY OF THE BIBLE | FROM THE MIDDLE AGES TO THE PRESENT DAY

Geddes MacGregor

ABINGDON PRESS  NASHVILLE & NEW YORK

32,613

A LITERARY HISTORY OF THE BIBLE

Copyright © 1968 by Abingdon Press

All rights in this book are reserved.
No part of the book may be reproduced in any
manner whatsoever without written permission of
the publishers except brief quotations embodied in
critical articles or reviews. For information address
Abingdon Press, Nashville, Tennessee.

JAN 22

Library of Congress Catalog Card Number: 68-11477

Scripture quotations unless otherwise noted are from the Revised Standard Version of the Bible, copyrighted 1946 and 1952 by the Division of Christian Education, National Council of Churches, and are used by permission.

Scripture quotations noted NEB are from The New English Bible, New Testament. © the Delegates of the Oxford University Press and the Syndics of the Cambridge University Press 1961. Reprinted by permission.

Acknowledgment is made to the following for the material quoted in Chapter 33: University of Chicago Press for *The New Testament, An American Translation* (Edgar J. Goodspeed); the American Baptist Publication Society for the *Centenary Translation of the New Testament* (Helen B. Montgomery); Mr. E. A. Knoch for the *Concordant Version of the Sacred Scriptures, New Testament;* Harper & Brothers for *The New Testament in Modern English* (James Moffatt); the Macmillan Company for *The New Testament* (Francis Aloysius Spencer) and *The New Testament in Modern English* (J. B. Phillips); the Johannes Greber Memorial Foundation of Teaneck, N.J., for *The New Testament: A New Translation and Explanation Based on the Oldest Manuscripts;* the Moody Press for *The New Testament* (Charles B. Williams), used by permission of Moody Bible Institute of Chicago; the A. J. Holman Company of Philadelphia for *The Holy Bible from Ancient Eastern Manuscripts* by George M. Lamsa; the E. P. Dutton Company for *The New Testament in Basic English;* the Confraternity of Christian Doctrine for *The New Testament . . . Translated from the Latin Vulgate,* copyright 1941; the Reorganized Church of Jesus Christ of the Latter Day Saints for *The Holy Scriptures, Containing the Old and New Testaments* (Joseph Smith, Jr.); Sheed & Ward for the *New Testament* in the translation of Monsignor Ronald Knox, copyright 1944, Sheed & Ward, Inc., New York. Used with the kind permission of His Eminence the Cardinal Archbishop of Westminster; Zondervan Publishing House for the Berkeley Version of *The New Testament* (Gerrit Verkuyl); the Book Society of Canada for *The New Testament from the Greek Text* (Ivan Panin); *The Month,* London, for *The Westminster Version of the Sacred Scriptures* (Cuthbert Lattey); Letchworth Printers, England, for *The New Testament* (T. F. Ford and R. E. Ford); the Watchtower Bible and Tract Society of Pennsylvania for the *New World Translation of the Christian Greek Scriptures;* Longmans, Green & Company for *The New Testament, A New Translation in Plain English* (Charles Kingsley Williams); Dennis Dobson, London, for *The Authentic New Testament* (Hugh J. Schonfield); the Wm. B. Eerdmans Publishing Company for *The New Testament: An Expanded Translation* (Kenneth S. Wuest), used by permission; Doubleday & Company for *The Jerusalem Bible* (Alexander Jones), copyright © 1966 by Darton, Longman & Todd.

SET UP, PRINTED, AND BOUND BY THE
PARTHENON PRESS, AT NASHVILLE,
TENNESSEE, UNITED STATES OF AMERICA

TO THE MEMORY OF MY MATERNAL GRANDMOTHER

J A M E S A N N A   M a c K I N N O N
1828-1920

among a family of nine children sole survivor beyond infancy

who showed me the beauty of speech and the truth of faith
by teaching me the 23rd psalm
when she was approaching ninety
and I was not yet three

PREFACE

The present work is designed for the intelligent general reader, including the college undergraduate, not for professional scholars in the field of biblical studies, though I hope that some of these may find it occasionally convenient for reference in certain areas of their work.

I have tried above all to simplify an exceedingly intricate story. For this I have perhaps one advantage. Though I have enjoyed the privilege of an academic theological training, including, of course, the necessary linguistic skills, I am a philosopher to trade and certainly not at all a professional biblical scholar. So I may claim a sort of amateur status and therefore a sympathy with and understanding of my audience—those general readers who approach the Bible not as specialists but as amateurs. Nevertheless, the distinction between professional and amateur must not be pressed too far. The scholarly study of the Bible as literature is an increasingly complex and learned engagement. It cannot be separated, as some may imagine, from the pursuits of historians and the preoccupations of philosophical and historical theologians. The palaeographical and archaeological skills and the mastery of the ancient tongues that is their prerequisite are of course indispensable to even the most modest pretension to biblical learning. The use of literary and scientific skills is not peculiar, however, to students of the Bible; nor is he who affects to study the Bible without talent or training less arrogant or ridiculous than he who would essay a study of astronomy without mathematics, or who thinks he can know Dante without Italian or Montaigne without French. Competence in English studies, perhaps the most difficult of all literary and linguistic pursuits, requires, among other rarer talents and skills, a mastery of at least Anglo-Saxon, Early Norse, Old German, Medieval Latin, and Modern French. The quantity of linguistic arrows in the biblical student's quiver is probably neither greater nor less; nor is their variety. The scholarly methodology proper to the humanities, though it may vary here and there from field to field, is essentially one, and the Bible, whatever else it is or is not, is at the very least an aspect

7

of humane learning. Herein lies, indeed, the motivation of my book and, indirectly, one of its themes. Herein also lies my excuse for the title, which otherwise would be pretentious.

If I seem sometimes harsh in my observations on the more obscurantist among past curial and other administrative activities in the Roman Catholic Church, it is because my admiration for the sanctity and learning of so many of my friends in that Communion is such that I am disappointed when I find them, as happens more rarely nowadays, tolerant of a hierarchy that has so often so patently lacked the very lively mind of that Church. In pointing to Rome's past I forget neither the past bigotries nor the present pravities of the nominal heirs of the Reformation. Nor have I axes to grind for traditionalism or against it. I had no lack of sympathy with that eminent biblical scholar, the late Sir Frederic Kenyon, when twenty years ago he chided a celebrated "radical" of the day for straining "out meticulously every traditional gnat, while swallowing without a qualm any number of anti-traditional camels." [1] I believe as he did that "Scholars must free themselves from the obsession that the presumption is against the traditional." [2] Nevertheless, antitraditionalism is at least as much the soul of faith as it is of skepticism. In the thirteenth century St. Thomas was at least as antitraditionalist as were, in the sixteenth, Luther and Calvin, and perhaps in some ways, as a thirteenth-century "modernist," more radically so than either of them. Be that as it may, the need today for radical reflection on the Bible as literature is acute. Not only must the believer think again; the skeptic must divest himself of the presuppositions traditionally accounted proper to his antitraditionalist profession.

The scope for error of detail in a work of this compass is practically boundless, and human frailty virtually excludes the possibility of its total elimination. I shall be gratified if only such blemishes are not numerous. Professional historians will be quick to notice that my statements and interpretations are often unsupported by evidence. They will also see the impossibility of furnishing evidence for everything in a book that covers so much ground in so relatively little space.

Notoriously numerous are books upon the Bible. Mine does not purport to present radical novelties, and biblical scholars will easily perceive my debt to other works; but I believe that, both in treatment and in scope, my book differs from all other books on its subject, including an earlier one of my own. The material it exhibits is not available elsewhere in any single volume; nor is the story it tells recounted elsewhere in the same way. I have drawn heavily, in some places, however, from that earlier

---

[1] Frederic G. Kenyon, *The Bible and Modern Scholarship* (London: John Murray, 1948), p. 45.

[2] *Ibid.*, p. 51.

book of mine, *The Bible in the Making,* published in the United States and Canada by Messrs. J. B. Lippincott Company and in London by Sir John Murray. To these publishers is abundantly due an acknowledgement of the gratitude I hereby express for their magnanimity in freely granting me permission to use these materials as I have used them.

I wish to acknowledge also the helpfulness of various persons mentioned in the footnotes, and also of others not mentioned in loco who, on both sides of the Atlantic and one side of the Pacific, have answered particular questions. These include Professor George D. Kilpatrick, D.D., of Oxford, Dr. Hellmut Lehmann-Haupt, Dom Molaise Meehan, O.S.B., the late Professor Arthur Darby Nock of Harvard, the Right Reverend Ian T. Ramsey, Lord Bishop of Durham, the Very Reverend Charles L. Warr, G.C.V.O., Dean of the Thistle, and Dom Eleuthère Winance, O.S.B. More particular still is my debt to two of my colleagues in the former Graduate School of Religion, University of Southern California, of which I was Dean: Dr. Eldon J. Epp (now of the Classics Department of that University) and Dr. Gene M. Tucker (now of Duke University Divinity School), who each read at least a chapter of the book and offered suggestions, as a New Testament and an Old Testament scholar respectively, besides giving me the support the entire faculty of that school so loyally brought to our common academic aims and professional responsibilities.

GEDDES MACGREGOR

CONTENTS

CHAPTER | *Introduction*

To George Herbert the Bible was, as it has been to many others, a priceless treasure, "the book of books, the storehouse and magazine of life and comfort." To Voltaire it was, as William Cowper tells us, his jest book. Some believers have accounted it the directly dictated Voice of God. Other believers have found in it a revelation more indirect yet no less normative as a guide in the pilgrimage of life. Some unbelievers have been content to shrug off the whole biblical literature as a relique of bygone superstition, harmless and no doubt once serving a useful function but irrelevant to our own times. More militant unbelievers have seen in it only an expression of religion as once defined by Reinach: "an assembly of scruples impeding the free exercise of our faculties."

Critical scholarship on the Bible, though it had a long history of forerunners even before the eighteenth-century Enlightenment, did not begin in full earnest till the last decades of the nineteenth century. Many factors played their part in the development of modern scholarship on the Bible; but perhaps none has been so important as the gradual recognition among scholars that the Bible, whatever else it may be, is a literature. The exact extent of its influence is, of course, incalculable; but it is, to say the least, one of the most influential literatures in human history. The Bible is by no means the oldest literature in the world. Even its oldest parts are much less ancient than, for instance, the Vedas. In the thousand years we call the Middle Ages it was revered with much lip service; but in an age when literacy was not widespread, comparatively few persons could have read it, and because of the Hebrew cast of thought it expresses, it was a very difficult literature for even the best of medieval Christian scholars to understand. Even when, under the influence of the Reformation, Bible reading came to be encouraged, more people owned Bibles, no doubt, than read them. Yet today the Bible is by any standard such a best seller that its readership, even at the lowest estimate, must be enormous. The Bible societies alone distribute twenty-five million copies of it, complete or in part, every year. The American Bible Society, since its inception in 1816, has distributed about half a billion copies of the Scriptures. This society, with its British counterpart, older by twelve years, and the score of other Bible societies associated with them, have among them caused substantial parts of the Bible to be translated into over eleven hundred languages. The rate of distribution has steadily increased. By no means all Bibles are read that are distributed, and agents of these societies report having found it used in some missionary outposts for such purposes as rolling tobacco into cigarettes. Nevertheless, there is abundant evidence for its being seriously used. The Revised Standard Version alone, since it appeared in 1952, has sold at an average rate of about a million copies a year. The New English Bible, a version in a more colloquial sort of English and intended for private reading rather than for use in public worship, similarly took the book trade by storm throughout the English-speaking world. To say the least, there is certainly no evidence that interest in the Bible has abated.

The remarkable pervasiveness of the influence of the English Bible on English literature and of its cadences on cultivated English speech are widely recognized. Ignorance of the Bible would be a formidable barrier to comprehension of even so revolutionary a twentieth-century work as Joyce's *Ulysses,* since this epic integrally reflects the pattern of the Roman Mass, which is saturated with Scripture. The Bible has also exerted an immense influence, however, apart from the English-speaking world. Its role in Jewry is unique. Not for nothing are the Jews called "the people of the Book." That book, the Hebrew Bible, is their Sacred Scriptures; but it is also their classical literature. Not only to the Jew who is faithful to his religious precepts, but also to the less observant Jew, the Bible is the literature that has moulded his Jewish consciousness. In the Catholic Christian tradition the Bible has always been, as we shall abundantly see, of fundamental importance. To the bishops and theologians of the Roman Catholic Church, which claims the allegiance of more than half a billion inhabitants of our planet, the Bible is accounted the documentary basis of every theological doctrine, and consequently of every official act, as well as of all true piety. In St. Peter's Basilica, written in letters six feet high upon a frieze under the drum of the dome whose internal diameter is 138 feet, is the appropriate verse of Scripture: TU ES PETRUS ET SUPER HANC PETRAM AEDIFICABO ECCLESIAM MEAM ET TIBI DABO CLAVES REGNI COELORUM.[1] Awareness of the fundamental importance of the Bible was reflected in the celebrated encyclical of Pope Pius XII, *Divino afflante,* which laid upon all priests the express duty of encouraging among the faithful "a knowledge and love" of the Bible. In the Eastern Orthodox Churches the Bible so permeates the liturgy that, as the Confession of Dositheus (1672) clearly proclaims, without Scripture "it is impossible to be Orthodox at all." All troparia[2] should be gathered from it, and they should end in a Scriptural

---

[1] Matthew 16:18.

[2] A troparion is a liturgical hymn. Sung by the choir, it plays an important role in the Eastern Orthodox liturgies. It was in use in Alexandria as early as about A.D. 400.

14

verse. Even under the Crescent of Islam the Bible is not without veneration. For Muslims believe that Moses and Jesus were among the great prophets of God, and God, according to Muhammad, had punished Jews and Christians alike for rejecting the message of the biblical prophecies. So although throughout the great Arab and Islamic world the Koran [3] has premier place, being accounted the Word of Allah, the Bible also commands attention and respect.

The Bible is all sorts of a book. It is, indeed, a whole library of books, representing the gamut of human interests and emotions. Some of its ideas are primitive; others are very sophisticated in terms of the age in which they were conceived. Because it treats of the mystery of man, it deals with the crudest aspects of sex as well as the most sublime ecstasies of love; it treats of war and peace, of joy and mourning, of life and death. It contains pure poetry and witty epigrams, straight narrative (not always impeccable), racy letters (not always grammatical), biographies, embryonic essays, mystical visions, dramas, ethics, revelations, and even metaphysical disquisitions. It exhibits within itself a long development of thought, culture, and conduct. On its pages is written the law of an ancient people. Within its covers can be learned the sentiments and customs, the whole corporate movement and life of all-too-human societies living precariously on the edge of the death-dealing desert. Parts of it are written for the harp; parts are for private reading as one reads a long-awaited letter at the family breakfast table; parts are rather more like a school lecture; much of it is proclamation—the proclamation of what is held to be eternal truth vital for living human life to the full and for perceiving man's ultimate destiny. All of it relates to the structure of the corporate life of society; yet all expresses much more the triumph of the individual spirit that emerges out of life.

It is this message to the anguished individual in his struggle for interior personal liberation that gives the Bible much of its perennial appeal. To millions of devout men and women of every race and language the Bible has spoken the final word of warning and encouragement, of enlightenment and hope, and to those who enjoy such a vision the Bible has, of course, unique significance. It is also, however, as much the basis of our humanist heritage as are Socrates and the Stoics, and it is therefore, if only for that reason, eminently worthy of study by all who engage in any form of literary pursuit.

Since our concern in the present book is to be with the literary history of the Bible from the Middle Ages to modern times, I propose to treat questions about the original Hebrew and Greek text, insofar as I try to treat them at all, only as these questions seem to arise naturally and to

---

[3] The more exact transliteration, preferred by Arabic scholars, is *Qu'ran*. But in English *Koran* has the sanction of custom.

demand discussion in the course of the story. I shall not attempt to provide here even the cursory introduction to such matters to be found in the earlier chapters of a previous book of mine.[4] Much less do I intend (nor could I even pretend) to undertake an adequate account of the extremely complex and highly specialized critical study of the original biblical text and its interpretation, which in any case would take longer to tell than does even the story ahead of us. My purpose is, rather, to begin with the Bible as it is found in Western Europe about the year A.D. 500, and to follow its literary history, more especially but by no means exclusively in the English-speaking world, down to the present day.

Nevertheless, for the sake of those readers who may be unfamiliar with certain rudimentary facts about the Bible that may seem to others too obvious or well known to need stating, I make the following observations before turning to the next chapter to begin our story.

The Hebrew Bible, which to this day is the Bible of the Jews and is at the same time venerated by Christians under the designation "Old Testament," was written over a period of roughly a thousand years before the Christian era. It did not, however, take anything like its present form till comparatively late within that period, and not until the Jewish Synod of Jamnia about the end of the first century A.D. were the contents of the Hebrew Bible officially settled. The term used by the Jews at the present day to designate these Sacred Scriptures is *Tanak,* a word formed out of the initial consonants of the three divisions that together constitute the whole: (1) *Torah,* the Revealed Law, consisting of the Pentateuch or first five books of the Bible; (2) *Neviim,* the Prophets, consisting of the writings of those men who are accounted the prophets of Israel, such as Amos, Hosea, and Isaiah; and (3) *Kesuvim,* the Writings, consisting of all the rest of the literature that does not fall into either of the preceding categories, such as the Psalms, Job, and Proverbs. All three divisions are part of the Sacred Scriptures; but to Jews the Neviim are more sacred than the Kesuvim, and the Torah is the most sacred of all. Traditionally attributed to Moses, it has for long been recognized by scholars to be of composite origin. Indeed, the whole Hebrew Bible as it had come down to the Jews by, say, the time of Jesus, was the result of long and very complicated processes of editing and re-editing. It represents many strands of tradition.

The most influential Greek version of the Hebrew Bible is the Septuagint, the precise origin of which is a matter of learned contemporary controversy. For our purpose it is sufficient at present to know that it was available at the time of Jesus and was used by the Greek-speaking

---

[4] *The Bible in the Making* (Philadelphia: J. B. Lippincott Co., 1959).

Jews of the day. It contains, besides the books of the Hebrew canon, various others known in the English-speaking world as the "Apocrypha," [5] such as Wisdom, Tobit, and Ecclesiasticus. The early Christian writers inherited the Septuagint and commonly quoted the Old Testament books from that Greek version.

The New Testament, written in Greek, is also the result of an editing process, though the process took place within a very much shorter time. The Epistles constitute the earlier part of it, and the earliest of them is dated by scholars about twenty years after the death of Jesus. The Gospels as they have come down to us were written after Paul's death about A.D. 65., and all the books of the New Testament, with the exception of II Peter, a very late book, had probably been written by A.D. 120, though they had not been collected by that time in their present form; nor had they acquired anything like their present status among Christians. They were at first simply part of the growing literature of those who followed the Christian way; but at least by A.D. 150 and probably much earlier they were already being used, especially the four Gospels, in the solemn and joyous celebration of the Church's liturgical worship. In the East there was for many centuries no universally fixed view of what constituted the New Testament. The general tendency there was to include much other Christian literature. In the West, however, the New Testament canon was substantially formulated by about A.D. 200. Translations into Syriac and Latin were made, and a considerable number of manuscripts of the version now known to scholars as the Old Latin were circulating by the time of Jerome, whose Vulgate eventually superseded all other Latin texts and became the official Bible of the Church in the Middle Ages at the outset of which our story will now begin.

---

[5] The term "apocrypha" was not intended originally to carry any reproach. It was used, rather, to designate those books that were of scholarly or ecclesiastical interest, yet were not for regular use in worship. The extension of the term to designate certain writings that grew up in the Christian Church is misleading. In *this* context it does mean "spurious" or "not to be taken seriously."

*Aquinas was once asked, with what
compendium a man might become learned.
He answered, "By reading of one book."*
—Jeremy Taylor

CHAPTER 2 *The Bible and the Medieval Mind*

The period commonly called the Middle Ages has neither a clear beginning nor an abrupt end. Its exact demarcation is impossible. It is convenient, however, to use the year A.D. 476, the date of the fall of the Western Empire, to mark its inception, and the year 1492 to indicate its close. Irrespective of this convention, it is important to bear in mind that we are dealing with a period of about a thousand years. It takes little reflection to see that we must expect to find, in such a long period of human history, a wide variety of attitudes and a considerable development of outlook and thought. If one considers how remote is our own age from that of even the relatively recent early decades of last century, when Jane Austen was writing, a generation after the American War of Independence, one will expect to find a vast difference in the background and outlook of, say, the Roman monk, Flavius Magnus Aurelius Cassiodorus (*c.* 485–*c.* 580), who was among those who defended the use of secular learning in the study of the Bible, and that of the English scholar-bishop Robert Grosseteste (*c.* 1175-1253), who like some other scholars of his day was making studies of the Hebrew Psalter seven hundred years later.

The contrast between the face of Europe in the days of Cassiodorus and by the time of Grosseteste leads us to expect the enormous difference of outlook that in fact we find. In the early period of the medieval millenium the ravages of war produced widespread anarchy and barbarism that left their blight for centuries. Intellectual life was meager. Outside the monasteries it scarcely existed at all. The modern student who goes to Europe in search of the architectural and other glories we associate with the Middle Ages may well wish he could see Chartres at its dedication in 1260, or Florence as it was when Dante (1265-1321) walked its streets. Yet if he could be transported back to the Europe of even only two centuries earlier, he would find almost none of the landmarks apart from which it is difficult for us to imagine the Middle Ages at all. He would find, for the most part, only the rudest of dwellings, and in making even short journeys from place to place his life would be often in great danger. By the time of Dante, on the other hand, he would be in a different world, a world already graced by much evidence of a most lively culture. In Paris, Oxford, and elsewhere he would see friars and other scholars engaged in rigorous and subtle disputation. Nor would he by any means find himself always breathing the hothouse atmosphere of "sacred studies" or the incense-filled air of the "ages of faith." He would encounter minds as skeptical and "secular" in their way as any he would be likely to meet on a modern university campus. Dante's age was as much an age of doubt as it was an age of faith.

For all that, no book was more studied throughout the Middle Ages than was the Bible. This fact is what makes so peculiarly absurd the popular legends of the Protestantism of a century ago, depicting the neglect of the Bible to have been such that Luther accidentally "discovered" one in an attic, overlaid with centuries of dust! Nothing could be farther from the truth since the Bible, in one form or another, was read by all who could read. It is true that some read it in a wholly devotional and uncritical fashion, as do many today read it. By others, however, notably monks such as the Benedictines in the ninth century, canons regular such as the Victorines in twelfth-century Paris, and friars such as the thirteenth-century Dominicans and Franciscans, it was approached also with much more academic eyes and the use of the best scholarly tools of the day. Not only were psalms chanted daily by monks in quire, and portions of the Gospel and other parts of Scripture read to the people on Sundays; in school and cloister the Bible was a basic educational text. The lad who went to get a primary education got it through learning to read the psalms. As he advanced to a study of the trivium (grammar, rhetoric, and dialectic) and even the quadrivium (music, arithmetic, geometry, and astronomy), which together constituted the seven liberal arts, the Bible was still used to some extent as a teaching instrument. As for the student who went on to theological studies, the Bible was the basis of all his work. His teacher's use of it would be governed, of course, by the advances made in the liberal arts, and this kind of learning varied much as the medieval period proceeded.

The Bible was a text for every kind of student. It was also, however, a book that was held to contain the basic documents of the Church and represented the foundation of the faith in written form. The Church conceived herself to be the guardian of the tradition it contained, so that churchmen, however learned, felt bound to protect the Sacred Page (*sacra pagina*), the Word of God (*verbum Dei*), from irreverence. Generally speaking, literacy in the Middle Ages had almost nothing to do with social rank. It was proper for a cleric to read and write, as it is now proper for a dentist to fill cavities or a pharmacist to mix drugs. Princes and barons were no more expected to be literate than were farmers and peasants. They might *happen* to be literate, as a modern American oil tycoon might happen to keep a volume of Greek odes for

19

bedside reading or pun subtly in French with his agent in Paris; but it was similarly unusual. Men of aristocratic birth or rank were expected to know how to handle a sword, not a pen. They were armigerous, not literate. Till the fourteenth century it was exceedingly rare for a layman of any social class to know how to read or write.

This does not mean the laity knew nothing of the Bible. A devout layman would have a great deal of secondhand knowledge about it, acquired from listening to sermons and homilies and from studying the bountiful supply of didactic representational art that he could find in churches and monasteries. He would be taught to see allegorical as well as literalistic meanings in the Bible, and if he were at all intelligent, he would have no difficulty in allegorizing. Such a layman lacked the tools, however, to cope with clerical discussions on the Bible. He might try to enter into one; but he would soon find himself lost, as indeed even the educated modern layman finds that the discussions of professional biblical scholars today are generally over his head. He lacks not only the languages that modern biblical scholars must possess but also the scientific methodologies in which they are trained. The medieval layman, lacking the ability to read and write, was in much the same case in terms of the learning of his day. He was not entirely cut off from what was going on among scholars; but he lacked the tools to take part in it.

While this state of affairs prevailed, the Church allowed wide latitude in the discussion of matters relating to the Bible. In the earlier centuries of the Middle Ages biblical study was fairly simple. Then, as philosophical reflection developed and contact with Jews and Arabs was made, it became more complex. In the twelfth and thirteenth centuries the exegesis of Scripture comes to be a specialized study in which highly critical methods are used by obviously very lively minds. These exegetes do anything other than just hand down traditions; they raise questions, invent problems, and propose solutions, using all the learning at their command, which by this time was very considerable, though not always quite accurate.

By the fourteenth century the Church had entered into a different situation. Now, especially in Italy, laymen were becoming much more capable of holding their own in such matters. Their knowledge, however, was often still very imperfect, and some of them were also in danger of the wilder and more unscholarly forms of allegorizing. Clerical scholars by this time had learned that they had to cope not only with the new lay interest in the Bible and the by no means inconsiderable toleration by the Church of lay expositors; they had to meet, for example, the new challenge of philosophical and other objections from "secularistic" thought such as the philosophical speculations of the various followers of Averroes (the heterodox Muslim, Ibn Rushd, 1126-1198), the peasant literalism of many Waldensians (the followers of Peter Valdes or Waldo, who died in 1217), and the occultist fancies of the Albigenses (Cathari) who during the twelfth century, when their influence was at its zenith, had menaced the survival of Christendom. When a scholar like John Wyclif (*c.* 1329-1384) raised radical problems in his interpretation of the Bible, conservative churchmen were now much more on their guard than they would have been a century or two earlier when such questions were raised and discussed within a more limited circle.

It is not difficult to see, then, how varied was the period we call the Middle Ages. Many developments took place in the course of centuries of the arduous toil that transformed Europe from a savage wilderness into a highly developed culture and relatively well-ordered society. This stupendous result was not easily accomplished. It was due to the intensity of the faith of a comparatively small number of people, and that faith, we shall see, took its inspiration from and was constantly sustained by the Bible.

There was another kind of variety, however, in the Middle Ages. If within that millenium you take any particular brief period and ask what was going on then, you will find a pattern that is in its way as variegated as that which is to be found in the whole panorama of medieval history. When St. Benedict and his small band of companions left Subiaco for Monte Cassino about A.D. 525, what was going on in their secluded little community was quite atypical of the rest of the society it eventually transformed. While the great universities were being developed at the zenith of the intellectual life of the Middle Ages, many priests were so ill educated they could hardly stumble through the Mass.

The renowned church built by St. Fulbert, Bishop of Chartres, which was reconstructed within a few decades after the fire of 1194 had destroyed all but crypt and towers, is today one of the most resplendent witnesses in stone both to the robust vigor and to the delicate subtlety of medieval culture. All classes shared in its rebuilding. In the north transept, for instance, the quire windows were given by various knightly and other donors, while the aspidal windows were mostly donated by trade guilds: the bakers, for example, provided the Moses window; the clothiers, Daniel and Jeremiah; the butchers, Ezekiel and David; and the bankers two windows, one depicting St. Peter and another with scenes from the life of John the Baptist. The lore of the Bible is so extensively portrayed both in sculpture and in glass that the cathedral of Notre Dame de Chartres may well be called a Bible in stone. The great humanistic tradition that Christianity inherited from Greece and Rome is likewise woven into the church fabric. It is as though the siliceous limestone quarried in Berchères had attained its own kind of life and im-

21

mortality from the sculpting of Scripture upon it, causing the richest heritage of pagan antiquity to bloom into a gorgeous flower in honor of the Blessed Lady who bore the Redeemer of mankind. Of Notre Dame de Chartres Napoleon is said to have declared that one could not see it and easily remain an atheist. Such are the harmony and proportion, the confident good taste and delicate restraint, that there is not a hint of vulgarity in the enormously rich splendor of the church, which cost, for its building, both the sacrifices of industrious craftsmen and the munificence of kings.

We have seen how great was the darkness, social and intellectual, into which Europe was plunged after the Fall of the Roman Empire, and how many centuries it remained in anarchy and barbarism. How, then, could a largely unlettered society so comparatively soon bring forth a mighty thinker such as Thomas Aquinas, an epic poet and incomparable literary artist such as Dante, and an exquisite monument such as Chartres, all reflecting a strength of purpose and above all a delicacy of imagination surpassing anything that we in our far more advanced and informed society seem able to achieve?

There are, of course, many reasons—reasons too complex to be dealt with here. One of them, however, is widely overlooked and is, I believe, very noteworthy. The men of the Middle Ages were largely unlettered, and even the literate among them lacked the innumerable mechanical and other external devices we possess today to assist us in making notes and records. To an extent that is almost unimaginable to modern man, they had to depend upon their memories. These memories were therefore perforce prodigiously well trained. We, even the most gifted of us, have by comparison no memories at all. We fear, not without reason, to clutter our minds with anything we can possibly jot down. Medieval people, lacking these technological tools we take so much for granted that we can hardly imagine what it would be like to be deprived of them, made use of mnemonic devices. Simple people would use, of course, relatively simple devices. The learned, however, used elaborate ones. The invisible gymnastics in which they engaged stagger our modern imaginations. A typical mnemonic device of bygone ages was the "memory theatre." You first set before your mind a vast theatre. You then furnished it with the images you wished to store for future use according to the order in which you wished to recall the corresponding ideas you intended to verbalize. These interior acrobatics of the mind may have held back progress in some matters; but they gave people an immense capacity for bringing forth and arranging images. The learned could by such means instruct the unlearned. The unlearned, though without the ability to read or write, would have been able to hold in their minds an astonishing amount of material. Even illiterate people might learn long passages by rote, while the lettered committed to memory enormous quantities of literature.[1]

At the time of the restoration of Chartres, Roger Bacon flourished as a champion of experimental science. Both Chartres and Roger Bacon were far removed from the basic life and attitudes of the mass of mankind. One might name many activities as expressions of thirteenth-century culture, and one would find they represented only peculiar facets of the life of the period, as Tennyson, Darwin, and the Crimean War would represent aspects in the life of Victorian England. To say, then, that the Bible played a special role in the life of the Middle Ages would be misleading if this conveyed the notion that it dominated the thoughts of men as it does not dominate men's thoughts now. The truth remains, however, that the Bible was accepted—for the most part very uncritically —as a literature which, for all the mystery attending it and the incomprehension that much of it evoked, was taken by everybody who knew of it at all, scholar and peasant alike, to be the most impressive body of literature that had come into the Latin heritage.

---

[1] For an admirable full-scale study of this neglected subject, see Frances A. Yates, *The Art of Memory* (Chicago: University of Chicago Press, 1966).

The tools wherewith I labor and
earn my bread are Paternoster, *and my*
primer Placebo *and* Dirige, *and sometimes*
my Psalter *and my* Seven Psalms.
—Langland, "Piers Plowman"

CHAPTER 3 *The Psalter in Medieval Life*

We have seen that the book of Psalms, by far the greatest anthology of lyrical poetry in the Hebrew Scriptures, had a long history before it received anything like its present form. Traditionally attributed to King David, it represents a wide variety of date and authorship. Some psalms are comparative latecomers to the Tanak, the body of Hebrew Scripture; others contain verses that reflect the ideas of comparatively early Hebrew mythology. In one of the "Songs of Asaph," God stands up in the midst of the other gods and, rebuking them for their unjust judgements and their evident partiality towards the wicked, urges them to mend their ways by bringing justice to the weak and the fatherless and by rescuing the needy.[1] Another carries traces of the old Babylonian account of the victory of the god Marduk over the sea monster Tiamat:

> Thou didst break the heads of the dragons on the waters.
> Thou didst crush the heads of Leviathan.[2]

Some psalms exhibit great lyrical beauty. Others are, from a purely literary point of view, comparatively pedestrian. No psalm received a place in the anthology unless it was supposed to have religious edification. On this account, literary excellence was incidental; yet because the best expression of the most profound religious ideas is always intensely beautiful, the book of Psalms that eventually took shape was well stocked with masterpieces of Hebrew lyric poetry. How many of the psalms were liturgical in origin, and to what extent, is obscure; but, at any rate, by the time of Christ the book of Psalms had acquired much liturgical importance. In the Jewish liturgy down to the present day the Hebrew Psalter is the very stuff of Jewish daily and festival liturgy, and every observant Jew delights in it as the songbook of his faith.

What is at first sight much more astonishing is the unique importance of the role the psalms have played in Christian life. Perhaps still more astounding, however, is the peculiar and abiding beauty of Latin, English,

[1] Psalms 91:1-4.
[2] Psalms 74:13-14.

and other translations of the psalms, which, as we shall see, have not only moulded Christian life but deeply affected the history and literature both of continental Europe and the English-speaking world. To the vast majority of Christians, Hebrew has been an unknown tongue; yet the book of Psalms has spoken more surely and directly to the hearts of the simplest than any other book in the Bible except the Gospels. Translations of any literary composition, poetry or prose, at the best generally miss the genius of the original. The great Latin and English versions of the psalms, which have won such extraordinary affection and have exerted such profound influence upon princes and peasants alike, exhibit many technical defects; yet as literary expressions they have acquired in their own right positions of unique literary importance, to say nothing of their individual religious influence and power. They contain singular qualities not to be found in the Hebrew itself. The Anglican Psalter, which is from a revised translation of Coverdale that antedated the King James Version of 1611 by about seventy years, is extraordinarily unlike the Hebrew Psalter in language, feeling, and tone. Yet it has taught the minds and touched the hearts of millions of English-speaking people whose ears its very English cadences have so long delighted. At the head of each of the psalms, as they are printed in the Book of Common Prayer, is a Latin phrase, the opening words of the psalm in its ancestral form in the medieval Latin Psalter, which is also in its own way no less far removed from the original Hebrew yet has a most compelling splendor of its own.

That Latin Psalter was the basic nourishment of the minds and hearts of men during the thousand years we call the Middle Ages. One might even call it a literary sacramental that both supported and adorned every one of the official sacraments and prayers of the Church. It was also basic pabulum in literary instruction. To be reminded that the regular daily praise of the monastic community consisted predominantly in the recital or chanting of the psalms is only to begin to appreciate the role these played in medieval life. They still constitute one of the greatest liturgical inheritances of the Latin Church. The Roman Mass itself begins with a psalm, and the letter and spirit of the Latin Psalter permeate it both as a literary and as a liturgical form. The Psalter is also the principal substance of most of the various rites and ceremonies of the Church outside the Mass. The words of the Asperges or Ceremony for Blessing with Holy Water, for instance, are, apart from the Collect, straight out of the Latin Psalter. Every rite and sacrament, indeed, from Baptism to the Office for the Dead, from the Marriage Service to the Exorcism of Devils and even the Litany of the Saints, exhibit the Psalter's omnipresent influence.

The novice, upon taking his vows and being admitted into the monastic community, sang three times with outstretched arms the verse of a psalm: *Suscipe me secundum eloquium tuum, et vivam.*[3] The rule of silence was based upon the verse of a psalm: *Dixi: custodiam vias meas, ut non delinquam in lingua mea.*[4] The ordering of the daily recitation of the Psalter was founded upon the Psalter itself: the psalmist proposes to praise God seven times a day.[5] In the middle of every night, by candlelight and often in freezing cold, at the sound of a bell that had once been cast to the singing of a psalm,[6] the monks rose to continue the singing of the Psalter. For again the directive was implied in the Psalter itself: "At midnight I rise to praise thee."[7] When a brother was sick and seemed dying, the entire community, summoned by those tending him, who gave the signal by loud raps on a board, dropped whatever task they had in hand so as to hasten to his side to bring him fraternal comfort in his loneliness and pain, singing the penitential psalms[8] in his ears as he passed from this earth in the peace of the cloister where he had spent his life, having loved "the habitation of thy house, and the place where thy glory dwells."[9]

That life, to which Europe owes almost all that brought her out of primitive savagery and disastrous disorder to the artistic grace, intellectual vivacity, and comparative physical safety of a cultured and well-ordered society, was guided by one principle above all others. This principle, upon which the well-being of every monastery and convent depended, was written in a Latin verse of incomparable beauty, dignity, and power from the same never-failing source of medieval inspiration: *Ecce quam bonum et quam jucundum, habitare fratres in unum.*[10] Well might they, indeed, behold with the psalmist "how good and pleasant it is for brethren to dwell together as one." It was through such fraternal unity that the psalms they loved had become the very tide of their lives, through which they largely conquered and subdued the terrors of the mad and hideous world that had been bequeathed to the age of St. Benedict by the meaningless pagan decadence of the dying and rotting Rome, once the most splendid wonder of the world.

Nor were the illiterate peasantry who lived on the edge of that tide of medieval Latin psalmody untouched by its healing rhythm or un-

---

[3] Psalms 119:116 (RSV). In the Latin Vulgate, the numbering of the psalms differs slightly, so that the reference here, for example, would be Liber Psalmorum 118:116.

[4] Psalms 39:1.

[5] Psalms 119:164.

[6] Psalms 150.

[7] Psalms 119:62.

[8] The seven penitential psalms are psalms 6, 32, 38, 51, 102, 130, 143 (RSV); 6, 31, 37, 50, 101, 129, 142 (Vulg.).

[9] Psalms 26:8.

[10] Psalms 133:1.

moulded by the lofty teaching it contained. Whatever else of the Bible reached them in their own dialect or tongue, they would know some of the Psalter. Whatever Latin they knew would include sonorous words from the psalms, such as the cry of the supplicant, *De profundis clamavi ad te* or *Domine, exaudi orationem meam,* or else the shouts of holy joy, *Jubilate Deo* or *Laudate Dominum omnes gentes.* And that, with the "right" heart the psalmist sought, might be worth more than much learning, which by itself does not always bring wisdom.

How was it that, of all the literature of the Hebrew Bible, the book of Psalms alone acquired such extraordinary influence and power?

To answer this question we need only be reminded of what we have already learned. When the Christian Church won the Gentile world, the Hebrew Tanak, in Greek translation, was taken over and revered with the Epistles and Gospels of the New Testament. Most of it, however, was far too antique and foreign, both in sound and pattern to mean much to the average man. Even the intelligent and devout who tried to read it would have found it trying. Among scholars only the most exceptional could honestly pretend to begin to uncover its mysteries, and they very imperfectly. The translation of the Old Testament into Latin helped to maintain and spread interest in it; yet language proved to be not the most fundamental obstacle to full comprehension. The real barrier was the foreignness of the thought, background, and structure. To Latin Christendom it could not but have seemed at least as strange and difficult as is an English translation of the Chinese classics to the average well-educated contemporary American. Of course, there were interesting human stories to be found to fire the imagination and entertain the mind—stories about men such as Samson and women such as Jezebel; but they seemed to need much allegorizing to make them edify or instruct. There was little internal clue to the meaning, such as one expected in a book. Moreover, the difficulty was compounded, even for the most intelligent reader, by the fact that the translators themselves had known too little about the spirit and inner structure of Hebrew literature to ease their readers' task. The Jews themselves had difficulties; but at least they were in the tradition that gave birth to the Hebrew Scriptures. As we shall see, very few medieval Christian scholars knew Hebrew.

The one exception to the medieval Catholic's difficulty with the Old Testament was the book of Psalms. It spoke straight to a man's heart in any language. For while much of the rest of the Tanak was bound up with the legends and the very peculiar history, laws and customs, of the Hebrew people, the Psalter, thoroughly Hebrew though in every way it was, expressed human longings and human joys whose appeal is universal. If the lyrical form of the Hebrew was lost, it received, in Latin, a new life. The music of the Psalter was in an ethical key played on a religious keyboard. The faith the Psalter uttered was a faith for the hearts of all men, depending upon no particular ethnic ritual or explicit theological teaching. The love it expressed was the purest and noblest love on earth—the communing of the individual soul with the highest he knows. So while Leviticus and Esther might puzzle and bore the most intelligent Roman beyond endurance, and even Hosea and Ruth leave him more or less reverently numb, most of the psalms in the Psalter, once they had been rendered for him into Latin, could make his whole spirit spring to life, almost as though he were discovering a hitherto unknown treasure within his own literature. St. Ambrose (*c.* 339-397) tells us that when other parts of the Bible were read in church, there was often restive talking among the people; but when the psalms were read, all were silent.

This universality in the Psalter was often noted and expressed by medieval churchmen. In A.D. 879, Pope John VIII was apprised of the proposal of Methodius and Cyril to translate the Bible into Slavonic. A rude alphabet, constructed for the purpose, was the origin of modern Russian script. The Pope approved, since the proposal seemed to be justified by the verse: "Let everything that breathes praise the Lord!" [11] While the New Testament was translated in its entirety into Slavonic, however, the Old Testament was represented by only the book of Psalms. The first known translation (contradistinguished from mere paraphrase) of any part of the Bible into Anglo-Saxon was also, inevitably, the Psalter —Aldhem's version of the psalms, written towards the end of the seventh century.[12]

The formal christianizing of Europe was a gradual process. In Scandinavia, for example, it did even not begin till eight hundred years after Christ. Everywhere, after the process had begun, its consummation took centuries and is of course accounted still incomplete today. In the first centuries of christianization, however, pagan customs, with all the power of conservatism behind them, offered the Christian missionaries competition and resistance. We need not be astonished, therefore, if we sometimes find in the course of the transformation of pagan ideas, Greek or Latin, Keltic or Teuton or Slavic, thick mixtures of primitive superstition covered with thin Christian veneers. Yet in the vast welter of lore and legend in which the Middle Ages abound, we constantly encounter the use of the psalms as a special instrument in the process of purification of Europe from the murkier elements of its variegated and often very primitive pagan past.

According to one such picturesque legend, when St. Patrick faced the power of the old paganism at Tara, the Psalms were used to great effect.

[11] Psalms 150:6.
[12] See below, p. 74.

28

The Keltic year closed with the spring equinox, and every third year the festival of Tara was held on the plain of Breg. It was a great occasion, attended by the various kings of Ireland, together with their retinue, their warriors, and their chariots. They took up their places at nightfall in nine triple circles, round the great pyre, while all Ireland awaited the lighting of the sacred flame from which, according to custom, every fire in the land was relighted. Then, to the horror of all the assembled grandees, a light appeared on the horizon. The Druids, outraged, set forth with their horses and chariots to seize the perpetrator of the sacrilege and bring him back to Tara for judgement. Upon a little altar in a rude hut on the hill of Slane they found the light that had distressed the kings. Before the light stood St. Patrick and his white-robed priests, celebrating Easter. As St. Patrick followed the Druids to Tara, he chanted the words of a psalm:

> Some boast of chariots, and some of horses;
> but we boast of the name of the Lord our **God**.
> They will collapse and fall;
> but we shall rise and stand upright.[13]

Then he spoke to the royal assembly with such power that all nature was still. The pagan pyre remained unlit. Only the light on the altar of the Christian chapel remained to greet the Easter dawn. The power of the Druids was broken.

The Golden Legend, one of the most popular in the Middle Ages, recounts that when Christ descended into hell to free the just there that awaited his coming, Satan quoted words from the Gospels that suggested hope that Jesus would still be won over to the kingdom of evil and death. Had he not admitted that his soul had been "very sorrowful, even to death"? Now, Satan thought, Jesus was ready to be captured. Then came a tremendous voice uttering the words of the psalm that was to be forever associated with Easter joy:

> Lift up your heads, O gates!
> and be lifted up, O ancient doors!
> that the King of glory may come in.[14]

The denizens of Satan asked: "Who is this King of glory?" [15] At this the psalmist himself, David, waiting with the other righteous ones, cried out:

[13] Psalms 20:7-8.
[14] Psalms 24:7.
[15] Psalms 24:10.

29

> Who is this King of glory?
> The Lord of hosts,
> he is the King of glory! [16]

Whereupon the gates of hell burst open and Christ appeared with a luminous splendor that lighted up the whole infernal prison. So, to the triumphant words of a psalm Christ drew from hell the righteous of all ages and every clime who had awaited him, and they rose with him victorious over death and hell. The Devil had used Christ's own words against him, and the effective reply came from the Psalter.

By modern standards the men of the Middle Ages were generally very ignorant of the natural sciences. A literalistic reading of the Psalter reinforced in medieval man his opinions about astronomy. Did not the psalmist say that the earth was fixed?

> Thou didst set the earth on its foundations
> so that it should never be shaken.[17]

The motion of Leviathan caused the tides and the gales that harass mariners.[18] These and many other medieval errors about astronomy were buttressed for those who sought astronomical instruction out of a book of religious poetry. Those medieval thinkers, and there were many, who were trying to make scientific progress in such matters, naturally had to face, as do pioneers in every age, the displeasure and threats of the less enterprising. Albert the Great (1193-1280), one of the keenest minds of the Middle Ages and St. Thomas' own teacher, being interested in chemistry and other such matters, was charged with divination. Such scientific pursuits did not seduce Albert, however, from his devotion to the Psalter. On the contrary, he found in it the proper attitude that a man ought to have who sought truth in any realm of human inquiry:

> To thee, O Lord, I call;
> my rock, be not deaf to me,
> lest, if thou be silent to me,
> I become like those who go down to the Pit. [19]

The Psalter could serve, then, every right mood of man. The joy at a royal coronation could be expressed with a psalm. A psalm such as the *Miserere* [20] served a hundred purposes; but it was especially appropri-

---

[16] *Ibid.*
[17] Psalms 104:5.
[18] Psalms 104:25-26.
[19] Psalms 28:1.
[20] Psalms 51.

ate for occasions of great sorrow and penitence. Men and women in the Middle Ages, feeling ever surrounded by a myriad evil powers, not least political wickednesses, had no difficulty in entering into the mood of the psalmist when he saw himself ensnared by doers of mischief and, having remembered the protection God had always afforded him, cried to him for help in the words: "My God, my God, why hast thou forsaken me?" [21] It was, of course, from the psalm that opens with these words that Christ quoted on the cross. In face of death the Christian called out, as did Thomas à Becket when his assassins slew him at Canterbury: *In manus tuas, Domine, commendo spiritum meum.*[22]

[21] Psalms 22:1.
[22] Psalms 31:5.

He who reads the Bible in translation
is like a man who kisses his bride through
a veil.—Hayyim Nachman Bialik

CHAPTER 4 *Hebrew Scholarship in the Middle Ages*

The custodians of Hebrew scholarship throughout the Middle Ages were, of course, the Jews. For a thousand years from the time of Jerome (*c.* 342-420), the first Gentile Christian Hebraist, Christian scholars were very largely dependent upon Jewish friends and teachers for such knowledge of Hebrew as they might and sometimes did possess.

First let us consider the condition of the Jew in the Middle Ages. Naturally, it varied considerably from time to time and from place to place, not least in respect of his isolation from the rest of society. Still, generally speaking, he was very much isolated indeed, and when he was less so, it usually turned out to be worse for him in the long run. In Spain, for instance, where he was less segregated, he was eventually led into far more cruel persecution than he had ever suffered before —probably worse than he was ever to suffer again till the rise of Hitler in the twentieth century.

After the destruction of the Temple at Jerusalem in A.D. 70, the dispersed Jews had wandered through many lands. For the preservation of their culture and their identity as a people, they had depended upon the Hebrew Bible, which nourished them and gave them hope. This special dependence upon their ancient literature was not, indeed, entirely new to them. Centuries before, during the Exile, they had already become "the People of the Book." Nevertheless, the Book was to become, after the fall of the Temple, more than ever the tie that bound them together.

Classical Hebrew, the language of the Bible, was an ancient tongue for the medieval Jew. Indeed, it had been already a little archaic by the time of Christ, when, in the synagogues of Palestine, the Torah would be expounded in Aramaic. The Hebrew of later times was an outgrowth of classical Hebrew. The transition was gradual. The later books of the Hebrew Bible already show movement into a style that is not quite classical, yet not quite the later Hebrew. For all that, the Bible continued to be quoted in the original, long after its language had become archaic in the everyday speech of the people. Eventually there was a desire to get back to the purity of the ancient literature in the classical Hebrew tongue. This ancient literature, the Hebrew Bible, had been in some measure overlaid and obscured by the vast output of rabbinic commentary upon it. The Talmudic scholars themselves, who were preoccupied with such exegetical exercises, were well aware of the danger. In the ninth century A.D, Gaon Saadya perceived more than did many of his contemporaries the importance of the Hebrew Bible as the keystone of all Jewish thought and learning. Saadya, a very great Jewish scholar, compiled a Hebrew dictionary and grammar, and also made a translation of the Hebrew Bible into Arabic, designed, of course, for Jews in the Arab world. This translation is still read by the Yemenite Jews. The first complete Hebrew dictionary in the Middle Ages was devised by Menahem ben Saruk in Tortosa, Spain, about the middle of the tenth century. Attention was drawn to its shortcomings by Dunash, Saadya's pupil, to the great benefit of Hebrew scholarship from a relatively early period in the Middle Ages.

The medieval rabbi was often very learned in the Hebrew Bible. To him his ghettoed people looked not only for the interpretation of its meaning but also for the custodianship of the purity of its text. The Jew in the Middle Ages, living in ghetto conditions, was naturally brought very close to this rabbinic tradition. More often than not he lived in very unnatural circumstances. In the daytime he might move about in the world outside his ghetto; every night at curfew he had to return to his own highly inbred society. Thus sheltered from the Gentile world, he was also cut off from the mainstream of the culture and civilization of his day. In such circumstances he turned to intellectual and artistic pursuits, thereby acquiring an aptitude for literature and the arts that has deeply and permanently affected the Jewish people, many of whose gifted sons have eminently exhibited the fruits of this tradition. Above all, however, the medieval Jew was constantly turned back upon the bond that held his people together. It was this bond, the Hebrew Bible and the rabbinic traditions associated with it, that meant more to him than all the other literary and artistic activities the pursuit of which may be said to have been unwittingly imposed upon him by the outside world in which, even at the best, he inevitably felt very much a stranger. He was aware of his Jewishness wherever he went, and the Hebrew Bible, however it might be read through mists of Talmud and Midrash, was the supreme symbol of that awareness. Without it, he would have culturally perished, feeling the world's door shut in his face; with it, he was able to recognize himself as heir to an incomparable treasure. He felt the possession of this heritage in a peculiar way, for though others in the world beyond his ghetto shared it with him in translation, he had inherited the text in its original language.

The medieval Jewish ghetto was an institution fully recognized by the state. It was a segregated society. Segregation was believed to be for the protection of the Jew as well as in the interest of all. Theoretically, the ghetto was an elective representative democracy. In practice, it was seldom if ever as much as this. The rabbi, the cantor, the beadles, and the ritual slaughterer were its important officials, and among these the rabbi's role was preeminent. A small council governed the ghetto, and this council, through various committees, administered the synagogues and the schools, organized the necessary charities, and assessed and collected all taxes, both those that had to be raised for the Gentile state and those that were needed within the ghetto itself. The rabbi, however, reviewed the decisions of this council and exercised very important judicial functions in civil matters, though the Gentile authorities rarely if ever permitted him to exercise criminal jurisdiction.

Medieval Jewry suffered great disabilities. As early as A.D. 419, a Christian council at Carthage had forbidden Jews to testify against Christians, and in 531 Justinian had reiterated this prohibition. Nevertheless, the Jews were not without powerful protection. In 598 Pope Gregory the Great established the principle that while they were subject to certain restrictions, they were also entitled to the fullest protection of the law and indeed to all the protection that Christian clemency ought to afford them.

Ever present, however, was the danger of mob violence due to ignorance and fear. All calamities, especially the more mysterious ones, such as plagues, fires, and the abduction of children, could be attributed, in vulgar superstition, to mischief caused by the Jews. These were not, of course, the only victims in bygone days of these dark dreads; under the Roman Empire Christians had been preeminent among the scapegoats for mysterious calamities. Moreover, the persecutions of Christians had been supported by pagan emperors who shared these superstitions, while medieval popes and bishops were usually much more enlightened in such matters than the flocks committed to their charge. Nevertheless, when vulgar superstition among ignorant Christians was aided and promoted by the sort of Jew who received Christian baptism out of spite against his own race and people rather than by way of genuine conversion to the Christian faith, the effect was indeed formidable. Such a Jew, it would seem, was La Rochelle, who in the thirteenth century brought charges to Pope Gregory IX to the effect that the Talmud contained wicked, dangerous, and seditious teaching. In France, copies of it were seized and examined by a commission of Dominicans and Franciscans who, aided by what Christians call a "converted" Jew acting as both chief prosecutor and as a sort of expert consultant, held a disputation with Jewish scholars of the day, on June 25, 1240. Copies of the Talmud were burnt. Eight years later Odo of Châteauroux ordered a reexamination of the Talmud, which was again condemned, and a series of extracts was compiled from it, on Odo's orders, purporting to justify the condemnation. There were many further examinations of Jewish books.

Nevertheless, but for the protection of the popes, the Jews, rather than their books, would have been burnt. When mysterious widespread calamities occurred, the Jews were sometimes indeed burnt by the frenzied mob, as we shall see. Always they were at the mercy of vulgar ignorance and prejudice. The stupid and misdirected zeal that drove some Christians to force Jews into receiving baptism certainly did not help matters.

From the highest authorities of the Christian Church the Jews did receive, however, considerable protection. In 1272 Pope Gregory X, echoing the principles laid down by Gregory the Great seven hundred years earlier, expressly decreed that Jews must not be coerced; nor must they be in any way ill treated, and "no one shall disturb them in any way during the celebration of their festivals, whether by day or by night, with clubs or rocks or anything else." In 1247 Pope Innocent IV had alluded to the unfounded and foolish fables invented by unworthy Christians, to the effect that Jews stole Christian children for human sacrifices. Gregory X again called attention to these slanderous tales among the vulgar and affirmed that there had even been Christians who pretended their children had been carried off, so that they might thereby falsely and wickedly injure the reputation of the Jews. He carefully explained that these stories against the Jews were without foundation and that their own laws expressly forbad them to do anything of the sort. He issued, therefore, in protection of the Jews, a papal decree that Jews seized under any such silly pretext should be freed at once and that there must be no further persecution of them. Finally, referring to "the wickedness and avarice of bad men" who disinterred and stole the bodies of Jews from their cemeteries in order to make their relatives pay a ransom for their return, he decreed that any Christians guilty of such wickedness should be excommunicated.

In spite of these salutary attempts to give Jewry at least a modicum of protection, lamentable popular ignorance often prevailed. When, in the middle of the fourteenth century, a terrible plague swept over Europe that seemed as though it would destroy all mankind, many ignorant people believed rumours that the Jews, ever bent on mischief, had caused the woe by a poison they had secretly introduced into the wells! In many places they were accordingly arrested and burnt; yet not, the chronicler Jacob von Königshofen assures us, at Avignon, "for the Pope protected them there." Some Jews at Berne, under torture, even "confessed" to the absurd charge. The city of Strasbourg, among others, was apprised of this. Though their civic leaders did not believe the stories wrung from the unfortunate victims and told the people they "knew no evil of them," the people nevertheless made such a commotion that in the end the Jews were either burnt by the citizens or else, being expelled from the city, were stabbed to death or drowned by stupid peasant mobs who, gloating over their prey, caught them. The citizens of Basel were so angered at the Jews that they staged a march on the city hall and compelled the council to take a solemn oath not only to burn the Jews but to allow no Jew to enter the city for the next two hundred years. Such is the power of mob ignorance and frenzy. Needless to say, it deeply alienated the Jew from the Christian Church, the nature of whose spiritual riches he could hardly be expected, in such circumstances, to appreciate.

In Spain, where the Jews had enjoyed a lot that was generally more favorable than elsewhere, the cruelties they eventually suffered in the massacres during the period between 1391 and 1411 were so great that many Jews lost heart and sought physical safety by resorting to external submission to Christian baptism. This move, however, by creating the fresh problem of the crypto-Jew, was the chief factor in bringing about the notorious Inquisition that was instituted in 1478. In 1498 the Jews were expelled from Spain where for so long they had enjoyed comparative liberty. Worse was to follow: within a century they were to be expelled from almost every country in Europe, and it was from the ashes of these persecutions that sprang the Jewish communities founded in England, Holland, and America. This part of the story of their sufferings belongs, however, to a period beyond that of the Middle Ages, our present concern.

It is against such a background that we must see the later development of Hebrew scholarship in medieval Jewry. The influence on all subsequent Jewish scholarship of Rabbi Solomon ben Isaac (1040-1105), known as Rashi from the initials of his designation and name, is not easy to exaggerate. His exposition of the Torah became a standard work that every educated Jew was expected to read. We shall see also how particularly important was his influence on medieval Christian scholars. Despite the limitations imposed upon the Jews by their social condition, Jewish scholarship flourished. In Provence were three pioneers, Joseph Kimhi and his two sons, Moses and David. David Kimhi (1160-1235) was the compiler of a Hebrew grammar and dictionary. These were so widely and so long influential that when at the close of the Middle Ages the great humanist Johann Reuchlin (1455-1522) made the first attempt of a non-Jewish scholar to compile a Hebrew grammar and dictionary, and sought the help of the rabbis of his own day, it was still to these works done by David Kimhi three centuries earlier that they directed him. He also influenced a Persian translation of the Bible made by a Jewish translator about the year 1400. It was about this time that Jewish translations of the Hebrew Bible began to be undertaken. In 1422 Rabbi Moses Arragel translated the Hebrew Bible into Spanish. To this and other Spanish translations, we must return later.[1]

Meanwhile, let us address ourselves to the question: To what extent did medieval Christian scholars engage in Hebrew studies, how good was their Hebrew, and in what manner did such Christian Hebraists acquire their knowledge and develop their skill?

First let us go right back to fourth-century Jerome, whose final and most important work included the translation into Latin of a very large portion of the Old Testament directly from the Hebrew. Jerome travelled in Syria and Palestine. His Hebrew teachers were Jews, one of whom only he names, Baranina, sometimes elsewhere designated Barrabanum. This teacher was so afraid of being seen teaching Jerome, a Christian, that he visited him by stealth at night. Jerome also refers to another, perhaps his principal Hebrew teacher whom he seems especially to have revered as "most learned" (*eruditissimus*), and from him Jerome learned midrashic methods and exegesis. Certain portions of the Old Testament demanded also a knowledge of Aramaic, which Jerome acquired under an anonymous teacher to whom he refers simply as "the Chaldee" (*Chaldeus*). There is no doubt that Jerome was a most diligent student of Hebrew. Indeed, he was more than this: he was so much influenced by the methods of his Hebrew preceptors that he personally follows them to a great extent in his own interpretations of the text. His indebtedness to Jewish sources and Jewish teachers raised many a Christian eyebrow. Jerome, a very ready and sharp-tongued controversialist, was quick to point out that Christian scholars neglected Hebrew at great peril to the soundness of their own Christian theology. It is not likely that many of his fellow Christians were adequately impressed by his insistence upon the need for Hebrew. Moreover, the degree of proficiency in Hebrew that Jerome actually attained is not clear. Almost certainly unparalleled among his Christian contemporaries, it was nevertheless probably quite average, not to say pedestrian, from the standpoint of the Jews who taught him. Hebrew is a very alien language to non-Semitic peoples, and before the development, after the sixteenth-century Reformation, of better teaching methods, probably not even the ablest Gentiles acquired a mastery of it that would have been accounted noteworthy in a Jew.

Not only was Jerome's knowledge of Hebrew unique among Christian scholars of his day. There was nothing like it among them for centuries to come. The knowledge of Hebrew sometimes attributed to early medieval English writers, such as Bede and Alcuin, may have been in fact minimal. One of Alcuin's more celebrated pupils, Rabanus Maurus

[1] See below, pp. 70-71.

37

(776 [or 784]–856), whom we shall have occasion to notice later,[2] does refer to help received from a Hebrew scholar, probably a contemporary. Rabanus, who was Abbot of Fulda and Archbishop of Mainz, used in his commentary on the Book of Kings certain passages containing Hebrew traditions. Paschasius Radbertus refers in his commentaries to the Hebrew text. The help he plainly must have received from Jewish scholars suggests at least some degree of factual foundation for the tradition that he was learned in Hebrew. By the eleventh century there is evidence that not a few Christian scholars acquired, through conversation with Jews, some knowledge of Hebrew; but whether it was normally substantial or only the merest nodding acquaintance with words and phrases is not easy to determine.

In the twelfth century, however, the more enterprising and original scholars begin to show a clear recognition of the need of Hebrew for an understanding of the Old Testament. In a man such as Robert of Cricklade, who was Prior of St. Frideswide's, Oxford, at the middle of that century and is noted for his wide learning, his travels, and his interest in the natural sciences, the knowledge of Hebrew attributed to him is very credible. At any rate, such a skill, though still unusual, was becoming less remarkable.

The twelfth-century renaissance of learning was stimulated by contacts with Greek writers in the Norman kingdom of Sicily and elsewhere; but it was due certainly no less to the impact of Arab and Jewish sources that were being made accessible in Spain, notably at Toledo. The English scholar, Adelard of Bath, translated works from the Arabic, including some books of Euclid. Such translation from a language as hitherto remote as was Arabic no doubt helped to make Hebrew seem less recondite than it had appeared in the past. Michael Scot, an important contributor to the history of the natural sciences in the Middle Ages, first appears at Toledo in 1217 as the translator of an Arabic work, and he had some knowledge of Hebrew as well. Pope Gregory IX commended his knowledge of Hebrew and Arabic. It seems clear that Michael Scot must have had contacts with Jacob Anatoli, who translated Arabic works into Hebrew. So it is unastonishing to find many twelfth-century Christian biblical scholars consulting rabbis about the interpretation of passages in the Old Testament.

In the thirteenth century the friars were transformed through various circumstances into the intellectual leaders of the day. As early as about the middle of the century they were devoting themselves to the study of Oriental tongues, partly to assist them in the missionary enterprise of converting Muslims and Jews, but also for reasons of pure scholarship.

[2] See below, p. 53.

Hebrew and Arabic studies were instituted at Barcelona in 1281, at which time Raymund Martini became lecturer in Hebrew studies there. This remarkable man appears to have been, for a Christian scholar of his time, a considerable Hebraist. He always quotes from Hebrew books in the original, providing also a Latin translation of his own making.

Robert Grosseteste, leader of the Oxford Franciscans whose house of studies he founded, was an ardent advocate of Hebrew as well as Greek studies. At Oxford there was at this time a considerable Jewish community, mainly consisting of the descendants of Jews who had come to England after the Norman Conquest. There is no doubt that Grosseteste was friendly toward the Jews at Oxford, and it is very probable that he learned Hebrew from a rabbi there. Nor is there any doubt that Hebrew was taught among the Franciscans at Oxford; but how often and how much we have no means of assessing. At the Sorbonne in 1319 a convert from Judaism was appointed to teach Hebrew and Syriac in Paris, and through a similar appointment at Oxford, with a stipend provided out of ecclesiastical properties, Hebrew was being taught there in 1321.

The greatest Hebraist among the Oxford Franciscans was indubitably Roger Bacon (*c.* 1214-1292), who was indeed in every way a most remarkable man. His knowledge of Hebrew probably exceeded that of any other Christian scholar of his day in the world, certainly of any in England. From a Jewish standpoint this may have seemed an easy win. It is difficult to determine how much Hebrew, precisely, would give one this preeminence. At any rate, not only was he a great Hebraist; he accounted Hebrew a wonderful repository of human wisdom, besides being the language in which God first revealed divine truths to man. He complains bitterly of the corruption of the Vulgate and pleads for much more serious attention to Hebrew studies. The principles of textual revision that he advocated may be discerned in the *correctoria* of the Latin text, to which we must turn later.

The strong pleas for Hebrew and other linguistic pursuits that were made by some of the thirteenth-century friars—the Dominicans no less than the Franciscans—led to papal support for various measures to promote such studies. In 1312 the Council of Vienna had expressly recommended the founding of chairs in Greek, Hebrew, Arabic, and other languages at the great university centers. In 1275 one scholar, Robert of Reading, was led by his love of Hebrew to profess the Jewish religion. In England, by the second half of the thirteenth century, we find a literal translation of the Old Testament from Hebrew into Latin, a large part of which is represented in surviving manuscripts to be found in the Bodleian and other Oxford libraries.

To Nicholas of Lyra (*c.* 1270-1340), a Franciscan, came to be attributed, after the Reformation, an influence over Luther that was much exaggerated. It came to be commonly said, with a catchy pun on Lyra's name, that if he had not sung, Luther would not have danced:

> Si Lyra non lyrasset,
> Lutherus non saltasset.

This is a crass overstatement, for there were many influences at work upon Luther. Still, Luther did borrow from Lyra's *Postillae perpetuae* (a commentary on the Bible), and Lyra, in turn, was indebted to the eleventh-century Rashi, the influence of whose work on subsequent Jewish scholarship has already been noted and will be further considered later on.[3]

Lyra's aim was, in its way, rather similar to that of Rashi. They were both concerned more for what they considered the "literal sense" (*sensus literalis*) of the text rather than the allegorical meanings that might be given it. Lyra enormously admired Rashi as the greatest of Hebrew doctors. Later chapters will be devoted to this very important question of literalism and allegory in the history of the Bible in the Middle Ages. Lyra, a regent master at Paris, was both a popular exegete and probably on the whole the best-equipped biblical scholar the Middle Ages produced. According to a much later French biblical scholar, the Oratorian priest Richard Simon (1638-1712), to whom among others may be attributed the beginnings of modern Old Testament criticism, no one since Jerome had contributed so much to understanding of the Old Testament as had Nicholas of Lyra. Curiously, it seems that Lyra, in spite of his Hebrew learning, did not know Greek. It has even been suggested that he was of Jewish origin; but while this may be a very plausible conjecture, there is no evidence for it, so far as I know. Paul of Burgos, who made additions to Lyra's *Postillae* about a century afterwards, was indeed, however, a converted Jew.

Perhaps enough has now been said to indicate the interest in and limitations of Hebrew scholarship among medieval Christians. The most significant point to be noted is that after the biblical legacy of Jerome to medieval Christendom, an interest in Hebrew studies would seem to be almost directly proportionate to general revivals of learning. It is at its height in the golden age of medieval Christian learning, piety, and culture, the age of St. Thomas and Dante, when in spite of the always smouldering if not erupting volcano of anti-Jewish mob fear and consequent violence, such studies were encouraged by the highest authorities in the Church and conducted by Christian scholars whose relations with their Jewish counterparts must have been friendly enough to make the pursuit of these studies possible.

[3] See chapter 6.

Fools make the text, and witty men
the commentaries.—Ferdinando Galiani

Bad commentators spoil the best books,
So God sends meat (they say), the devil cooks.
—Benjamin Franklin

CHAPTER 5 *Text and Commentary*

The language of the early Christians was Greek, and in the Greek Church the Bible was naturally handed down in Greek and is in use in Greek to this day. The early occupants of the See of Rome bore Greek names such as (in romanized form) Anacletus, Telesphorus, Eleutherus, Zephyrinus, and Callistus (d. *c.* 223), and Greek was used by Christians in Rome till well into the third century. Elsewhere in the West, for example in North Africa and southern Gaul, a Latin translation was needed sooner than it was needed in Rome, and it is known that in these two regions the Scriptures existed in Latin before the end of the second century. By A.D. 400 Latin texts were circulating widely and displayed great variation.

We have already learned that the Latin version of the Bible, known as the Vulgate, was the work of Jerome. It was completed by him in A.D. 404. It came to be known as the Vulgate, not so much because it was in the "vulgar" or "common" tongue, but rather because of its adoption, in Western Europe, as the "vulgar" or "common" edition. Jerome had undertaken the task because by his time there were, he declared, almost as many different Latin texts of the Bible as there were manuscripts. Jerome's efforts to provide Latin Christendom with a standard text were not unresisted. Churchmen are conservative, and those who had been using earlier Latin texts tended to cling to them. Even when such prejudices were overcome, corruptions in the text soon abounded. There were several reasons for this. The most obvious is that the copying out of the Bible by hand naturally fathered a multitude of scribal errors. There were also other variations introduced, however, as a result of memories people carried with them of the earlier texts to which they had become accustomed. Jerome's aim was therefore already in jeopardy as soon as he had accomplished his task.

Never throughout the Middle Ages did the Latin Church possess any standard or generally accepted text of the Vulgate such as is officially issued by the Roman Church today. Through the history of the textual revisions that led to the development of the text currently in use falls far beyond the medieval period, it will be both profitable and convenient to consider it briefly at this point before giving some account of the Latin text in the Middle Ages.

The first Bible of any kind ever to be printed was the celebrated Gutenberg Bible, an edition of the Vulgate published at Mainz, Germany, not later than the middle of August, 1456. About forty copies of it are known to exist. One of these, purchased for about $400,000, is in the Library of Congress. There is also in the Henry E. Huntington Library, San Marino, California, a fine copy whose fifteenth-century binding of stamped leather and metal bosses over heavy wooden boards enabled it to escape the "cropping" of pages that has been the fate of many precious old books. This edition came to be known as the Gutenberg Bible, being attributed to Henne Gensfleisch, a printer who assumed the name of Johann Gutenberg. He has generally been credited with having invented printing by movable type, perhaps the most influential event in history. The claim may need some modification, however, since undated fragments of early Dutch printing do exist, and they may antedate the Gutenberg Bible. The type for the Bible was cut by another printer, Peter Schoeffer. At any rate, what Gutenberg printed was a copy of the Vulgate Bible that had been circulating in manuscript form for a thousand years and had undergone many textual corruptions.

The division of the Bible into chapter and verse is an arrangement so familiar to the modern reader that he may overlook the fact that it is only a practical device invented in the Middle Ages. Stephen Langton (d. 1228), of whom more will be said presently, divided the Bible into chapters according to the arrangement which, arbitrary though it be, has proved very convenient. Division of the Bible into verses came later, at the end of the Middle Ages. In 1448 Rabbi Nathan devised such an arrangement for the Old Testament, and this was used in a Venice edition printed in 1524.

The first critical text of the Vulgate was that printed in Paris in 1528 by Robert Estienne (1503-1559), with later editions in 1532 and 1540. He tried to follow Jerome's text as closely as possible. In 1544 he began to print Greek and in 1550 published an important edition of the Greek New Testament, the earliest one to contain any sort of critical apparatus. The Sorbonne attacked him severely because of his annotations to the biblical text he published. Forced to flee in 1551 to Geneva, he espoused the cause of Calvin, and in the New Testament he published at Geneva that year he introduced the division of the chapters into verses according to the arrangement with which we are nowadays familiar.

When, in April, 1546, the Fourth Session of the Council of Trent declared the Vulgate to be the only authentic Latin text of the Bible, a new edition of it was eventually issued in 1590 with the authority of Pope

Sixtus V. This edition was intended to be unalterable; but as it turned out to contain a very large number of errors, it was as far as possible recalled from circulation, and in 1592 a revised edition was issued under Pope Clement VIII, with some three thousand corrections. Since Pope Sixtus had pronounced the 1590 edition to be unalterable, the revision issued in 1592 under Clement originally bore on the title page the words: *Biblia Sacra Vulgatae Editionis Sixti Quinti Pont. Max. jussu recognita atque edita.* Modern copies of the Vulgate, however, often bear the title: *Biblia Sacra juxta Vulgatam Clementinam,* and this revised edition of 1592 is nowadays generally referred to as the Clementine edition of the Vulgate. It departs from Jerome's text in a great many places. Attempts at further revision were for long hampered by papal prohibitions against such an enterprise. In 1743 an emended edition was printed by Domenico Vallarsi (1702-1771). Vallarsi, who had edited Jerome's writings in a series of eleven volumes, published in 1734-1742, produced an excellent work that superseded one that the Benedictines of the Congregation of St. Maur had published in Paris in 1693-1706. For the most part, Vallarsi's work has never itself been superseded.

Because of the continuing papal prohibition against emendation of the Bible that had been pronounced unalterable by Sixtus V and had been two years later altered under Clement VIII to the extent of three thousand corrections, Vallarsi was unable to send forth his revision of the Vulgate as a revised *text* of the Vulgate. He circumvented the prohibition, however, by publishing the biblical text as part of his definitive edition of the writings of Jerome. In more recent times there have been further attempts at producing a better Vulgate text, such as one of the New Testament made by John Wordsworth (1843-1911), Bishop of Salisbury, an Anglican scholar and one of the most eminent Latinists of his day. He published Matthew–Acts in 1889-1905, and a minor edition of the whole New Testament in 1911. In 1908 Pope Pius X authorized the making of a new edition, publication of which is still in progress, having begun with the issue of Genesis by the Vatican Press in 1926.

In view of the difficulty of arriving at a definitive text of the Vulgate Bible even in the five hundred years since the invention of printing by movable type, one may well imagine how great was the textual confusion in the preceding thousand years of the Middle Ages, during which the Vulgate, besides having had to face widespread practical opposition from conservative churchmen at the outset, had to be copied out by the hands of monastic and other medieval scribes.

Though knowledge of the Greek language had disappeared in the West by the beginning of the medieval period, there are exceptions to the general rule that ignorance of the biblical tongues prevailed throughout the early Middle Ages. The philosopher John Scotus Erigeno [1] (*c.* 810–*c.* 877), one of the few original thinkers of the earlier and darker period, knew Greek. Besides translating some useful works from the Greek, he discussed exegetical points arising out of his studies of the Greek text of Scripture and the Greek Fathers. Yet he was, like others, hampered in his work. We find him complaining of the lack of a Septuagint for reference. Remigius of Auxerre (*c.* 841–*c.* 908) knew at least enough Greek to write a few words and probably enough Hebrew to make some comparative studies. A psalter setting forth the Greek and Latin in parallel columns was written at the Abbey of St. Gall in 909. This abbey may have had contacts with Greek-speaking monks from southern Italy. There were a few Christian scholars even in that early period who consulted Jews and left behind them some evidence of having compared the Vulgate with the Hebrew text. As we shall see, such Jewish influence on Christian scholarship was, at a later medieval period, both extensive and very salutary.

Generally speaking, however, the Vulgate was all there was, and this was very much corrupted. Few of the few who could read at all knew anything of the Greek and Hebrew that lay behind it. In the whole period between Isidore of Seville (*c.* 560-636) and the ninth-century John Scotus Erigena, by far the most outstanding biblical scholar is Bede (*c.* 673-735). In England Bede is generally designated "the Venerable" and sometimes called "the father of English history." He knew almost no Hebrew, and though he knew and used Greek, his knowledge of it has probably been much exaggerated.

The reign of Charlemagne (768-814) encouraged a renaissance of scholarship. The Carolingian schools that were the outcome of this revival of learning after a long period of darkness were not remarkable, however, for originality of thought. Our gratitude to Charlemagne for his interest in learning—rare in a ruler in those days—ought not to blind us to his defects. His known annoyance with the Greek Empress Irene is likely to have inclined him to try to discredit Greek influences and to encourage a Western independence of all that seemed to be associated with the Eastern Christian tradition.

The declared purpose of Charlemagne's renaissance of learning was to prepare scholars for the study of the Bible and the Fathers. The prevalent ignorance, the extreme scarcity of books, and not least the textual corruption of such texts of the Scriptures as existed, were formidable obstacles to the Carolingian renaissance. No more appropriate gift can be imagined for Charlemagne when he was crowned Emperor on Christmas day in the year 800 than a copy of the Bible, with which

[1] See below, p. 54.

44

Alcuin (*c.* 735-804), the leading spirit behind the Carolingian revival, presented him.

Alcuin's work established, no doubt, a textual norm; but it did not by any means introduce a new, standard Vulgate text. At most it mitigated the textual corruption. Bishop Theodulf of Orleans (d. 821) produced another recension. There were several others in use, such as the Italian (Codex Amiatinus), dating from about 700, the Gallican (Codex Bigotianus), the Irish (Codex Armachanus), and the Spanish (Codex Cavensis), to say nothing of the remnants of Old Latin versions still in circulation. While the famine in books prevented even the most discriminating and fortunate scholar from having much choice of text, the average scholar would be glad to be able to lay hands on any text at all. Moreover, in the tenth century the Cluniac monks were fostering liturgical reforms which, while advancing the use of the Bible in sermons and in public devotion, resulted in a comparative neglect of biblical study till well into the eleventh century. In the cathedral schools, grammar, poetry, singing, and rhetoric were taught rather than theology. They were safer and raised fewer problems to distress the spirit and trouble the mind. There are even complaints that some masters admired the philosopher Boethius (*c.* 480–*c.* 524) more than the Bible.

The attitude towards the Old Testament Apocrypha in the early Middle Ages is noteworthy here. In the Eastern Church all the books of the Septuagint continued to be widely accepted for many centuries, and no sharp distinction was made officially till as late as 1672, when the Synod of Jerusalem decided that among the books not found in the Hebrew Canon, only Tobit, Judith, Ecclesiasticus, and Wisdom were to be accounted canonical Scripture. In the West, Jerome had made a distinction between the books not found in the Hebrew Canon, which he called the ecclesiastical books (*libri ecclesiastici*), as opposed to the canonical ones (*libri canonici*). In practice, however, the distinction was not much insisted upon. Certain writers, notably St. Augustine, made it; but generally speaking there was a great deal of haziness on the question. The Irish *Liber de numeris,* paraphrasing the *Decretum Gelasianum,* warns of apocryphal books that the Church does not recognize at all and refers to them as books that are not to be copied or read or received. The same *Liber de numeris,* however, places the pseudepigraphical books, III and IV Maccabees, along with the two books, I and II Maccabees (generally included in the Vulgate), as Holy Scripture. It has been shown that Latin translations of apocryphal literature were common during the early medieval period,[2] and all sorts of ideas from

[2] Dom Albert Siegmund, *Die Ueberlieferung der griechisch-christlichen Literatur* (Munich, 1949), pp. 33-48.

45

the apocryphal writings were handed down in oral tradition, and influenced thought. What is remarkable, indeed, is that their influence did not injure the prestige of the canonical writings. From the pseudepigraphical book of Enoch, for instance, came a host of ancient magical ideas connected with the number seven, such as that there are seven heavens and seven archangels (Gabriel, Michael, Raphael, Uriel, Sariel, Rumiel, and Panchel), and that man was created out of seven substances: flesh from earth, blood from dew, eyes from sun, bones from stone, intelligence from angels, hair from grass, soul from the divine breath.

In the monastic scriptoria, however, the reproduction of the biblical texts and the patristic commentaries, and the revival of interest in the Fathers that was brought about through the Carolingian renaissance, helped to mitigate the influence of the wilder ideas and to cause a more sober tradition to prevail. The Latin Fathers exercised a dominant influence; nevertheless, the Greek Fathers, in translation, were by no means unknown. The translations were for one reason or another deficient; but at least forty Greek writers were so transmitted and at least fifty of the translators were known.[3] Even such very inadequate patristic learning helped to anchor the early medieval biblical scholar to a tradition in which his biblical scholarship could be conducted in better perspective.

The practice developed—its eleventh-century beginnings are obscure —of making marginal or interlinear glosses to the text. Anselm of Laon (d. 1117) played an important role in this development, laying the foundation for later standard commentaries on the Bible. The biblical glossators usually remained anonymous, so that it is impossible to give a satisfactory historical account of the subject in even the most cursory fashion. What we do know is that the glossators pursued their work for practical ends, such as teaching. By about 1150 the Bible with glosses had become a fairly standardized production, and the practice spread from Paris to the rest of Western Christendom. Out of it came other forms of biblical commentary and a whole tradition of learned descanting upon the Bible for the purpose of guiding students to revered "authorities" and providing them with tools for clarifying the meaning of the text.

Much of this activity was directed towards exegesis, and there was much preoccupation with this to the detriment of concern for textual purity. Interest in the latter was nevertheless also developed, and books called correctories (*correctoria*) were written. These, in the compilation and diffusion of which the Dominicans and Franciscans played an important role, were designed to correct errors that had been detected in the current Vulgate text. The *correctoria* contained lists of variant readings as well as textual emendations. The *studium* of St. Jacques, in which

[3] See *Die Ueberlieferung der griechisch-christlichen Literatur.*

Hugh of St. Cher played a leading part and held a theological chair from 1230 to 1235, was especially celebrated for its work in the improvement of biblical apparatus and text.

It was about this time that the word *postilla* came to designate biblical commentary interposed as a continuous gloss between places in the text of the Bible. The word is perhaps derived from the Latin *postilla,* meaning "after those [words of Holy Scripture]," and it acquired a more precise meaning than "gloss" ever possessed. Gradually it acquired also a different character. Similar in form to the *postilla* were the *expositio* and *lectura.* By this time abridgements of the *glosa* are called *glosaria.* The *postilla* came to be regarded as an indispensable supplement to the gloss. It was about then also that the older expression for the Bible, "the Sacred Page" (*sacra pagina*), was going out of fashion. It was giving way to the terms "Bible" (*biblia*) and "Scripture" (*scriptura*).

Besides the more strictly textual and exegetical type of commentary, there were also theological observations and analyses that might be made. These had not always been distinguished; but gradually the theological questions (*quaestiones*) had occupied an increasingly larger place, and these *quaestiones* had come to be excerpted and circulated separately as *Quaestiones de divina pagina,* that is, theological questions about Holy Writ. This process is particularly notable in the work of Stephen Langton, one of the most distinguished scholars of his day at Paris and afterwards a cardinal (1206), Archbishop of Canterbury (1207), and a leader in the movement that led to Magna Carta.

Eventually, though the *quaestio* might be retained in the *postilla,* it acquired something of the function of a literary device. The Bible remained, of course, the solid ground from which the theologian, with his heritage of wisdom from Plato and his fashionable Aristotelian philosophical equipment, could take wing; but theological disputation acquired a special grandeur and dignity of its own, partly because the study of Scripture had become technical enough to be a learned groundwork for it, but more because of developments within philosophy and theology themselves.

As a consequence of the attention to commentary and text, a great change came about in the attitude towards learning and its relation to the devotional life of the individual and of the Church. In the old monastic tradition, Bible reading had been on the whole a very simple affair, being accounted largely a means for enabling the soul to turn inwards upon itself and upwards to God in prayer. Study and exegesis of the text had been so primitive at the time that they could not seem to distract a monk much from his prayer life. By the time of St. Bernard (1090-1153) the situation had already sufficiently changed to cause alarm to a conservative contemplative such as he. A monk could have

47

little rightful business with the study of the Bible were it not the better to incline him to prayer. "Reading," warns Gilbert of Holland, a Cistercian abbot, "ought to serve our prayer, prepare our mood, not encroach on our time and weaken our character." A good monk in this tradition would confess his excessive addiction to Bible reading as a fault that he ought to curb, giving himself over instead more fully to prayer and works of compassion. This was the sort of attitude St. Francis of Assisi (*c.* 1181-1226) had somehow inherited, and which he classically expressed in the celebrated advice he offered the novice: "When you have gotten a psalter, you'll want a breviary, and when you've gotten that, you'll sit on your chair like a great prelate, and you'll say to your brother, 'Fetch my breviary for me.'"[4] He told a novice that he also had once wanted books but had been shown a better way—books are for those who need to learn through parables; the children of Christ have direct illumination from the Gospel.[5] The fact that contemporary Bible study could be so contrasted with the devotional life was possible only because Bible study had already become in some measure a technical enterprise as well as the edifying pursuit and prayerful undertaking it had been in the earlier Middle Ages.

By the end of the thirteenth century, however, the Franciscan friars had come to be ranged with the intellectual avant-garde of the day, being, with the Dominicans, the leaders of scholarly life at the universities. A pious brother lamented, indeed, that Paris had destroyed Assisi. The Franciscans were also associated with social and political reforms disliked by the conservative monks of the older orders. One of these, the Lord Abbot of Peterborough (Grosseteste's abbey), writing of the year 1224, bewails that it was in that year, "O misery! O more than misery! The Friars Minor came to England." The Franciscans could be both learned expositors of the Bible and advocates of the simple life of holy poverty and booklessness; both barefoot mendicants and university professors; both literalistic preachers of the Gospel and academic theologians; both fervent mystics and promoters of the political interests of the papacy. They could be all these things because by this time the study of the Bible, through text and commentary, had become a very different pursuit from what it had been in Bede's or Alcuin's time. Bible reading was now much more than an aid to devotion or a prelude to mystical contemplation. It was a work that demanded great technical skill. The resolution of textual and exegetical difficulties required much training. Yet the Bible was still the one book without which there would be no theologizing at all, and indeed no university or school.

[4] "Intentio Regulae," *Documenta Antiqua Franciscana*, ed. L. Lemmens (Quaracchi, 1901), p. 93.
[5] Matthew 13:10-13.

It is well known that to the copying out of the Bible the medieval scribes devoted much patient labor. In the scriptorium a group of monks sat diligently taking down to the dictation of a brother monk the words of the biblical text, till a certain number of copies had been made. The examples of these most familiar to us from museums and illustrations are often extremely beautiful, being ornamented, gilded, and sometimes decorated with exquisitely delicate painting, showing the Bible scenes as the medieval artist-scribe imagined them. Such copies are artistic as well as bibliographical treasures. There were many other much less decorative copies made, however, especially after the revival of learning in the twelfth century, and there was an increasing demand for these more ordinary copies.

A very large number of medieval manuscripts of the Vulgate Bible belong to the thirteenth century, when the demand for copies for studious purposes had reached its peak. Many of these Bibles are quite small. The writing is compact, arranged in double columns to get as much as possible into a page, and there is none of the sumptuous decoration associated with the grand-style Bibles of the Middle Ages. Ornament, if present at all, is reduced to a minimum. These Bibles are obviously for scholarly purposes, not for fostering the kind of piety with which one might approach a rich icon. They are, rather, schoolbooks, and their abundance reflects, besides the salutary influence of St. Louis (1214–1270), King of France, whose scholarly interests led to the founding of the Sorbonne, the widespread attention among scholars in the thirteenth and later centuries to the academic study of the Scriptures.

I would not say that [God] appears
as he is, though he does not manifest himself
as something wholly other than that which
he is.—St. Bernard of Clairvaux

CHAPTER 6 *The Letter and the Figure*

Nobody, on reading that Jesus is a door,[1] wonders whether he be maple or mahogany. No one, however ignorant or stupid, has ever read the Bible "literally." Yet all persons, however intelligent or learned they may be, are in danger of literalism to the extent that they lack imagination or fail to exercise such as they have. Imagination is by no means proportionate to learning or even to intelligence. Many very simple people are highly endowed with the combination of imaginative and moral qualities that is conducive to religious insight, while other men, possessing a massive intellect and being well trained in the use of it, are singularly lacking in imagination. Life in our contemporary urban societies is so inhospitable to a contemplative attitude that even the most rudimentary forms of human imagination are soon atrophied.

Medieval layfolk, when they tried to understand biblical teaching, possessed, except in one respect, a considerable advantage over their counterparts in modern society. The exception is that they generally could not read at all, but had to depend upon clerics to dispense not only the interpretation but the text itself. Since apart from contemplating pictorial representations of the biblical stories, parables, and other teaching, they could hear at most only portions of the text, they could not, generally speaking, enter into any serious discussion of biblical interpretation. The singular advantage possessed by the average modern churchman in Los Angeles or New York is that he has access to English translations of the text. Yet this advantage is not so great as might appear, for these *are* only translations, as was the Latin Vulgate used in the Middle Ages. Moreover, even if the man of today could read the original text, he would still lack the historical learning and the highly specialized training in methodology necessary to put him on a fair footing with the modern biblical scholar.

In any case, neither he nor the illiterate layman in the Middle Ages has been able to escape the peril of misconstruing biblical ideas in terms of the thought of their respective contemporary societies. Indeed, here has been a pitfall even for modern scholars as well as for their medieval

[1] John 10:7, 9.

50

counterparts. As in our own days some "fundamentalists" have talked as though St. Paul had a New Testament in his pocket and some "liberals" as if Jesus were expounding a blueprint for modern democracy, so in the Middle Ages there was a general tendency to put Christ into a medieval Roman mould and to see all biblical teaching as an archaic and exotic yet universally appealing mode of expressing medieval ideals. The danger among medieval interpreters was not that the Bible should be approached too literalistically, but rather that allegorization should be allowed too much rein. From the scholars, with their greater access to the text, we should expect an influence restraining the wilder forms of allegorization. Very broadly speaking, this is what in fact we find in the history of the Bible in the Middle Ages.

These same scholars, however, in this very exercise of their proper caution, were open to the opposite danger of stultifying the meaning of the Bible and turning its teaching into a code of rules. Luther and other sixteenth-century Reformers, armed with some of the weapons of a new humanistic learning, believed that this is what had happened to a calamitous degree by the time they came on the scene. Their vision, only very partially fulfilled, was of a Reformed Catholic Church in which layfolk would be sufficiently well instructed to participate with the clergy in an appreciative understanding of the Bible. This understanding, while keeping pace with scholarly advances, would depend above all upon the imaginative vision that everyman must bring to the Bible if he is to benefit at all from the message it contains, the message that Christians have always believed to be of more crucial and more lasting importance than anything else in the world. No one who knows the historical facts can pretend either that the case of the Reformers lacked justification or that the outcome in the Reformed tradition has not been to repeat, perhaps in an even worse form, the very vices that disfigured medieval Latin Christendom in its use of the biblical heritage.

An example will illustrate the point I have in mind here. The sixteenth-century Reformers had complained of the tendency among the pious of their day to seek heavenly merit through external observances such as pilgrimages and fasts. At a later period, however, the heirs of the Reformation often fell into worse offences of the same kind. Some of them, for example, came to be, at one period of their development, strongly sabbatarian, insisting upon abstinence from travel and work on the Lord's Day with a rigor that not even an Orthodox Jew could easily excel. In Scotland, where sabbatarianism was especially cherished, a devoted churchwoman complained to her pastor about a tendency to laxity she had noted in the younger generation. To this her pastor responded by a timely reminder to his zealous parishioner:

"But you know that even our Lord broke the sabbath." [2]

"Yes," she snapped, "and I never thought any the better of him for it."

Surely the zeal of the lady's literalistic sabbatarianism had eaten up her vision of the central truths of her faith. More deeply religious people, however, have always seen beyond the letter to the life-giving spirit behind it. Allegory has been the chief instrument of such people in their reverent approach to a genuine understanding of the Bible.

That there is allegory in Scripture was by no means a novel discovery to the men of the early Middle Ages. At the outset they inherited the idea from the earlier Christian Fathers, notably Origen. In that earlier patristic period there was, indeed, such a strong awareness of the possibilities of allegorizing that the question had come to be, rather: What are the limitations that must be put upon it? In A.D. 430 Vincent of Lérins, in his *Commonitorium Primum,* had provided a normative rule in such matters. The Bible, the Church's basic text, is the Sacred Page, the Divine Law, the Word of God; but since it is liable to various kinds of misinterpretation, it is important that its interpretation be regulated. The rule is that it should be interpreted not according to private whim, but according to churchly understanding; not to help to grind the axe of this or that individual or group, but in the interest of the whole living Church. This rule, intended to prevent the wilder and more fanciful allegorizing, such as that which had delighted the Gnostics, demanded an appeal to history, to what has generally been taught by the Church: *ut id teneamus quod ubique, quod semper, quod ab omnibus creditum est.* It was normative throughout the Middle Ages. Yet practice varied widely, as we shall see, for the medieval scholars inherited also two traditions, that of Alexandria on the one hand and that of Antioch on the other. The Alexandrian tradition encouraged, within limits, a wide latitude in allegorizing. The Antiochene tradition discouraged this, inclining more to the anchoring of exegesis in history.

The reverence of churchmen for the Bible may be seen at the beginning of the medieval period. St. Benedict (*c.* 480–*c.* 550), founder of the great order of monks who bear his name and eventually became much celebrated for their scholarship, was personally more of an administrator than a scholar. Yet he appreciated scholarly traditions and ways. In the last chapter of his Rule, he wrote belittling his own work in comparison with the Bible, the perfect norm (*rectissima norma*) of human life. In contrast to his master, John Cassian, who had developed a fourfold level of interpretation—allegorical, tropological, analogical, and historical— Benedict approaches the Bible more practically, being perhaps quite unwittingly more Antiochene in his reading of it. The methods of the

[2] Matthew 12:1-14.

Alexandrian exegetes, with their interest in Platonic and Philonic allegorizing, were remote from his simple, practical Roman outlook. Gregory
the Great (*c*. 540-614) used allegory freely; yet his use of it differs decidedly from that of earlier Fathers such as Origen and Ambrose. Instead
of allowing himself to become involved in wild speculative fancies, he
generally prefers to find allegories that help him to draw either moral
or doctrinal lessons from the text. When the interests of orthodox doctrine permit or encourage more free allegorization, he can stray far beyond the given words. In Job, for example, he sees Arcturus, Orion,
and Pleiades as figures of the Church, her martyrs and her doctors. Yet
one rarely if ever finds Gregory indulging in allegory as a plaything. He
is an allegorist with a serious purpose, much influenced by Stoicism in
his ethical aims and seeking to be always Catholic in his doctrine. He
allegorizes only to edify.

Two ways of allegorizing are to be seen respectively in Bede and in
Alcuin. Bede exercises Gregorian restraint, making use of the patristic
tradition as a subordinate authority in understanding the scriptural
foundation, yet permitting himself also some independence when he feels
himself guided to do so by the Holy Spirit. Alcuin is inclined to rely
more exclusively on the Fathers. So much is to be found in St. Augustine,
in St. Ambrose, and other giants, that one need do no more, thinks
Alcuin, than walk reverently in their steps, humbly culling the flowers
they strew rather than trying to cultivate new blooms.

Many, such as the great Benedictine theologian and poet Rabanus
Maurus [3] and Walafrid Strabo (*c*. 808-849), followed Alcuin in this
exegetical tradition, and they certainly had no difficulty in disgorging
from the Fathers a wide variety of figurative interpretations of Scripture.
The Bible was never far from the minds of thoughtful men. Even the
heterodox monk Gottschalk (*c*. 805–*c*. 868), when he invoked St. Augustine and others in defence of his own high doctrine of double predestina-
tion that the Synod of Quiercy condemned in 849, was as rooted in the
Bible, as he knew it, as were to be the Calvinists and Jansenists who, in
much later times and with greater access to the sources, were to argue a
similar cause.

Some ninth-century exegetes disliked the tendency, however, of looking
to the ancient Fathers for guidance in allegorizing Scripture. Druthar
(d. 850) began his commentary on St. Matthew by observing that he
had sought to study the historical rather than any inward or higher
meaning in the Bible. He plausibly points out that one cannot pretend
to go beyond the historical till one knows what the historical is. Notker
the Stutterer (*c*. 840-912), a monk of St. Gall, reproached Bede for

---

[3] See above, p. 38.

having written interpretations of Scripture that were pleasant rather than good exegesis, as if it were always better to find an allegory even in the most straightforward narrative. The celebrated John Scotus Erigena [4] was critical of the very notion of that sharp distinction between a "literal" and a "spiritual" sense that had been inherited and taken for granted by Alcuin. Erigena preferred to see the need for cultivating a methodology in biblical interpretation that would find in the words of the Bible text itself (when understood in the light of historical evidences such as variant texts) the full range of all the meaning they were intended to convey and that should be expected of them. When Western monasticism was reorganized under the leadership of Odo of Cluny (879-942), the old Benedictine emphasis on the practical moral value of the Bible tended to be reinforced. Meditation upon the Bible, wrote Odo in the beginning of his *Collationes*, keeps a wise man steadfast in the midst of the turmoils of the world. On this view the Bible should be left to speak for itself. Let the monk, rather than study it critically or invent elaborate allegories from it, meditate upon it as he chants it in church. The chanting of the office (*divinum officium*) was, after all, a monk's principal daily duty. Surely God, who loves the faithful servant, will reward him with all the illumination he needs.

This attitude was highly influential throughout the monastic tradition in the Middle Ages; yet other influences strongly competed with it. Lanfranc (c. 1005-1089), who was no doubt a warm supporter of the Norman Conquest and who succeeded to the See of Canterbury, greatly promoted the copying out of the Bible in monasteries. His own attitude towards it, however, was very much that of Alcuin. He simply reiterated what the ancient Fathers had said. In his controversy with Berengar of Tours (c. 999-1088) on the nature of the eucharistic presence, which led to the latter's condemnation and the eventual triumph in Western Christendom of the doctrine of Transubstantiation, Lanfranc showed a reluctance to entertain any philosophical analysis of biblical ideas. Berengar had denied that there could be any material change in the bread and wine used in the Eucharist, preferring the view that Christ is ideally or figuratively present in these elements. To Lanfranc this kind of philosophical allegorizing of the Bible was to be treated as insolent pride. Yet it was an attempt to surmount a theological difficulty in terms of philosophical reflection. It was evidence of intellectual vivacity in approaching a serious problem arising out of the text of the Bible.

The program of the Victorine school was ambitious. Hugh of St. Victor (c. 1096-1141) was a theologian and mystic so deeply influenced

---

[4] See above, p. 44.

by the Neoplatonic tradition that had been transmitted through St. Augustine that he was sometimes called Alter Augustinus. According to Hugh, who wrote a commentary on the *Celestial Hierarchy* of the fifth-century mystical writer Dionysius, the mystic way leads one from ordinary natural thought (*cogitatio*) to an intuitive meditation by which one discovers the thoughts of God hidden under the veil both of the created universe and of the Scriptures. From this latter activity (*meditatio*) one proceeds to a greater purity of life, and finally to the pure, loving contemplation (*contemplatio*) of God.

The Victorines were indebted to the biblical scholarship of a school of French Jewish rabbis who followed the eleventh-century Rashi, who still commands among Jewish scholars to this day a high place as an interpreter of the Hebrew Scriptures and the Jewish Talmud. In opposition to the current practice of his time, Rashi had been inclined to a literal interpretation of the Hebrew Scriptures. We have seen that Rashi, whose commentaries, especially his commentary on Genesis, were used by Nicholas of Lyra, very indirectly influenced Luther. We have seen, too, that Christian interpreters of the Bible from the ninth century onwards owed much to Jewish scholars and often consulted them. In spite of the protection often afforded the Jews by the papacy, popular sentiment against them broke out periodically. While Rashi's commentaries were being burned in Paris during anti-Jewish riots in the thirteenth century, Christian scholars were engaged in translating them.

Under such influences as that of Rashi, Hugh of St. Victor, in spite of his own mystical inclinations, advised his students not to ignore, much less despise, the literal interpretation of Scripture, which is to be looked for before one attempts to discover allegorical meaning. "Do not despise," he counsels, "what is lowly in the Word of God." By "lowly" he refers to the literal meaning. No doubt he was well aware, from his own temperament and poetical genius, how wild and fanciful allegorizing may become, unless it is curbed. So he always prefers to look first for the literal meaning before attempting to discover allegory. He rebukes those who try to find mystical significance and profound allegory in a work such as Ecclesiastes, where none is intended. So he wished his students to accept the descriptions of Noah's ark quite literally, while at the same time explaining that they have also a mystical significance. For instance, the ark signifies the Church, which is the Body of Christ.

Andrew of St. Victor (d. 1175) was an even more extreme defender of the importance of literalism. He seems to wish to be emancipated from theological preoccupations and to delight only in the documents themselves. Just because he took the literal interpretation so seriously, he resorts to an elaborate explanation of the problem of harmonizing the two accounts of Creation in the first and second chapters of Genesis, and both of them with the text in Ecclesiasticus which proclaims that God created all things together.[5] Andrew's method, however, is historical in the sense that he is much less interested in metaphysical or theological reasons for any explanation that anyone may offer, than in historical considerations such as the purpose of the biblical writer. Placing the literal sense always before the allegorical, yet using the latter too, he is able to arrive at a conclusion that appears to him more satisfactory than that of the writers who allegorize freely in a theological or mystical interest. His conclusion may be perhaps even more fantastic in some cases, from a modern point of view; but it does reflect an historical sense in terms of medieval scholarship. He is disinclined, for example, to suppose that the story of Creation was directly revealed to Moses; it may have been handed down from Adam, orally or even in writing, and obtained by Moses after scholarly investigation.

Of Richard of St. Victor (d. 1173) we know much less. He appears to feel that Andrew was too much influenced by what the Jewish scholars were saying. If it were wrong to swallow wholesale allegorizing by Christians, it was certainly no less wrong to accept the utterances of Jewish scholars as though they had a special authority. One should respect the Fathers; yet one must also remember that there might be much of value and significance in Scripture that had escaped them. Often it would be the literal meaning itself that had eluded the Fathers.

We can imagine how lively was the debate in the twelfth century between those who tended to the more extreme forms of allegorization and those who preferred an historical method. That there should be as a normal part of the twelfth-century biblical education arguments for and against the literal interpretation of the "six days" of one of the Genesis accounts shows us only one aspect of the temper of the disputes of medieval scholars about the way in which the Bible should be interpreted. There was certainly no single view that prevailed concerning the right method, and though the medieval scholars lacked the tools we have today, they probably went about their task with neither more nor less diligence and honesty than modern scholars employ.

On the one hand we have the splendid eloquence, sublime mysticism, penetrating theological sense, and profound piety of St. Bernard (1090-1153), under whom the Abbey of Clairvaux became one of the chief centers of the Cistercian Order. Bernard's saintliness gave him great authority in the Church, and his severe asceticism commended him to his contemporaries. He was, however, an extreme allegorizer, whose sermons on the Song of Solomon represent various mystical reflections about God, angels, and the Church that are far removed indeed from

---

[5] Ecclesiasticus 18:1. The Vulgate reads "simul."

the literal sense of the book, which is quite erotic in character. When his allegories seem to carry him too far afield, he will stop short to try to discover moral edification rather than turn to any literal meaning the book might have. Joachim of Floris (d. 1202), one of the most extreme allegorists, developed, through his allegorization, a revolutionary doctrine of Church. On the other hand, in Andrew of St. Victor, we have what might be called, in terms of the day, an historic radicalism.

Nevertheless, there was always in the Middle Ages a strong tendency towards making the moral sense of Scripture supreme, and generally speaking this consideration dominated others. According to one writer, the foundation of Scripture is history, the walls are allegory, and the roof tropology, that is, an attention to the moral sense of Scripture which discloses to the reader how he ought to act. We might express this medieval emphasis by saying that the Bible is intended not only to instruct and enlighten the minds of men but also to move their hearts.[6]

---

[6] For a learned modern discussion of medieval ways of reading the Bible, see Henri de Lubac, S. J., *Exégèse Médiévale* (Paris: Aubier, 1959 ff.) .

*It is befitting Holy Scripture to
put forward divine and spiritual truths
through comparisons with material things.*
—St. Thomas Aquinas

CHAPTER 7 *The Thomist Solution*

We have seen that long before the Victorines, some scholars saw the danger of wild allegorizing. They felt there must be in the Bible a foundation of "literal" meaning. At the same time, the prestige of allegorical methods of exegesis was so great that it always tended to reduce the literal interpretation to a sort of second-class exegesis. Eucherius of Lyons (d. 449 [455?]) had used a scheme of "levels" of exegesis that had been suggested by the heritage from Origen and was to be for long normative. His words echoed down the Middle Ages: "The letter kills, while the spirit vivifies." So while there were many who insisted, in Antiochene fashion, upon the necessity for accounting the literal sense basic, this did not remove from their minds the characteristic early medieval conviction that when a scholar went about his exegetical task, it was only when he reached the figurative and spiritual kinds of interpretation that he was able to show his best quality as a Christian scholar. After all, every architect knows that though in the construction of a building everything depends upon the foundations, yet it is what rises above them that his critics approve or condemn, and that makes him a great architect or otherwise.

Of course, the matter is not really so simple. The sharp distinction between "literal" and "figurative" is unsatisfactory, if only because even the most literalistic kind of language is in some way or to some extent figurative. When we read that David lifted up his voice,[1] are we to understand that he elevated his larynx in his throat, or is this just a way of saying he cried or shouted? Then, if this is a metaphor, does this take the passage out of the set of "literal" statements and place it in the collection of "figurative" ones? Have we moved into figurative exegesis, or are we still with the letter of the Bible? Then again, suppose we are dealing with a parable such as the one about the good Samaritan. An intelligent, but untutored child, even, can see that the point of the story lies beyond the bare rapportage of events. Is the scholar obliged to go back to the "literal" sense and drearily expound the text accordingly, as "simple" narrative, before allowing himself to allegorize as even the child can do?

[1] II Samuel 3:22.

Such difficulties were not overlooked by medieval scholars even in the earliest period; but these scholars had no effective or conclusive way of dealing with them. It was against the rules of good theological debate for an argument to be presented in the form of a spiritual or figurative interpretation unless the disputant in the argument could substantiate his point in terms of the literal sense. In the hinterland of other fields, such as canon law and political theory, there was no such clear understanding. So the question might arise, for instance, whether one might invoke an allegorical interpretation of the Bible as one's defence in arguing for, say, the rights of the Church over the state. Again, there were often disputes between the monks and the secular clergy on canonical questions which, though not highly theological, were of practical importance to both sides. Certain priestly rights, such as the right of receiving tithes, had never been claimed by the monks in St. Benedict's day; but the time came when the monks claimed them and the secular clergy contested their claim. In a record of such a dispute, the secular priest uses the following argument: in the Bible, the tribe of Levi exclusively enjoyed the right to such tithes, and the tribe of Levi, being the priestly tribe, is represented in Christianity by the priests, not the monks. The monastic answer to this argument ran thus: the story of Isaac may be understood allegorically, as meaning that Abraham's sacrifice of Isaac prefigures the sacrifice of Christ; but as Isaac deprived Esau of his birthright, so the avaricious secular clergy are deprived of their privilege, which goes instead to the monks, who in the biblical story are prefigured by Jacob.[2] This monastic argument, which includes seeing the Church in Rebecca, who preferred her favorite son to him who had right by primogeniture, could be made to seem plausible in such a dispute (for the monk had ethical right on his side), though it would have been untenable in a strictly theological debate unless it could have been shown to have a foundation in the "literal" use of the Bible.

Such arguments seem farfetched today, and indeed they probably seemed a little farfetched even in the twelfth century. The difference is that there was not at that time the same objection as there would be today to their being farfetched. The Bible was the Church's fundamental document, and from it one could expect specific guidance in theological and doctrinal matters; but one could not expect such specific guidance in practical questions relating to contemporary social, political, and legal matters. There, in the absence of canonical authority in legal codices, tradition, or custom, the Bible could be invoked; but in the nature of the case the invocation must be directed to allegorical interpretations.

[2] R. Foreville and J. Leclercq, "Un débat sur le sacerdoce des moines au XII° siècle," *Studia Anselmiana. Analectica monastica,* XLI (1957), pp. 8-119.

Had the Antiochene approach prevailed in the early Middle Ages, making the Church more thoroughly literalistic in its attitude to the Bible, the result would have been very different. Either the Bible would have lost its prestige as the fundamental document of the Church, or else the Church would have been forced into an extremely narrow legalism that would have altered the character of all its institutions and deprived it both of its humanizing and intellectual power, and of its capacity for fostering, corporately and individually, a rich devotional life. The twelfth century was to see, in fact, what dangers could attend excessive literalism, not least when the Bible was translated into the vernacular, read by simple people, and used in special pleading for a particular point of view.

For instance, when Peter Waldo or Valdes, a rich merchant of Lyons, asked a theologian for guidance to heaven, the latter directed him to the Gospel story of the rich young ruler who, desiring perfection, was told by Jesus to sell all his goods and give the proceeds to the poor. In 1176 Waldo, deciding to take this counsel, paid his creditors, provided for his wife and children, and proceeded to distribute the rest of his wealth among the poor. Then, with a copy of the New Testament in the vernacular, he followed closely the directions it provided in regard to dress and other matters. Obedient to the appropriate Gospel injunction, he wore no shoes and carried no purse as he went forth begging his daily bread. As he gained followers, he enjoined them to follow him in the same practice, literally obeying the details of the Gospel injunctions.

The movement he led, which had many of the features that were to characterize the early followers of St. Francis of Assisi half a century later, was at first approved by the Pope. Then the Waldenses, attaching themselves more and more to the kind of literalistic method of Bible reading that had inaugurated their movement, began to preach with or without local episcopal approval, and they were eventually excommunicated. They went out in twos, according to what they accounted an express requirement in the teaching of Jesus. They memorized large portions of the New Testament in the vernacular, upon which they meditated in an independent and literalistic fashion without regard to the problems in biblical exegesis that were posed by the scholarly standards of their time. They condemned as "Pharisees" the scholarly commentators who used allegory. The Franciscans, though in many ways of the same spirit and with similar ideals, were soon to play an important role in purifying the medieval Church of many of the laxities that disfigured her. Their schools were to become, by the end of the thirteenth century, one of the liveliest intellectual forces in Europe, not least in England. The Waldenses, on the contrary, remained obscure down to comparatively recent times.

60

The Albigenses, or Cathari, who represented a movement of a very different sort, flourished extensively in the twelfth century in southern France and northern Italy and Spain. Also emerging as a protest against ecclesiastical corruptions, which were of a particularly deplorable character in these regions, the Albigenses taught a dualistic philosophy that made them appear sometimes like a resuscitation of old life-negating heresies in the Church, sometimes like another religion altogether. Broadly speaking, they regarded Satan as the author of the material world and God as the author of the spiritual world they believed to be at war with it. Some actually committed ritual suicide (the *endura*), either slowly by self-starvation or by a more expeditious method such as blood-letting. Far from seeing any unity in the Bible, the Albigenses took the Gospel according to St. John as their special charter, and while they used the New Testament generally, they accounted large portions of the Old Testament to have been inspired by Satan.

At this time there were many Bibles circulating in the vernacular, and it is well known that the medieval Latin Church sometimes opposed their use. What is often ignored is that these popular Bibles were generally well interlarded with various fanciful and apocryphal stories that were not in the biblical text at all but had been added by what we should nowadays call occultist groups by way of providing more "biblical" support for their doctrines than they had been able to find in the Bible itself. Such compositions, in French or German, sometimes in versified or dramatic form, bore little real resemblance to the Bible, and even the less extravagant books of this kind, such as the *Historia Scholastica* of Peter Comestor, written about 1175, and the *Speculum* of Vincent of Beauvais, of the next century, contained much apocryphal material.[3]

It was against such a background of abuse of the biblical text either by fanciful allegorizing or, worse, by shameless tampering on the one hand and obscurantist literalism on the other, in contrast to an increasingly well-grounded tradition of scholarly moderation in learned circles, that the universities grew. As the new order of friars, notably the Franciscans and Dominicans, began to dominate the intellectual scene, a mature and restrained interpretation of Scripture was carried out in the great centers of learning, notably at Paris and Oxford.

By far the greatest figure in all this, as in much else in the golden age of medieval thought, was St. Thomas Aquinas (1225-1274). Not only had he a vast familiarity with the Latin Bible; he regarded Scripture as the foundation of all theological studies. To him is attributed the

[3] Cf. Steven Runciman, *The Medieval Manichee* (Cambridge: Cambridge University Press, 1947), pp. 167-68.

saying: I am a man of one book (*homo unius libri*). His great *Summa Theologiae* begins with an examination of the role of Scripture as a channel of human knowledge of God, and before coming to the end of even the first *quaestio* or section of his vast work, he approaches crucial subjects such as the use of metaphor in Scripture and the various senses in which Scripture may be read.

Addressing himself to the question of the use of metaphor in the Bible, he considers first, in accordance with the usage of the schools, the chief objections. It would seem that metaphors are proper to poetry, accounted the least intellectual activity, and should have no place in the scientific presentation of theological truths, such as might be expected of the Scriptures, as the fundamental documents of the Church. The Bible is supposed to manifest truth, so why would this be hidden under figurative language? Moreover, the higher creatures are in the order of being, the nearer they approach the divine likeness, so that one should expect to find represented in the Bible the noblest rather than the lowliest of creatures; yet the contrary is often the case. In answer, St. Thomas points out that it is natural to man to attain to the highest, most intellectual truths, through sensible things because (as Aristotle taught) all our knowledge originates in the senses. The fifth-century mystical writer Dionysius had said: "We cannot be enlightened by the divine rays except they be hidden within the covering of many sacred veils." The Bible is for all. Therefore, the spiritual truths therein are properly expounded under the figure of corporeal things, so that even the simplest minds can learn the truths in their own fashion though they cannot grasp them in an intellectual way. The function of metaphor in poetry is different. Poetry uses metaphors because it is intended to please, and such representations are naturally pleasing. The Bible uses metaphors, however, for a nobler purpose, and in terms of this purpose they are necessary. The fundamental purpose of the Bible is to give man a knowledge of God.

Then St. Thomas comes to his final answer to the objectors. As Dionysius taught, it is to be noted that the veil of sensible imagery does not extinguish or exclude the ray of divine revelation.[4] The truth so far remains that *it does not allow the minds of those to whom the revelation has been made to rest in the likenesses, but raises them to the knowledge of intelligible truths.* The very hiding of truth in figures, says St. Thomas, is useful for the exercise of thoughtful minds and is a defence against the scorn of unbelievers. He recalls the Gospel injunction: "Do not give dogs what is holy."[5]

[4] Cf. Augustine: "Light, even though it pass through dirt, is unsullied." (*Lux, etsi per immunda transeat, non inquinatur.*)

[5] Matthew 7:6.

Here is the very spirit of the Thomist view of the Bible. It is not only a treasure-house for the learned. It is a mine for all. It demands study and may be studied at various levels. The revelation of God it contains (for God is its author) is concealed from the idle inquirer, the lazy or superficial reader, and above all from the man of ill will who does not really want to find it and, being afraid that his conscience will be searched out by it, affects to scorn it. The sublime truths it proclaims are revealed in proportion to the diligence, the studious love, that is brought to it. So while it stretches up to God on the one hand, it is grounded deep in the common things of earth, where, reaching the simplest man and showing him God, however obscurely, it can lead him to his final destiny which is the eternal enjoyment of God.

Proceeding at last to a solution to the problem of "levels" of meaning in the Bible, which he undertakes in the last article of this introductory prologue, before launching into his philosophical and theological exposition of the doctrine of God, St. Thomas again raises the objections in customary style. The Bible should state truth without danger of fallacy, and where there are different senses or levels of meaning, there exists a confusion that leads to the destruction of clear argument. Moreover, there is no plain rule about what the supposed levels are; while St. Augustine has one sort of fourfold scheme (history, etiology, analogy, and allegory) in his interpretation of the Old Testament, there has grown up another fourfold scheme (historical or literal, allegorical, tropological or moral, and anagogical or spiritual), so that there seems to be not even common agreement among the authorities. Besides, where do parables—so important in the Bible—fit into either scheme?

St. Thomas replies that words have a primary meaning: they signify things, historically or literally. In the Bible, however, the things signified have also a further spiritual or figurative meaning, and this spiritual sense has a threefold division, as follows. (1) According to the writer of the Epistle to the Hebrews,[6] the Old Testament itself is a figure of the New; (2) according to Dionysius, the New is itself a figure of future glory;[7] and (3) according to the New Law, Christians believe that whatever Christ has done is a type of what ought to be done by us. In these three kinds of figure we see the threefold division of the spiritual or figurative sense of Scripture. To the extent that the Old Testament prefigures the New, there is the allegorical sense of Scripture. To the extent that the things that signify Christ are also signs of what ought to be done by us, there is the tropological or moral sense. To the extent that they signify that which relates to future glory, there is a higher allegorical

[6] Hebrews 10:1.
[7] *Ecclesiastical Hierarchy*, 2.

(spiritual or anagogical) sense in Scripture. The biblical writers may intend only the historical or literal sense; but God, who "by one act comprehends all things by his intellect" and who is ever speaking through the Bible, so addresses the reader spiritually, beyond the literal or historical signification.

This is at once the culmination of medieval thought on, and the classic medieval solution of, the problem of the relation of the literal to the figurative in the interpretation of the Bible. The role of both literal and figurative is vindicated in terms of this solution. St. Thomas builds the gigantic edifice of his theological system upon it. While his treatment is inevitably, from the standpoint of contemporary studies in the philosophy of language, an inadequate formulation of the problem as well as an inadequate solution, it still provides a basic key to the understanding of the Bible. On the one hand, the language of the Bible is often quite commonplace, for this kind of language is proper to the circumstances that surround its writing. On the other hand, by the same token, the language of the Bible, taken as a whole, *must* be odd because the purpose it serves, the revelation of God's truth to needy man, is as odd as odd can be.

The novelty and subtlety of the Thomist solution may elude us. Its schematic form is not notably different from that which, bequeathed by Origen, had already been traditional in the Latin West for eight hundred years. What St. Thomas did with the traditional schema was, however, highly original. While holding the Bible to be inspired by God, he noted that it was written by men. God's meaning permeated what they wrote; but there was also a meaning intended and conveyed by the writers themselves. The latter is the "literal" meaning, through which God's meaning, the spiritual one, shines. When a scholar approaches the Bible, his ears ought to be attuned to the voice of God, so that he may perceive the spiritual meaning God conveys to such ears; but as a scholar his primary task is to consider the intention of the biblical writer himself. In expounding this he must take into account the biblical writer's use of metaphor and other figurative language, *all of which belongs to the "literal" or "fundamental" meaning of the Bible.* In other words, as we might say, God uses the Bible as a basic melody and sings his own descant upon it to those who have ears to hear these celestial notes. The descant is, of course, what makes the Bible the special joy of Christians, sustaining and guiding them along the pilgrimage of life; but the scholar's task is to attend to the basic melody, so that God's voice beyond it may have, so to speak, good ground to work on.

St. Thomas is naturally anxious to show that the "literal" sense of Scripture can be very rich and interesting, full of poetry and imagery. The Bible could be read with literary profit and often delight on this account alone, even by a person deaf to the descant. It seems clear from the method he adopts in his own commentaries that he wished to get away from the old heritage from Alexandria that the "literal" sense is necessarily inferior, being "flesh" rather than "spirit." No, the literal sense is also manifestly spiritual. The biblical writers used metaphors and similes, allegories and parables, as do any other literary artists, and these not only stimulate and delight the imagination, as does all good artistry, but also may instruct and edify as does all humane learning.

This scholastic solution of the problem, though not unresisted, gradually gained universal acceptance. By the middle of the fourteenth century the old methods of argumentation had gone entirely out of favor, having given place to a new attitude that implied that the exegete had plenty of important work, calling for qualities of imaginative skill as well as learning and patience, without going into the mystical allegories that might be extracted from Scripture by those who sought them there. The difference of exegetical method soon becomes apparent in fourteenth-century commentators. Even the Song of Solomon, which had been always traditionally very much allegorized as referring, for instance, to Christ and the Church, now came to be treated more historically. Of course something edifying had to be found in it; but this was supposedly discovered in the intention of the author himself. Solomon—so it was thought—might have expressed his own feelings in a secular love song in order to get over to his readers an idea of the love that God bears towards his own people. God is married to Israel.

By the time that Nicholas of Lyra came to his task, armed with the tools of some of the Jewish scholars of the day, it seemed possible to a Christian scholar to enunciate certain criteria by which a specifically Christian interpretation of the Old Testament might be made. Broadly speaking, it was as follows. An Old Testament passage might be so interpreted only if it had been already so interpreted in the New Testament itself, or if the ancient rabbinical authorities allowed a messianic type of interpretation, or if the passage itself was clearly more easy to understand in a Christian than in a Jewish setting. On these principles, he was able to treat only about one psalm in six as referring specifically to Christ.

At Paris and Oxford such relatively advanced methodologies gained favor for a time. As the spirit of scholasticism declined, however, people went back to the old methods without the simplicity of heart and mind that had made these methods honorable in their day. Many paid lip service to St. Thomas but were disobedient to the vision he had offered of true piety through honest scholarship. By the fifteenth century, when practical corruption in the Church was crying out to heaven for radical reform, scholarly use of the Bible had fallen so low, the example of

St. Thomas notwithstanding, that only drastic reform could bring back the kind of intellectual life that would eventually make possible a new understanding of the Bible. The Reformation was far from bringing this about all at once; but by that time new tools were available to the Reformers. These tools enabled them to make fresh beginnings in the solution of the problem St. Thomas had so well mapped out in his day and, within the limitations of the thirteenth century, so skilfully treated.[8]

---

[8] St. Thomas sets forth the basic principles of his teaching on the nature and use of the Bible in his *Summa Theologiae*, I, 1, 1-10.

*Everywhere I sought rest and found
none, save sitting in a nook with a book.*
—Thomas à Kempis

CHAPTER 8 *Vernacular Manuscript Bibles in the Middle Ages*

The original languages used in the Bible were of course at one time vernacular tongues; that is to say, the Bible was written in the language of the people. We have seen that versions were subsequently produced to meet the needs of particular communities to whom these tongues were foreign or otherwise unintelligible. The Georgian, Gothic, and Slavonic Versions are examples. Latin itself was once a vernacular tongue. The translation of the Bible into such languages resulted in its transmission in various versions.

In the present chapter, however, we are to be concerned not with such versions, but with the translations of the Bible into vernacular tongues other than English that are now actually spoken in Western Europe today, or that were archaic forms or the immediate ancestors of these modern languages. We shall see that, contrary to what is often imagined, the Bible was extensively translated in the Middle Ages into such languages as French, German, Italian, and Spanish, as well as English, centuries before the Reformation. To the story of the vernacular Bible in England, a separate chapter will be devoted.

The principal version in the West was, of course, the Vulgate. Throughout the Middle Ages, Latin was the language universally employed in the West as a scholarly medium. Its use continued, indeed, in scholarly circles for long after that. Every serious medieval student of the Bible approached his subject, therefore, with a knowledge of Latin as his most fundamental tool. It was only after the Reformation that there was any *widespread* popular study of the Bible in vernacular tongues such as English and German, by which time all serious biblical scholars had turned to such use of the Hebrew and Greek originals as had become available. Even then, the Latin Vulgate was consulted. It was among the secondary tools used, for instance, by the seventeenth-century team of translators who produced the King James Version.

In the Middle Ages people were nevertheless by no means without any knowledge of the Bible in the common speech with which they were familiar in the marketplace. Printing by movable type was not invented till the middle of the fifteenth century, when the celebrated edition of the Vulgate commonly called the Gutenberg Bible was printed, showing men what marvels the new invention could accomplish. Between then and the birth of Luther in 1483 there were already, as we shall see,[1] many printed translations of the Bible, in whole or in part, into various vernacular tongues. When Luther began his translation of the Bible into German in 1521, no fewer than eighteen editions of a German version had already appeared.

Long before the invention of printing, however, numerous manuscripts of the Bible in various vernacular tongues had been circulating during the Middle Ages. Fragments survive from the earlier medieval period, showing that even before Charlemagne such biblical translation into the everyday language of the people was not at all unknown.

Fragments amounting to twenty-five leaves survive that pertain to an eighth-century manuscript of the Gospel according to St. Matthew, in Latin and German. This manuscript belonged to a monastery at Monsee, Bavaria, and the translation is in a Bavarian dialect. The St. Gall manuscript, dating from the second half of the ninth century, of a translation of Tatian's Diatessaron or "Harmony of the Gospels" into an East Frankish dialect of German provides further witness to the existence at an early date of basic biblical materials in the German vernacular. It is known that Notker Labeo, a monk of St. Gall who died in 1022, translated the books of Job and Psalms, with a commentary, and of his work the Psalms survive. The arrangement of his work, with the Latin, the German, and the commentary arranged interlinearly, sentence by sentence, points to this work's having been intended for study rather than devotion. Williram, Abbot of Ebersberg, who died in 1085, translated with commentary the Song of Solomon. This was a popular work, and it survives in several manuscript forms. The translation is a very free one, but once again in a good German style.

There are further manuscripts showing the continuation of this sort of work in the twelfth and thirteenth centuries, and in the fourteenth we find the beginning of a vast number of translations. There is evidence for the existence of well over a hundred biblical manuscripts in German pertaining to the fifteenth century alone. One of the manuscripts, the *Codex Teplensis,* so called from the Norbertine or Premonstratensian [2] monastery of Tepl in Bohemia, reflects Waldensian, but almost certainly not exclusively Waldensian, origin. The Wenzel Bible, so called after the German king of that name, containing most of the Old Testament

[1] See chapter 12.

[2] The Premonstratensians are the Order of Canons Regular founded by St. Norbert in the twelfth century, who from the color of their habit are sometimes called White Canons.

translated by Martin Rotlev in the last decade of the fourteenth century, is a splendid work in six elaborately illustrated volumes.

The story of printed versions belongs to a later chapter of this book;[3] but a note on the earliest printed Bible in German may be useful at this point. It was at one time a matter of controversy; but according to W. Walther, one of the most eminent experts in this field, it was certainly the one printed at Strasbourg by Mentel, a copy of which at Stuttgart states that it was printed in 1466, and another at Munich that it was bought on June 27 of that year for the sum of twelve gulden.

The oldest known manuscript containing any translation of biblical texts into a French vernacular is a Latin Bible of the eighth century that includes a few glosses in the vernacular. It could hardly be expected at a much earlier date, since French had by then only somewhat recently emerged as an independent *lingua romana rustica*. In 813 the Synod of Tours ordered the Latin homilies to be translated into that vernacular tongue. After the emergence of two distinct vernacular tongues, the *langue d'oil* of the north and the *langue d'oc* of the south (the ancestor of the Provençal dialect surviving to this day), the *langue d'oil* appeared in four different dialects, of which three (Norman, Picard, and Burgundian) gradually gave place to the French of Paris, which achieved linguistic supremacy in the fourteenth century, having to a great extent supplanted by that time even the *langue d'oc* of the south.

As early as the twelfth century, however, we find a manuscript of considerable portions of the Bible, mostly in the Norman dialect, but partly in the *langue d'oc*. Thereafter we find numerous French psalters and manuscripts of various portions of the Bible. By the end of the twelfth century we begin to hear of considerable portions of the Bible translated by or for the Waldensians; but there are many other such manuscripts that show no Waldensian connection at all. These manuscripts were intended for regional use, being in dialects not understood over the whole country.

The first complete French Bible appears in the second quarter of the thirteenth century. It was made at Paris by a team of translators and shows unevenness in quality and style. While the translators seem to have used several Latin manuscripts, the principal basis of their work was evidently a copy of the Vulgate text revised by scholars of the University of Paris. The contemporary Roger Bacon gives the year 1226 as the date of that Paris revision. In the Bibliothèque Nationale are an imperfect copy of this French Bible that may be dated about the middle of the thirteenth century and a perfect one that may be assigned to about the end of the fourteenth.

[3] See chapter 12.

In the first half of the fourteenth century there was also an Anglo-Norman French version made in England. A revision of this, providing a text independent of the great thirteenth-century French version, was made in the diocese of Reims, probably about the middle of the fourteenth century. There is also the so-called Bible of Charles V, of which a manuscript in the Bibliothèque Nationale gives a revised text that contains the entire Old Testament.

There is evidence that points to the translation of portions of the Bible into the Italian vernacular about the time of Dante's (1265-1321) infancy or youth. No manuscripts survive, however, that are to be dated earlier than the fourteenth century, and there is evidence in these of the influence of the thirteenth-century French Bible. One of the most eminent authorities on the history of the Bible in Italian, S. Berger, has shown that there is an especially close connection between the Italian texts and those emanating from Provence. The earlier Italian translations of portions of the Bible were very probably for devotional use. The portions were generally such books as the Psalms, the Wisdom literature, and the Gospels. Later, however, the work was completed, probably by Dominicans in the fourteenth century. There are several extant manuscripts belonging to the fourteenth and fifteenth centuries; but the only surviving one that contains the entire Bible in Italian is one of Neapolitan origin that may be dated about the end of the fifteenth century. It is now in Paris in the Bibliothèque Nationale.

The predominant dialect in the medieval Italian manuscripts of the Bible is Tuscan; but Venetian is sometimes found, and there seems to have been an independent Venetian text of the Gospels. The authorship of the medieval translations of the Bible into Italian is not easy to determine. Various names—such as those of the Dominican friar Domenico Cavalca of Pisa who died in 1342, John of Tavelli who, born in 1386, became Bishop of Ferrara, James of Voragine, and others—have been associated with the translation of the Bible into Italian; but the part they played in the work is obscure.

In Spain, the existence of manuscripts of the vernacular Bible by the year 1233 is attested by the decree passed by Juan I, King of Aragon, that no one, cleric or lay, was to have in his possession a copy of the Bible in the vernacular tongue. Alphonsus the Wise, however, who reigned 1252-1284 and who favored the translation of the works of antiquity into Spanish, is said to have ordered a translation of the Bible from the Vulgate. A sort of paraphrase of at least parts of the Bible was produced in his time. Gradually, actual translations were made, of which many fourteenth- and fifteenth-century manuscripts survive.

The influence of medieval Jewish scholarship is conspicuous in the Spanish versions. In particular must be noted a fifteenth-century manuscript in the Escurial, consisting of a large portion of the Old Testament, including the Psalms. These purport to have been, and evidently were, translated from the Hebrew in the thirteenth century, probably at Toledo, by Herman, known as a translator of Aristotle. The second half of the Bible is contained in another manuscript, dating from the fourteenth century. This may be a text going back to a very early date, since it exhibits the influence of the Gothic Version. The translation, or rather revision, ordered in 1422 by Luis de Guzman, Master of the Order of Calatrava, and executed by Rabbi Moses Arragel of Maqueda, near Toledo, with the assistance of Franciscan scholars within the next few years, is a splendid piece of work. Sometimes called the Bible of the Duke of Alba, it naturally reflects the translator's knowledge of Hebrew. There are also, however, several medieval Spanish manuscript translations of the Vulgate, such as the one presented by Cardinal Quiroga to Philip II, before the earliest printed edition of any part of the Spanish Bible. The celebrated Ferrara Bible, published in 1553, and other Spanish printed versions will be considered later on.

There is a Portuguese counterpart to the Spanish scriptural paraphrase produced under the inspiration of Alphonsus the Wise. Evidence also exists to show that a Portuguese version of certain portions of the Bible, such as the Gospels, the Acts, and some of the Old Testament books had been made possibly as early as the fourteenth and almost certainly by the second quarter of the fifteenth century. There are no printed translations into Portuguese till very late in the seventeenth century.

The history of the vernacular Bible in the Netherlands also begins with scriptural paraphrases; but by the second half of the fourteenth century we begin to have manuscripts that point to the existence of a Flemish version, based on a translation from the Vulgate, as early as about the end of the thirteenth century. The anonymous Flemish translator indicated that the work of translation into the vernacular had been undertaken despite the disapproval of such enterprises by many people, both among the clergy and among the layfolk. The objections were not entirely unheeded, however, for apparently certain passages were omitted as likely to mislead simple people, such as the Deuteronomic provision of the death penalty for a bride whose lack of virginity her husband could prove to the elders.

As we turn to Scandinavia, we must bear in mind that Christianity was not introduced into the Scandinavian lands till the ninth century and met with little success till late in the tenth, so that we must not expect even the beginning of vernacular translations till comparatively late. Sweden was not christianized till the twelfth century. There is mention of a Swedish translation from the Vulgate of a part of the Bible, probably the Pentateuch, as early as the beginning of the fourteenth century. Other parts of the Bible were later translated into Swedish before the Reformation, all from the Vulgate; but there is no evidence of a complete Swedish Bible until after the separation of Sweden from Denmark in 1523. There is in Copenhagen, however, a fifteenth-century manuscript containing the first half of the Old Testament in a close translation from the Vulgate into Danish. This may reproduce a version current even as early as the preceding century. There are also several Danish manuscripts of the Psalms and of various fragments of the Bible.

The Bohemians, having contacts with the Slavs of the East who had several Slavonic versions at a very early date, may have had at least parts of the Bible in their vernacular tongue even as early as the tenth century. The earliest known manuscripts are the Wittenberg and the Clementine Psalters, which belong to the fourteenth century. There can be no doubt, however, that considerable portions of the rest of the Bible existed in the Bohemian tongue by that time. The translators of that period used the Vulgate text as their basis; but they probably also in many cases consulted such of the Slavonic versions as might be available to them. John Wyclif, with whom is associated the great medieval English manuscript version of the Bible, testifies that the wife of Richard II possessed a Bible in three languages, one of which was Bohemian.

John Huss, Wyclif's Bohemian admirer and counterpart, who was martyred in 1415, not only revised and corrected the Bohemian Bible but through his work on it rearranged the alphabet and remodelled the spelling of the Bohemian language. Many other revisions of the Bohemian Bible were made, and there were many manuscripts of the Bible and of the New Testament that show the use of the Vulgate as their basis before the appearance of the first printed Bohemian Bible in 1488.

The earliest known translation of the Bible into Hungarian dates from the beginning of the fifteenth century. It is attributed to two Franciscans who, under persecution, fled to Hungary from Bohemia. The various fragments that survive indicate that it must have contained at least a substantial part, if not all of the Bible. There was also a Hungarian translation by Ladislaus Batori, who died about the middle of the fifteenth century. The earliest book of any kind to be printed in the Hungarian language was a translation of the New Testament Epistles.[4]

⁴ See below, p. 105.

CHAPTER 9 *The English Bible in the Middle Ages*

England is exceptional in having no printed vernacular version antedating the Reformation. It has nevertheless a long history of vernacular versions in manuscript. The story of the English Bible is generally said to begin with Caedmon, who died in the year 680. Caedmon was a laborer who eventually became a monk. Since he translated nothing, he is not, strictly speaking, a contributor to the history of the translation of the Bible into the English tongue; nevertheless, he plays such a distinctive part in the embryonic stage of English Bible translation that he is of more than ordinary note. The story has been handed down to us by his contemporary, or near contemporary, the great early medieval English chronicler and biblical scholar, Bede.

When Caedmon was a laborer at the monastery of Whitby in the north of England, about the year 670, it was the custom in the evening to call for songs. Caedmon, being apparently a shy man, is said to have avoided this invitation by leaving the table just before his turn came. The story goes that one night, after he had so done, he lay down on his straw and fell asleep. In his sleep he was addressed by a visitant who said to him: "Caedmon, sing *me* something!" Caedmon explained that he was no good at that sort of thing; but, encouraged by the visitant, he burst forth into a song of praise in his own Northumbrian dialect. The song Caedmon sang was subsequently written down. A scriptural paraphrase, it may be the first native growth of English literature.[1]

Several chroniclers tell of Bede's work on the translation of the Bible. John Purvey, a disciple of Wyclif writing seven centuries after Bede, says of him that "if worldli clerkis loken wel here croniclis and bokis, thei shulden fynde, that Bede translatide the bible." There is no evidence for any extensive translation of the Bible by Bede; but Cuthbert, his contemporary, gives us a picturesque account of his death, at which time, he says, Bede was engaged upon the translation of the Gospel according to St. John. On the eve of the Feast of the Ascension, as Bede lay dying, he went on dictating to his disciples, urging them to write as quickly as they could. The following morning he was reminded that more remained to be done. Throughout the day he continued, despite interruptions. That evening he was reminded of a sentence that needed finishing. When

[1] On early English biblical materials, see M. C. Morrell, *Old English Biblical Materials* (Knoxville: University of Tennessee Press, 1965) .

he had dictated the needed words, the scribe observed, "Now it is finished." To which Bede replied: "Thou speakest truly; it is finished." Then, having bidden his friends to lay him down on the stone floor of his cell, he died peacefully with a prayer on his lips.

Very early manuscripts survive that give the Psalms and Gospels in Anglo-Saxon. A version of the Psalter, contained in a manuscript in the Bibliothèque Nationale, has been generally attributed to Aldhem, the first Bishop of Sherborne, who died in 709. The first fifty psalms are rendered into prose; the others are in verse. Here is a specimen, representing the first two verses of the one that is numbered psalm 103 in the King James and Revised Standard Versions:

> Bletsa, mine sawle, blidhe drihten;
>   and all min iuneran his thæne ecean naman!
> Bletsige, mine sawle, bealde dryhten!
>   ne wylt thu ofergeottul æfre weordhan.

A free translation of portions of Exodus and Acts was also made by King Alfred. Aelfric "the Grammarian" (c. 955–c. 1020), who became Abbot of Peterborough in 1004 and Archbishop of York in 1023, made from the Latin a metrical, abridged version of the Pentateuch and several other portions of the Old Testament. One of the best known of the earlier translations into Anglo-Saxon apart from the Latin text is a copy of the Gospels that is now in the library of Corpus Christi College, Cambridge. Dating from about A.D. 1000, it is a copy of a text known to have been circulating in the southwest of England at least fifty years earlier.

For about two hundred years after the Conquest in the eleventh century, there is little sign in England of translation of the Bible into the vernacular. The language, through the incorporation of Norman words, underwent considerable change. Anglo-French was the language of the law courts. The educated classes tended to be more content than ever to have Latin as the language of the Church. The people's knowledge of the Bible at this time must have been meager at best, being mostly confined to what they might be able to glean from the occasional homilies at Mass, and such rhyming paraphrases and fragmentary vernacular portions as they might be fortunate enough to hear.

The clergy were little better. Many must have corresponded fairly well to the priest of the celebrated story of a much later date who, chided for saying *mumpsimus* for *sumpsimus* in the prayer at the first ablution of the Mass, replied: "My *mumpsimus* is as good as your *sumpsimus!*" A visitation of seventeen parishes in Berkshire in 1222 revealed that five of the clergy did not know enough Latin to limp through the Mass. Nor are we to suppose that the better educated priests were necessarily better versed in the Bible. They could often be in some respects even more remote from it than were their less instructed brethren. The people had to depend, for the most part, upon priests who could hardly read the Bible themselves, let alone expound it to the people. Chaucer (*c.* 1340-1400) has satirically immortalized the English scene he knew in the fourteenth century, and there is certainly every reason to believe it had been no better and in some ways had been worse in the two hundred years succeeding the Norman Conquest.

On the other hand, one must not exaggerate the plight of the layfolk in those days. The devout could follow, and in their own way understand, the essential meaning of the great transaction presented to them, however fumblingly, with the aid of representational art and the lively and robust imagination that contact with the soil and the wonders of nature can bring to the most illiterate peasant. It must be remembered that the Church of that period, for all its preoccupation with penances and pilgrimages, was not encumbered by the peripheral devotions of the late medieval Church. Still less was it like the post-Reformation Roman Church, whose reactionary spirit all but smothered the ancient and early medieval liturgical rhythm and led eventually to emphases on such non-liturgical devotions as Corpus Christi processions, Quarant'ore devotions, litanies to the Sacred Heart, hymns in honor of the Immaculate Conception, rosaries of innumerable kinds, including one in honor of the Seven Dolors of the Virgin, and novenas to the Holy Ghost, the Holy Face, and the Immaculate Heart of Mary, to the point of making modern Roman liturgical reform extraordinarily and unnecessarily difficult. Least of all was the medieval Church of Dante's day decimated by the prosy chitchat that disfigures so much modern "Protestant" worship, making the Bible seem alien if only by reason of the demands it makes upon the poetic imagination. Perhaps, then, it was not so difficult in those days for the devout but unlettered peasant to feel himself, at Mass, in the presence of his Maker and touched by the grace of his Redeemer, as it is for most people today to feel this in the fussy drabness of Protestant worship.

I have elsewhere [2] told the story of how an illiterate yokel in modern times followed a church service that others found unfamiliar by thinking, as his father had taught him, of three colors—black for our unworthiness and sin; red for the cleansing gift of Christ's blood; and white for the result. Here is, after all, the quintessence of the Bible as Christians understand it, as well as of the Mass, making available to such a man, whose humility had taught him self-respect, insights that are too often "hid from the wise." Nevertheless, the twelfth-century English laborer was deprived of many spiritual riches through his lack of access to the

[2] See *The Coming Reformation* (Philadelphia: The Westminster Press, 1960), pp. 127-28.

Bible in its plentitude. This access was to mean much to his descendants of a later age.

Vernacular translations of the Psalter and some other scriptural materials were made in Anglo-Norman sometime before the end of the twelfth century, and some are inclined even to the view that the entire Bible was translated into Anglo-Norman in a literal prose version. This Anglo-French or Anglo-Norman was the language of the ruling class after the Norman Conquest of 1066. There is evidence that Old English manuscripts of the Gospels were copied in the twelfth century, so they were presumably read by some people; but generally speaking the Conquest so changed spoken English that Old English was now unintelligible. From the end of the twelfth or the beginning of the thirteenth century a work called the *Ormulum* makes its appearance. It consists of a poetical version of the Gospels and Acts, with a commentary, and it receives its name from the monastic translator Orm or Ormin. Only one manuscript of this translation, which may even possibly be the original, is known to exist. It is in the Bodleian Library, Oxford. From the mid-thirteenth century there are metrical versions of the Psalms and of various other books, notably Genesis, and there were prose versions of the Psalter in English dialects of the Midlands and the North.

The Psalter made by Richard Rolle of Hampole (*c.* 1295-1349) is especially noteworthy. Richard, a native of Yorkshire, went to Oxford and (according to the result of research into the records of the Sorbonne by Dom N. Noetinger) later to Paris to complete his theological studies as a priest. From about 1326 he lived as a hermit, preaching against the wickedness of the time, and eventually settled near Hampole, near Doncaster. He is of considerable interest as one of the first English writers to use the vernacular as well as Latin in his writings. He was a scholar and a poet, and his commentaries show considerable skill and learning in terms of the methods of the day.

A version of the principal New Testament epistles was made towards the latter part of the fourteenth century, evidently for the use of monks and nuns. Acts and part of Matthew were added later, and there is a prologue summarizing biblical history from the Creation to the Giving of the Law. It is in Early Middle English.[3]

The fourteenth century was a period of widespread turmoil for the whole of the Church in the West. From 1309 till 1377, the papacy was removed from Rome to Avignon. A papal court in France helped to undermine the influence of the papacy in England, where France was

[3] A specimen is given in chapter 33. On the history of the English Bible from Bede to Wyclif, see the article by H. Hargreaves in the Bulletin of the John Rylands Library, XLVIII (January, 1965), 118-40.

accounted the traditional enemy. Antipapal feeling was expressed in two important English enactments in the fourteenth century, the Statute of Provisors in 1351 and the Statutes of Praemunire, passed in 1353, 1365, and 1393, in restraint of appeals to the papal court and, finally, in prohibition of the promulgation in England of papal bulls. In Germany parallel sentiments found expression in 1338 when the electors asserted their right to choose a king without the necessity of papal confirmation. In England, after military victories at Crecy and Poitiers, came the "Black Death," a terrible plague that killed half the population in the middle of the century, resulting in a dearth of laborers and a consequent struggle by the laboring classes to obtain better wages, culminating in the Peasants' Revolt. By this time, moreover, English was coming back into favor among the upper classes, replacing Anglo-French.

This was Chaucer's England and the scene of the labors of John Wyclif (*c.* 1329-1384), the greatest, perhaps, of all the pre-sixteenth-century Church Reformers. With the activities of Wyclif and the Lollards, as his disciples were called, is associated the vernacular English of the Bible that circulated in manuscript as the only translation of the Bible available in the English tongue till the time of Tyndale and Coverdale, whose translations came after the Lutheran Reformation on the continent of Europe.

Wyclif, born into a manorial family, is closely associated throughout his life with Oxford. He soon gained a considerable reputation as a philosopher, attacking both Scotus and Occam. His rise to fame was due to his two works, *De Dominio Divino* and *De Civili Dominio,* in which he taught that since true lordship (*dominium*), such as was claimed by bishops, for example, depends on grace and is precluded in the present state of the Church, the Church should be disendowed and its material property confiscated. He fiercely attacked the Church that Chaucer satirizes, ridiculing fat-bellied monks, the scandalous holding of ecclesiastical benefices in which the incumbents rendered no service at all, and other abuses such as the popular saint-cults that gave rise to foolish superstitions far removed from the teaching contained in the Bible, and indeed from the best theological tradition of the Church. His views developed to the point at which, in the *De Potestate Papae,* written towards the end of his life and denouncing the claims of the papacy as without foundation in the Bible, he taught that the Gospel is the sole criterion of the conduct of the Pope.

There is no doubt that he encouraged the translation of the Bible into the vernacular. He expressly pled for this in a tract, pointing out that if the French, overcoming hindrances, should have a Bible in their own tongue, why not the English? "Also the wurthy reume of fraunse,[4] not-with-stondinge alle lettingis, hath translatid the bible and the gospels with othere trewe sentensis of doctours out of lateyn in-to freynsch, why shulden not engliysche men do so? as lordis of englond han the bible in freynsch, so it were not ayenus[5] resoun that they hadden the same sentense in engliysch; for thus goddis lawe wolde be betere knowun & more trowid for onehed of wit,[6] & more acord be be-twixe reumes."[7] Another tract, possibly by Wyclif but more probably by a disciple, denounces those who seek to keep the Bible from being translated into English. Such wicked men "crien opynly that secular men schullen not entirmeten[8] hem of the gospels to rede it in heir modir tonge, but heere her gostly fadris preche & do after him in alle thingis; but this is expresly ayenst goddis techynge." Wyclif, who in his last years had been appointed to the incumbency of Lutterworth, died on December 31, 1384.

The part Wyclif actually played in the work of the translation of the Bible traditionally attached to his name is obscure. To say the least, it was less than was for long popularly supposed. To Nicholas of Hereford is to be attributed the greater part of the translation into English of the Old Testament in the manuscript in the Bodleian Library, Oxford. Nicholas, while a Fellow of the Queen's College, Oxford, became an ardent Lollard and began to preach Wyclif's doctrines in 1382. After much persecution he fled to the continent of Europe, but later returned to England, where he resumed his Lollard activities. After becoming Chancellor of Hereford Cathedral, he resigned in 1417 to spend the last few years of his life as a Carthusian monk. He died about 1420. The author of the translation of the New Testament and the rest of the Old, in the Bodleian manuscript mentioned, is unknown, though this part of the work has been traditionally ascribed to Wyclif himself.

A later revision was made, probably by John Purvey (*c.* 1353–*c.* 1428), whose remarks on Bede have already been noticed.[9] Purvey was a close associate of Wyclif and till the end of his days a faithful exponent of his doctrine. There is no doubt, at any rate, that if he did the work of the revision, he did not do it alone. The prologue refers to the translator's having worked with others. The purpose of the work, it says, was "to saue alle men in our rewme,[10] whiche God wole haue sauid, a symple creature hadde myche trauaile, with diuerse felawis and helperis, to gedere manie elde biblis, and othere doctouris, and comune glosis." It

---

[4] realm of France
[5] against
[6] believed for unity of meaning
[7] realms
[8] interfere
[9] See above, p. 73.
[10] realm

also mentions a debt to Nicholas of Lyra, already noticed earlier in our present study. "On the elde testament," he writes, Nicholas of Lyra "helpide ful myche in this werke." The team appointed for the final revision "manie gode felawis and kynnynge [11] at the correcting of the translacioun."

The Vulgate was, of course, the only text available, and the translation in the Wyclif Bible follows it very closely. Moreover, the style is uneven: parts are very stilted with many Latinisms, while other parts are charmingly colloquial. The educated modern reader has no difficulty with "boyschel," which in the context he can easily enough recognize as an antique spelling of "bushel"; but words such as "gemels" (from the Latin, *gemini*) for "twins" are less obvious, modern space probes notwithstanding. Here is an example from a familiar passage, the opening words of Psalm 23 (according to the numbering of the King James and Revised Standard Versions), as rendered in the translation ascribed to Nicholas of Hereford: "The Lord gouerneth me and no thing to me shal lacke; in the place of leswe where he me ful sette. Ouer watir of fulfilling he nurshide me; my soule he conuertide."

The Wyclif Bible was enormously popular, attaining an astonishing circulation for a book issued before the days of printing. The Lollard preached wherever he could get a hearing. You might have heard him in a field or in a lane. Such a "poor preacher," as the Lollard was often called, prepared the hearts and minds of his hearers for a reform of the Church they would never see, but in which their great-grandchildren might perhaps take part.

Prominent among the causes of unrest that favored the spread of Lollardy was papal pressure on England and the growth in the nation of a desire for independence from the papacy. The vested interests of the English Church were nevertheless obviously endangered by Wyclif's teaching, and the Wyclif Bible met with ferocious opposition in many quarters. Those who read it were liable to forfeiture of "land, cattle, life and goods." Archbishop Arundel, writing to Pope John XXIII [12] (Baldassare Cossa), complained that Wyclif, in his attack on the Church, had crowned his evildoing by the production of a new translation of the Bible into the vernacular tongue. This was described as the work of Antichrist.

Wyclif, thanks to favorable circumstances and his influence in court circles, escaped martyrdom at the stake. His followers were not always so fortunate. Preaching against vested ecclesiastical interests was a hazardous occupation in those days. It could end by the roasting of the preacher. Many of the Lollards were effectively silenced after the passing of the

[11] cunning; that is, knowledgeable and skilful
[12] See below, p. 91.

act, in 1401, *De haeretico comburendo*. This act provided that persons holding heretical views were to be arrested and tried by the Canon Law of the Church. If the bishop found them guilty of heresy, they were to be handed over to the secular courts who would cause them "to be burnt that such punishment may strike fear into the minds of others." The practice of burning heretics by the secular authorities on the demand of the Church had been established long before this date, and one of the Lollards, William Sawtre, was actually so martyred before the passing of the act in 1401. It was nevertheless the first time that the English Parliament had provided legislation supporting the practice. The act, later repealed, was to be revived by Mary Tudor, in whose reign hundreds were to suffer under it in the Reformation cause, before its final repeal by Elizabeth I.

The Lollards, in spite of persecution and the terror of the provisions of *De haeretico comburendo,* continued their work, the greatest strength of which lay in the dissemination of the English Bible. Ordinary people, men and women, were beginning to find in the Bible hope for a way out of the mess that the Church seemed unable, not to say unwilling, to clear up. In the preface to the revised version of the Wyclif Bible is a prayer that reflects the spirit of the Lollards at its best, as well as the circumstances in which they labored: "God graunte to us alle grace to kunne [13] wel and kepe wel holi writ, and suffre ioiefulli sum peyne for it at the laste." Joyfully or no, many did indeed suffer for the English Bible at that time. Some were burned with copies of it round their necks.

Copies of the English Bible were so eagerly sought that people paid well for even the loan of one. It is said that a load of hay was the price for an hour's use of it each day for a course of reading. The price was not unreasonable. A copy of such a manuscript represented an enormous amount of labor. Moreover, copyright was not safeguarded in those days, and a borrower, if he chose, might surreptitiously copy considerable passages while the book was briefly in his possession, and make a profit on the result, for people were only too glad to pay a high price for even only a few sheets of the much sought-after translation of the Bible into their mother tongue.

There is said to be, indeed, an ancient Irish decision on the subject of copyright in such manuscripts. The story goes that in the sixth century St. Columba, on a visit to St. Finian, had obtained permission to read the latter's Psalter. This was granted, and every night, while the old saint slept, the young saint was hard at work in the chapel where, according to the legend, a miraculous light enabled him to continue all through the night till at last he had copied the whole manuscript and was the proud possessor of a Psalter of his own. St. Finian, dis-

[13] know

covering what his guest had done, was very angry and argued that the latter's action was unlawful. The dispute was referred to King Diarmad, who gave the decision that "as to every cow belongs her calf, so to every book belongs its son-book." Columba, losing his Psalter, was so indignant at the adverse royal judgement that, according to the legend, the incident afforded him one of the reasons for his leaving Ireland.

Be that as it may, copyright was not easily safeguarded in the days of English Lollardy. Many copies of parts of the vernacular Bible probably owed their existence to its infringement. No doubt they brought hope and joy to innumerable hearts, showing countless men and women that in the Christian faith lay riches far beyond the compass of what they knew of it in the ordinary teaching and preaching of the Church. Over a hundred and fifty copies of manuscripts of the Wyclif Bible survive to this day. Let one reflect that, apart from the various causes of loss throughout the course of more than five hundred years, the authorities had burned as many copies as they could lay hands upon. That so many copies survive even to this day is evidence of a very extensive circulation in Lollard England.

The Wyclif Bible was intended for plain folk, not for scholars or nobles. Its language, at its finest, anticipates some of the best-loved phrases in the versions with which we are more familiar. "Strait is the gate, and narewe is the way," apart from the spelling, is indistinguishable from the phrase we know so well in the Sermon on the Mount. Likewise the Wyclif Bible gave us "the beame and the mote" and "the cuppe of blessing that we blessen." Sometimes its language is more beautiful in its simplicity than even the language of the King James Version that has so profoundly influenced the linguistic as well as the religious inheritance of the English-speaking world. "Blessed are the meek, for they shall inherit the earth" is the King James rendering; but the Wyclif Bible had said this with a sharper ring: "Blessed be the mylde men, for thei shuln welde the errthe." What a promise to the survivors of the Black Death in Chaucer's England!

Lollardy was naturally also used as a cover for types of social revolt that were far from the spirit of Wyclif. All such movements are in danger of being so abused. The spiritual effect of Wyclif was nevertheless widespread and enduring. Lollard teaching spread to Scotland. Two men charged with Lollardy went to the stake in Scotland long before the burning, in 1528, of Patrick Hamilton, the first native Scottish martyr in the Reformation cause. A manuscript translation of the Wyclif Bible into Scots was made by Murdoch Nisbet about the year 1520, a year before Luther's excommunication and forty years before the establishment in Scotland of the Reformed Church, in which accomplishment John Knox was to play the leading role.

CHAPTER 10 *The Sixteenth-Century Biblical Renaissance*

The movement for the Reformation of the Christian Church, though it comprises a long series of tendencies, events, failures, and achievements occurring in Western Christendom between the fourteenth and the seventeenth centuries, reached its explosive zenith in the sixteenth. It cannot be described as a failure or a success, for it was conspicuously both. That is to say, in contrast to the many attempts at the reform of Latin Christendom that had been the deep concern of all sincere and educated churchmen for more than a hundred years before Luther was born, the events of the sixteenth century were attended by many widespread, spectacular, and enduring successes; yet in terms of their leaders' very comprehensive aims, they were also failures, since they failed to bring about the fundamental goal of the Reformers, the *total* reformation of the Catholic Church, which according to all ancient orthodox Christian teaching is one and indivisible because it is accounted the earthly instrument of the one true God and, as the Bible has it, "the Body of Christ." [1]

Though the Reformers failed to bring about the total reform of the Catholic Church, as had been their dearest wish and firm intention, the influence of their movement has been in every way immense. It was enormous in extent, since Rome lost the allegiance of most of northern Europe, including England and Scotland, and but for little more than an historical accident would have lost also that of France. Even where, as in the lands of Italy, Rome maintained her authority, Reformation ideas exerted an influence more considerable than is generally remembered. Almost nowhere was the authority of Rome not seriously threatened.

In the long run, however, far more impressive than the extent of the influence of the Reformation in terms of "territorial gains" has been the depth of the influence of the Reformation heritage in terms of its effect upon the life of the whole Christian Church. From the first this manifested itself in many ways, not least of course in the profound spiritual vitality it fostered where Reformation ideas seized the hearts and minds of men, but also in the remarkable effect of the Reformation

[1] See Ephesians 4:1-16.

in hastening reforms already begun under the blessing of Rome as well as by stimulating others. The astonishingly rich and vigorous ecumenical movement we are witnessing in our own time is, of course, its outcome. The task of this movement, as seen from both "Roman" and "Protestant" eyes today, is to consolidate the riches that came out of the various programs of reform, while overcoming the impoverishments that also by any reckoning attended them.

Perhaps the best known, though unfortunately also one of the most misunderstood, effects of the Reformation was the new attitude fostered among "Protestants" toward the Bible. "The BIBLE, I say, the BIBLE only, is the Religion of Protestants," wrote a seventeenth-century English divine.[2] Words such as these, wrested from their contexts, have caused a great deal of confusion and misunderstanding about the work of the Reformers in regard to the Bible.

They have tended to encourage the promotion of absurd legends that till not very long ago were exceedingly common among ill-informed heirs of the Reformation and are by no means yet extinct. One of the more fantastic of these "Protestant legends" is the story that in the Middle Ages the Bible was for centuries hidden away and buried, so that the Church, by keeping the Bible out of men's reach, could exercise power over the minds of men without fear of their discovering the spiritual strength the Bible gives the individual who thereby obtains the means of revolt against ecclesiastical oppression.

According to a picturesque development of this legend that has already been mentioned, a young friar, Martin Luther, had the good fortune to come across, while rummaging among cobweb-laden books in the attic of his monastery, a copy of the Bible which, when he had read it, changed his life and enabled him to bring about the Protestant revolt against the old subjugation under the heel of Rome! This legend is no less cheap or ridiculous than its Roman counterpart that Luther, beset by scruples and compulsions arising out of an imperfect mastery of his own moral and spiritual life, brought about the Protestant Reformation by determining to lead a revolt against the whole Catholic Church in order that he might break his religious vows and marry a nun! Except among the very ignorant, neither legend is so readily believed as was the case even a century ago; but both recall to our remembrance the astounding degree of misunderstanding about the Reformation that has been deliberately introduced on both sides of the "Protestant-Catholic" controversy.

Three observations must be made upon the "Protestant legend." In the first place, we have seen how exceedingly powerful was the Bible

[2] William Chillingworth, *The Religion of Protestants. A Safe Way to Salvation* (1637).

in medieval life. No one who attends to the historical facts, whether he regards them as a misfortune or as a blessing for the Middle Ages, can fail to see the absurdity of the notion that at the end of that Bible-steeped period the Bible stood in any need of being "discovered in an attic."

In the second place, the term "Protestant" is singularly unfortunate because it is peculiarly and radically misleading. It was by a mere accident that it was coined. When, in the sixteenth century, Germany was divided between those who followed Luther's lead and those who still preferred submission to the Rome that condemned him, it became necessary to reach a practical *modus vivendi*. At that time in human history, the notion of religious toleration within the same region had not been developed in the form in which we understand it today. The principle was gradually evolved, therefore, that the prince of each territory should determine which side, within his own domain, would prevail. This principle was eventually expressed in the well-known maxim, *cujus regio, ejus religio;* that is, the religious allegiance of a territory would follow the religious allegiance of the prince of that territory. This principle was adopted in 1555 in a treaty known as the Peace of Augsburg. As early as 1526, however, it had been in effect devised by the Diet of Speier, which decreed that each prince should order ecclesiastical affairs within his territory according to his own conscience. In 1529, when the Diet met again at Speier, the proceedings happened to be controlled by a strong majority supporting the papacy, and legislation was passed putting an end to the toleration of Lutherans in all regions recognized as officially faithful to the papacy, while at the same time insisting upon the principle of toleration for the supporters of the papacy in all Lutheran territories. In protest against this ludicrously unfair arrangement, six princes and fourteen cities lodged a formal *protestatio* to the Archduke Ferdinand on April 19, 1529. As a result of this document, those who supported the cause of the Reformation of the Catholic Church came to be dubbed "Protestants."

The name so accidentally given them at the time becomes objectionable when generally applied to the heirs of the Reformation, if only because it is a mere outmoded nickname disproportionately perpetuating an exceedingly trivial incident in the enormously long and profoundly involved series of events in the Reformation process. It is also singularly unsuitable and inadequate as an expression of the characteristic aim of the Reformers, which was anything other than to create a "new" Church, let alone a new sect. The Reformers' aim was much more far-reaching. It was nothing less than the total reform of the One Catholic Church. Precisely for this reason it must be acknowledged that, despite the great moral and spiritual influence of the Reformation, the Reformers' principal aim has so far been unfulfilled. The ecumenically minded hope that it will be fulfilled in what is sometimes called in contemporary ecumenical discussions "the Coming Great Church." This hope can be fully realized only by what I have elsewhere optimistically called "the Coming Reformation." [3] The movement we call "the Reformation" is unfinished. It included a new attitude to the Bible, and it must lead to an ever deepening understanding of the function of the Bible in the Church before the full organic unity that is the final aim of every contemporary ecumenical enterprise can be achieved. The accomplishments of Rome's Second Vatican Council are a contribution to the hoped-for realization of that aim, which nevertheless still looks distant.

In the third place, misunderstanding fostered by identifying the Reformation with the "discovery" of the Bible in the sixteenth century does point, however, to a grain of truth in the Luther legend. For the Church's use of the Bible was, indeed, a lively point of controversy in the sixteenth century. It was the preoccupation, for example, of writers on the Roman side, such as John Driedo (*c.* 1480-1535), who took up his pen against the Reformers. Driedo is a most interesting writer, too little known [4] and yet an excellent protagonist of the Roman side in the sixteenth-century controversy. While accounting the Bible the inspired Word of God, Driedo insisted, as would all modern scholars on both the Reformation and the Roman side, that the Gospel is the testimony of the primitive Church about the nature and life of the Church. Speaking much of "apostolic traditions" and "the apostolic tradition," he developed a view of the relation of the Bible to the Church. According to him, the authority of the universal Church throughout the ages is the foundation of the relationship between Church and Bible, and a continuing function of the Church is to clarify the Bible. This is not in the least different from what the Reformers taught, except on one point. They insisted that though it is indeed the function of the Church to interpret the Bible, the authority of the Bible for Christians is not derived from the authority of the Church. The true Church, they taught, *hears* the voice of Christ, its own "Spouse and Pastor," and does not presume to exercise authority *over* that voice.

This emphasis on the independent authority of the Bible for Christians gave Reformation teaching its peculiar character and power. Far from attempting to diminish in any way the importance of the Church in the life of Christians, it did bring out an idea largely overlooked or undeveloped in practice in the Middle Ages, that the Bible possesses

[3] See *The Coming Reformation.*
[4] His work is the subject of a dissertation by John L. Murphy at the Gregorian University, Rome, published under the title *The Notion of Tradition in John Driedo* (Milwaukee: Seraphic Press, 1959) .

an autonomous and indirect spiritual authority as the individual's heritage in the Community of Faith that is the Church. Indirectly, however, this Reformation emphasis has also had another effect—one more closely related to the humanism that was the Reformer's principal ally apart from the life of the Church and one that is crucially important in this our own contemporary situation. The Bible has become, in a secondary sense, everybody's heritage. So it has become possible to invite the skeptic outside the Church as well as the churchman inside it to look at the Bible for whatever illumination he may perchance find there. The Bible has become not only the book *of* the Church; not even only the book *to* the Church; but also everyman's book. Whatever role it may be supposed to play in the eternal salvation of this man or that, it is everyman's book, for good or ill. One of the most remarkable indirect accomplishments of the Reformation is having put into effect this attitude to the Bible, as a spiritual mine open to all. In spite of the special treasures churchmen may claim to find in it, and in spite of the great learning that is necessary for an understanding of its many technical difficulties, it is a book to which all men may go directly with abundant profit. There is no need to keep it out of anybody's hands. For such is the faith the Reformation has engendered, that believers are willing to let God speak also to unbelievers through the book that contains, they are confident, his own Word.

Again, there was *in theory* nothing in this that was wholly contrary to the attitude of the Middle Ages; but medieval thinking about the Bible could not have expressed the situation in that way. When, at the close of the Middle Ages, the Reformers began to talk about the Bible as they did, there was resistance among those who had not yet been intoxicated by the spiritual power, vitality, and freedom that the sons of the Reformation found in the Reformers' message about the Bible. The Bible might have been translated into a hundred tongues though the Reformation had never taken place. It might quite possibly have become, even, a great bestseller of the new age of printing. But without the Reformation it could not have affected the hearts and minds of men as in fact it did.

It is true and not surprising that, even where the Reformation has exerted its greatest influence, the Bible has remained a closed book to many. The story is told of the farmer whose son was asked by the pastor whether they had such a thing as a Bible in the house. The son, remembering the large leather-bound volume that was at that time a conventional appurtenance of the American home, replied: "You mean the book Pop sharpens his razor on?" Old-fashioned Bibles of that sort sometimes helped to minister to men's shaving needs in a day when razors were open in fact and Bibles too often open only in theory; yet for all that, the Reformation not only opened the Bible to millions but, through the new attitude it brought to bear upon the Bible, gradually altered the whole face of Western culture. Among much else, it may almost be said to have brought the modern German language into literary being. Through its effect upon the use of the Bible, it also eventually transformed and immeasurably enriched the English tongue.

The theological teaching of the Reformers accorded with the dictum of Cyprian (d. 258) that "he cannot have God as his Father who has not the Church for his Mother." Nevertheless, they characteristically insisted no less that the Church is not the Mother of God's Word but is born of this. "The Church," wrote Luther, "is a daughter born of the Word, not the Mother of the Word." [5] To Luther the power of the Bible is something revealed to the reader by the Holy Spirit of God, and what is revealed there above all, by that Spirit, is that the center of the Bible is Christ. Christ is, he says, *punctus mathematicus sacrae scripturae,* the mathematical point of Holy Scripture.[6] Calvin was no less christocentric in his interpretation of the Bible. In his principal work, *The Institutes of the Christian Religion,* he quoted the New Testament nearly twice as often as the Old—the Old Testament 1,755 times and the new 3,098.[7] Both Luther and Calvin, however, admitted the immense debt they owed to the humanists, whose interest in the Bible sprang from a renaissance of all learning. The sixteenth-century Renaissance was, indeed, one of the many founts whence sprang the Reformation movement that conveyed the Bible to mankind with an astonishingly new vigor and power.

There is a task ahead of us before we can be ready to turn to an examination of the history of the great translations of the Bible that spring from the Reformation movement. For a full understanding of the motive that lay behind this epoch-making work, we must understand more precisely the magnitude of the Reformation spectrum and how deep are its roots in the Catholic Church out of which it emerged and whose corruptions it was intended to cleanse. Humanist and Reformer went hand in hand in conveying the Bible to everyman and encouraging everyman to read it, whether with the eye of faith as the Word of God to man, or through a lens ground rather to a skeptic's prescription. Through such a lens it can still be seen as at least part of the great literature of mankind. The humanistic Renaissance to which the Reformers owed so much was among the most important allies of the Reformation; but the roots of the biblical Renaissance went far deeper, even, than this. It is these deeper roots we must now briefly explore before turning to the mainstream of our story.

---

[5] *Werke* (Weimar ed.) , XLII, 324: Lectures on Genesis, 7:16-24.
[6] *Ibid.,* II, 439.
[7] Henri Clavier, *Etudes sur le calvinisme* (Paris: Fischbacher, 1936) , p. 87.

*I should wish that all good wives
read the Gospels and St. Paul's Epistles;
that they were translated into all languages; that
out of these the husbandman sang while
ploughing, the weaver at his loom.*—Erasmus

CHAPTER II *Roots of the Biblical Renaissance*

The intellectual achievements of the thirteenth century, notably of St. Thomas Aquinas, set that century apart as the Golden Age of medieval life. Thereafter comes a marked intellectual decline. This is by no means to say there was no important thought to succeed that of Bonaventure, Thomas, and Scotus. Nevertheless, the scholastic type of intellectual activity that had been chiefly responsible for the growth of the universities deteriorated soon after these acquired their great prestige as centers of a new kind of intellectual ferment such as Europe had never before witnessed. Spiritual and intellectual leadership passed to others—to a new type of mystic, for instance, and to the great fourteenth- and fifteenth-century humanists, such as Boccaccio (1313-1375) in the former century, and Laurentius Valla (1405-1457), Marsilio Ficino (1433-1499), and Pico della Mirandola (1463-1499) in the latter—all in their way precursors of the great humanist associates of the Reformation movement, such as Johann Reuchlin (1455-1522), Desiderius Erasmus (*c.* 1466-1536), and Jacques Lefèvre d'Etaples (*c.* 1455-1536).

Meanwhile, the successors of the thirteenth-century schoolmen degenerated on the whole to the point of the discussion of useless puerilities. There were indeed great scholastic minds even then. Durandus a Sancto Porciano, for instance, and Nicholas of Autrecourt may be rightly accounted in certain respects the medieval forerunners of Locke and Hume respectively. Nevertheless, the late medieval scholastics often did treat futile questions in a mechanical and unoriginal manner. I have never found evidence that anyone actually asked the celebrated question attributed to this period of medieval decline: "How many angels can dance on the point of a needle?" It hardly exaggerates, however, the absurdity of the questions then raised, and it fails, moreover, to reveal the full extent of the dreariness of the treatment such questions frequently received. Scholasticism, which had been a thrilling intellectual adventure, became an idle game.

The apparent decline of Christendom towards the end of the Middle Ages was by no means, however, only a decline in the vigor of its academic pursuits. All over Europe Christendom seemed to be in decay. The sun that was setting in the West appeared to be no less surely setting in the East. After the middle of the fourteenth century, not only were all the Eastern Churches except the Russian losing numerically and territorially; there was almost no sign of new intellectual life there at all. The Nestorians and Jacobites in Asia suffered from political oppression and persecution, shrinking in some cases to the point of extinction. Before the might of Islam, Armenians, Copts, and others, all suffered in varying degree. In 1389 a large number of Christians, men and women, who had renounced their faith under pressure, marched through the streets of Cairo denouncing Islam and uttering cries of repentance for their apostasy from Christianity. They were beheaded, and a new persecution of Christians began. By the end of the fourteenth century most of the Balkan peninsula had been conquered by the Ottoman Turks, and though there was valiant Christian resistance there to Turkish rule and, except in Albania, no extensive Christian capitulation to Islam, Christianity in the Balkans was much weakened in various ways.

Constantinople, the great bulwark of Christianity in the East and the focal point of the hopes of the Eastern Orthodox Churches, eventually fell in 1453 to the Ottoman Turks. On the eve of the final assault upon the ancient Christian capital, the Christian emperor, the patriarch, and their allies from the Christian West took Holy Communion in the cathedral of Saint Sophia. The following day the emperor was killed in action. The Turkish ruler, Muhammad II, entered the city, where in the same ancient Christian shrine a Muslim service was conducted in thanksgiving to Allah for the victory of Islam in Christianity's ancient holy place, and some decades later, St. Sophia was turned into a mosque. Today, under modern Turkish rule, it is little more than an ill-kept museum, despite the ancient glory it still reflects.

Meanwhile, the Turkish armies pressed on, till by the middle of the sixteenth century they had brought within the Turkish hegemony all the Balkans, except for inaccessible little Montenegro and a strip of the Dalmatian coast. The Turkish Empire now encompassed the Euphrates Valley in the East and embraced a huge expanse of territory that covered Asia Minor, Syria, Palestine, and Egypt. In Africa it reached Morocco, in Europe Hungary, and at one time the Turks even achieved an incursion, though brief and limited, into the Italian peninsula itself. The might of the Turkish invaders seemed irresistible, and in face of it Christendom, all sacrifices and martyrdoms notwithstanding, inevitably lost vast numbers of its children.

To those who had the fortitude to carry their fears to a logical conclusion, it must have seemed only a matter of time till the entire world should come under the Crescent of Islam and the odious rule of the Turks. In Asia Minor, to which St. Paul had journeyed to the Christian communities there, Christians captured and enslaved by the Turks sometimes voluntarily submitted to Islam in an effort to mitigate their sufferings. Others, more favorably placed, changed their religion in order to curry favor with their Muslim lords. Compulsory conversion also occurred, however, and on a large scale; young men forcibly subjugated to Islam were enlisted in the Turkish army, and the best of them were selected for service in the elite Turkish fighting unit, the Janissary Corps. That Eastern Orthodoxy survived at all in such circumstances is astounding.

In the course of the Crusades in which Christians from Western Europe went forth on a holy war to try to stem the tide of the Turkish conquest of Christendom, Latin Christians made contact with their separated brethren in the Eastern Churches, and out of these contacts grew a movement by the papacy to bring the Eastern Orthodox Churches into communion with Rome. These attempts met with some occasional, limited success, resulting in the existence today of various relatively small so-called Eastern Uniate rites within the Roman Catholic Church.

By the period now under discussion, Western Christendom was also, as we shall presently see, for other reasons in a seriously weakened state. Yet partly in spite of and partly because of this, the papacy continued its efforts to persuade the Eastern Christians to submit to the papal claims. The authority of the papacy, greatly undermined in the West, would have been enhanced by a successful attempt to bring Eastern Christians within the Roman obedience. Some Eastern Christians, harassed by their Turkish oppressors and desperate for help, sought compromise with Rome as a last hope. In 1438 and 1439 ambiguous agreements were reached. The resulting decrees were proclaimed. But they were signed only with reluctance by Eastern bishops, formally repudiated by the Eastern patriarchs, and overwhelmingly opposed by the Eastern Orthodox faithful who, even at the cost of losing the military aid they so badly needed, refused to pay the price of renunciation of their independence of Rome. Hatred and distrust of the papacy were to be further aggravated. Only very limited military help from the West was given to the beleaguered city of Constantinople. After its fall in 1453, when the very heart of Eastern Christendom seemed to have fallen irretrievably into Muslim hands, opposition to the papal claims, among the vast majority of the Eastern Orthodox Christians, increased. Relations between East and West deteriorated further, and Orthodox dislike and distrust of Rome have continued to this day. Even in face of modern forms of religious persecution in Soviet Russia and notwithstanding both the intense strife and confusion among Orthodox Churches today, on the one hand, and, on the other, the prevailing climate of ecumenical lovemaking, the Orthodox Churches continue to account themselves the One Indivisible Church, rejoicing in their independence of Rome.

In the West, during this medieval period, the fortunes of the papacy fell to their nadir. The Latin Church in Western Europe still looked, thanks to her inheritance of the ancient Roman mania for organization, by far the best-ordered stronghold of the Christian religion. Yet not only had she become seriously weakened; she was led into a state of anarchy and confusion that deeply distressed all thinking churchmen. True, there was some profound vitality within the *congregatio fidelium,* the congregation of the faithful people who in the last resort constitute the life of the Christian Church; but it seemed hidden and ineffective. The hierarchical structure of the Church was endangered by the obvious decline in the prestige of the papacy. The beginning of this decline may be traced to the removal of the papacy in 1309 from Rome to Avignon where it was to remain till 1377—the period of that exile that Boccaccio called, in a phrase later used also by Luther in another connection, the Babylonian Captivity of the Church.

The Popes during this period were for the most part personally much better men than many of their successors in the ensuing century; but their position was exceedingly difficult, and for a generation afterwards the Church was rent and further embarrassed by the presence of rival popes, latterly three at a time, each claiming the allegiance of all Christians and each receiving the support of some. This, the Great Schism, lasted from 1378 to 1417. It undermined order in Latin Christendom and wreaked havoc upon the life of the Church. Sincere men everywhere, not least scholars and especially the influential leaders at the University of Paris, sought to end the turmoil and disorder by means of a General Council of the Church, which would put the House of God in order, cleansing it of corruption and bringing reform. Both intellectual and moral reforms were sorely needed.

Various attempts were made to end the anarchy by the convocation of such a Council. In 1413 the Council of Constance was convoked by Pope John XXIII [1] at the instigation of the Roman Emperor Sigismund. It is necessary to explain here that there were at this time three rival claimants to the papacy: John XXIII (Baldassare Cossa), Benedict XIII, and Gregory XII. Since the Roman Church today does not recognize this John XXIII as having been a rightful pope, it was appropriate in modern times for the successor of Pius XII, on assuming the name John, to be designated John XXIII. The choice of name alluded, of course, to the fifteenth-century situation.

Designed to end the Great Schism, the Council of Constance met from 1414 till 1418. It claimed that its decisions, being the decisions of a General Council of the Church, were binding on all Christians, including

[1] See above, p. 79.

91

the Pope. The Council also condemned doctrines that had been taught by John Wyclif, ordered his body to be removed from consecrated ground, and also handed over John Huss, Wyclif's Bohemian admirer and counterpart, to the secular authorities to be burned at the stake. The failure of the Council of Constance to effect any genuine reform of the Church increased the feeling among many earnest and thoughtful churchmen that the reform of the Church could not be brought about by any constitutional means but required something more drastic.

Further attempts ensued to attain reform by conciliar means. Generations passed. Things went from bad to worse. By the end of the fifteenth century, ecclesiastical life at Rome had reached its lowest. Even a scholarly and relatively honorable pope like Sixtus IV saw his task more as making the papacy politically strong and influential in Italy than as reforming the Church or being the spiritual leader of the world. Others were much worse—so much worse that when Innocent VIII appointed one of his illegitimate sons a cardinal, he was acting almost as he was expected to act. Some of the cardinals lived exceedingly worldly lives, keeping mistresses, gambling, hunting, and entertaining in the manner of secular princes.

It was not the first time in the history of the Christian Church that worldliness had sapped the spiritual authority of the papacy. The corruption now spread, however, to all aspects of the life of the Church. The monks, for example, who at various times had relaxed their discipline, had been nevertheless a great leaven, generally speaking, in the Church's life. It had seemed as though, whenever they had needed reform, God had raised up a leader to reform them. Among the ancient orders, only one, the Carthusian, boasts that it was "never reformed, because never deformed." After the middle of the fourteenth century, however, the influence of the monks largely evaporated. They seemed no longer reformable. When the Black Death had taken a large toll of their numbers, they were sometimes able to recoup their losses; but their moral life generally kept on deteriorating. More ominous still, there seemed to be almost no sign of the impetus to self-reform that had saved monastic life and institutions in earlier times. Elsewhere in the Church the moral tone was low. Bishops provided rich benefices for their numerous illegitimate offspring, and the holders of such benefices often absented themselves from their duties, getting poorly paid substitutes to do the work instead. So far as could be judged by any intelligent and informed person trying to look rationally, even sympathetically, at the whole situation, Christianity must have seemed, at any rate as a religion having any recognizable association with the New Testament, to be declining so fast that final extinction was inevitable and was unlikely to be long postponed. The Church was the standard butt of literary satire. The Church of God had become a harlot. By the end of the fifteenth century, people were no more shocked to hear the Church called a whore than people today are shocked to hear politics called a game.

Among many the Church was nominally accepted as a traditional institution that could not well be disturbed but was to be disregarded as an instrument of moral or spiritual power. Others, whom this sorry spectacle inexpressibly saddened, voiced pious acceptance of the Church's structure and machinery; but they looked increasingly to foci of spiritual strength within the Church that seemed to be present in spite of, rather than because of, the Church's hierarchical structure and traditional design. A new kind of mysticism, warm, individual, deeply spiritual yet practical and humane, captured the attention and interest of many.

Women began to play a more important role. Though many of the mystics of the late fourteenth and fifteenth centuries were men, women were prominent in the movement for the cultivation of a new life of interior devotion. Women became increasingly prominent, indeed, in all movements of spiritual vitality within the Church. Various popular devotions were developed, such as the Stations of the Cross. Vernacular hymns began to play a considerable role in lay devotions. Preaching came into its own.

In spite of the outrageous general corruption, there were glimmers of light. In some places, notably in Spain, attempts at reform began to meet with some success; but everywhere a new spirit was awakening with springlike freshness amid the cheap chuckles and ribald grimaces of the impious, and the long-suffering groans of the faithful who for a century had cried, "How long, O Lord, how long?" and who had had to bear a sense of the absence of God, the excruciating silence that seemed the voice of eternal nothingness, with only their faith to support them in their pain.

The new spirit came from the fifteenth-century humanists. These *umanisti* were generally religious and sometimes very deeply religious men at heart; but they were thoroughly impatient of the scholastic mould of thought and the legalism of the Curia and other agencies of the Church. As poets, they saw everything with a poet's eye, not a canonist's or theologian's. Some of them regarded themselves, indeed, as a sort of unofficial priesthood of the Church—a priesthood of poetry and literature in the service of the spiritual life that comes from God. They felt that God spoke more clearly through their media than through the rotting structure of the Church's official agencies. Scorning both the decaying methodologies of the schoolmen and the stultified pattern of the monastic life that had for long been the medieval ideal, they sought spiritual vitality and salvation by a consecration of their lives to the literary and poetic ideals of their humanism. This spirit of the *umanisti*

93

and their attitude to the Church are by no means without parallel in our contemporary situation.

The roots of fifteenth-century humanism went deep into the ancient world; but it was thoroughly steeped in Christian dyes. The *umanisti* could lay claim to be in the succession of Socrates and the Stoics; but they were generally Christian in their values and ideals, and they certainly often devoted themselves to these with no less fervor than that which monks and hermits, knights and friars, had brought to the fulfilment of their respective ideals.

In this humanism were many strains, however, some essentially religious, some fundamentally frivolous. What characterized them all was a preoccupation with the original texts of antiquity, and an interest in using the power of literature to return to these sources rather than to depend on ecclesiastical or any other kind of authority and tradition. To him who would learn about Plato, the humanist's advice was of this sort: pay little attention to what even the most revered scholars tell you about him—go, learn Greek, get the earliest text you can find, and read him for yourself.

It was this attitude, more than any other factor in the fifteenth-century situation, that prepared the way for the explosive events of the sixteenth-century Reformation, with all their limitations and failure, and with all their enduring success and abiding intellectual and spiritual power. To many hoarse with crying, "How long?" the spirit of the humanists seemed sweet and refreshing indeed. Might it not be the very Breath of God, the Holy Spirit himself? It seemed the Dew of Heaven coming at last to water the parched earth and bring life out of even the Valley of Dry Bones that the late medieval Church had become.

For through the humanists, men learned to look to the sources not only for their understanding of Plato and Cicero but for their understanding of the Bible. The humanists encouraged men to forget not only the *glossae* and the *postillae* but, looking beyond the Vulgate text itself, to go back to the original Hebrew and Greek. The spread of this enterprise among the increasingly large number of people undertaking it, and also among the multitudes they influenced, greatly undermined confidence in the Vulgate.

The plight of the Church in the late fifteenth century recalls to us in many ways, indeed, the conditions and problems of the Christian Church today. Our contemporary situation has for long seemed hopeless to many thoughtful people. The anarchy and ecclesiastical stultification, Protestant, Roman, and Orthodox, and the widespread stupidity, ignorance, and stubbornness of churchmen have led to the identification of Christianity, in the minds of many, with reactionary stupidity and sloth. At last there is some hope of the fulfilment of long unrealized ecumenical dreams; yet not all are convinced that this fulfilment will be in time to undo the wicked wrongs of the past or to cure the theological ignorance of the multitudes who are more ready to sit on a wall of the churchyard than to kneel on a *prie-dieu* in the church.

Ours was, indeed, *mutatis mutandis,* the prevalent climate on the eve of the Reformation. The one star that seemed to spiritual men to shine ever and ever more brightly in the night of gloom was the hope, due chiefly to the inspiration of the humanist renaissances, that there was a new way of reading the Bible itself. Through the capture by the individual of this supreme constitutional document of the Christian Church, men and women might attain the inner, spiritual freedom promised by Christ to all who "know the truth."

The introduction in the sixteenth century of the trilingual discipline of Hebrew, Greek, and Latin was the fruit of a long development. It suddenly burst into flower, aided by many circumstances, notably the invention of printing in the middle of the fifteenth century. We have already considered at length both the limitations and the progress of Hebrew scholarship in the Middle Ages. The study of Greek was a different case. Though in southern Italy it may have never really died out, ignorance of Greek was quite general in the Middle Ages. Its humanistic cultivation began in Italy in 1360. It was already being taught at Florence with government sponsorship in 1397, by Manuel Chrysoloras (*c.* 1355-1415), translator of Homer and Plato. The founding of the Platonic Academy at Florence about the year 1442 was largely due to the influence of Georgius Gemistus Plethon (*c.* 1355-*c.* 1450), a native of Constantinople attending the Council of Ferrara and Florence.

The impetus to Greek studies came, then, from Italy, which before the age of the great Quattrocento humanists had already produced a Cimabue, a Giotto, and a Fra Angelico. Quattrocento painting included Filippo Lippi, Botticelli, Ghirlandajo, and the incomparable Leonardo da Vinci; its sculptors, Ghiberti and Donatello; its architects, Brunelleschi, Bramante, and the still young Michelangelo. To the Quattrocento belonged Nicholas of Cusa, a profound, antischolastic philosopher and a Roman cardinal, and Savonarola, the great Italian prophet and reformer who was martyred as a result of the fickleness of the mob. This was the Italy of Marsilio Ficino, a priest and humanist with an immense ardor for Plato and a belief that the greatest need of the time was a return to the original Christian sources. From this Italy, too, sprang the ideas that were to find expression in great humanists elsewhere, such as Johannes Reuchlin (1455-1522) and Desiderius Erasmus.

Reuchlin's interest in Hebrew studies had been partly inspired by Pico della Mirandola (1463-1494), who besides being a Greek scholar knew also Hebrew, Aramaic, and Arabic, being interested in the Cabbala, a curious system of Jewish theosophy which purported to reveal mysteries through an esoteric method of interpreting the Hebrew Bible. Pico della Mirandola had learned Hebrew from a prominent Italian Jew, Elias del Medigo (1463-1489); his interest in the Cabbala came from another Jew who had come to Italy from Constantinople, Jochanan Aleman. Reuchlin first learned Hebrew from Jacob Jehiel Loans, physician at the court of the Emperor Frederick III. Later he pursued his study of Hebrew at Rome under Obadiah ben Jacob Sforno, also a physician. By 1497 Reuchlin was already teaching Hebrew privately at Heidelberg, and he eventually became the first scholar in Europe to put the study of Hebrew by Gentiles on a sound footing. He was the first Christian to explore Hebrew grammar scientifically, and to him is to be ascribed in very large measure the impetus for the enormous spread and genuine development of Hebrew studies in Europe in the sixteenth century. His *De rudimentis hebraicis,* published at Pforsheim in 1506, shows both his independent judgement and his indebtedness to the grammar devised three centuries earlier by David Kimhi. His arrangement of words alphabetically rather than by roots marked an important development in the tools of the Hebraist.

Reuchlin's work was epoch-making. His bitter conflict with the Dominicans clarified the position of those who, like him, sought to put the whole spectrum of learning in the biblical tongues at the service of religion. Christian thought, which in the thirteenth century had had philosophy as its handmaid (*ancilla*), now had another and, many felt, a better servant at its disposal.

It was this fresh outlook that gave rise, at seats of learning, to the widespread establishment of the trilingual discipline, Hebrew, Greek, and Latin. Perhaps the most remarkable of all of these trilingual institutes was the one founded by Cardinal Ximenes at Alcalá or, as the Romans called it, Complutum. In this city a university had been founded in 1500, and within this was established in 1528, as an integral part of the university, a trilingual college named after St. Jerome. Already, however, the great Complutensian Polyglot Bible had been published in 1517 and received a papal license in 1520.

Notice has already been taken in earlier chapters of the peculiarity of the biblical tradition of Spain in the Middle Ages, and more remains to be explained later concerning some of its fruits. Upon a collation of Spanish biblical manuscripts the Hebrew text of the Complutensian Polyglot was based. In the Old Testament, each page is set forth with the Hebrew, the Vulgate Latin, and the Septuagint. The Septuagint was provided also with an interlinear Latin translation, and at the foot of the page the Targum, with a Latin translation in parallel columns. This remarkable work was followed by a spate of similar polyglot editions of the Bible. Also available to sixteenth-century biblical students were many Jewish editions of the Hebrew Bible. The first portion to be printed was the Psalter, published in 1477, probably at Bologna. Five years later editions of the Pentateuch began to appear, and in 1494 a complete Hebrew Bible appeared at Brescia, from the press of Soncino. There were other and better texts of the Hebrew Bible published in the sixteenth century. The Soncino Bible is of peculiar interest, not only because it was the first to be printed, but because its text was the one used by Luther in his translation of the Bible into German.

England was in the vanguard of the new learning that brought about the introduction of the trilingual discipline. Richard Foxe (1448[?]–1528), Bishop of Winchester, founded Corpus Christi College, Oxford, in 1517, as an expression of his zeal for the new learning. Readerships were established in this college in Greek and Latin, and a similar appointment in Hebrew would have been made but for difficulties that were probably connected with the high favor enjoyed at this time by Cardinal Wolsey. Wolsey had founded Cardinal College, which was later refounded by Henry VIII and named Aedes Christi, Christ's House, now known officially as Christ Church and, colloquially, The House. The first Hebrew teacher at Oxford, so far as is known, was Robert Wakefield, who also taught Hebrew briefly at the University of Louvain at a trilingual college founded there shortly after the death in 1517 of Jerome Busleiden, who bequeathed the necessary money for it. Another English Hebraist, Robert Sherwood, also taught Hebrew very briefly at Louvain. Foxe fostered the study of Greek and Hebrew at Cambridge, too. There, through his inspiration, Lady Margaret founded Christ's and St. John's Colleges, at both of which the trilingual discipline was to be included. In respect of Hebrew studies, Cambridge was put on a similar footing to Oxford by Robert Wakefield's brother. In Wittenberg, Vienna, and elsewhere, the trilingual movement was likewise vigorously promoted. At Paris it was encouraged by Francis I, who founded a chair of Hebrew at the Sorbonne in 1531, the first occupant of which was Francis Vatablus, among whose many distinguished pupils is to be numbered Antoine Chevalier (1523-1572), who came to England in the reign of Edward VI and was encouraged by Cranmer to teach Hebrew privately at Cambridge. Forced, like so many others, to leave England upon the accession of Mary Tudor, Chevalier received an appointment to teach Hebrew at Strasbourg. He returned to England later and eventually obtained an official appointment in Hebrew at the University of Cambridge, counting among his pupils the interesting Hugh Broughton, of whom we shall hear much more in connection with the King James Version of the Bible.

Erasmus had published an edition of the Greek New Testament, accompanied by his own Latin translation, as early as 1516. By 1535 there had been four revisions of it. In 1528, at Lyons, was published the literal Latin rendering of the Hebrew text by the Dominican Sanctes Pagninus, and a second edition of this appeared at Cologne in 1541. This work was to be extensively used, not least by one of the great figures in the story of the translation of the Bible into English, Miles Coverdale. Not only was the stage set, then, for the full flowering of the biblical Renaissance; the tools, rough though they may have been by modern standards, were for the first time abundantly available to those scholars who wished seriously to pursue the tasks opened to them by that enlistment of the new learning in the service of Christian piety that was to become eventually yet another expression of the long-standing marriage between humanism and the Christian faith.

In this brief glance at the background of the biblical Renaissance, it has been possible only to hint at its scope. Many facets have gone unmentioned; innumerable forces, political and religious, have been ignored. Even in such a rapid glance at the background of this biblical Renaissance, however, we have been able to sense the temper of the day. More intelligible to us now are reports about the overwhelming joy the Bible brought to every man who read it with the new eyes available to him and who, even if illiterate, could now hear it with new ears.

Great men in the Middle Ages had taught men's minds and touched their hearts. Men and women had lived and laughed, suffered and died all the better for the culture the medieval period had gradually evolved; yet a combination of circumstances—many wholly beyond human control—had led to an impasse. The sun of medieval glory had set, and each man, stumbling alone in the darkness, had to find his own way into freedom and light. The Bible, read by the individual with the methodological spectacles the humanists had furnished, proved to be the way out. Reading and hearing the Bible in the new way did lead many to exaggerations and misunderstandings that have tended to undermine the vitality of the Reformation heritage ever since. Some were half-blinded by the dazzling brightness the Bible seemed to cast upon their path. Some wanted to grasp it like a jewel or swallow it like a pill. Others, wiser and more reverent, prized its treasure too highly not to see it as the very mine of God's unsearchable riches. It is this last attitude that accounts more than anything else for the immense consecration of heart and mind to the Bible that the Reformation inspired. All the circumstances, however, worked together to bring about the sixteenth-century biblical Renaissance: the ecclesiastical decadence of the late medieval Church, the invention of printing, and the failure of attempts at conciliar reform, as well as the humanists' diligence and the Reformers' zeal.

*Printing—the art that conserves
all arts.*—Inscription on the façade
of the house in Haarlem, Holland, that
belonged to Lourens Koster

CHAPTER 12 *First Printed Bibles in the Vernacular*

It is a commonplace of history that the invention of printing by movable type is generally associated with the printing of the celebrated forty-two line or Gutenberg Bible, an edition of the Vulgate Latin, in 1456. Less well known is the fact that numerous editions of the Bible and of portions of the Bible in the vernacular tongues of Europe appeared soon thereafter and long before the birth of Luther in 1483. The English language was an exception; there was no printed edition of the English Bible till several years after the condemnation by Leo X, on June 15, 1520, of forty-one of Luther's theses by the papal bull *Exurge Domine,* and his excommunication, on January 3, 1521, by the subsequent bull, *Decet Romanum Pontificem.* In view of this and of the special interest that the English Bible holds not only for the English-speaking world but for the history of biblical translation as a whole, the English Bible will be much more extensively considered later on.[1] In the present chapter will be treated only translations into vernacular tongues other than English.

A copy in the Munich Library of an edition of the Bible in German, printed by Mentel at Strasbourg, but bearing no date, states that it was purchased for twelve gulden on June 27, 1466.[2] This, as has already been noted, is the earliest known printed edition of the Bible in German. An edition by Eggestein, also undated and also printed in Strasbourg, appeared a few years later, probably in or about the year 1470. Two further undated editions, both printed in Augsburg, one by Pflanzmann and the other by Zainer, may be assigned to about the year 1473. One copy of a Swiss edition, probably printed in Basel, bears the date 1474. Numerous editions follow, and by the time Luther was engaged upon his translation of the Bible, eighteen printed editions of the Bible in German had appeared, fourteen in High German, four in Low German. The text of these editions apparently belongs to the same family, all relating to the first known printed German Bible published by Mentel at Stras-

[1] See chapters 13 ff.
[2] See above, p. 69.

bourg. Between 1473 and the end of the century many German psalters appeared, having the same text, as had also a German edition of Job published in 1488 and one of the Apocalypse published in 1498. The last five editions of the complete High German Bible that preceded Luther's seem to depend on a revision made by Koburger, printed at Nuremberg in 1483.

Before Luther undertook the German translation of the Bible that was to have such an important role both in German literature and in the biblical Renaissance, he had already translated various sections of the Epistles and Gospels, and some of the Psalms. In 1521 he determined to translate the entire Bible, and in September of the following year, at Wittenberg, appeared the New Testament, which on account of the month of its publication came to be known as the *Septemberbibel*. In less than sixty years thereafter, no fewer than seventy editions of this New Testament had appeared. Luther then addressed himself to the more formidable task of translating the Old Testament. In 1523 the Penta-teuch appeared; but it was not till 1534 that his complete translation of the Bible, including the Apocrypha, was published.

Germany became a nation only in modern times. In Luther's day it was a collection of principalities without formal unity. Yet there was in the hearts of the German peoples a growing sense of a common bond that was still too vague to command the expression they felt it deserved. Luther was very much a German. He loved his people and had a natural and spontaneous understanding of their needs. His translation of the Bible into his native tongue reflects this affectionate sympathy with his people, their aspirations, and their still unuttered aims. This is in-dubitably among the most important reasons for its immense influence and epoch-making success. The measure of its influence is indicated by the fact that while in Luther's day there were many distinct dialects of German, the vernacular he used became the predominant one and the basis of the modern German language. Its success was reflected also in the fact that it was destined to be not only the basis of the versions used in the Low Countries and the Scandinavian lands but also, indirectly, in some sense a model for all vernacular translations, since it showed the literary world what could be done by a translator who thoroughly understood the needs of his own people.

In terms of the tools available to him, Luther's work was scholarly and independent. He used the Brescia edition of the Old Testament that had appeared in 1494, and of course the Greek New Testament of Erasmus, besides the Septuagint, the Vulgate, and various other con-ventional tools. Naturally, Roman Church critics made the most of the defects, and in time his text was in various ways revised. The opposition that was encountered in making these revisions is in itself a testimony to the literary power and spiritual influence of Luther's German translation. In the sixteenth century it was almost without a competitor. The nearest approach to this was the Zürich Bible of 1530, most of which was heavily indebted to Luther. Even the later edition of this Bible, published in 1548 and claiming to incorporate revisions based upon comparisons with the original Hebrew, did nothing to shake the popularity of Luther's work; nor have the later and better revisions of the Zürich Bible seriously affected this.

The earliest German translation on the Roman Catholic side, Beringer's New Testament, published at Spires in 1526, was virtually a reprint of Luther's. In 1527 Emser's New Testament appeared, containing some changes, many showing preferences for the Vulgate; but again the text remained largely that of Luther's. Dietenburger, a Dominican, produced a Bible in 1534, also largely indebted to Luther, and in 1537 Luther's own celebrated antagonist, Johann Maier of Eck (1486-1543), brought out a German Bible in which the Old Testament followed the older German Bibles and the New Testament Emser's. Eck's work likewise shows little originality, and is moreover in inferior German. After the sixteenth century there were many attempts at other translations of the Bible into German; but the dominance of Luther's work has always remained characteristic of the German scene.[3]

In the first printed French Bible the text of the thirteenth century was adopted. It was edited by Julien Macho and Peter Farget and published at Lyons in 1477. A later one, printed by Verard, is undated, and the date cannot be accurately estimated, though this Bible certainly belongs to the late fifteenth century. It embodied a revision made by John de Rely, confessor to Charles VIII. In 1523 Jacques Lefèvre d'Etaples, known also as Jacobus Faber or Stapulensis (*c.* 1455-1536), brought out his edition of the New Testament in French, published at Paris by Simon de Colines. It was followed by the Psalms in 1525 and finally, in 1528, by the Old Testament. Lefèvre, a French priest and humanist influenced by Nicholas of Cusa and Marsilio Ficino (whom he had met in Italy), had been condemned by the Sorbonne for heresy in 1521, and his apparent sympathy for the Reformation cause had forced him to flee to Strasbourg in 1525. In fact his attitude resembled that of Erasmus: he did not accept the doctrinal emphases that were fashionable in his day among those who espoused the Reformation cause;

[3] On the German versions see: H. Bornkamm, "Luthers Übersetzung des Neuen Testaments" in *Luthers geistige Welt* (3rd ed.; Gütersloh, 1959), pp. 263-71; A. Freitag, "Die Zainerbibel als Quelle der Lutherbibel" in *Theologische Studien und Kritiken*, C (1927-1928), 444-54; P. H. Vogel, *Europäische Bibeldrucke des 15. und 16. Jahrhunderts in den Volkssprachen* (Baden-Baden, 1962), pp. 23-51; G. Eis, *Frühneuhochdeutsche Bibelübersetzungen. Texte von 1400-1600* (Frankfurt a.M., 1949).

but he understood the meaning of the Reformation and was much affected by Reformation ideas, while never formally repudiating Rome. He obtained the protection of the Queen of Navarre. His translation of the Old Testament is largely based on the Vulgate and may be regarded as a revision of the medieval French text rather than an entirely fresh translation.

Calvin's cousin, Olivetan (*c.* 1506–1538), made a translation of the Bible that has had great influence in France. Olivetan's real name was Pierre Robert. He was dubbed "Olivetanus" because, it is said, of his habit of burning the midnight oil.[4] Having learned Hebrew and Greek at Strasbourg, he preached to the Waldensians in Piedmont from 1532 to 1535, and in order to carry out his missionary enterprise he translated the Bible into French. Olivetan's translation was published at Neufchâtel in June, 1535, with prefaces contributed by Calvin. His work was in some ways a masterpiece of its kind. The extent of his knowledge of Hebrew has been disputed; but at any rate he shows that, for his day, his translation methods were critical in respect of the Old Testament. In respect of the New, while he made some use of the Greek, he leant very heavily on Lefèvre's edition. There were many editions of Olivetan's Bible, and even a "purified" version prepared at Louvain for Roman Catholic use and published in 1550. Comparatively few changes were actually made in this edition; but the work, having thus obtained a Roman blessing, acquired acceptability even beyond the Reformed Church and went into several editions. Meanwhile, Olivetan's translation, as eventually revised and published at Geneva in 1588, became the accepted, traditional text for French-speaking heirs of the Reformation. It went into a great many editions in the course of the seventeenth and eighteenth centuries. An important further revision was made by Osterwald and published at Amsterdam in 1724.[5]

Two independent editions of the New Testament in Italian were published in 1471. Through the influence of the Reformation movement, Brucioli undertook the translation of the Bible into his native language. His New Testament was published at Venice by Giunti in 1530, the Psalms in 1531, and the whole Bible in 1532. Brucioli's knowledge of Hebrew was probably very limited. In any case, his sympathy with the Reformation cause brought about the condemnation of his

---

[4] *Olivetum,* an olive yard, in allusion to the oil lamps.

[5] On the history of the French versions see: W. J. van Eys, *Bibliographie des Bibles et des Nouveaux Testaments en langue française des XVme et XVIme siècles* (2 vols.; Geneva, 1900-1901); E. Reuss, "Fragments littéraires et critiques relatif à l'histoire de la Bible française" in *Revue de Théologie* (Strasbourg, 3e série; vols. III-V, 1865-1867); E. Pétavel, *La Bible en France* (Paris, 1864); E. Mangonot, "Françaises [Versions] de la Bible" in *Dictionnaire de la Bible,* ed. Vigouroux, II (1895), cols. 2346-73.

work by Rome, which in 1535 put it on the Index of Prohibited Books. Nevertheless, it was the basis of the version produced by Marmochino, a Dominican, who by bringing it into conformity with the Vulgate made it less odious to Rome. Diodati (1576-1649), a scholarly Italian whom Beza appointed to teach Hebrew and Greek at Geneva, produced a version of the Bible in Italian, published in 1607. This, the most important Italian translation of the Bible, was and has remained the accepted version for Italians in the Reformation heritage. Such was the power of the papacy in Italy that the ban issued by Pius IV in 1564 against reading the Bible in the vernacular was not lifted till 1757, so that Brucioli's version could hardly have much competition.[6]

A Spanish Bible traditionally attributed to Boniface Ferrer was printed near Valencia in 1478. A version of the Pentateuch in Spanish was published at Venice in 1497 by Jewish exiles there. We have already seen that for various reasons Spain had a special tradition in regard to Bible translation. Towards the end of the fifteenth century, largely due to the personality and work of Cardinal Ximenes, the Church in Spain was in many ways less corrupt than elsewhere in Europe. In the history of the early printed versions in Spanish, the so-called Ferrara Bible has a unique place.[7] The work of two Portuguese Jews, Duarte Pinel and Jerome de Vargas, it was based upon the translation done by Rabbi Moses Arragel in 1422.[8] Containing the whole of the Old Testament except Lamentations, it was published in 1553. The papal prohibition against reading the Bible in the vernacular was supported in Spain by the Inquisition, so that not till after the middle of the eighteenth century was there any effort by the Church to provide a translation of the Bible in Spanish. There were, however, some translations of the Gospels and other parts of the Bible that are found in the liturgical books of the Church.

In Portugal, on the other hand, there was no printed version of the Bible till Ferreira d'Almeida brought out his Portuguese New Testament in 1681. He continued his work on the translation of the whole Bible, and what he had left unfinished at his death was completed by others by 1712.

In the Netherlands an edition of the old Flemish manuscript translation was printed at Delft in 1477, and within the next thirty years the

---

[6] On Italian versions see: A. Vaccari, "Bibbie protestanti e Bibbia cattolica" in *Civiltà Cattolica*, LXXIV (1923), 343-51; S. Minocchi in *Dictionnaire de la Bible*, ed. Vigouroux, III, cols. 1026-31; A. Hauck in *Realencyklopädie für protestantische Theologie und Kirche*, III, 141.

[7] On the Ferrara Bible see: Cecil Roth, "The Marrano Press at Ferrara" in *Modern Language Review*, XXXVIII (1943), 307-17; S. Rypins, "The Ferrara Bible at Press" in *The Library*, 5th series, X (1955), 244-69.

[8] See above, p. 71.

Psalms were published seven times. In spite of the Inquisition, Luther's German New Testament was promptly translated into Dutch and an edition published at Antwerp as early as 1522. This was followed by other Dutch New Testaments printed in Switzerland, and in 1525 an edition of the Old Testament was published at Antwerp, based partly on what was available of Luther's German text and partly on the version already printed at Delft. In 1546, after several editions of the Dutch Bible had appeared, the printer was executed for having included in the notes statements accounted heterodox. Editions of the New Testament that had the approval of the Roman Church appeared in 1527, followed by the whole Bible in 1548. This, by Nicholas van Wingh, had the approval of the Faculty at Louvain and the support of Charles V. It was prefaced by a discourse on Protestant errors. Revised later, it was frequently reprinted. Before the end of the sixteenth century, several rival versions of the Bible in Dutch had been printed.

In Scandinavia, the King of Denmark, Christian II, had the New Testament translated by his secretary, Hans Mikkelsen, and this version, published at Leipzig, appeared in 1524. Two Danish versions of the Psalter were published in 1528. One of these was by C. Pedersen (1480-1554), whose work is of such historical and literary importance that his role for Danish has often been compared with Luther's role for German. His version was based on the Hebrew and the Vulgate. It was printed first at Antwerp and then later at Copenhagen. The following year Pedersen published an edition of the New Testament based on the Mikkelsen translation but with the help of Luther and Erasmus. Other translators brought out portions of the Bible, and in 1550 the first complete Danish Bible appeared. It was the work of Pedersen and others in the Copenhagen theological faculty and had been undertaken at the command of Christian III, which provided for a close adherence to Luther's version. It was followed by a second edition in 1589.[9]

Sweden was separated from Denmark in 1523. In 1526 the first Swedish New Testament appeared, printed at Stockholm by the royal press. It is ascribed to either Laurentius Andreae or Olaus Petri, who both played important roles in the Swedish Reformation. Based on Luther's work, it also shows the influence of Erasmus and the Vulgate. Sweden was the first Scandinavian country to get a complete Bible in its own language. The Swedish Bible, ascribed to Olaus or Laurentius Petri, perhaps more probably the latter, was published at Uppsala in 1541. It is very much influenced by Luther's version, and though there were various other

[9] On the Danish Bible see: C. T. Engelstoft, "Om Udgaverne og Udgivningen af den danske Bibeloversaettelse fra Reformationen til vore Tider" in *Nyt theologisk Tidsskrift* (1856) ; P. H. Vogel, "Danische und norwegische Bibelübersetzungen seit der Reformation" in *Internationale kirchliche Zeitschrift,* XLIV (1954) .

Swedish versions, this one remained substantially the Bible of the Church of Sweden till 1917, when a version based on modern critical editions of the Hebrew and Greek texts was authorized by King Gustav V.

The New Testament was translated into Icelandic by Oddur Gottskálksson and printed at Roskilde, Denmark, in 1540. The Gudbrand Bible, so called after Bishop Gudbrandur Thorláksson, who translated most of the Old Testament, using the German and the Vulgate, was published in 1584. For the New Testament it depended largely on Gottskálksson's translation. Through Bishop Rothovius a Finnish Bible was printed in the seventeenth century.

In Hungary the first book to be printed was a translation of the New Testament Epistles, and in the course of the sixteenth century there were various translations of the Bible in whole or in part. The first Hungarian version of the New Testament to be made from the original Greek was published in 1541. It was the work of Johannes Sylvester, who had studied at Wittenberg under Melanchthon. Several books of the Bible were translated into Hungarian by the Calvinist Gáspár Heltai between 1551 and 1565, and in 1590 the complete Bible appeared in Hungarian, translated by Gáspár Károlyi, who had studied at Wittenberg and was also a Calvinist. This scholarly version, though there were revisions of it, remained the accepted one for heirs of the Reformation in Hungary. A Roman Catholic version in Hungarian by György Káldi was printed at Vienna in 1626.

The first printed Czech New Testament appeared in 1475, several years before Luther was born. The place of printing is uncertain. The first complete Bible in Czech was published at Prague in 1488, based on John Huss's revision of the text. It was superseded by a Czech Bible printed at Venice in 1506. Several other versions followed. The translation of the Bible undertaken by the Moravian Brethren (Unitas Fratrum), who detached themselves from the doctrinal disputes that troubled Bohemia, exerted an immense influence on Czech history, language, and literature. Published in six volumes between 1579 and 1593, it came to be known, from the place of printing, as the Kralice Bible, and its place in Czech history and literature is comparable, *mutatis mutandis,* to the place of the King James Version in the English-speaking world. A Roman Catholic version made by Jesuits, printed at the Jesuit College at Prague in three volumes in 1715, and known as the St. Wenceslas Bible, it remained for long the standard Roman Catholic version in Czech.[10]

The Sárospatak Bible, called also the Bible of Queen Sophia, is a

[10] On the whole subject of the Council of Trent and vernacular Bibles, see the article by R. E. McNally in *Theological Studies,* II (1966), 204-27.

Polish translation of the Czech version. Under Lutheran influence the Gospels in Polish appeared at Königsberg in 1551-1552. There was a Roman Catholic version published at Cracow in 1561. This, a translation from the Vulgate, was quickly overtaken by a sumptuous and very scholarly version printed in 1563 at Brest Litovsk, which was a translation from the original tongues by a committee of Calvinists and Socinians.

As early as 1551, some detached portions of the Bible had been translated from the Latin Vulgate into the Welsh tongue. The function of these translated passages is reflected in the fact that they were called passages "appointed to be read in Churches in the time of Communion and Public Worship." In 1562 Elizabeth's Parliament enacted that the Bible, "containing the New Testament and the Old," should be translated into Welsh. After the translation into Welsh had been "viewed, perused, and allowed by the Bishops of St. Asaph, Bangor, St. David's, Landaff and Hereford" (the dioceses affected), the Welsh Bible was to be "printed and used in the Churches by the 1st of March, in the year 1566, under a penalty, in case of failure, of forty pounds, to be levied on each of the above Bishops. That one printed copy at least of this translation should be had for and in every cathedral, collegiate, and parish church and chapel of ease throughout Wales, to be read by the Clergy in time of Divine service, and at other times for the benefit and perusal of any who had a mind to go to church for that purpose, as the inhabitants of Wales, being no small part of the realm, are utterly destituted of God's Holy Word, and do remain in the like, or rather more, darkness and ignorance than they were in the time of Papistry."

The translation of the Book of Common Prayer into Welsh was also ordered, and pending the availability of the Bible and the Book of Common Prayer in Welsh, the clergy of Wales were required in public worship to make use of such translations as already existed of the Lord's Prayer, the Creed, the Litany, the liturgical Epistles and Gospels, and the like, as directed by their bishops. It was further provided that every church in Wales should also possess an English Bible. Less gratifying, no doubt, to the more ardent lovers of the Welsh language, was one of the declared purposes behind this provision, namely, "that such as do not understand the English language may, by conferring both tongues together, the sooner attain to the knowledge of the English tongue."

The Welsh Bible was by no means ready by the appointed date; but the following year, 1567, saw the appearance of the first Welsh New Testament. It was a black-letter edition printed in quarto by Henry Denham, constituting a handsome volume of 399 leaves. The chapters were not divided into verses. There is a lengthy epistle in Welsh by the Bishop of St. David's, and a dedication in English to "the most vertuous and noble Prince Elizabeth, by the Grace of God of England, France, and Ireland, Queene, defender of the Faith, etc." This masculine designation of Queen Elizabeth, perpetrated unwittingly or otherwise, anticipated the popular saying of a later generation, to which reference will be made in a later chapter, that King Elizabeth had been succeeded by Queen James. The translation was done by three men. Richard Davis, Bishop of St. David's and one of the panel appointed for the translation of the Bishops' Bible, translated into Welsh the Epistle to the Hebrews, the second Epistle to Timothy, both Epistles of St. Peter, and the Epistle of St. James. Thomas Huet, Precentor of the same diocese, was responsible for the translation of the Apocalypse, while the rest of the New Testament was done by William Salesbury.

The whole Bible in Welsh eventually appeared in 1588. Printed at London by Christopher Barker and containing the Apocrypha as well as the Old and New Testaments, it included a lengthy dedication to the Queen in Latin, signed by William Morgan. It is sometimes called "Morgan's Bible." The chapters are divided into verses. Printed in small folio, it contains 555 leaves. The title reads:

Y Beibl Cyssegr-Lan, Sef yr hen Destament a'r Newydd.

A revision of this Welsh Bible was undertaken early in the seventeenth century by Richard Parry, Bishop of St. Asaph's, and was printed in folio at London by Norton and Bill in 1620. It is a black-letter edition. The first octavo edition of the Bible in Welsh appeared in 1630, also printed at London, but in Roman type. Throughout the seventeenth and a large part of the eighteenth centuries there were only two folio and four octavo editions of the Welsh Bible, and the total number of copies available probably represented only about a tenth of the population of Wales at that time.

A translation of the New Testament into Irish, begun in 1573 by two clergymen of St. Patrick's Cathedral, Dublin, constitutes probably the first biblical translation into Irish Gaelic.[11] They were John Kearney and Nicholas Walsh. The latter was elected to the See of Ossory in 1577 but continued with the translation work till 1585, when he was assassinated in his own house by stabbing. Some years earlier the two translators had been joined by another, Nehemias Donellan, who went on with the work till he became Archbishop of Tuam in 1595. In 1603, the year

[11] On the subject of translations into Irish and Scottish Gaelic I am much indebted to a Gaelic scholar who is learned in this field, the Reverend T. M. Murchison, D.D., Minister of St. Columba Summertown, Glasgow, Scotland, who not only obtained for me out-of-print materials but put at my disposal his own personal notes. Perhaps the best published account is Donald MacKinnon, *The Gaelic Bible and Psalter* (Dingwall, Scotland: The Ross-shire Printing and Publishing Company, Ltd., 1930).

of the Union of the Crowns, Bishop William O'Donell [12] published an Irish translation of the New Testament, presumably using the foundation already laid by the three aforementioned pioneers. It bore a dedication, in English, to King James, after whom is named the most celebrated version of the English Bible, and of whom much more will be said later.

The translation of the Old Testament into Irish was begun in 1630 by Bishop Bedell of Kilmore and Ardagh, with assistance from Mortogh O'Cionga, said to be the best Keltic scholar of his time, and Dennis O'Sheriden. Political foes of O'Cionga caused him to be thrown into prison at the age of eighty, and Bedell, till his death in 1642, had to continue the work without O'Cionga's help. His manuscript was preserved, though his successors in the See took no interest in it. Meanwhile, the Honourable Robert Boyle printed at his own expense a copy of O'Donell's Irish translation of the New Testament, instituting at the same time a search for Bedell's manuscript of the Old. Eventually, early in 1686,[13] the first Old Testament in Irish, revised by various persons including William Huntingdon, who had a knowledge of Semitic languages, was published. So far, the Irish Bible had been printed in Keltic characters. An edition transliterated into Roman script was prepared by Robert Kirk and published in 1690 in one small volume with glossary and chapter headings. The New Testament of this edition was published at Glasgow in 1754.

Scottish Gaelic is traditionally the language of the Scottish Highlands and Islands. The eastern parts of the Highlands, however, had been sufficiently bilingual in the sixteenth century for the Bible to have been received there when it first became available in its English dress. Elsewhere the parish ministers had to make their own translations as they expounded the Bible in public worship. The Gaelic language is, of course, to be distinguished from Scots, spoken in the Scottish Lowlands. The latter has an affinity with English, while Scottish Gaelic, like Welsh, is a Keltic tongue, though unlike Welsh it has a common ancestry with Manx and Irish. Scottish Gaelic was distinguishable from Irish, by this time; but the two languages were sufficiently akin for mutual comprehension.

As we are about to see, the Bible was not completely translated into Scottish Gaelic till the beginning of the nineteenth century. To help Gaelic-speaking parishes in Scotland, copies [14] of the Irish Bible, *faute de mieux*, were sent to them, and these were so welcomed that the

---

[12] Later Archbishop of Tuam.

[13] The title page bears the date 1685; but the book did not actually appear until 1686.

[14] MacKinnon, in *The Gaelic Bible and Psalter*, gives 200 as the number; others say as few as 80.

parish copy often circulated from home to home during the week, before being returned to the church on Saturday evening for use the following day in public worship.

The first book to be printed in Scottish Gaelic appeared in 1567. It was the Book of Common Order.[15] The translation was by John Carswell, Bishop of the Isles. By the middle of the seventeenth century, the Synod of Argyll, Scotland, had begun work on the translation of the Bible into Scottish Gaelic; but no part of it was ever printed, and the manuscript is not known to be extant. In 1659 the first fifty psalms were printed in a metrical version, done by ministers of the same Synod. The whole Psalter appeared in 1694, and in 1767 the first Scottish Gaelic version of the New Testament was published. The translation was the work of James Stuart and others. There was a second edition in 1796, made by the translator's son John, by which time parts of the Old Testament had appeared, mainly the work of the latter, except for Isaiah–Malachi, which was done by John Smith; but the last part was not completed and published till 1801. Many editions of the Gaelic Bible, in whole or in part, have since been issued, including, in 1875, a Roman Catholic version of the New Testament in colloquial Gaelic, made from the Vulgate by Father Ewen MacEachen and revised by Father Colin C. Grant.

Manx is the Keltic tongue proper to the Isle of Man, an island 220 square miles in area lying between England and Ireland and of great historical interest. The language, akin to both Irish and Scottish Gaelic, is closer to the latter. The nonbiblical literature in Manx is slighter than that in other Keltic tongues. In 1748 Bishop Wilson caused a translation into Manx by W. Walker of the Gospel according to St. Matthew to be published. The Gospels and Acts appeared in 1763 in a version that Wilson had begun and his successor Bishop Hildesley revised. In 1767 came the Epistles and Revelation, and in 1773 the Old Testament, which was the work of twenty-four scholars. An edition of the complete Bible, consisting of only forty copies, was published in 1775 by the Society for the Promotion of Christian Knowledge, and in 1819 the British and Foreign Bible Society published an edition of five thousand copies of the Manx Bible.

---

[15] Commonly called "Knox's Liturgy" after the Scottish Reformer, it embodied the law of the Church of Scotland in respect of worship, from 1564 till 1645. The first edition had been printed at Edinburgh in 1564.

CHAPTER 13 *The First Printed New Testament in English*

Though copies of Wyclif's translation of the Bible into English had been circulating in England in manuscript since the time of the Lollards, no printed translation into English was published till eight years after Luther had posted his theses on the door of the church at Wittenberg. The printing of this translation of the New Testament by William Tyndale (*c.* 1494-1536) was begun at Cologne and completed at Worms in 1525. The following year copies of it arrived in England.

William Tyndale was an Oxford man. He had gone up to the University about the year 1510 and had studied at Magdalen Hall till 1515. He later studied at Cambridge, shortly after Erasmus had left it. The Oxford of Tyndale's day had already been affected by the humanist Renaissance. Men such as John Colet (*c.* 1466-1519) had been deeply influenced by the humanists at Florence and elsewhere. Oxford was undergoing a change. While the older scholars had been content with the traditional medieval pattern of learning and had continued the practice of quoting the old authorities in the customary fashion, the newer scholars, such as Colet, were quoting directly from the sources, which included both Plato and the Bible. The new method was exciting. When Colet was lecturing on the Epistles, for instance, his students felt them come alive for the first time. They must have been as excited as would be a spectator at a modern art exhibition who, faced with what he took to be an incomprehensible "abstract" painting, suddenly saw in it lively human faces swathed in mysterious light. We are told in the quaint language of the day that Tyndale, who was profoundly affected by such influences, used to read privately to groups of students and others at Oxford "some parcel of Divinity." In the course of this he endeavoured to employ the new methods to instruct them "in the knowledge and truth of the Scriptures."

It was not unnatural that a young man so fired by the possibilities that lay before a scholar armed with the new methodological tools should conceive the ambitious idea of translating the Bible into English. No doubt this dream was not very far from the thoughts of many of his friends who had likewise been caught up by the excitement of the new kind of learning. The Bible was a gigantic undertaking. Tyndale determined, however, to make a beginning by translating the Greek New Testament. Erasmus had expressed the wish that the Bible should become so familiar to the common people that bits of it would be sung by men and women working in the fields. Tyndale conceived a more ambitious form of the aspiration. He hoped that the plowboy should come to know his Bible better than now did his priest.

The time was not propitious in England for even the partial fulfilment of Tyndale's ambition. In 1408, at Oxford, Convocation had passed a constitution forbidding any man, under pain of the "greater excommunication," to translate any part of the Bible into English without authority from a bishop. Though much had happened since then, the official attitude to the translation of the Bible remained much the same. Henry VIII had been on the English throne since 1509 and had received at his own request from Pope Leo X in 1521 the title *Fidei defensor,* "Defender of the Faith," borne by all British sovereigns to this day. It is a title of the same kind as *Christianissimus,* formerly taken by the kings of France. At a later date, Henry's desire for divorce was to lead him to break with Rome; but in the early fifteen-twenties, when Tyndale was contemplating his task, Henry was showing great outward zeal for the defence of the papacy and vigorous opposition to the Reformation cause. In fact throughout his whole life he had never more than an accidental connection with the English Reformation, which was led by men of a very different sort. The identification of Henry VIII with the Reformation movement in England is largely due to misunderstanding or misrepresentation of the nature of that movement, which has so profoundly influenced English and American life and conduct.

Thomas Wolsey (*c.* 1474-1530), who had just missed the papal throne, wielded tremendous power in England. In those days it was expected that great prelates should live in splendor. Cardinal Wolsey's pomp, however, exceeded all ordinary custom. He lived like a great king. Having enjoyed the favor of Henry VII, he gained the favor also of Henry VIII, under whom he became, in 1514, Archbishop of York. The following year, two new dignities had been bestowed upon him, one secular, the other ecclesiastical. He became Lord High Chancellor of England and at the same time a Cardinal of the Roman Church. From all these sources he derived huge revenues, and he used them in lavish display. He was sometimes attended by as many as four thousand horsemen, including nobles, prelates, and knights, and his ordinary establishment at Hampton Court numbered about a thousand persons. Twelve chaplains, a physician, four legal advisers, two secretaries, and a herald-at-arms attended his table, as well as other courtiers. Naturally, he was not inconspicuous in his opposition to the Reformation.

It was during Wolsey's heyday of favor with Henry VIII that Tyndale, after leaving Cambridge, went as tutor to the household of John Walsh, a Gloucestershire knight. The position was a pleasant one, affording the young scholar time for pursuing his studies. The manor house was beautifully situated in the sleepy Cotswolds. The family extended every courtesy and hospitality to the clergy, who were frequent guests at their table in the hall of the manor. Tyndale, excited by his new learning, sometimes got into arguments with the other guests, and as he was already, despite his youth, remarkably learned compared with the average clergyman of the day, it was inevitable that he should generally win, and no less inevitable that in winning he should often displease the other disputants. Those who, like Lady Walsh, probably did not follow the arguments well on either side, thought Tyndale rather presumptuous in his attitude. She chided him about it, asking how he could possibly be qualified to argue about the Bible with "much better placed" clergymen who, she supposed, must know more than he. When, echoing Erasmus, he went so far as to say to one of these clerical guests that he would one day cause even the commonest plowboy to "know more of the Scripture than thou dost," no doubt Lady Walsh took it as the idle boast of an uncommonly opinionated young man.

Tyndale, opinionated or no, was determined to go ahead with his translation of the New Testament. He was more determined than prudent. Hoping for the episcopal support required by the Convocation of Oxford, he went up to London in 1524, seeking to interest prominent churchmen in his project. He hoped that Cuthbert Tunstall (1474-1559), then Lord Bishop of London, would help him; but he was disillusioned. The Bishop was hospitable but not encouraging. "Room enough was there in my Lord's house for belly-cheer; but none to translate the New Testament."

It was now evident to Tyndale that the only hope of fulfilling his aim was to leave England and work on the continent wherever he could find support. He stayed for a time in Hamburg. Then, unable to find a printer there, he went on to Cologne in June, 1525. The project of printing a translation of the Bible was at this time highly suspect, of course, and could only be attempted with the help of sympathizers with the Reformation cause, for it was so closely identified with this cause that enemies would do all they could to stop it. The work of printing, therefore, had to be kept very secret.

The secret was in fact well kept for a time, and the work progressed. Then the printers tactlessly bragged that they were printing a work that would throw England into revolution. This boast came to the ears of a zealous enemy of the Reformation, John Cochlaeus, who invited some of the printers to his house. Having duly plied them with drinks, he extracted from them the information that three thousand copies were

112

being printed (a large number in those days) and that ten sheets had already been struck off. Cochlaeus had no difficulty at Cologne in finding means to plan to destroy Tyndale's work. Cologne happened to be in several ways a stronghold of the enemies of the Reformation cause. It was there that, in 1479, were printed the first two books to bear the *imprimatur* that is to this day a familiar expression of the system employed by Rome in censoring books. It is said that a priest in Cologne had such a distaste for Erasmus that he kept a picture of him in his study, so that he could occasionally vent his hatred by spitting on it.

Tyndale, however, having been warned of the danger, succeeded in making off with the quarto sheets already printed. He took a ship up the Rhine and reached Worms, the city already well known as the scene, only a few years earlier, of Luther's celebrated defence of his position. Worms, where sympathies for the Reformation cause had already been roused, provided Tyndale with the opportunity of completing, without hindrance, the work of printing the New Testament in English.

There was no doubt in Tyndale's mind that Cochlaeus would apprise the English authorities and that these would be on the lookout for the quarto sheets that might arrive in England. What could Tyndale do? Once the authorities knew to expect copies, they would look out for them and would certainly confiscate them all. The demand was enormous. There were people who would have been willing to pay almost any price for one. When Spalatin, a friend of Luther, said the English would have paid a hundred thousand pieces of money for a single copy, perhaps he exaggerated; but there was at any rate no doubt that the market was so good that Tyndale could have sold a printing of three thousand copies over and over again at a very high price if only he could have put them on the market.

In an attempt to foil the English authorities, Tyndale got the printer, Peter Schoeffer, to do an anonymous octavo edition as well. This edition, being without notes, could be and was printed very quickly. It is believed that about three thousand copies of the quarto edition were also printed. Of this only a fragment consisting of thirty-one leaves of Matthew is known to be extant. This fragment is in the British Museum.

Early in 1526 the first copies of the first printed English New Testament were smuggled into England. The price was half a crown a copy, a relatively high price for a book in those days. It represented a mason's wage for five days. Still, it seems inexpensive when we recall that it was only half what people in Wyclif's day had been willing to pay for *borrowing* a manuscript copy of the latter's translation for an hour a day.

The opposition of the English authorities was ferocious. The Bishop of London called the translation a "pestiferous and most pernicious poison." The book was publicly burned at St. Paul's Cross, and the bishops even subscribed money to buy up all available copies. As we shall see, many thousands of copies were eventually printed. Yet so thoroughly did the authorities contrive to exterminate the book that apart from the solitary extant fragment, already mentioned, of the quarto edition, only two copies of the octavo edition have survived. One, which lacks only the title page, is in the Baptist College at Bristol, England, and the other, an imperfect copy, is in the library of St. Paul's Cathedral, London.

There is no doubt that one of the chief reasons for the vehement hostility to the book was Tyndale's growing association with sympathizers to the Reformation cause. He had had some association with Luther at Wittenberg. The form of Tyndale's edition, with its black-letter Gothic type, single column, prologue, prefaces, and other features, suggested the influence of Luther's German counterpart. At any rate, Sir Thomas More charged that the translation contained errors and that many of these were wilful and intended to promote heresy. Where the bishops would have liked "penance," for example, which is suggested by the Vulgate phrase *poenitentiam agite* (literally, "do penance"), Tyndale, translating from the Greek, wrote "repent." The Bishop of London claimed he could find three thousand errors. This was a gross exaggeration and an entirely unfair charge. The number of real errors was in fact remarkably small, in the circumstances. Tyndale, whose scholarly integrity is incontestable, wrote to a friend: "I call God to record against the day we shall appear before the Lord Jesus to give a reckoning of our doings, that I have never altered one syllable of God's word against my conscience nor would do, this day, if all that is in the earth, whether it be honor, pleasure, or riches, might be given me."

The translation is in fact, from more than one point of view, a very good one. Generally speaking it is racy and direct while being at the same time a work that reflects the best scholarship of the day. It was an enormous improvement on Wyclif's. For one thing, it was from the original tongue. Tyndale used the Greek text of Erasmus which, though not perfect, was the best available text of the original Greek. In the second place, it was in the free, idiomatic English of the day. Its influence not only on the King James Version of the following century but on the subsequent history of the English Bible is considerable. Indeed, the King James Version was to be, as we shall see, more conservative than Tyndale's had been. Twentieth-century translations have sometimes reverted to felicitous words and phrases of Tyndale's that the King James Version rejected. For example, the Vulgate use of *caritas* suggested "charity," which is a familiar feature of the King James Version. Tyndale, however, used "love" as do most modern English versions. The effect may be seen from an example of a very well-known passage as translated by Tyndale. It is taken from his revision of 1534, which is about to be considered here, as reprinted in the sumptuous edition edited by N. Hardy Wallis and published in 1938 by the Cambridge University Press for the Royal Society of Literature.

Though I spake with the tonges of men and angels, and yet had no love, I were even as soundinge brasse: or as a tynklynge Cymball. And though I coulde prophesy, and vnderstode all secretes, and all knowledge: yee, yf I had all fayth so that I coulde move mountayns oute of ther places, and yet had no love, I were nothynge. . . . Love suffreth longe, and is corteous. Love envieth not. Love doth nott frowardly, swelleth not dealeth not dishonestly, seketh not her awne, is not provoked to anger, thynketh not evyll, reioyseth not in iniquite. . . . When I was a chylde, I spake as a chylde, I understode as a childe, I ymagened as a chylde: but assone as I was a man I put awaye childesshnes. Now we se in a glasse even in a darke speakynge: but then shall we se face to face. . . . Now abideth fayth, hope, and love, even these thre: but the chefe of these is love.

Nowadays well-bred controversialists conduct even the most acrimonious disputes in language that is not less effective for being happily restrained. In Tyndale's day there was no such polite convention. Public controversies were conducted like a cockfight. Yet though Tyndale naturally engaged in controversy according to the conventions of his own time, his language was less coarse than that of his antagonist Thomas More. Tyndale distrusted More, thinking him an opportunist ready to enlist his pen in the service of his own advancement. Probably More was not the timeserver Tyndale supposed. When, later, More had succeeded Wolsey as Lord Chancellor of England, his opposition to Henry's divorce was to cost him his head, which was easily lost in the service of that monarch. More is now officially enrolled in the calendar of the saints of the Roman Church, having been canonized in 1935 by Pope Pius XI. More's language towards his opponents lacked nothing of the fashionable robustness of the day. He called them "hell hounds that the devil hath in his kennel" and "apes that dance for the pleasure of Lucifer." He called Tyndale a "develish drunken soul" saying that "this drowsy drudge hath drunken so deep in the devil's dregs that if he wake and repent himself the sooner he may hap to fall into the mashing fat and turn himself into draff [hogwash] that the hogs of hell shall feed upon." Whatever the twentieth-century *advocatus diaboli* in More's canonization at Rome may have thought about this sort of language, no modern Englishman would account it, even allowing for the literary fashions of a bygone age, a masterpiece of English understatement.

Tyndale had had the support of London merchants from the beginning. It was probably in the home of one of these, Humphrey Monmouth, that he had first essayed his translation. Now these London merchants, particularly Augustine Packynton, came to his aid, raising money to purchase copies. These were in turn rapidly bought up by the Bishop and burned. This arrangement was remarkably convenient. It pleased both Tyndale and the bishops. It pleased the bishops because it satisfied their ire. Tyndale was pleased on two counts. In the first place, it showed up the bishops as destroyers of Holy Writ. In the second place, and of urgent practical importance, it kept Tyndale in funds. As an old chronicler put it, the Bishop of London thought he "had God by the toe, when indeed he had the Devil by the fist." At any rate, copy after copy of Tyndale's New Testament poured into England as fast as they could be bought and burned.

So Tyndale continued his work of translation. It was his hope to complete the whole Bible. In 1530 he issued the Pentateuch translated from the Hebrew with marginal notes, some of which are bitter.[1] The five books of the Pentateuch were printed at Marburg, and apparently one at a time, for Genesis and Numbers are done in black letters while Exodus, Leviticus, and Deuteronomy are in a type more like that to which we are nowadays accustomed. In 1531 Jonah appeared. There is one copy of both Jonah and the Pentateuch in the British Museum.

In the fall of 1534 Tyndale, now living in the free city of Antwerp in a house established there for him by some of his London friends, published a revision of his New Testament. This contained introductions to each chapter and a much-improved marginal commentary. He also corrected the text. The Greek underlying this edition remained close to the text of the editions by Erasmus that had been published in 1519 and 1522. The 1534 revision of Tyndale's English New Testament became the basis for all future revisions. Though founded on a Greek text that was shown later to have defects, it is a masterpiece of its kind. Occasionally there are echoes of Wyclif in it. Tyndale also consulted several other versions, including of course both the Vulgate and Luther's German; but his writing is marked by such freshness and vigor that it is clearly and strikingly a work of singular originality. Great has been its influence on subsequent editions. It has been estimated that basically, in respect of those portions of the Bible on which he labored, at least eighty per cent of the language used in all subsequent versions designed for Church use, down to our own times, is straight out of Tyndale.

---

[1] A reprint of Tyndale's Pentateuch has been published recently: *William Tyndale's Five Books of Moses called The Pentateuch* (Carbondale: Southern Illinois University Press, 1967). It contains collations and prolegomena by J. I. Mombert and is newly introduced by F. F. Bruce.

In the preface to the Revised Version of the New Testament, completed in 1880, the debt to Tyndale was expressed as follows: "That Translation [the King James Version of 1611] was the work of many hands and of several generations. The foundation was laid by William Tyndale. His translation of the New Testament was the true primary Version. The Versions that followed were either substantially reproductions of Tyndale's translation in its final shape, or revisions of Versions that have been themselves almost entirely based on it."

Tyndale's work as a translator was more than matched by his work as a reviser. The changes he made in the 1534 revision exhibit meticulous care, being designed sometimes to attain closer agreement with the Greek text, sometimes to achieve more vigorous or idiomatic English, sometimes in the interest of uniformity, always with scholarly caution and literary skill. Examples, illustrating the felicitous phrases introduced into Tyndale's revision that have since become particularly familiar to the English-speaking world, are as follows: In 1525 Tyndale had written, "Blessed are the maynteyners of peace," which in 1534 he changed to "Blessed are the peacemakers." "And ye shall fynd ese [ease] unto your soules" became "And ye shall fynd rest unto youre soules." "The faveour of oure lorde Jesus Christ" became "The grace of oure Lorde Jesus Christ." Perhaps most strikingly of all, "Beholde the lyles of the felde" was turned into the now especially beloved "Considre the lylies of the felde."

The first title page reads:

> The ne-
> we Testament /dyly
> gently corrected and
> compared with the
> Greke by Willyam
> Tindale: and fynes
> shed in the yere of ou
> re Lorde God
> A.M.D. & xxxiiii
> in the moneth of
> Nouember.

The second title page reads:

> The ne-
> we Testa-
> ment.
> Imprinted at An-
> werp by Marten
> Emperowr
> Anno. M.D. xxxiiii.

The appearance of Tyndale's revision in 1534 seemed timely. It was just then that under the Act of Supremacy the jurisdiction of the Pope in England was officially repudiated. That jurisdiction had been in fact long resented, however, and the formal break did not produce as much of a change as might have been expected. The climate of opinion towards the translation of the Bible into English did change, however. Anne Boleyn desired a copy, and the magnificent one presented to her is now preserved in the British Museum. Meanwhile, the improvement in the climate of opinion about englishing the Bible did nothing to abate the malice against Tyndale. His enemies had not forgotten him. In 1535 a man called Henry Philips, having secured his confidence by various means, including even the borrowing of money from him, betrayed him. Through the treachery of Philips, who had borrowed forty shillings from Tyndale just before kidnapping him, the author of the first printed New Testament in English was handed over to officers of the Emperor Charles V, who was pledged to destroy the Pope's enemies. The fact that Henry VIII was now nominally a supporter of the Reformation cause did nothing to help Tyndale. Henry, a notoriously ruthless monarch, was much more interested in what he could get out of the Reformation than in what he could contribute to it. No doubt he could have stayed the hand of Tyndale's English persecutors if he had chosen to do so; but he would not lift a finger. By now death had stilled Wolsey's angry pride; but Henry's selfish indifference had the same practical effect.

Tyndale was therefore taken to the castle prison at Vilvorde, a town that lies between Brussels and Malines. There for eighteen months he suffered conditions to which we have only too clear a testimony in a sad letter of his, a copy of which is preserved in the British Museum. Written in his cell, it contains an appeal for a warmer cap, "for I suffer extremely from cold in the head, being afflicted with a perpetual catarrh, which is considerably increased in the cell; also a piece of cloth, to patch my leggings. My overcoat has been worn out. My shirts also are worn out. I also wish his [the jailer's] permission to have a candle in the evening; for it is wearisome to sit alone in the dark."

Notwithstanding his sufferings in the castle prison, he continued his work, which at the time of his death was completed as far as II Chronicles. At last, however, on October 6, 1536, he was led forth to the stake. He who had left his native England to provide it with the Bible in his maternal English tongue uttered in a loud voice an eloquently brief prayer, the words of which were for many years to echo from his exile into every English home. His prayer was: "Lord, open the King of England's eyes."

They strangled him and burned him at the stake.

*I have nether wrested nor altered so
moch as one worde for the mayntenaunce of any maner
of secte.*—Coverdale's Dedicatory Epistle

CHAPTER 14 *Coverdale and the First English Bible*

The first complete printed English Bible was published in October, 1535, while Tyndale was in the castle prison at Vilvorde and about a year before his martyrdom. It was the work of Miles Coverdale (1488–1568), a Yorkshireman born probably in York. Coverdale was not at all a scholar of Tyndale's quality, and with characteristic and becoming modesty he was always eager to disclaim any such pretensions. The first Coverdale Bible was printed on the continent. The name of the printer and the place of printing have been much disputed. Nineteenth-century scholarship was inclined to decide in favor of Christopher Froschover, Zürich, who certainly printed a later issue; but many other places and printers were plausibly suggested. More recently, scholars equipped with better bibliographical tools have argued against Zürich, favoring rather Marburg or Cologne. There is now strong though not conclusive evidence in favor of Cologne as the place, and of Cervicorn and Soter as the printers. The date of its first appearance in England has been likewise the subject of learned dispute. It is a complicated question; but there is now evidence that a printed copy of *part* of it, together with a copy of Coverdale's dedication to the King, was actually in England a month or two before publication. Under a law enacted by Parliament in 1534, no alien might sell foreign books in England, so Coverdale's continental supporter, of whom something will be said presently, was obliged to find an English distributor to whom to sell the sheets. The distributor, James Nicolson, would, in turn, bind and distribute the copies. Nicolson hoped to include on the title page a formal royal licence. Though, as we shall see, this was denied, the Coverdale Bible was nevertheless published.

How did it come about that Coverdale, whose Bible was first printed while Tyndale was still alive, should live to the age of eighty, being buried under the altar in the chancel of the church of St. Bartholomew, London, commemorated by a brass inscription in Latin elegiacs for the uprightness of his life, while Tyndale had been long since cruelly killed and burned at the stake? The circumstances must be inspected more carefully before an answer to this question can be made intelligible.

There is no doubt that hostility toward the translation of the Bible had been very marked in England since the time of the Lollards. The hostility had been largely independent of the attitude of English churchmen toward Rome. The ecclesiastical authorities in England had been frightened by the rapid growth of Lollardy, and though memories of the Lollards were growing dim by Tyndale's time, they were still lively enough to make the idea of Bible translation suspect. At the same time, however, the situation was beginning to change. The views of the humanists were beginning to pervade the most influential circles in the English Church. There was a fairly general feeling, not only among the bishops, but also among prominent laymen who happened to have the King's ear, such as Sir Thomas More, that something should be done. The question was: How should it be done, to what extent, and with what precautions? In other words, they recognized that England would be behind the times if nothing were done to provide for a translation of the Bible; but the old fears of what Lollardy might do were still powerful enough to cause them to approach the question with great caution. In these circumstances, Tyndale's New Testament was odiously embarrassing to the authorities. They knew they should be doing something about the matter of Bible translation. Suspicious of the idea, however, they were sure it ought to be carefully controlled. Above all, they were certain that whatever was done in the matter should be done by the ecclesiastical authorities, so as to make it seem plain to all that the initiative in implementing any such progressive decision came from them. It was therefore eminently necessary to vilify Tyndale's translation and to discredit the translator. It was desirable for them also to destroy not only the books but their author. In the summer of 1531 Tyndale had issued a challenge to the King. If only the King would license an English Bible, no matter by whom it might be translated, Tyndale would desist from his controversial activities and submit dutifully to his sovereign. How could such a proposal have been acceptable to the authorities? It would have made it plain that Tyndale had forced their hand. The King did not reply, and as late as the end of 1534 fifteen of the New Testaments were burned by order of the Lord Chancellor of England.

In 1532, however, Thomas Cranmer (1489-1556) had become Archbishop of Canterbury. Cranmer, who accepted this office reluctantly, was to become the King's chief instrument in the overthrow of papal jurisdiction in England. Toward the end of 1534, Cranmer, with the support of the Convocation of Canterbury, asked the King (a) to adopt certain means for the control of suspected books; (b) to nominate a body of "good and learned men" to translate the Bible and to have the fruit of their labors "delivered to the people for their instruction"; and (c) to order that henceforth no layman should presume to dispute upon the Bible or the Catholic faith.

Apparently Cranmer was entrusted by the King to attend to the matter of the translation himself and set about discharging his duty in the matter. Why he failed to achieve even a New Testament is obscure. There was some opposition to the project, notably by John Stokesley, Bishop of London. At any rate, it failed.

Meanwhile, others had been working independently, without any official authority, on the translation of the Bible. William Roye, who had been Tyndale's secretary till the spring of 1526, declared in a letter written the following year that he had begun work on the translation of the Old Testament and sought the prayers of "the right noble estates" and "all other of the town of Calais" to pray the Lord that he might be granted strength of mind and body to complete his task. Roye never produced anything of the promised translation in print. Nor did Tyndale expect this of him. In 1528 he wrote of Roye that the latter "promised more a great deal than I fear me he will ever repay."

George Joye (1495 [?]–1553), on the other hand, did put out between 1530 and 1534 the first printed versions of five books of the Old Testament and, in 1534, an attempted revision of Tyndale's New Testament. The latter, published anonymously and containing emendations unauthorized by Tyndale, naturally angered the latter and was the occasion of a bitter quarrel between Tyndale and Joye. To a second edition of the work that had offended Tyndale, Joye added a translation, under his own name, of the Liturgical Epistles drawn from the Old Testament. The historical importance of Joye consists in his being the first person to translate and publish an English printed translation of a considerable portion of the Old Testament, including the Psalms. There is no doubt that Joye's scholarship was not at all of Tyndale's caliber. Not only does he borrow freely from Tyndale; whenever he deserts Tyndale, he nearly always follows the Vulgate. He shows little concern for accuracy and often takes off on his own to indulge in paraphrastic and sometimes periphrastic effects that appeal to him as picturesque or dramatic. The picturesque and dramatic are not attainable by such undisciplined means, and rarely are Joye's flights successful, though a few have affected the later history of the English Bible. It is to him, for instance, that we owe the use of the word "backslide." Generally speaking, however, his abilities are of a very ordinary sort compared with Tyndale's, and he lacks, moreover, the modesty to avow this.

It is just this modesty that is so welcome in Coverdale. In May, 1532, a paraphrase of the Psalms known as the Campensis Psalter (*Psalterium Campensis*) was published. It was the work of John Campensis, Professor of Hebrew at Louvain. Two copies of an English translation of this survive, one printed at Antwerp in 1535, now in the library of Lincoln Cathedral, and one at London in 1539, now in the British Museum. Though the translation is anonymous, there is the strongest internal evidence that Coverdale was the translator. At any rate, the translation of the Campensis Psalter was well received. Its success probably encouraged Coverdale to go on to the production of a whole English Bible —a much weightier enterprise. This is the work that was completed and printed in October 1535.

Who encouraged and financed Coverdale in this project? The evidence is not beyond dispute; but it is extremely probable that it was one Jacob van Meteren, a merchant in Antwerp sympathetic to the Reformation cause. Seventy-four years later this merchant's son, Emmanuel, testified to this effect in a dispute relating to the Dutch Church in London. It is known that Coverdale was in Antwerp in 1535, and it is reported that while Jacob van Meteren was temporarily in England on business in that year, his wife, pregnant and nearing the time of her delivery, was troubled by the intrusion of officers with a warrant to search for forbidden books. As the officers rummaged through the house, they stumbled several times on the chest containing the fatal evidence; yet they ended by failing to discover it. The wife, who during this operation had been terror-stricken lest the evidence of her husband's active support of the Reformation cause should come to light, devoutly gave thanks for the divine protection she believed she had been granted and promised God in her heart that if her baby should be a son she would have him named Emmanuel, God with us.

It is fairly certain that when a sample of the Coverdale Bible was presented to the King shortly before the work was due to be published, the King reluctantly allowed it to be printed, though without the formal royal licence that the English printer, James Nicolson, had desired.

The martyrdom of Tyndale has already been accounted for. His action had offended both the King and the bishops. We may be sure that even if he had not offended them, Henry VIII would have been entirely uninterested in saving Tyndale's life, unless he could have seen a selfish advantage in doing so. All that is easily understood in view of Henry's gifts for making his interest in religion always serve his dominating concern for his own selfish ends, whether of pleasure or of power. It still remains difficult to understand why he should have tolerated Coverdale's Bible. When Tyndale's execution took place unhindered, the English authorities were neither more nor less well disposed to the Reformation cause than when Coverdale's Bible had received the King's reluctant consent the previous year.

How, then, is the toleration of Coverdale's Bible to be explained? Though Coverdale used Tyndale's text for the New Testament and Pentateuch, he modified the terms that were objectionable to the authorities. He also excluded all controversial matters from his notes and prologues. His Dedicatory Epistle was couched in polite language. These expressions of his tractable disposition probably helped to mollify the King and the bishops. Another, perhaps more important part of the explanation seems to lie in the circumstance that the Queen, Anne Boleyn, who happened to be in the King's favor at this time, was genuinely concerned for and well disposed to the Reformation. She was very much interested in the translation of the Bible into English, and it seems she had secretly received a copy of Tyndale's New Testament. Evidence points to her having used her influence with the King in respect to the Coverdale Bible, and it is possible that but for her intercession it would have fared no better than Tyndale's New Testament. There is at any rate no doubt that she ordered a copy of Coverdale's Bible to be placed on the "desk of her chamber" so that it might be read by others, and she personally went to read it at this desk herself. There is some evidence, too, that she extracted from the King permission to have the Bible in English set up in all churches in a place where it might be read by all who could read. Coverdale's Bible never attained any status of this kind however; nor was Anne Boleyn long able to exercise her influence on its behalf, for she soon fell out of favor, was arrested, and was beheaded less than three weeks after her arrest. The promise to have the Bible placed in churches had been made; but probably those who, having the King's ear, desired its implementation deemed it more prudent not to press the question after the Queen had fallen out of Henry's favor. At any rate, little more is heard of the Coverdale Bible for many years, though there were several printings. The Queen's efforts were not entirely in vain, however. They had a direct influence, for, as we shall see, another translation was licensed in 1537, and in 1539 yet another was actually authorized for setting up in churches. This was at the height of Henry's reign, about the time of his marriage, in 1540, to Anne of Cleves. Such was Henry's personal fickleness and the divided state of England at that time on the subject of the Reformation, that a foreign visitor exclaimed:

"What a country is this! On the one side they are hanging the Pope's friends; on the other they are burning his enemies."

Meanwhile the Coverdale Bible pursued its way quietly. What sort of translation was it? What were his sources? Since Coverdale had known little Hebrew or Greek and had readily admitted his incapacity to translate the Bible from the original sources, he had done the best he could do in these circumstances. He used Tyndale's translation freely for the New Testament and the Pentateuch. For the rest, he depended mainly on the Vulgate and on Luther's German version, as representing two sources, Roman and Lutheran, respectively, that were available to him. The Vulgate was the version that had been familiar to him from his earliest years. By the time that he was at work on his translation, its defects had become more and more known in the scholarly world of the humanists. Erasmus had brought out, in 1516, a revised text of the Latin New Testament that was more conformable to the best scholarship of the day, and in 1528 an Italian Dominican friar, Sanctes Pagninus, learned in Hebrew, had provided a revised Latin New Testament of Erasmus. Naturally, Coverdale made extensive use of the labors of Pagninus.

The Swiss, desiring a Bible in their own dialect, provided themselves with a translation that was printed at Zürich in 1524–1529 by Froschover in three folio volumes. This Swiss Bible had been translated from Luther's German in respect of the New Testament and about three quarters of the Old, that is, from Genesis to the Song of Solomon. Because the Swiss had been eager to have the complete Bible in their own dialect, they had felt unable to wait for Luther to finish his German version. So the translation of the rest, the Prophets and the Apocrypha, had been independently undertaken by the Zürich divines and by Leo Juda respectively. There had been a 16mo. reprint of this Swiss Bible, followed by an octavo edition, very slightly revised, in 1530. Then in 1531 had come the third edition, in folio, magnificently reproduced with many woodcuts and considerably revised. Coverdale made extensive use of this third edition of the Swiss Bible; but he also used a fourth edition published in 1534 and containing some further revisions which he sometimes follows in englishing the Bible.

These, then, are the "five sundry interpreters" mentioned by Coverdale in his Dedicatory Epistle to the King: Tyndale, the Vulgate, Luther, Pagninus, and the Swiss Bible. Coverdale could not claim, as did Tyndale, that he "had no man to counterfeit, neither was holpe with englyssche of any that had interpreted the same, or soche lyke thinge in the scripture beforetyme." Generally speaking, Coverdale used his "sundry interpreters" wisely. He followed Luther's example in segregating from the rest of the Old Testament the books that had not been included in the Hebrew canon. He inserted these "apocryphal books" at the end. Later English translators in turn followed Coverdale here, when they did not entirely omit the Apocrypha.

The text of the title page is enclosed in a woodcut border by Holbein. It reads as follows:

BIBLIA
The Bible / that
is, the holy Scripture of the
Olde and New Testament, faith-
fully and truly translated out
of Douche and Latyn.
into Englishe.
MDXXXV.
S. Paul II. Tessa. III.
Praie for us, that the worde of God maie
have fre passage, and be glorified. &c.
S. Paul. Col. III.
Let the worde of Christ dwell in you plen-
teously in all wyssdome &c.
Josue I.
Let not the boke of this lawe departe
out of thy mouth, but exercyse thyselfe
therein daye and nighte &c.

The border is composed of four blocks. At the top is the tetragrammaton, the sacred name of God in Hebrew, set in the midst of the rising sun, with Christ on the right hand and Adam and Eve on the left. The bottom block of the border shows Henry VIII, bearded, seated, and crowned, with the royal arms of England at his feet. In Henry's right hand is a drawn sword, leaving his left hand free for the dispensing of the Bible to the mitred bishops assembled at his right. On his left are kneeling nobles. In the side block at the left are scenes from the Old Testament (Moses giving the tables of the Law, and Ezra reading the Law to the people), while in the one at the right are scenes from the New Testament (Christ giving the commission to the disciples, and Peter preaching on the day of Pentecost).

In the dedication, the errors of "the blind bishop of Rome" are denounced, with special reference to his suppression of the Bible and his undermining of princely authority. The King is praised as a true defender of the Faith and as favoring the Bible, the Word of God that is the true instructor of men of all classes. Coverdale speaks with becoming modesty of the manner in which he had undertaken the task of translation. After alluding to his "simple and rude labour," he expresses his devotion to Henry as his liege lord and the "chief head" of the Church of England. He invited Henry to correct or improve the translation or even reject it altogether, should Henry's "godly wisdom" so dictate. The same modesty that graces the dedication appears in the prologue, where, having pondered his linguistic shortcomings, he refers to his great dependence on the work of others and prays God that the inadequtae work he has done may stimulate others to do better.

The first English Bible ever printed in England appeared in 1537. It was a second edition of Coverdale's. This folio edition was "Imprynted in Sowthwarke for James Nycolson." It was declared on the title page to be "newly ouersene and corrected," and it contained a dedication to King Henry, as in the first edition, except that changes in the monarch's domestic life necessitated a slight alteration: the name of "dearest just wyfe and most vertuous Pryncesse Quene Anne" had to become "Quene Jane." So we have the following:

> The right & just adminstracyon of the lawes that God gaue vnto Moses,/and vnto Josua: the testimonye of faythfulnes that God gaue of Dauid: the/plenteous abundaunce of wysdome that God gaue vnto Salomon: the lucky/and prosperous age with the multiplicacyon of sede which God gaue vnto A/braham and Sara his wyfe, be geven vnto you moost gracyous Prynce, with/your dearest just wyfe, and moost vertuous Pryncesse, Quene Jane, Amen./

In 1538 an edition of Coverdale's New Testament was published in 16mo. Of this only a few copies are extant. One of these, in the British Museum, contains an interesting manuscript note to the effect that this copy belonged to Queen Elizabeth I. I have not had an opportunity of seeing this note, of which the following is a description by J. R. Dore:

This small book was once the property of Q. Elizabeth, and actually presented by her to A. Poynts, who was her maid of Honour. In it are a few lines of the Queen's own hand writing and signing. Likewise a small drawing of King Edward the 6th when very young (of Windsor Castle) and one of the knight in his robes. The view of Windsor measures 3 5/8 in. by 2 3/8 in., and gives a view of the castle from Windsor Park. Several deer and hares are represented in the foreground, and the grass is of a very bright green colour. The sky and most of the building have become much darkened by discoloration of the paint with which they were depicted; but a red fence skirting the park, a gate with steps down to the park, and the gilt-tipped towers of the castle beyond, are all distinctly visible. The drawing of the knight, about 3 in. by 12 in. in size, displays greater artistic skill than that of Windsor Castle. Below it is this manuscript note. "This is actually a drawing of King Edward the Sixth. I. W. May, 1768. He likewise drew the Castle of Windsor on the other side of fore-going Leafe." The next leaf bears the following writing:

"Amonge good thin (in Q. Elizabeth's handwriting)

"Liber Roberti Grove
ex dono Thomae Field
Martii 20mo 1709

"Liber Thomae Gibbon
ex dono Roberti Grove
1714

"N.B.
The Worthy Dr. Gibbon, faithfully
assured me that the hand writing on
the other side this Leafe was really
Queen Elizabeths & I believe it
    having many Letters of her writing
                J^{no} Waller."

Upon the other side of the same leaf is the very interesting entry by Queen Elizabeth herself, as follows:

"Amonge good thinges
I prove and finde, the quiet
life doth muche abounde,
and sure to the contentid
mynde, ther is no riches
may be founde
    Your lovinge
      maistres
      Elizabeth."

It appears that the word "friend" had been written after the word "lovinge" in the seventh line of the above, but it has been partially erased, and the word "maistres" in the line below looks very much like an insertion. The writing is in Elizabeth's fine bold hand.

The titles of each book are printed in red, and each page has a red lined border. The cross and half-cross, intended to show the beginning and ending of the appointed Epistles and Gospels, the running titles, and initial letters are also printed in red.

There are numerous woodcuts. Gothic type. It has marginal references. Pointing hands are introduced to mark passages on which notes at the end of the chapters are appended.[1]

In 1538 Nicolson brought out a quarto reprint of Coverdale's New Testament, with the Vulgate text in parallel columns. The purpose was

---

[1] J. R. Dore, *Old Bibles* (2nd ed.; London: Eyre and Spottiswoode, 1888), pp. 95 ff.

apparently to give the clergy an opportunity of checking for themselves with the Latin to which they had been accustomed. The title is as follows:

> The new tes/tament both in Latine and/Englyshe ech correspondent to/the other after the vulgare texte com/munely called S.Jeroms. Fayth/fully translated by Myles/Couerdale/Anno./M.CCCCC. xxxviii. Jeremie xxij./Is not my worde lyke a fyre sayeth the/Lorde, and lyke an hammer that/breaketh the harde stone?/Printed in Southwarke/by James Nicolson./Set forth wyth the Kyn/ges moost gracious licence.

At the time Nicolson published this edition, Coverdale was in Paris. Being dissatisfied with it, he caused a corrected edition to be issued with the following title:

> The new testament both in/Latin and English after/the vulgare texte:/which is red in/the churche./Translated and corrected by My/les Couerdale: and prynted in/Paris, by Fraunces Regnault,/M.CCCCC. xxxviij./in November.

The cost of this corrected edition was probably borne by Edmund Bonner, then Archdeacon of Leicester and Bishop-elect of Hereford. Bonner, who later became Bishop of London, was much interested in the cause of the dissemination of the Bible in English. Coverdale explained, in the dedication of this edition, the reason for his having made it:

Trueth it is, that this last lent I dyd with all hūbleness directe an Epistle vnto the kynges most noble grace: trustinge, that the boke (wher vnto it was prefixed) shulde afterwarde haue bene well correcte, as other bokes be. And because I coulde not be present my selfe (by the reason of sondrye notable impedimētes) therfore inasmoch as the new testament, which I had set forth in English before, doth so agree wyth the latyn, I was hartely well contēt, that the latyn and it shulde be set together: Prouyded allwaye, that the correctour shulde followe the true copye of the latyn in anye wyse, and to kepe the true and right Englishe of the same. And so doynge, I was contēt to set my name to it. And euen so I dyd: trustinge, though I were absent and out of the lande, yet all shuld be well. And (as God is my recorde) I knew none other, till this last Julye, that it was my chauce here in these partes at a straungers hande, to come by a copye of the sayde prynte. Which wan I had perused, I founde, that it was disagreable to my former translacion in English, so was not the true copye of the latyn texte obserued, neither the english so correspondent to the same, as it ought to be: but in many places both base, insensyble, and cleane contrary, not onely to the phrase of oure language, but also from the vnderstondynge of the texte in latyn. Wherof though no man to this houre did write ner speake to me, yet for as moch as I am sworne to the trueth, I will favoure no man to the hinderaunce thereof, ner to the maynteyning of anything that is contrary to the ryght and just furtheraunce of the same. And therefore as my dewtye is to be faythfull, to edifye, and with the vttermost of my power to put awaye all occasions of euell, so haue I (though my businisse be greate ynough besyde) endeuoured my selfe to wede out the fautes that werein the latyn and English afore: trustinge, that this present correction maye be (vnto them that shall prynt it herafter) a copye sufficient.

Notwithstanding the publication of this edition in Paris in November, 1538, Nicolson, at the end of the year, issued a reprint of the Latin-English New Testament that Coverdale had found unsatisfactory. In the title, however, the name of "Johan Hollybushe" was substituted for that of Coverdale, as the translator.

In 1550 a quarto reprint of the Coverdale Bible was printed by Christopher Froschover of Zürich and published by Andrew Hester of London. Froschover's own copy, bearing his autograph, is in the Public Library at Zürich. This Bible is a reprint of the 1537 folio and bears the following title, ascribing the translation to Thomas Matthew:

> The whole Byble/that is, the Olde and New/Testamente, truly and purely/translated into Englishe/by Mayst Thomas Mathewe./Esaie j. Hearcken to, ye heauens: and thou earth/geaue eare: for the LORD/ ✠ speaketh. ✠/Christ. Frosch. Imprinted at Zürych by Chrystoffer Froshower.

The reason for Froschover's ascribing this reprint to Thomas Matthew is obscure. As we shall see in our next chapter, the Bible commonly known as "the Matthew Bible" or "Matthew's Bible" was a separate work, done by John Rogers. It has been suggested, however, that Froschover would have had at least one reason, in 1550, for using Matthew's name in his reprint of the Coverdale Bible. By that time the situation had changed. Henry VIII had been succeeded by the boy-king, Edward VI, during whose reign the Reformation cause was in high favor. There was no longer any restriction against publishing the Bible in England. On the contrary, publishers may have been troubled, rather, by the normal difficulty of selling copies. With this in view, Froschover may have used the name of Thomas Matthew as a selling device, because, as we shall see, the Bible so designated had by that time acquired a status the Coverdale Bible never possessed: it had become the first English Bible to have obtained the royal licence, which Henry VIII bestowed upon it. It may have seemed profitable to Froschover to give his product the name associated with a Bible that had the royal licence, rather than the name associated with a Bible that had enjoyed only permissive status.

Sheets of the Froschover Bible were reissued by Richard Jugge of

London in 1553; but thereafter no reprint of it appeared until the nineteenth century.

A note about sixteenth-century book practices is in place here. It should be remembered that in the sixteenth century the author or translator of a book had as little to say about what appeared on the title page as a modern writer has about what appears on the jacket of his book. The publisher drew up the title page and put on it whatever he thought would promote the sales. Wherever this is the custom, the author or translator is not to be accounted responsible for departures from truth. One might as well hold people responsible today for what press reporters say about them in the newspapers. If the reporter cannot extract something newsy out of the opinions he elicits in an interview, he must either look elsewhere or improve upon the opinions provided. He often finds the latter easier and more expedient. The publisher may find enough in a book to make the jacket exciting; but what if he cannot? Then he must concoct something, whether it is in the book or not, or at any rate he must turn the truth into a saleable phrase. Sixteenth-century practice was not essentially different, except that books did not have jackets, so the title page was the publisher's preserve.

Bibliographical Note to Chapter 14

To the reader who wishes to pursue in greater detail the contribution of Coverdale to the history of the English Bible is recommended a scholarly work of great value by J. F. Mozley, *Coverdale and His Bibles* (London: Lutterworth Press, 1953). Such is the role of George Joye that for long he was understandably but regrettably neglected by scholars. This state of affairs has now been remedied. Charles C. Butterworth, who before his death had called attention in more than one of his books to the not inconsiderable importance of Joye, had begun a separate monograph on him, and when he died before this was far from complete, the work was taken up by Dr. Chester, who, with Dr. Mozley, had urged him in the first place to undertake it. The result is an excellent study: Charles C. Butterworth and Allan G. Chester, *George Joye* (Philadelphia: University of Pennsylvania Press, 1962). See also the editorial article "Miles Coverdale and the English Bible" in the *Bulletin of the John Rylands Library*, XIX, July, 1935.

Your highnesse never did anythinge
more acceptable to God . . . than when your
majestie lycenced and wyled, the moost
sacred Bible, contaynge the unspotted and
lively word of God, to be in the Englyshe tonge
set forthe to your highnesse subjects.
—Taverner's Dedicatory Epistle

CHAPTER 15 *The Matthew and the Taverner Bibles*

Coverdale's Bible, first published in 1535, was, we have seen, the first complete English Bible to be printed. In 1537, a competitor appeared on the scene, whose title attributed the translation to Thomas Matthew and which is commonly known as the Matthew Bible. There was, in fact, no such person. The work was that of John Rogers, a friend of Tyndale and his literary executor, who either assumed the name of Thomas Matthew when at Antwerp or adopted it as a pseudonym to conceal or disguise the then very damaging fact that a large part of the translation Rogers put forth was his friend Tyndale's. Rogers used what had already been printed of Tyndale's work, together with the manuscripts the latter had left him. These comprised portions of the Old Testament that Tyndale had completed in prison before his execution. For the rest Rogers simply relied upon Coverdale.

The title is as follows:

⟨The Byble,/which is all the holy Scrip/ture: In whych are contayned the/Olde and Newe Testament truly/and purely translated into En/glysh by Thomas Matthew.
⟨Essaye j./Hearken to ye heauens and/thou earth geaue eare: For the/Lorde speaketh/M,D, xxxvii./
Set forth with the Kinges most gracyous lycēce.

The royal licence did not confer on the Matthew Bible any authorization for its being set up and publicly read in churches; but it did afford complete protection to those who read it privately. Coverdale's version, though permitted and even quietly encouraged, was never so licensed. How was it that the Matthew Bible, so deeply indebted to the detested Tyndale, and edited by his literary executor, was so readily granted the royal licence?

The explanation reflects the labyrinthine complexities of the technique of face-saving which, though by no means peculiar to England or the sixteenth century, was a highly developed sixteenth-century English art.

In 1537 Richard Grafton brought a copy of the Matthew Bible to England. On August 4, 1537, Archbishop Cranmer wrote Thomas Cromwell sending him a copy of this Bible that had just come into his hands and which he commended as "very well done" and "dedicated unto the king's majesty, as farther appeareth by a pistle unto his grace in the beginning of the book." Cranmer wrote that he liked it "better than any other translation heretofore made," and he politely requested that Cromwell should obtain of the King a licence to enable it to be sold and read by everyone "without danger of any act, proclamation or ordinance heretofore granted to the contrary, until such time that we the bishops shall set forth a better translation." The remoteness of the possibility of improving upon the version now submitted was expressed in Cranmer's declared opinion that such an improvement was not expected to occur "till a day after doomsday."

Within a week Cromwell had secured the royal licence, and on August 13 Cranmer wrote him his warm thanks. It may seem a bold, not to say daring action to have presented the King with a book containing so much of Tyndale; but it was really a deft move. Henry was by this time disposed to look favorably upon the translation of the Bible. Alienated from Rome, he had already shown himself willing to tolerate Coverdale's Bible, and so long as he was not made to appear guilty of mistakes or misjudgements in the past, there seemed no reason why he should not now formally give the royal licence to a Bible commended to him by his advisers.

In fact, only a few years later Henry found the English Reformation going too fast for his liking. Death was decreed against anyone who denied transubstantiation, and a man was hanged in London for eating meat on Friday. This sentence seems severe in light of Rome's permissiveness about abstinence today; but these precautions were to ensure no public controversies about religion. There was no objection to private opinions that might be held on these subjects, so long as they did not issue in open controversies that might disturb the peace of the realm. After all, though Henry had repudiated the authority of the Pope in England, he had not so much abolished papal power as he had assumed it for himself. He wished his pronouncements upon religion to be unchallenged, for he could ill afford to tolerate religious strife between "Catholic" and "Protestant"; but in exercising papal power in England his concern was to order England's religion to his political advantage. He had no interest in what men might think privately, one way or the other, in the presence of God, whom he did not account in any way a rival to his authority.

At any rate, in 1537 Henry was disposed to encourage the widespread feeling that it must be possible to make an acceptable translation of the

Bible, and since the Matthew Bible was presented to him as the best available at that time, he gave it his licence.

John Rogers, the editor of the Matthew Bible, was born near Birmingham about the year 1500. He was graduated from Cambridge in 1525 and seven years later obtained the incumbency of a London church. After two years there he left for Antwerp, in 1534, where he met Tyndale and other friends of the Reformation cause. While in Antwerp he married a kinswoman of the wife of Jacob de Meteren, Coverdale's promoter. By his marriage to this Flemish lady, Adriana de Weyden,[1] Rogers had eight children. After six years in Antwerp he left for Wittenberg, where he matriculated on November 25, 1540. There he met various Lutheran divines, coming especially under the influence of Melanchthon.

On the death of Henry and the succession of Edward VI to the English throne, he felt that the time was ripe for return to England. Many exiles returned to England about this time. It was about this time, too, that John Knox, the Scottish Reformer, embarked upon his years of labor in England for the Reformation cause that flourished under Edward VI before Scotland was ready for Knox's leadership. On May 10, 1548, John Rogers was presented to an English ecclesiastical living, and on August 24, 1551, he obtained the prebendal stall of St. Pancras at St. Paul's Cathedral, London. He afterwards became Rector of Chigwell, Essex. The advent of Mary Tudor to the English throne soon put an end to his labors. On August 16, 1553, the Lords of Council ordered John Rogers, *alias* Matthew, to be confined to his residence at St. Paul's Cathedral, charged with being a seditious preacher. On February 4, 1555, he was burnt. Under Henry VIII, Rogers had been the first to have his Bible officially licensed in England. He was now, under Bloody Mary, first in the procession of the three hundred Protestant martyrs to suffer death during her brief, wicked, and unforgettable reign.

The printed matter of the Matthew Bible measures 6½ by 11¼ inches, with about two thousand marginal notes in addition, occupying one inch of space on either side of the text. There are 1,110 pages and about a hundred woodcuts. The woodcuts before Psalms and Proverbs occupy the entire breadth of the page.

The marginal notes are drawn chiefly from the work of Lefèvre d'Etaples and Olivetan, whom we have met in an earlier chapter. The text, however, was as much Tyndale's as could be. Coverdale was used only where Tyndale was not available. In 1538 a second folio edition of the Matthew Bible appeared, and this is now much rarer than the first. In 1540 an edition in 16mo. in five volumes was printed by Robert Redman, and in 1549 a very accurate reprint of the original first folio

---

[1] Later anglicized "Pratt."

was issued at London "By Thomas Raynalde and William Hyll, dwelling in Paules Churche yeard." Explanations of terms are provided, such as the following for the Book of Exodus: "Ephod, is a garment somewhat lyke an amyce, saue the armes came thoroe and it was gyrd to," and "Arcke, a cofer or cheste as oure shrynes, saue it was flatte and thee sameple of oure shrynes was taken thereof."

Another folio edition of the Matthew Bible appeared in the same year, edited by Edmund Becke and printed in London "by Ijon Daye, dwelling at Aldersgate and William Seres, dwelling in Peter College." Issued on August 16, 1549, it incorporated some now unpalatable notes by the editor, such as one on I Peter 3, in which husbands are instructed as follows how to treat their wives: "And yf she be not obedient and healpfull vnto hym [he] endeaoureth to beate the feare of God into her heade, that therby she maye be compelled to learne her dutie, and to do it."

The Matthew Bible was superseded within two years by the Great Bible, to which the next chapter will be devoted. Nevertheless, there was an issue of it by Nicholas Nyll as late as 1551. During its two-year reign it reached a great many people, encountering varying degrees of commendation and condemnation. There were not nearly enough copies to go round the churches, and in any case many country parsons were too poor or too indifferent to buy one.

In 1539, the year of the appearance of the Great Bible, another version was published in folio that might have received greater acclaim had it not been overshadowed by that formidable competitor. This was the version by Richard Taverner (*c.* 1505-1575), a lawyer by profession who later, under Edward VI, when preachers were scarce, obtained a licence as a lay preacher. Taverner evidently knew Greek well but not Hebrew. In his youth at Christ Church, Oxford, he had been in trouble for reading Tyndale's New Testament. The title of Taverner's Bible is as follows:

> The Most/Sacred Bible/Whiche is the holy scripture, con/teyning the old and new testament,/translated into English, and newly/recognised with great diligence/after most faythful exem/plars, by Rychard Taverner.
>
> ☞ Harken thou heuen, and thou earth gyue/eare: for the Lorde speaketh. Esaie i./
>
> ☞ Prynted at *London* in Flete strete at/the sygne of the sonne by John By/ddell, for Thomas Barthlet./
>
> ☞ Cvm Privilegio/ad imprimendum solum./M.D. xxxix./

It was dedicated "To the most noble, most mighty, and most redoubted prynce, Kinge Henry the viij."

Like the more celebrated Great Bible, Taverner's Bible is a revision of the Matthew Bible; but his revision is much less thoroughgoing. Many of Taverner's revisions, however, are very good ones, and in his apparatus, drawn mainly from the Matthew Bible, he is restrained, omitting the more pointed references to Church corruption. The changes he made often provided more vigorous renderings or more idiomatic English. So Christ is called our "spokesman with the Father" rather than our "advocate." Where Tyndale had said that Christ "obteyneth grace for our sins," and the King James Version calls Christ "the propitiation for our sins," Taverner says: "For he is the mercy-stock for our sins." Where, at Luke 12:29, the King James Version has "neither be ye of doubtful mind," and the twentieth-century New English Bible has "you are not to worry," Tyndale had put: "neither climb ye up on high." For this Taverner wrote: "and be not carried in the clouds."

Taverner, though an ardent subscriber to the Reformation cause, was not a seeker after martyrdom. He was at home at Oxford, among men of "the new learning," and it is related by Anthony à Wood that when Taverner was a law student in London, "his humour was to quote the law in Greek when he read anything thereof." When he got into trouble with Henry VIII and was sent to the Tower of London, Taverner did not stay long there. He submitted to the King and was restored to the royal favor. Then, during Mary Tudor's reign he quietly disappeared from public life and so lived to return to it under Elizabeth, preaching at St. Mary's Oxford, and becoming High Sheriff of the County, before his death in 1575.

Though Taverner's version was overshadowed by the appearance of the Great Bible, it is possible, as some scholars have suggested, that it had some independent influence on later Bibles, such as the Douai and the King James Versions. The evidence for this, however, seems inconclusive, to say the least. Most of the words and phrases in Taverner that find their way into these versions have already appeared in versions other than his. Some of his renderings in the New Testament were indeed, however, adopted in later versions, notably his use of the word "parable" for "similitude," and the "express image" (Heb. 1:3) which he borrowed from the phrase *expressa imago* of Erasmus. At any rate, competition from the Great Bible notwithstanding, there was apparently sufficient demand for Taverner's as late as a decade after its first appearance and the appearance of the Great Bible that dwarfed it. In 1549 an edition of Taverner's Bible was issued in five duodecimo volumes by Daye and Seres. The purpose of issuing it in so many separate parts was declared to be a practical one for the convenience of those who could not afford the outright purchase of the entire Bible at one time. It was a sort of sixteenth-century pay-as-you-go plan.

The Byble in Englyshe, that is to say,
the content of all the holye scrypture.—Title of
the first edition of the Great Bible

CHAPTER 16 *The Great Bible*

When the Matthew Bible appeared, the English authorities were already aware that a royal licence enabling people to read the Bible privately in English without fear of reprisals was not enough. This was only a temporary measure. What was needed was an English Bible authorized for public use in churches. Yet whatever this more official English version was to be, it must not be so blatantly indebted to Tyndale as were all existing printed versions. It is one thing to say, "You are permitted to read this book," or even, "In reading this book you have the King's protection"; it is another to say, "This book is authorized for public use in church." So far there was no English Bible so authorized, and it was plain that one must be provided, however distasteful the idea might be to some of the bishops.

It was natural that the authorities should look to Coverdale to provide what was needed. He was a man of peaceable disposition. He had experience of Bible translation, and even though he was not as well qualified as some, he could be trusted, and of course he could obtain whatever technical help he might need. Coverdale had for long been the friend of Thomas Cromwell, who is so closely associated with the project of making the Great Bible that it has sometimes been named Cromwell's Bible, after him.

Coverdale's instructions were to take the Matthew Bible as his basis and do with it whatever might be needed to make it acceptable for the purpose in view. When the work was begun, Cromwell was in high favor and enjoyed great power in England, being the King's Vicar-General. It is said that as such he treated the bishops with much haughtiness. At any rate, he was eventually disgraced and executed in July, 1540, the year after the first edition of the Great Bible had appeared. Charged with having enriched himself with bribes taken to pervert justice and with other offences, he was condemned under the Act of Attainder without trial—poetic justice, since it had been he who had devised this process for others. Awaiting execution in the Tower, he wrote to the King abjectly: "With heavy heart and trembling hand of your Highness most miserable prisoner, and poor slave, I cry for mercy, mercy, mercy." Even his friend Cranmer favored his execution.

When the Great Bible was being planned, however, Cromwell, at the height of his power, was Coverdale's patron. That neither Coverdale nor his associates could always count on Cromwell's support when it was most needed is evident from the correspondence.

Richard Grafton and Edward Whitchurch were chosen as publishers. They had brought out the Matthew Bible and were an obvious choice. They were Englishmen, respected members of the city companies, men of assured standing and able to bear the cost of the venture, which apparently they were called upon to do. It seems, however, that Cromwell did make some contribution out of his own budget, or at any rate provided an advance.

So ambitiously was the project conceived that Cromwell felt there was not in all England paper good enough or printers sufficiently skilled to produce the sumptuous edition that was desired. In admitting this to the French ambassador, he remarks also that in France "books are dispatched sooner than in any other country." Another reason for printing in France has also been suggested, namely, to circumvent dangers to the project that could well attend it in England where some of the bishops might be hostile to it and use their influence with the King to impede its fulfilment. Of course Cromwell was well aware of this danger and endeavoured to forestall it by obtaining from the English King his request to the French King to grant his permit and licence to have the Bible printed in France. In the British Museum there is a document in which the King of France grants such a licence to Grafton and Whitchurch, enabling them to have the Bible printed in France and transported to England, provided that it should contain no "private or unlawful opinions." Unfortunately, this document is undated, so that its precise force is obscure. At any rate, the phrase about unlawful opinions practically voided any protection it might be supposed to give, for in France the Inquisition could still do almost anything it pleased under cover of that comprehensive phrase. It was almost as though the French King should have granted a licence to print the book as long as he did not find it desirable to stop it.

As early as June 23, 1538—by which time Coverdale had been in Paris with Grafton for about a month, staying with their printer, Francis Regnault—they were already writing to Cromwell, complaining of their being "daily threatened" in the pursuit of their task, and invoking his aid. It is fairly certain that Cromwell did little or nothing for them, for a letter from Whitchurch to Cromwell survives (unfortunately also undated but apparently written from London) in which he deplores the latter's failure to obtain adequate protection for "our purposed work." Be that as it may, Coverdale and Grafton did send with their letter of June 23 evidence of progress: two sets of printed sheets, one on fine paper and the other on parchment. More followed in August, and in September they sent Cromwell a progress report in which they predicted the completion of the work within a few months. We find, however, that in October the new English ambassador to France, Bishop Edmund Bonner, is writing to Cromwell complaining of difficulties experienced by those engaged in the production of the new Bible. Nevertheless, the work continued till mid-December, when Coverdale and his associates, apprised of grave dangers impending, wrote hurriedly to Cromwell, explaining their plight and sending him by the hand of Bonner some more printed sheets by way of salvaging what they could before disaster overtook them.

On December 17, 1538, the Inquisitor-General for France ordered Francis Regnault and others engaged in the printing of an English Bible to desist immediately, forbad them to dispose of the printed sheets now in their hands, and cited them to appear before him. Regnault appeared before the Inquisitor's court and was charged with heresy. Coverdale and Grafton fled to England, leaving behind them twenty-five hundred of their Bibles, which were of course confiscated by the French authorities. These Bibles were no doubt incomplete, and what happened to them is obscure, though it seems that some were burnt, and it is certain that Cromwell conducted negotiations with the French authorities for several months in hope of retrieving those that remained. Whether they were ever recovered or not is less clear; but there is some indication, at least, of their having been returned to Grafton in November, 1539. Before then, however, Coverdale and his associates succeeded in conveying the type and printing equipment to London where the work was resumed, being completed there in April, 1539. The conveyance of the printing facilities from France to England appears to have been done quietly, even secretly; yet there is no evidence at all that the French King sought to prevent it. To a letter written on February 29, 1539, to the French ambassador to London by the Constable of France is appended a declaration of the King of France. This is to the effect that, while he does not profess to judge whether the English Bible be good or bad, and so is not willing to impugn it, he sees no reason why it should be printed in Paris when it could very well be printed in England.

Why, then, should there ever have been such hostility in France to the printing of a Bible that was destined for use in another realm? Francis of France wished to keep on good terms with Henry of England. Only a few years earlier he had encouraged Lefèvre's French version. Why should there have been any objection on the French side to the printing of a Bible few Frenchmen could read and that could have little interest, therefore, for the vast majority of the French king's subjects? The explanation lies in the fact that the hostility came much less from the French authorities than from some of the English bishops and others who were antagonistic to the scheme and were intriguing through agents in France and at Rome to put difficulties in the way of its publication. In other words, the source of the trouble was theological opposition from certain quarters in England, supported, of course, by the Inquisition in France, rather than from the French authorities themselves. There was at this time widespread opposition in England to a vernacular Bible, and when the Great Bible was eventually published, there was still need for considerable public education in the acceptance of the idea, as is attested by the injunctions and laws that were required to force it into circulation. Even late in 1541 we find Thomas Becon complaining that in spite of the fact that men were now free to read the Great Bible "even in the churches," the sacred volume was sometimes, like the pulpit, covered in dust. In the customarily violent language of the time he goes on to remark: "So little pleasure have these filthy swine and currish dogs in that most sweet and singular treasure." Moreover, in spite of the injunctions, some country churches had no Bible at all. Where neither the parson nor any literate layman actively encouraged its purchase, this would generally be deferred on one pretext or another. Since the majority of the people could not read, nothing would be done.

Nevertheless, where it was once installed, it often attracted much attention. Indeed, there were ugly cases of disturbances, followed by reprisals, for example, when a young tailor, John Porter, read aloud from the Bible to groups of friends and was later accused of heresy and allowed to be starved to death. Often, however, it exerted its influence quietly, firing the imagination of men and moving their minds.

Two prepublication copies in vellum of the first Great Bible exist today, one at St. John's College, Cambridge, and the other in the National Library of Wales, and it is to be presumed that these are parchment copies such as are mentioned in the letter sent by Coverdale and Grafton to Cromwell on June 23, 1538. The copy at St. John's is generally believed to be Cromwell's personal copy, though there seems to be no conclusive evidence that this is the case.

The first edition, published in April, 1539, was indeed a noble volume, well meriting the name Great Bible. Splendidly printed on very large paper, it bore a frontispiece said to be designed by Holbein, depicting a singularly ascetic Henry VIII handing a Bible to Thomas Cromwell on one side and on the other Archbishop Cranmer. (Cranmer had in fact no share in either the translation or the publication, though he wrote a celebrated preface that appears in the second and subsequent editions.) Lower down in the picture, Cranmer is presenting a copy to a kneeling priest, while on the other side is to be seen Cromwell giving one to a group of noblemen. At the bottom is a more crowded scene, in which a priest is preaching to a group of the common people. From the mouths of these people unconvincingly proceed ribbons containing the words

VIVAT REX: Long live the King! Behind the loyal subjects rises the sinister outline of Newgate Prison. From this those not currently in the royal favor enjoy a view of the proceedings impeded only by prison bars. In the clouds immediately above Henry's royal, not to say glorified, head nestles God, clearly accorded a slight precedence over the monarch, though not in any way to suggest any diminution of or limitations upon the King's Majesty. Surely the artist must have quietly enjoyed himself in the fulfilment of his appointed task.

The title of the first edition reads:

⁋ The Byble in/Englyshe, that is to saye the con/tent of all the holy scripture, bothe/of ye olde and newe testament, truly/translated after the veryte of the/Hebrue and Greke textes, by ye dy/lygent men, expert in the forsayde/tonges./⁋ Prynted by Rychard Grafton & Edward Whitchurch./Cum priuilegio ad imprimen/dum solum./1539./

The Bible in English, that is to say, the content of *all* the Holy Scripture! Think of a man who, unable to read, asks a literate friend to tell him what is said in the title. As his friend slowly enunciates the exciting words, such a man must feel then, if ever, an incitement to learn the art of reading. For once he has mastered that art he can hope, given time and patience, to read the entire Bible. His fathers have been able to hear occasionally bits of the Bible—a part of a chapter of an "Epistle of Holy Paul" or this or that from the "Holy Gospels." The man himself may have heard of New Testaments or even Bibles in the common English tongue and may have perhaps seen one and furtively heard a friend read a little of it in private. But now openly, in the parish church itself, is the *whole* Bible. If only he could read, here would be the opportunity to get to the bottom of the matters the great men of the day are fighting about. So long as he had the good fortune to live near a parish church that obeys the injunction to possess a copy, he could go and read it for himself, once he had mastered the art of reading.

Nor was it only in churches that it could be read. Anyone who could muster ten shillings could obtain an unbound copy for himself, and for twelve shillings a bound one. These were the official prices; but there is evidence in the books of the churchwardens that copies were sometimes sold for much less—near five shillings. This was about the price paid by the parish of Ashburton, for instance, for "a new booke called a Bybyll." The same parish also paid eightpence "for a chaine for fastenynge the sayde booke." Around those who possessed a private copy and could read it, others, less gifted, would eagerly come to listen. For in spite of the indolence and disinterestedness of the many of whom Thomas Becon was complaining, there were others whose minds and hearts it enchanted as no other book had ever done. Indeed, the popularity of all other forms of literature, even the lascivious alehouse tales, seems sometimes to have waned in competition with the rich diversity of the texture of the Bible and the robust vivacity of its style. Men could not fail to observe that the Bible was all sorts of a book, varying from the aphorisms of Proverbs to the apocalyptic visions of Revelation, from the narrations of Chronicles to the mighty prophesyings of Amos.

There were no explanatory notes or comments in the Great Bible. Coverdale had hoped, indeed, to provide these in later editions. Such notes had been prepared and in the prologue there is an allusion to this intention: "We have added many hands in the margent of this Byble vpon which we purposed certen godly annotacyons, but for so moch as yet there hath not bene suffycient tyme mynystored to the Kinges moost honorable councell for the ouersyght and correcyon of the sayde annotacyons, we wyll therfore omyt them tyl their more conuenient leysour."

No doubt the King indicated his desire that the notes should remain omitted, for they were never provided in any of the later editions. There are, however, pointing hands in the margin and text, indicating passages Coverdale accounted obscure and therefore in need of annotation.

The first edition has certain very distinctive features. The wrists of these pointing hands have ruffles; in later editions they have cuffs. The stars in the first edition have all six points, while in later editions some of them have five. The woodcuts of the first edition are supported by a border on each side; in later editions the woodcuts have no borders. In the first edition the New Testament title page has a border of six woodcuts absent from other editions, and the title page of the Apocrypha (called Hagiographa) has a border after the manner of the principal title page, which is not the case in later editions.

The first edition was followed by six others in the next two years, three in 1540 and three in 1541. The second edition, published in April, 1540, bore a preface by Cranmer. It also included a considerable amount of revision by Coverdale, especially in the poetical books of the Old Testament. The third was issued in July, and the fourth is dated November, 1540, in the colophon, though the title has 1541. This edition is declared to have been "overseen and perused" by two English bishops, Cuthbert Tonstall and Nicholas Heath. The remaining editions appeared respectively in May, November, and December, 1541. Of course, among surviving copies many, probably most, are mixed; that is to say, they contain parts from more than one edition. Certain tests are used to determine to which edition particular leaves belong—not an easy bibliographical enterprise.

141

O Gracious God, and most merciful father, which hast vouchsafed us the rich and precious jewel of thy holy word, assist us with thy spirit, that it may be written in our hearts to our ever- lasting comfort, to reform us, to renew us, according to thine own image; to build us up, and edifie us into the perfect increasing of thy Christ, sanc- tifying and increasing in us all heavenly vertues. Grant this O heavenly Father, for Jesus Christs sake. Amen.—Prayer prefixed to the text of the Geneva Bible

CHAPTER 17 *The Geneva Bible*

Though it was during the reign of Henry VIII that the jurisdiction of the Pope in England was formally repudiated, we have seen that the Reformation was by no means much in Henry's debt. The reign of his successor, the precocious boy-king Edward VI, was much more propitious for the Reformation cause; but it soon gave place to that of Mary Tudor, whose succession in 1553 drove shiploads of English refugees to the continent of Europe. Some of these fugitives from the Marian terror were attracted to Geneva, the Swiss city by the lake, where a community was being moulded by Calvin into the cosmopolis that John Knox, the Scottish Reformer, was to describe as "the most perfect school of Christ since the days of the Apostles." Be that as it may, there was on that Swiss lakeside a climate of freedom not easily obtainable elsewhere at that time. Many learned men were congregated there, including The- odore Beza, the greatest living biblical scholar. French scholars there were working on the French Bible that was to become the official version for the Reformed Church in France.

That the English-speaking exiles in Geneva should have produced a revision of the Great Bible is as might be expected. In Geneva they could produce their work unhampered by the grave difficulties which, as we have seen, had beset such enterprises elsewhere, even in compara- tively favorable circumstances. The leading figure in the work was William Whittingham, Calvin's brother-in-law, who was the principal if not the sole translator of a duodecimo English New Testament issued on June 10, 1557, by Conrad Badius of Geneva.

Whittingham was born at Lanchester, near Durham, in or about 1524. Educated at Brasenose College, Oxford, he became a Fellow of All Souls in 1545, and moved two years later to Christ Church. Having gone

142

to Frankfort in June, 1554, he married on November 15, 1556, Catherine Jacquemaine, Calvin's wife's sister. Later, at Geneva, he eventually succeeded John Knox in 1559 as minister of the congregation of English-speaking exiles there, returning to England the following year to become, under Elizabeth, Dean of Durham, an appointment he obtained through the influence of the Earl of Leicester.

The title page of his New Testament reads as follows:

> The Nevve Testament of ovr Lord Iesus Christ. Conferred diligently vvith the Greke, and best approued translations *with the arguments as wel before the Chapters as for euery boke and Epistle, also diversities of readings and the most profitable annotations of all harde places, whereunto is added a copious Table.*

Below this is a woodcut representing Time with scythe and hourglass, drawing out of a well a female figure. On the right of the woodcut are the words: "God by Time restoreth Truth." On the left: "and maketh her victorious." Below all this are the words: "At Geneva. Printed by Conrad Badius M.D.LVII."

Whittingham's New Testament is rare, and no second edition was printed. It exhibited some interesting features, notably the division of chapters into verses and the use of italics to mark words not in the Greek. An innovation of Whittingham that proved convenient and popular, being adopted in the earlier editions of the Geneva Bible, was the use of Roman in place of old English or black-letter type. He borrowed very considerably from Tyndale. His version is, indeed, more a revision of the latter's work than an independent translation. Nevertheless, there are distinctive renderings. For example, in the account of Joseph's first reaction when he heard Mary was with child (Matthew 1:19), Tyndale has written: "Joseph her husbande beynge a perfect man, and loth to make an ensample of her, was mynded to put her away secretly." This was followed in the Matthew and the Taverner Bibles. Coverdale had: "Joseph her hosband was a perfecte man/and wold not bringe her to shame/but was mynded to put her away secretly." Whittingham's rendering was: "Then Joseph her housband being a just man, and loth to make her a publike exemple of infamie, was mynded to put her a way secretly." In this he was followed by the Geneva Bible, except that this omitted the words "of infamie."

Whittingham also rendered psalms into English metrical form, some of which were included in the version by Sternhold and Hopkins. This version was in use in the Church of England till it was supplanted by Tate and Brady's version of the metrical psalms, which was in general use in Anglican worship in the early nineteenth century and still not uncommon even as late as Gladstone's time. Whittingham's poetic gifts were very limited, however. His metrical rendering of the first verses of the Nisi Dominus (Psalms 127, RSV) represents his better work:

> Except the Lord the house do make,
> And therevnto do let his hand:
> What men do build it cannot stand.
>   Likewise in vaine men vndertake,
> Cities and holdes to watch and ward,
> Except the Lord be their safeguard.
>
> Though ye rise early in the morne,
> And so at night go late to bed,
> Feeding full hardly with browne bread
>   Yet were your labour lost and worne,
> But they whom God doth loue and keepe
> Receiue all things with quiet sleepe.

The crowning glory of the labors of the English-speaking exiles at Geneva was the publication, on April 10, 1560, of the first edition of the Geneva Bible. Some of the exiles, now free to return to England under Elizabeth, had remained to help in the final stages of the work. In several respects it was an improvement on previous translations. In the Old Testament it followed the Hebrew more closely than had its predecessors. It was in quarto and therefore easier to handle than many Bibles were in those days. The use of Roman type, which we have seen was introduced by Whittingham, was of considerable convenience. Though the invention of printing had fostered the spectacle trade, optical prescriptions were still fairly simple, and Roman type was much more easily readable than the old black letter. Moreover, though division into paragraphs was by this time customary, further division into verses was not. Rabbi Nathan in 1448 had used a method of verse division in a Venice edition published in 1524, and this had been adopted in a Latin Bible printed in 1528, which also used a similar method for the New Testament. In 1555 Robert Estienne of Paris had issued a Bible in which the same verse division was used for the Old Testament but a different one provided for the New. The Geneva Bible followed Estienne's arrangement. This was likewise a great convenience to students of the Bible, and also to the general reader. Finally, though the Geneva Bible followed the customary practice of providing notes to the text, the notes it provided were less violently controversial than was usual in that age.

The publication of the Geneva Bible was timely, and it achieved enormous popularity. It was the Bible of Shakespeare and the Bible of the Pilgrim Fathers. A copy actually used on the *Mayflower* is preserved at Harvard. The Geneva Bible appeared just about the time of the abolition of papal jurisdiction in Scotland in 1560, and an Act of the Scottish Parliament made it compulsory for every householder whose income was above a certain sum to buy a copy. The first generation of Scotsmen to enjoy the benefits of the Reformation was reared exclusively upon this version. In England it was never in any sense an authorized version; nevertheless it was imported from Geneva and widely used in private houses. In Elizabeth's reign alone there were sixty editions of it, despite the fact that it lacked her official approval. By the middle of the seventeenth century the number of editions had doubled.

Here is the title of the first edition:

> The Bible/and/Holy Scriptvres./Conteyned in/the Olde and Newe/ Testament. Translated accor/ding to the Ebrue and Greke, and con- ferred with/the best translations in diuers languages./with moste profit- able annota/tions vpon all the hard places, and other things of great/ importance as may appeare in the Epistle to the Reader./
>
> Feare not, stand stil, and beholde/the saluacion of the Lord, which he wil shew to you this day. Exod. 14, 13.
>
> At Geneva/Printed by Rovland Hall/M.D.LX.

There is a woodcut on the title page, showing the Passage through the Red Sea, and a dedicatory epistle is provided later on:

> To the Moste Ver/tvovs and Noble Quene Eli/sabet, Quene of En- gland, France ād Ireland, &c., Your hum/ble subjects of the English Churche at Geneua wish/grace and peace from God the Father, through /Christ Iesvs our Lord.

Also published in 1560 was a New Testament issued in 16mo. whose text is not that of Whittingham's but follows exactly that of the first edition of the Geneva Bible. The notes are, however, shorter. This New Testament is without a printer's name; but the printer was probably Rouland Hall of Geneva. Such was the popularity of the Geneva Bible that for three quarters of a century from the time of its publication no single year passed without an edition, either in folio or in quarto or in octavo. In the year 1599 alone ten separate editions were printed. The last quarto edition printed in England appeared in 1615 and the last folio in 1616. By that time the King James Version, published in 1611, was available; nevertheless, as we shall see, this version by no means im- mediately superseded the Geneva Bible, which for some time continued to enjoy enormous popularity. After 1616 many editions of it were printed in Holland by Joost Broerss of Amsterdam and other printers. After the Geneva Bible ceased to be printed in England, about 150,000 copies of it were imported from Holland for English household use.

The printing of an English Bible on foreign soil was naturally always attended by the danger of errors, and partly on the pretext that such errors were dangerous, Archbishop Laud eventually forbad the importation of copies of the Geneva Bible. The reason for his dislike of it ran deeper, however: in England this version was associated with the Puritan party that Laud opposed. His prohibition of its importation was among the charges brought against him at his trial in 1644 that led to his execution on Tower Hill on January 10, 1645.

The Geneva Bible, on account of its rendering of Genesis 3:7, in which it relates that Adam and Eve "sewed fig leaves together and made themselves breeches," has often been nicknamed "The Breeches Bible." "Breeches" was not, however, entirely a novel rendering. Wyclif's version, which had circulated in manuscript before the Reformation, reads: "And whan yei knewen yat ya were naked ye sewiden ye levis of a fige tre and madin brechis." Moreover, in the "Golden Legend," printed by William Caxton at Westminster and issued on November 20, 1483, and containing a translation of the Pentateuch and most of the Gospels, the corresponding verse reads: "And thus theye knewe then that they were naked/and they toke figge leuis and sewed them to gyder for to couere theyr membres in maner of brechis." This was by no means the only verse of the Geneva Bible, however, to contain such a peculiarity. Peculiarities are to be found on almost every page.

Other editions of the Geneva Bible contained errors that similarly gave rise to particular designations. For example, at Matthew 5:9, in an edition published in 1562, the word "peacemaker" was printed "placemaker." This edition therefore came to be known as "The Placemaker's Bible," and sometimes "The Whig Bible." A later edition was known as "The Jesus Church" Bible because at I John 5:20 the words "Jesus Christ" were erroneously printed "Jesus Church." More serious was the misprint of an edition 1610, which at John 6:67 reads "Judas" instead of "Jesus." Perhaps more remarkable than the presence of such errors is the fact that in these comparatively early days of printing there were not more.

The exegetical notes in the Geneva Bible often reflected partisan bitterness. For example, at Revelation 9:3 we read that: "Locusts are false teachers, heretiks, and worldlie suttil prelates, with Monkes, Friars, Cardinals, Patriarkes, Archbishops, Bishops, Doctors, Baschelers, and Masters which forsake Christ to mainteine false doctrine." As we have seen and shall see further, however, the provision of such polemic interpretative notes was characteristic of many Bibles of this period. The Douai version was similarly provided with annotations expressive of hostility to the Reformation.

The Apocrypha was generally included in Geneva Bibles; but in the editions published in 1599 it was more usually omitted.

The first Geneva New Testament to be printed *in England* was an octavo edition which appeared in 1575. Its title page reads as follows:

> The/Newe Te/stament of/ovr Lord Iesvs/Christ./Conferred with the Greke,/and best approued/translations. VVith the arguments, as vvel before the/chapters, as for euery Boke and Epistle./Also diuersities of readings, and/most profitable annotations of all harde places: vvhere/ unto is added a co/pious Table./
> Imprinted at/London by T.V. for Christopher Barker./Cum privilegio.

This edition has certain peculiarities. For instance, for "babe" and "babes," which occur frequently in other Bibles, are substituted the words "childe" and "children." It was printed at London for Christopher Barker by Thomas Vautroullier. Christopher Barker obtained by purchase a patent from Queen Elizabeth, giving him the exclusive right to print Bibles. Between 1576 and 1587, very few editions of the Geneva Bible printed in England have any other publisher's name. Thereafter, till 1599 we have "Deputies of Christopher Barker," and from then till 1618 Robert Barker's name generally appears.

By modern standards, critical biblical scholarship in the sixteenth century was still at a rudimentary stage. Nevertheless, scholars in those days were not as innocent of it as might be supposed. The authorship of the Epistle to the Hebrews provides an interesting case. Traditionally ascribed to St. Paul, its authorship was questioned in early times; but it continued to be attributed to him. Its non-Pauline authorship is now taken by modern scholars as certain. Yet as late as 1914 a biblical commission that had been established at Rome, consisting of a committee of cardinals, assisted by consultors, ruled that it was substantially Pauline, despite the internal evidence that had by then convinced modern scholars against this possibility. This ruling, though not held to be infallible, was accounted binding upon the conscience of all Roman Catholic clergy and laity.

The Epistle was also ascribed to St. Paul in the title provided not only in the King James Version, but even in the Revised Version of the New Testament published in 1881. Its presence there no doubt led many people unskilled in such matters to suppose it to be a matter of loyalty to the text to insist on its Pauline authorship. The late Henry Sloane

Coffin, President of Union Theological Seminary, New York, once told me he had heard in an obscure place of worship in England a sermon, by a preacher whose training left something to be desired, which began: "I am to speak to you about the Hepistle of Paul to the Ebrews. There are some wot syes that the Hepistle of Paul to the Ebrews weren't written by Paul. Well, I syes, if the Hepistle of Paul to the Ebrews weren't written by Paul, 'ow did 'e get 'is nyme at the top of it, I'd like ter know?"

The sixteenth-century editors of the Geneva Bible were much better informed, as the following statement, customarily prefixed to the Epistle in Geneva Bibles, will show:

THE EPISTLE TO
the Ebrewes.

THE ARGVMENT.

Forasmuche as diuers, bothe of the Greke writers & Latines witnesse, that the writer of this epistle for iuste causes wolde not haue his name knowen, it were curiositie of our parte to labour muche therein. For seing the Spirit of God is the autor thereof, it diminish nothing the autoritie, althogh we knowe not with what penne he wrote it. Whether it were Paul (as it is not like) or Luke, or Barnabas, or Clement, or some other, his chief purpose is to persuade vnto the Ebrewes (whereby he principally meaneth them that abode at Iersualem, and vnder them all the rest of the Iewes) that Christ Iesus was not onely the redemer, but also that at his comming all ceremonies must haue an end: forasmuche as his doctrine was the conclusion of all the prophecies, and therefore not onely Moses was inferior to him, but also the Angels: for they all were seruants, & he the Lord, but so Lord, that he hathe also taken our flesh, & is made our brother to assure vs of our saluacion through him self, for he is that eternal Priest, whereof all the Leuitical Priests are but shadowes, & therefore at his comming they oght to cease, & all sacrifices for sinne to be abolished, as he proueth from the seuenth chap. ver. 11, vnto the 12. chap. ver. 18. Also he was that Prophet of whome all y Prophetes in time past witnessed, as is declared from the 12. chap. ver. 18 to the twentie & fiue verse of y same chap. yea, & is the King to whome all things are subject, as appeareth fro that ver. 25. to the beginning of the last chap. Wherefore according to the examples of the olde fathers we must constantly beleue in him, that being sanctified by his iustice, taught by his wisdome, & gouerned by his power, we may stedfastly & courageously perseure euen to the end in hope of that ioye that is set before our eyes, occupying our selues in Christian exercises, that we may bothe be thankeful to God, and duetiful to our neighbour.

The first Bible printed in Scotland appeared in 1579. It was based upon the folio edition published at Geneva in 1562. The title page reads:

148

The Bible and Holy Scripvres conteined in the Olde and Newe Testament Translated according to the Ebrue & Greke, & conferred with the beste translations in diuers languages (∴) With moste profitable annotations vpon all the hard places of the Holy Scriptvres, and other things of grete importance mete for the godly Reader. God save the King. Printed in Edinbvrgh Be Alexander Arbuthnot, Printer to the Kingis Maiestie, dwelling at ye Kirke of feild. 1579. Cvm gratia et Privilegio regiae maiestatis.

The text runs from Genesis to II Maccabees. Then follows the New Testament, the title of which is as follows:

The/New Testament/or ovr Lord Ie/svs Christ./Conferred diligently with the Greke, and best approued translations in diuers languages/

This title is followed by the Scottish arms with the words "God save the King" at the sides. The imprint is: "At Edinbvrgh printed by Thomas Bassandyne, MDLXXVj. cvm privilegio." The text is in Roman type.

The difference between the name of the printer given in the principal title page of this edition of the Bible and the name borne on the New Testament title page requires explanation. On April 14, 1568, a licence to print the Bible in Scotland had been issued to R. Lekprevik in the following terms:

Ane Letter maid with auice of my Lord Regent, to Robert Lekprevik ovr Souerane Lordis imprentare Given granted and committed to him ful license priuilege and power To imprent all and haill ane buke callit the Inglis bybill, imprintit before at Geneua, and that continuallie induring the space of tuenty yeires nixt following the dait hereof. Chargeing all and sindrie imprintaris, writtaris, and utheris, his hienes liegis within this realme That nane of thame tak vpoun hand to imprint or caus be imprintit be quhatsumeuer persoun or persounis within this realme in ony tyme heireftir induring the said space vnder the panis of confiscatioun thairof The said buke callit the Inglis bibill viz. samony as salhappin to be imprintit and payment of the soume of twa hundreth pundis money of this realme &c. At Glasgw the fourtene day of Aprile, The yiar of God. 1568.

For some reason this printer did not use his privilege. On June 30, 1576, a similar licence was granted to Ballantyne, who undertook the task. In order to raise money for it he took into partnership a wealthy burgess, Alexander Arbuthnot, whose name appears on the title page. They were accorded the patronage of the General Assembly of the Church of Scotland, which ordered every parish in the land to purchase a copy of the Bible they would produce, and to pay five pounds for it in advance. The price of the Bible was fixed at a sum less than that figure by 6s.8d:

this difference represented the amount charged for expenses incurred. The Bibles were not delivered till three years after payment of this advance. Salomon Kerknett was brought from Flanders to be employed as the printers' composer, at a weekly wage of forty-nine shillings. The partnership was not a happy one. It was dissolved before the work was completed; hence the difference noted above in the principal title page of the Bible and that of the New Testament, the former bearing the name of Arbuthnot and the latter Ballantyne's. Unfortunately, Bassandyne, who died before the work was published, left no account of the dispute between him and his partner Arbuthnot.

The Scottish authorities were determined to see that the Bible was made known to the people. They were not content to order a copy in every parish, or even with the enactment that every householder with an income over a certain sum must purchase one. They appointed searchers to see that the law was obeyed. Householders were required to produce their copy of the Bible, and if they could not, they were fined a sum double the amount authorized as the subscription price and several times the amount for which a Bible could actually be bought. The searchers were thorough. There was no use borrowing a Bible when they were known to be coming. The searchers would require that the copy bear the name of the particular householder under inspection.

These methods may seem to us today to have been intolerably coercive; but the circumstances were different. The authorities took the Bible seriously as the basic document for a Christian land. It was their responsibility to see that every step was taken to make practicable the education of the people in the Bible. After all, we accept today without question compulsory automobile inspections by the State, and a sixteenth-century Scottish Privy Councillor, if he could talk with us, might well point this out. The measures he employed in his day for forcing an illiterate and backward people to provide themselves with the tools for their moral and mental improvement, to say nothing of their eternal salvation, were, to say the least, as much in the public interest as, and no more coercive than, the arrangements to which we are accustomed and which we accept as indispensable to our safety on the public highways.

Whatever one may think of the methods by which ownership of the Bible was imposed on the Scots, one need not be a Christian to perceive that benefits eventually accrued to the Scottish people as a result. Scotland on the eve of the Reformation was, like Ireland, one of the most backward nations in Europe. Church and State were singularly corrupt there, even for those days. As a result of the measures taken to promote education in the Bible, Scotland (unlike Ireland, which the Reformation hardly touched) enjoyed within a comparatively short time the fruits of that education, acquiring on their account considerable fame. She became, like Holland, eventually, an example of a small nation in which the benefits of education were obvious and effective in bringing her to the forefront in the affairs of the modern world. The legend of universal theological education in Scotland is based upon an absurd exaggeration. That Edinburgh, in her Golden Age in the late eighteenth and early nineteenth century, was one of the leading literary centers of Europe is nevertheless beyond dispute. Students flocked to Edinburgh because of her repute as a center of letters. Many, like Benjamin Constant, abundantly sang her praise, and indeed she has continued to attract literary people to the scene of the curiously haunting spirit that still broods over her eighteenth-century graciousness, long after her literary fame has been eclipsed by her reputation for medical and other concerns.

In 1576 appeared a revised version of the Geneva Bible, the first edition of which was in small octavo. This was the work of Laurence Tomson, who was in the service of Sir Francis Walsingham, Secretary of State to Queen Elizabeth. It is generally known as "Tomson's New Testament," and its title page reads:

> The New Testament of our Lord Iesvs Christ, translated out of the Greeke by Theod. Beza. Wherento are adjoyned briefe Summeries of doctrine vpon the Euangelistes and Actes of the Apostles, together with the methode of the Epistles of the Apostles: by the said Theod. Beza.
>
> And also short expositions on the phrases and hard places, taken ovt of the large annotations of foresayd Author and Ioach. Camerarius, by P. Loseler Villerius. Englished by L. Tomson.

Below a woodcut representing the appearance of the angels to the shepherds, and the words "Beholde I bring you tidings of great ioy that shalbe to all the people. Luk. 2.10." appear the words:

> Imprinted at London by Christopher Barkar dwelling in Poules churchyeard at the sign of the Tigres head. 1576. Cum privilegio.

A second edition was printed in 1577 by Christopher Barker. Both editions are scarce; the second is particularly rare. Tomson's revision attained immediate and considerable popularity and was frequently reprinted. In Geneva Bibles printed from the year 1587, it was generally substituted for the Geneva New Testament, though the latter was also being sold separately after that time.

Strong sentimental attachment to the Geneva Bible caused a demand for it in English Puritan households long after the King James Version had won general acceptance. Gradually, however, both in Scotland, where it had been in general use, and in England, where its use was never so universal, the demand gradually waned.

A curious survival is to be noted. A volume of selected passages from the Geneva Bible was issued for Oliver Cromwell's troops in 1643. It was entitled:

> *The Souldiers Pocket Bible: containing the most (if not all) those places contained in holy Scripture, which doe shew the qualifications of his inner man, that is a fit Souldier to fight the Lords Battels, both before the fight, in the fight and after the fight.*

About fifty thousand copies of reissues of this were circulated in the interests of morale during the American Civil War.

The Ilande on the VVest coast,
of late founde by Christopher Colombo.
—Bishops' Bible

CHAPTER 18 *The Bishops' Bible*

The great popularity of the Geneva Bible and its superior scholarship had made it from the first a formidable competitor to the Great Bible. It was far too much associated with a particular Church party, however, to win general acceptance. Soon after Elizabeth succeeded to the throne in 1558, the need was felt for a version that would be generally accepted in the Church of England. At the direction of Matthew Parker, Archbishop of Canterbury, a new translation was ordered, which was eventually issued in 1568. In 1571 the English Church Convocation ordered all churchwardens to obtain a copy of it for their churches, and in the year following a revised version, containing some corrections, was published. This Bible remained the official Church of England version till the publication in 1611 of the King James Version, the most important of all, to which naturally much more attention must be given later.

Archbishop Parker, who was personally a considerable biblical scholar, seems to have been at first favorably disposed to the Geneva Bible; but powerful opposition to it was an insuperable obstacle to its official adoption. He sought assistance of others in the work, much of which he eventually entrusted to a panel of translators, mostly, but not exclusively, bishops of the English Church. One of the peculiarities of the version produced is that in folio editions the initials of the translators are appended to the individual portions (or "parcels," as they were called) for which they were responsible. The bishops, in accordance with a still-observed English custom, used the Latin designation of their respective Sees, so that the Bishop of St. Davids, for example, signing R. Meneven, has R.M. for his initials. Thus:

Pentateuch: William Alley, Bishop of Exeter (W.E.)
II Samuel: Richard Davies, Bishop of St. Davids (R.M.)
II Chronicles: Edwyn Sanders, Bishop of Worcester (R.W.)
Job and Proverbs: Andrew Pearson, Canon of Canterbury (A.P.,C.)
Song of Solomon: Andrew Perne, Canon of Ely (A.P.,E.)
Lamentations: Robert Horne, Bishop of Winchester (R.W.)
Daniel: Thomas Cole, Bishop of Lichfield and Coventry (T.C.,L.)
Malachi: Edmund Grindal, Bishop of London (E.L.)
II Maccabees: John Parkhurst, Bishop of Norwich (J.N.)

Acts and Romans: Richard Cox, Bishop of Ely (R.E.)
I Corinthians: Gabriel Goodman, Dean of Westminster (G.G.)

Much of the work was personally executed by Archbishop Parker himself, and the whole under his direction. Because of the preponderance of bishops in the panel, the resulting version came to be known as "The Bishops' Bible." Published in 1568, this Bible was formally sanctioned by Convocation and a copy presented to the Queen on October 5 of that year. It immediately superseded the Great Bible as the authorized version for the Church of England; yet it cannot be said to have been successful in terms of its aims. The Geneva Bible retained an overwhelming popularity in England and remained, of course, the only Bible of the Scots. For every edition of the Bishops' Bible there were about five of the Geneva Bible. The comparative failure of the former was not undeserved. Though Parker was an able scholar, his not particularly distinguished panel was accorded too little time. In spite of Parker's supervision, the result was uneven, especially in the Old Testament.

The first edition, in folio, bears, within a border, the title: "The holi Bible conteynyng the Olde Testament and the newe." There is a copperplate engraving of the Queen, and at the bottom are a lion and a dragon with the Latin text: *Non me pudet Evangelii Christi. . . .* ("I am not ashamed of the Gospel of Christ. . . ."). After various preliminary materials is placed Parker's preface in Roman type, followed by Cranmer's prologue in black letter. The imprint reads: "Imprinted at London in povvles Church-yarde, by Richard Jugge, printer to the Queenes Maiestie. Cum priuilegio Regiae Maiestatis."

The second edition, in quarto, appeared the following year. On the title page we find, in the upper part, an engraving of the Queen enthroned, between representations of Justice and Mercy. Lower down are Prudence and Fortitude, whose hands reach out to uphold her throne. Below the royal feet are the words: "The holi bible." At the bottom is the representation of a preacher wearing a bishop's chimere, and the words: "God save the QVEENE."

The second folio edition, which appeared in 1572, is commonly called "The Leda Bible" because several of the initial letters used in the New Testament in this edition are enlivened with woodcuts designed for the illustration of Ovid's *Metamorphoses,* and the one used for the Epistle to the Hebrews represents the ancient Greek legend of Leda and the Swan. In Greek mythology, Leda was the daughter of Thestios, King of Aetolia, and the wife of Tyndareus, King of Sparta. Zeus, father of the gods, having fallen in love with her, used his divine power to transform himself into a swan in order to prove irresistible to the lady of his desire and accomplish her seduction. He was successful, and the children of their union, the Dioscuri, half gods, half mortals, are supposed to have appeared in storms in the form of the electrical phenomenon later known as St. Elmo's fire. This picturesque illustration can hardly be accounted the most fitting adornment for the Epistle to the Hebrews in a Bible designed to supersede the Great Bible and to replace the Geneva Bible that was in so many respects so much superior. That such curiously pagan features in this edition should have met with disapproval is hardly astonishing. They were never repeated.

Not only in the woodcuts of this edition of the Bishops' Bible, however, was fancy allowed to run free. Some of the notes found in the Bishops' Bible are hardly less unrestricted. Among the notes to other editions is one, for instance, relating to the ninth verse of the forty-fifth psalm, where Ophir is taken to be "the Ilande in the VVest coast, of late founde by Christopher Colombo; from whence at this day is brought most fine golde."

The Leda Bible was, as we have seen, the third edition (second edition in folio, and often called the second folio edition) of the Bishops' Bible. The succeeding editions appeared as follows: fourth, in quarto, 1573; fifth, in folio, 1574; sixth, in folio, 1575; seventh, in quarto, 1575; eighth, in quarto, 1576; ninth, in quarto, 1577; tenth, in octavo, 1577; eleventh, in folio, 1578; twelfth, in folio, 1584; thirteenth, in quarto, 1584; fourteenth, in folio, 1585; fifteenth, in folio, 1588; sixteenth, in folio, 1591; seventeenth, in folio, 1595; eighteenth, in folio, 1602; and nineteenth, in folio, 1606. This, the last edition, is very rare.

The New Testament of this version was frequently printed by itself. There were at least five separate editions; the first two, one of them in quarto, were printed by Jugge in 1570, bearing his customary device, a pelican feeding her young, supported by Prudence and Justice. The last edition appeared in 1619 and bears the following title:

> The New Testament of our Saviour Jesus Christ, faithfully translated out of the Greeke, with the Notes and Expositions of the darke places therein, Mat. 13.
>
> > "The Pearle which Christ commaunded to be bought,
> > Is here to be found, not else to be sought."
>
> Imprinted at London, by Bonham Norton and John Bill, Printers to the King's most excellent Maiestie MDC. xix.

Woodcuts representing the Four Evangelists by their traditional emblems (a man for Matthew, a lion for Mark, an ox for Luke, and an eagle for John) adorn the corners. At the sides are two female figures and at the bottom the royal arms and crown.

The text of this edition differs from the others, and there are copious notes. Some of these are explicitly anti-Roman. One of the beasts in the Apocalypse, for example, which "cometh ovt of the earth," is identified with "the pompe of the romish bishops. He pretendeth to be a lambe." It is affirmed that the whole eighteenth chapter of the Apocalypse "intreateth moost principallye against the seconde regimente of Rome, that is the papisticall kingdome, which vnder the pretence of the name of Chryste, hath dealte so cruelly against all faythfull Christians, and the euangelicall Kyngdome of God."

The Bishops' Bible included a new version of the Psalter. Nevertheless, many editions replaced it with the version used in the Great Bible. The latter version of the Psalms used in the English Book of Common Prayer to this day is almost identical with that of the first edition of the Great Bible. The quality of the Bishops' version may be fairly estimated from its rendering of the nineteenth psalm:

> The heauens declare the glorie of god: and
> the firmament sheweth his handie worke.
>
> 2. A day occasioneth talke thereof vnto
> a day: and a nyght teacheth knowledge
> vnto a nyght,
>
> 3. No language, no wordes, no voyce of
> theyrs is hearde, yet theyr sound goeth into
> all landes and theyr sayinges vnto the endes
> of the worlde.
>
> 4. In them he hath set a tabernacle
> for the sun, which commeth forth as a bryd-
> grome out of his chamber and rejoyceth as a
> giaunt to run his course.
>
> 5. His settyng foorth is from the vtmost
> part of heauen, and his circuite vnto the vt-
> most part thereof, and there is nothing hyd
> from his heate.
>
> 6. The law of God is perfect, conuerting
> the soule: the testimony of God is sure
> and geueth wysdome vnto the simple.
>
> 7. The statutes of god are right, and re-
> ioce the heart: the commaundement of
> God is pure, and geueth light vnto the eyes.

8. The feare of god is sincere and endureth
for euer, the iudgementes of god are trueth,
they be iuste at all poyntes.

9. They are more to be desired then golde
yea then muche fine golde, they are sweeter
then honye, and the honycombe.

10. Morouer, by them thy seruant is
well aduertised: and in kepyng of them
there is a great rewarde.

11. Who can knowe his owne errours?
Oh clense thou me from those that I am not
priuie of.

12. Kepe Thy seruaunt also from pre-
sumtuous (sinnes) let them not raigne ouer
me: so I shall be perfect and voyde from
all heynous offence.

13. Let the wordes of my mouth, and the
medetation of my heart be acceptable in thy
sight: O God my strength and my redeemer.

Despite its literary inferiority, the Bishops' Bible is nevertheless of considerable historical importance since, as we shall see, it was the version used as the basis for the elaborate revision undertaken by the seventeenth-century translators who produced the King James Version. That they, being tied by their rules to a version as undistinguished as was the Bishops' Bible, were nevertheless able to bring forth a version of such extraordinary felicity and power may seem paradoxical. To this seeming paradox attention will be paid in a later chapter.

CHAPTER 19 *The Douai-Reims Version*

We have seen much earlier that for centuries before the Reformation, the Bible had been not only read but also critically studied in terms of scholarly tools then available. In the late Middle Ages, however, the Church in the West had been both threatened by the armies of Islam and torn by internal strife. That it was in need of reform was questioned by none. Even among those most sympathetic to it and most deeply committed to the Catholic Christian faith, its institutions were the butt of satire. The sense of the need for reform was especially strong in intellectual circles, and innumerable attempts were made to deal with the situation. Long before Luther appeared on the scene, a thoroughgoing program of reform had been begun, notably in Spain. Nevertheless, it was far too slow to deal with even the most elementary moral and spiritual demands of the *congregatio fidelium,* the body of the faithful in which, according to ancient Catholic Christian teaching, the life of the Church flows. The effects of the humanist Renaissance, which had often expressed itself in a deeply religious mood, eventually made possible a movement of reform whose spiritual resources were far beyond the capacity of many to understand. The outworn methods and machinery of Rome proved entirely inadequate for dealing with the march of events. Before Rome could provide even a token program of reform, the Church had taken the matter into her own hands. The result was that a short time after Luther had nailed the ninety-five theses to the church door in Wittenberg on October 31, 1517, Rome was left immeasurably shorn of her spiritual, to say nothing of her intellectual, influence.

The immediate sources of the spiritual power of the Reformers were complex; but one of the most striking was the new way of approaching the Bible. The movement that had begun in Spain and that was continued within the Roman Church was notably expressed in the Council of Trent, which lasted for nineteen years, from 1545 to 1563. Not unnaturally, it took on extremely defensive and reactionary aspects. The breach between those who wished the thoroughgoing program of the reform of the Catholic Church that was led by men such as Luther and Calvin and those who continued to seek another way that would conserve more of the medieval pattern of her institutional life inevitably widened. Among the latter was a deep piety and often delicate devotion; yet they failed to understand the profoundly Catholic spirit of the Reformers, and particularly their attitude to the Bible.

By the time the Council of Trent closed in 1563, the authorities of the Roman Church had by no means given up hope of destroying the Reformers' work. In England, where the work of the Reformation had proceeded in a curiously reluctant way, being much confused by political events, the situation was unique. Some of the conservative English families remained loyal to Rome throughout the vicissitudes of the English Reformation, and have so remained to this day. The house of Norfolk, England's premier dukedom, is an outstanding example.

The attitude of the Roman Church toward the reading of the Bible by the common people was at this time ambivalent. The Bible was unequivocally declared to be, and always to have been, the most fundamental document of the Christian Church; yet the Pope claimed to be in possession of an ecclesiastical dominion giving him the means of directing the consciences of all men with infallible certainty. In principle, therefore, while there was by no means any fundamental objection to the translation of the Bible into the vernacular, there might well be very grave practical reasons against it, especially, of course, when the translation was done without the approval of the ecclesiastical authorities at Rome. To say the least, among those who felt especially committed to a Roman *pietas,* there had never been any widespread zeal for the translation of the Bible into the vernacular, and there had been not infrequently a radical suspicion of such enterprises. Yet now the Roman authorities were alarmed by the influence of the English Bible, and most of all by its influence on the decreasing minority of Rome's adherents in the English-speaking world. This minority possessed no English Bible approved by Rome, yet were surrounded by Bible readers. The Roman authorities were naturally alarmed lest the influence of the Geneva Bible and other versions should in time alienate them from their Roman allegiance. In these circumstances there was nothing for the Roman authorities to do but foster the production of a translation to which they might hope to give their own kind of ecclesiastical approval. It was natural, too, that they should wish to see any such translation provided with notes such as might help English-speaking adherents of Rome to hold their own in that theological controversy that was such a popular pastime of all parties in the sixteenth-century ecclesiastical scene.

It happened that in 1568 a college had been founded at the Flemish town of Douai, now in France, by William Allen (1532-1594) for the purpose of educating English-speaking sons of the Roman Church. Allen had been a Fellow of Oriel College, Oxford, and later Principal of St. Mary's Hall. He left England in 1561 to go to Louvain, returning to England the following year and being forced into exile in 1565. Believing that the English people were still at heart preponderantly inclined to Rome, and that the Reformation need have only an ephemeral success in England, he devoted his attention to the training of missionary priests who would one day return to England, he hoped, to bring back the people to the Roman obedience. It was for this purpose that he founded several colleges on the continent of Europe, including, besides Douai, one at Rome and one at Valladolid. Created cardinal of the Roman Church in 1578 by Pope Sixtus V, he was also appointed Archbishop of Malines; but it seems that this latter appointment was not confirmed. Through his political support of the Spanish attempt to invade England in 1588, he ended by provoking widespread hostility in England. He concluded his life at the college in Rome that had been among his foundations.

From Douai, Allen issued a vigorous stream of Roman propaganda. Among his projects was the production of an English Bible. To his inspiration was due the version that was eventually produced and became for centuries the standard translation for English-speaking Roman Catholics. His chief associates engaged in this work were also Oxford men: Gregory Martin, Thomas Worthington, and Richard Bristowe.

In 1578 the college was obliged for political reasons to move from Douai. Its students found refuge in Reims, and it was there that the first edition of the New Testament was issued in 1582. The title reads:

The/Nevv Testament/of Jesvs Christ, trans/lated faithfvlly into English,/out of the authentical Latin, according to the best cor/rected copies of the same, diligently conferred vvith/the Greeke and other editions in diuers languages: VVith/ARGVMENTS of bookes and chapters, ANNOTA/TIONS, and other necessarie helpes, for the better vnder/standing of the text, and specially for the discouerie of the/CORRVP-TIONS of diuers late translations, and for/cleering the CONTRO-UERSIES in Religion, of these daies:/IN THE ENGLISH COLLEGE OF RHEMES./

Psal. 118.

Da mihi intellectum, & scrutabor legem tuam &
custodiam/illam in toto corde meo.

That is,

Giue me vnderstanding and I vvill search thy lavve, and/vvill keepe it vvith my vvhole hart./

S. Aug. tract. 2, in Epist Ioan./Omnia quae legentur in Scripturis sanctis, ad instructionem & salutem nostram intente oportet/audire: maxime tamen memoriae commendanda sunt quae aduersus Haereticos valent plu/rimum: quorum insidiae, infirmiores quosque & negligen-tiores circumuenire non cessant./That is,/Al things that are readde in holy Scriptures, vve must heare vvith great attention, to our/instruction and saluation: but those things specially must be commended to me/morie vvich make most against Heretikes: vvhose deceites cease not to cir/cumuent and beguile al the vveaker sort and the more neligent persons./Printed at Rhemes,/by Iogn Fogny./1582./Cvm privilegio.

160

The translators point out, in their preface, that the practice of translating the Scriptures into the common tongue of various peoples is ancient. This was indeed what St. Jerome did. They are at pains to justify their having translated from the Latin Vulgate rather than from the original languages. They cite its antiquity and the fact that it was corrected by St. Jerome and commended by St. Augustine, being used and expounded by the ancient Fathers. Claiming that it is the most grave and the most majestic of all the versions and is such an exact rendering of the original Greek that even the Calvinist Beza commended it, they assert it is purer than any Greek text then available. They also defend the retention of certain technical words. A feature of the Rhemish New Testament, as it is sometimes called, is its tendency to keep such words rather than to try to put them into a more English form.

The version immediately excited much hostility in England. It is said that about five years after its appearance, when Mary, Queen of Scots was required to swear upon the Scriptures that she had not plotted against the life of Queen Elizabeth, the Earl of Kent declined to allow her to take the oath on the Rhemish Version, on the ground that, being "a popish Testament," it was "of no value" in taking such an oath.

Queen Elizabeth's searchers seized and confiscated many copies. Priests found with a copy in their possession were imprisoned. The attitude of the English authorities is exhibited in a black-letter tract issued by Cecil, Lord Burleigh, entitled: "The Execution of Justice in England, for maintenaunce of publique and Christian peace, against certeine stirrers of sedition, and adherents to the traytors and enemies of the Realme, without any Persecution of them for questions of Religion, as it is falsely reported and published by the faurors and fosterers of their treasons." Another tract, entitled "A declaration of the favourable dealing of Her Majesty's Commissioners," provides some insight into the nature of the persecution of Roman priests in England at this time. It is claimed that a certain priest who was tortured with the rack "was charitably used, and never so racked but that he was presently able to walke." The warders whose office it was to discharge such duties were charged to use the rack "in as charitable maner as such a thing might be." So fiendishly cruel were the tortures to which all parties were ready to subject their victims, that perhaps the claim was not entirely unfounded that this "charitable maner" of using the rack was relatively humane. It might be so accounted when compared with, say, the burning of Patrick Hamilton by the Roman authorities in Scotland in 1528, when in the howling gale of a northern winter day the first lighting of the fire only scorched the left hand and side of the face of the scholarly young gentleman. It had to be relighted six times while a Dominican friar tried to get him to say *Salve Regina* and was answered by three black-

161

ened fingers held up by the now speechless victim, in token of his faith in the Triune God, till at length the fire became "vehement" and so ended six hours of unthinkable torture.

The fame of the Rhemish New Testament was, by a curious irony, promoted through the polemical attack launched upon it by William Fulke (1538-1589), Master of Pembroke Hall, Cambridge, and a bitter English antagonist of the Roman cause. Fulke undertook to refute the work of the Rhemish translators, to which end he caused to be printed at London, by the deputies of Christopher Barker, the Bishops' New Testament and the Rhemish version in parallel columns, with annotations and refutations at the end of each chapter. The title of Fulke's work, which was in folio, is as follows:

> The text of the New Testament of Jesus Christ, translated out of the vulgar Latine by the papists of the Traiterous Seminarie at Rhemes, with arguments of books, chapters and annotations, pretending to discover the corruptions of divers translations, and to cleare the controversies of these dayes.
>
> Thereunto is added the translation out of the original Greeke, commonly used in the Church of England, with a confutation of all such arguments, glosses, and annotations, as containe manifest impietie, of heresie, treason and slander against the Catholike Church of God, and the true teachers thereof, or the translations used in the Church of England; both by auctoritie of the Holy Scriptures, and by the testimonie of the ancient fathers.

It is probable that Fulke did more to make the work of the Douai-Reims translators known than did any of those whom he was concerned to refute. As we have seen, the Bishops' Bible was by no means the best English translation that had so far seen the light, and in comparison with it, the Rhemish New Testament did not show up so badly as might have been the case. But for Fulke, the latter might not have had even the modest influence it did eventually exert upon the King James and other later versions.

The Rhemish New Testament exhibited grave shortcomings. In the first place, though the translators did consult the Greek, their work was essentially a translation of the Latin, and they consequently reproduced many of the notable shortcomings of a Latinization of the Greek. Moreover, this proceeding was often in accordance with their partisan interests. An example will illustrate this. As has been already noted, the Vulgate uses, for the injunction "repent," the Latin phrase *poenitentiam agite*, which means "do penance." This is by no means a fair translation of the Greek; but it accorded well with the aims of the Rhemish translators, who wished to reassert the emphasis on penitential works such as barefoot pilgrimages and the wearing of hairshirts—works that had characterized much medieval Latin piety but were capable of resulting, as the Reformers believed they did result, in a grave distortion of the ideals of the Christian life. The Rhemish New Testament, though not entirely without merit, was vitiated by such avowedly polemical enterprises. This aspect of its purpose was most blatantly expressed in the notes, which were not only highly controversial but often calculated to indoctrinate the reader with exceedingly fanciful interpretations of passages that were the object of current controversy. The English of the Douai-Reims translators was also, as we shall see, infelicitous and not infrequently ridiculous. Sometimes it was not English at all.

In 1593 the college was able to return to Douai, and in 1600 a second edition of the New Testament was issued, the title of which reads:

> The/Nevv Testament/of Iesvs Christ faith-/fvlly translated into English,/out of the authentical Latin, diligently conferred with the/ Greeke, and other Editions in diuers languages: VVith Ar/gvments of bookes, and chapters: Annotations,/and other helpes, for the better vnderstanding of the text,/and specially for the discouerie of Corrvptions in di/uers late translations: and for cleering Controver/sies in Religion of these daies: By the English/College then Resident in Rhemes./Set Forth the second time, by the same College novv/returned to Dovvay. VVith additions to one nevv Table of Heretical Cor/rvptions, and other Tables and Annotations somevvhat augmented./
> Search the Scriptures, Ioan 5.
> Giue me vnderstanding, and I will search thy law: and/wil kepe it with my whole hart.
> *Psalm* 118, *v.* 34./
> S. Augustin, Tract 2, in Epist. Ioan.
> Al things that are readde in holie Scriptures
> &c.
> Printed at Antvverp
by Daniel Vervliet
1600
VVith Privilege.

In this edition "our Aduersaries" were charged with "corrupting the Greeke it selfe, vvich they pretende to translate," and asserts that "The blessed Confessour, Bishop Tonstal noted no lesse than tvvo thousand corruptions in Tindals translation, in the Nevv Testament only. VVherby, as by these fevv here cited for examples, the indifferent reader may see, hovv vntruly the English Bibles are commended to the people, for the pure vvord of God." Those who were not of the Roman party in the controversy were to be accounted heretics, and it was affirmed that "No heretics haue right to the Scriptures, but are vsurpers: the Catholike Church, being the true owner, and faithful keeper of them. Heretics abuse them, corrupt them, and vtterly seeke to abolish them, though they pretend to the contrarie. Yet do they vaunt themselves of Scripture exceedingly, but they are neuer the more to be trusted for that. The cause why, the Scriptures being perfit, yet we use other Ecclesiastical writings and traditions."

This second edition is well printed in Roman type. The text is not divided into verses; but on the inner margin, within a black line, verse numbers are placed, and beyond this are references to parallel passages, while on the opposite margin are the notes, of which more is to be said later.

At the end of the book of Acts is a table purporting to set forth the lives of Saints Peter and Paul, after which follows the following remarkably uncritical account of the development in the early Church of the credal statement commonly called the Apostles' Creed, which, though its doctrine may be argued from New Testament evidence, is considered by modern scholars to be of gradual and comparatively late development, being not designated by its present title till nearly the end of the fourth century:

Before they departed one from an other al twelue assembling together, and ful of the Holy Ghost, eche laying downe his sentence, agreed vpon twelue principal Articles of the Christian faith, and appointed them for a rule to al belieuers: VVhich is therfore called and is THE APOSTLES CREDE: *Not written in paper, as the Scripture, but from the Apostles deliuered by tradition.* VVhich, as of old, so at this day al solemnely professe in their Baptisme, either by them selves or by others: and al that be of age and capacitie, are bound to know and beleeue euerie article of the same. VVhich are these that follovv:

THE APOSTLES CREDE
or
Symbolvm Apostolorvm

1. I beleeue in God the Father almightie, creator of heauen and earth
2. And in Iesvs Christ, his only Sonne, our Lord.
3. VVho was conceiued by the Holy Ghost, borne of the Virgin Marie.
4. Suffered vnder Pontius Pilate, was crucifed, dead and buried: Descended into hel.
5. The third day he rose againe from death.
6. Ascended into heauen: sitteth at the right hand of God the Father almightie.
7. From thence he shal come to iudge the quicke and the dead.
8. I beleeue in the Holy Ghost.
9. The holy Catholike Church: the communion of saincts.
10. Remission of sinnes.
11. Resurrection of the flesh.
12. Life euerlasting.   Amen.

A third edition, in duodecimo, was issued in 1621 by James Seldenflach of Antwerp, and a fourth edition, in quarto, by John Cousturier in 1633. There was no further edition till 1738.

Meanwhile, the translators had been at work on the rest of the Bible, which appeared in its entirety for the first time in two volumes published respectively in 1609 and 1610 at Douai, whither, as we have seen, the college had by this time returned. The title of this first edition, which is in quarto, reads as follows:

> The Holie Bible Faithfully translated into English ovt of the avthentical Latin. Diligently conferred with the Hebrew, Greeke, and other Editions in diuers languages. With Argvments of the Bookes, and Chapters: Annotations, Tables: and other helpes, for better vnderstanding of the text: for discouerie of corrvptions in some late translations: and for clearing Controversies in Religion.
> By the English College of Doway.
> Haurietis aquas gaudio de fontibus Saluatoris.
> Isaiae,12.
> You shal draw waters in ioy out of the Sauiours
> fountaines.
> Printed at Doway by Lavrence Kellam,
> at the signe of the holi Lambe.
> M.DC.IX.

The delay in the appearance of the whole Douai Bible is explained by "our poore estate in banishment." Again the choice of the Latin Vulgate, rather than the original biblical tongues, as the basis for translation is defended on the pretext that the available texts in these languages do not properly represent the original. The charge was by no means entirely unfounded, since at that time the texts of the original that were available were from sources less ancient than had been used by St. Jerome. As we shall see later, manuscripts were to come to light shortly after the issue of the King James Version that made even that translation out of date, and in much more recent times a large body of manuscript and other evidence was to be made accessible to modern scholars.

On the other hand, the translators write as if they had full confidence in the purity of the Vulgate. For reasons we have considered at an earlier stage of the present work, this confidence was unwarranted. "VVhy we translate the Latin text, rather then the Hebrew, or Greke, which Protestantes preferre, as the fountaine tongues, wherein holie Scriptures were first written? To this we answer, that if in dede those first pure Editions were now extant, or if such as be extant were more pure then the Latin, we would also preferre such fountaines before the riuers, in whatsouer they should be found to disagree." Then, after some comparisons of recent English translations follows a dedicatory address to the entire English-speaking world:

VVith this then we wil conclude most deare (we speake to you al, that vnderstand our tongue, whether you be of contrarie opinions in faith, or of mundane feare participate with an other Congregation; or professe with vs the same Catholique Religion) to you al we present this worke: dayly beseaching God Almightie, the Diuine VVisedom, Eternal Goodnes, to create, illuminate, and replenish your spirites, with his Grace, that you may attaine eternal Glory, euery one in his measure, in those manie Mansions, prepared and promised by our Sauiour in his Father's house. Not only to those which first receiued, and folowed his Diuine doctrine, but to al that should afterwardes beleue in him, and kepe the same preceptes. For there is one God, one also Mediatour of God and men: Man Christ Iesus. VVho gaue himself a Redemption for al. VVherby appeareth his wil, that al should be saued.

From the English College in Doway, the Octaues of al Sainctes, 1609.

The title of the second volume is similar to the first, except for the opening words, "The seconde tome of the Holie Bible," and the use, in place of the quotations from Isaiah, of another from II Peter 1:21: *Spiritu Sancto inspirati, locuti sunt sancti Dei homines,* duly translated, "The holie men of God spake, inspired with the Holie Ghost." Then follows the date, M.DC.X.

A second edition of the Old Testament in the Douai Version was issued in 1635 at Rouen by John Cousturier. Apart from slight changes in spelling, the text is a reprint of the first edition; but while the first edition relegated the verse numbers to the margin, the second edition embodies them in the text. The pages of the second edition have, moreover, a double black line enclosing the text.

The sales and distribution of the Douai Bible were meager. The English Roman Catholic minority for whom it was specially intended were spiritually unprepared for it, and it lacked any intrinsic merit that might have helped to foster an interest in it. One of the marginal notes characteristically declared that "the holy Scriptures to carnal men and Heretickes are as pearls to swine." Those who claimed to be alone excluded from this condemnation seemed, however, to be making the scantiest use of the pearls. The Douai Bible, far from being widely used, was not even well known. The New Testament fared a little better; but it owed a good deal of its very modest success to the polemics of Fulke against it. English Roman Catholics were generally content to be Bible-less. Throughout the seventeenth and eithteenth centuries they generally remained so, despite the dissatisfaction of the more scholarly among their bishops and priests during these trying days when Roman Catholics in England were subject to grievous restrictions that were only very gradually mitigated till their almost complete removal in 1829 by the Roman Catholic Relief Act.

Between 1633 and 1738 not a single edition of the Rhemish New Testament appeared. Among the improvements made in the fifth edition, published in the latter year, may be mentioned one that illustrates what scope for improvement there was in the literary style of the Douai-Reims translators. The young follower of Jesus whom the twentieth-century New English Bible describes as having "nothing on but a linen cloth" (Mark 14:51) was described in the 1738 edition of the Rhemish New Testament as "cloathed with linnen cloath over his naked body"—surely an improvement upon the original Rhemish rendering: "clothed with sindon upon the bare."

One of the best known among the un-English Latinisms of the Rhemish New Testament was the phrase used in the translation of the difficult passage in Philippians in which the humiliation, or as modern theologians would call it, the *kenosis,* of Christ is asserted. The King James Version follows Tyndale, who had said that Christ "made him silfe of no reputacion" (Phil. 2:7). The Vulgate had rendered the Greek verb ἐκένωσε by the nearest that Latin seemed able to do, *exinanivit,* which the Rhemish translators offered to the English-speaking public in the phrase "he exinanited himself," which was as bad English then as it is now. In later revisions of the Rhemish New Testament this was changed to "he emptied himself," the phrase now used in the modern Revised Standard Version. The twentieth-century New English Bible says he "made himself nothing."

Yet the Rhemish New Testament was not invariably artificial in its style or wholly given over to its theological Latinity. Occasionally, and especially when doctrine did not seem to be involved, it could be exceptionally straightforward and even robust. For instance, Rhoda,[1] the girl who was so overjoyed at Peter's unexpected escape that when he appeared at the door she ran inside to announce the news instead of letting him in, is called in many of the old versions, including Wyclif's and Tyndale's, a damsel or damozel. In the twentieth-century New English Bible she is a maid. The Rhemish New Testament, however, called her a "wenche."

The literalism that had made most of the Rhemish New Testament sound unnatural to English ears is even more marked in the Old Testament of the Douai Bible. The language, more often than not stilted, is sometimes entirely unintelligible as was to be conceded by later Roman Catholic translators such as Cornelius Nary, whose version was to appear in 1718. Perhaps a patient reader may make sense of the rendering of Ruth 1:21: "Noemi came from the land of her peregrinations," though

[1] Acts 12:13.

167

no one accustomed to the genius of the English tongue would account it a masterpiece of English prose. We have more excuse for despair when we read that "hearing I heard Ephraim going into transmigration" (Jer. 31:18). Even the most valiant reader, however, must surely give up in face of the rendering of Numbers 6:17: "The ram he shal immolate for a pacifique hoste to the Lord, offering withal the baskette of azymes, and the libamentes that by custom are dew."

The Douai Version has occasionally been nicknamed "The Rosin Bible." This sobriquet has its origin in the word used for balm in the well-known question, "Is there no balm in Gilead?" Here is the passage (Jer. 8:18-22) as it appeared:

18. My sorow is aboue sorow, my hart mourning within me. 19. Behold the voice of the daughter of my people from a farre countrie: Is not our Lord in Sion, or is not her king in her? Why then haue they prouoked me to wrath in their sculptils, and in strange vanities? 20. The haruest is past, somner is ended; and we are not saued. 21. For the affliction of the daughter of my people I am afflicted, and made sorowful, astonishment hath taken me. 22. Is there noe rosin in Galaad? or is there no phisition there? Why then is not the wound of the daughter of my people closed?

Apart from the polemical proclivities of the translators, expressed both in the text and even more patently in the notes, its technical defects as a translation were, in the circumstances, to a great extent inevitable. Its style, however, alien to the genius of English and almost wholly lacking in rhythm, made it unsuitable either for public worship or for private devotional use. Since the translators were Englishmen, trained at Oxford, these shortcomings can hardly be accounted accidental. They reflect, rather, the failure of partisans of the Roman Church of the time to grasp the significance of the deep currents of spiritual life that ran below the events associated with the Reformation, and the nature of the role the Bible played in nourishing that life.

A glance at a psalm particularly familiar to the English-speaking world both in the King James Version and in the older English version preserved in the Book of Common Prayer will illustrate fairly the shortcomings of the Douai Bible as it appeared in the first decade of the seventeenth century. It appears there, of course, as the twenty-second psalm, following the Vulgate numbering. The text, with the original notes, reads as follows:

1. The Psalme of Dauid

2. Ovr (*a*) Lord ruleth me, and nothing shal be wanting to me: in place (*b*) of pasture there he hath placed me.

(*a*) Christ the good pastor gouerneth, protecteth, (*b*) and feedeth his faithful flocke.

3. Vpon (*c*) the water of refection he hath brought me vp: he hath (*d*) conuerted my soule.

(*c*) Baptisme of regeneration (*d*) which is the first iustification.

He hath conducted me vpon (*e*) the pathes of justice (*f*) for his name.

(*e*) Gods precepts which the baptised must obserue. (*f*) Saluation is in the name and power of Christ, not in mans owne merites.

4. For, although I shal walke in the (*g*) middes of the shaddow of death, I wil (*h*) not feare euils: because thou art with me.

(*g*) In great danger of tentation to mortal sinne, (*h*) yet by Gods grace we may resist.

Thy (*i*) rod and thy (*k*) staffe, they haue comforted me.

(*i*) Gods direction and law is streight, (*k*) and strong.

5. Thou hast prepared in my sight (*l*) a table against them that truble me.

(*l*) Christ hath prepared for our spiritual foode the B Sacrament of the Eucharist.

Thou (*n*) hast fatted my head with oyle: and my (*o*) chalace inebriating how goodlie is it!

(*n*) Christian souls are also strengthened by the other Sacraments. (*o*) The B Sacrament and Sacrifice of Christs bodie and bloud.

6. And thy merce shal folow me (*p*) al the dayes of my life.

(*p*) Continual and final perseuerance is by Gods special grace

And that I may dwel in the house of our Lord, (*q*) in longtitude of dayes.

(*q*) in eternal life.

To what extent and with what limitations this was improved in the course of time may be judged from the text of the corresponding passage in a Douai Bible of the mid-nineteenth century:

The Lord ruleth me: and I shall want nothing. 2. He hath set me in a place of pasture.

He hath brought me up on the water of refreshment: 3. he hath converted my soul.

He hath led me on the paths of justice, for his own name's sake.

4. For though I should walk in the midst of the shadow of death, I will fear no evils, for thou art with me.

Thy rod and thy staff, they have comforted me.

5. Thou hast prepared a table before me, against them that afflict me.

Thou hast anointed my head with oil; and my chalice which inebriateth *me*, how goodly is it!

6. And thy mercy will follow me all the days of my life.

And that I may dwell in the house of the Lord unto length of days.

CHAPTER 20 *"Queen" James*

By far the greatest event in the history of the English Bible was the publication in 1611 of what came to be known in England as the Authorized Version and, more generally, the King James Version of the Bible. Historically it is the most influential version of the most influential book in the world, in what is now its most influential language. The background of this version and the circumstances attending its composition deserve more than an ordinary share of our study.

The most obvious fact about this version is its association with King James. How did it come to bear his name? What part did he play in the project? The better we are able to answer these questions, the more remarkable it becomes that to such a man we are indebted for the appearance of such a book.

James's mother was the beautiful, far-famed, and ill-starred Mary, Queen of Scots. Mary, a few days after her birth in 1542, had inherited the Scottish throne. Brought up at the court of France, she married, when scarcely sixteen, the precocious, sickly, and half-witted fourteen-year-old Dauphin Francis. The wedding had been attended by intentionally spectacular festivities because for over two centuries no dauphin had been married on French soil, and the Guise family wanted to show the world that by the marriage now being solemnized they had virtually brought Scotland within the hegemony of France.

Mary, dressed in a blue velvet robe covered with silver lilies and precious gems and wearing on her head a diamond tiara worth several fortunes, had been conducted to the altar of Notre Dame de Paris by the King of France. Opposite the great West Door of Notre Dame a vast amphitheater had been erected. There was a gallery hung with blue velvet and adorned with golden lilies. At the door of the ancient cathedral had assembled the prelates of France with the papal legate, the Cardinal Archbishop du Bellay. There were bands to play music for the crowds, and halbadiers to guard the arrival of the royal wedding couple. After Nuptial Mass and the dinner at the old palace of the Tournelles, there had been a ball. As Mary, with her shy and bilious boy-bridegroom, danced a stately pavan, her seven-and-a half yard train was carried for her by a courtier. The guests had been entertained by singing girls, hobbyhorses caparisoned in gold, white ponies drawing pagan gods. As six galleons passed by the marble table at which the various princesses sat, a prince leapt out and gallantly "captured" the lady of his choice. Poor Francis, no doubt a little nervously, dutifully carried off his own princess, the future Mary, Queen of Scots. Mary eventually came to her Scottish throne as a nineteen-year-old widow, shortly after the triumph of the Scottish Reformation for which she had no sympathy and, despite her high intelligence, little understanding. A few years later, in July, 1565, with the Pope's approval, she married her cousin, Henry Stuart, Lord Darnley.

By this time there was much gossip at court about Mary's private life. An Italian *valet de chambre* at the Scottish court, David Riccio, had been advanced with noticeable speed to the position of secretary and adviser to the Queen. One evening in March, 1566, when she was six months pregnant, she had been sitting at supper in the palace of Holyrood House, Edinburgh, with Riccio and some of the ladies of the court, when a band of armed men burst in upon them and demanded that Riccio accompany them. Riccio had screamed hysterically and, clutching Mary's skirt, had then been dragged off and killed with such violence that it is said fifty dagger wounds were later found on his corpse. The following year Darnley had been murdered by, or under the direction of, the Earl of Bothwell, and a few weeks after Mary had subsequently married him, angry bystanders who saw her taken prisoner by some of her nobles roared after her in the streets of Edinburgh, "Burn the whore!" The child Mary had carried in her womb that evening when Riccio had been murdered was James, the prince who was later to give his name to the version of the Bible that has so greatly influenced English literature and so deeply moved the hearts and minds of many generations of men and women.

He became James VI of Scotland. When the crowns of England and Scotland were united in 1603, he became also James I of the United Kingdom. As a child, his principal tutor had been George Buchanan, the greatest of the Scottish humanists and a supporter of the Reformation of the Catholic Church in Scotland. Buchanan had already served as tutor to the young Mary, Queen of Scots, and on her disgrace he had sat in judgement against her with the English commissioners at York, playing some part in her condemnation. It was against Mary's wishes that Buchanan had been appointed, in 1570, tutor to her three-year-old son, James.

Buchanan found in him an able pupil, and he imparted to him a taste for languages, literature, and theology that was by no means universal in princes. His pupil was precocious. His interest in literary and theological pursuits was genuine enough; but it was accompanied by a most unfortunate range of qualities. He grew up to seem odd and pedantic to those engaged in the conduct of State affairs. His temperament was an effeminate one. He was inordinately vain; yet it was not the sort of vanity one might expect of a monarch of those days. It was entirely remote, for example, from the vanity of the eighth Henry of England. Though his use of "kingcraft," as he called it, met with some practical success in Scotland, he was never popular in his native land. How could he be? He was openly proud of his virtuosity in guile. Even for the sixteenth century such an attitude was curious. A prince might engage in double-dealing; he was hardly expected to boast of it as a virtue proper to his exalted station. Nor does a man make it easy for even his most sympathetic friends to like him when he allows his mother to be beheaded, as did James, with scarcely any serious protest. The sixteenth century was accustomed, indeed, to cold-blooded intrigue. Even so, the Scots found it hard to stomach James.

If his Scottish subjects, in reluctantly putting up with him, had found him hard to understand, to the English he was beyond comprehension. His English subjects had been extraordinarily eager to welcome him to the throne of England. So fearful had they been of what they might get in succession to Elizabeth, they were disposed to like James. Such was their mood that they would almost have welcomed him had he had two heads rather than two crowns. James characteristically delighted in the flattery with which they greeted him. He took it as further evidence of his mastery of kingcraft. This flattery notwithstanding, his English subjects soon found their new sovereign unendurable. He was enigmatic. He was ridiculous. His habits were slovenly, and he seemed wholly lacking in royal dignity and bearing. Yet so well disposed were the English and so ready to put up with almost anything that none of these shortcomings entirely exhausted their patience. It was his particular kind of vanity that was beyond their endurance.

Feminine vanity is often forgiven because of the womanly enchantment accompanying it. James had all a woman's vanity without anything of the feminine charm. He talked endlessly on subjects that interested none but himself. He showed that he was willing not only to discard all ethical principles whenever the occasion seemed to him to call for this, but also (which was even worse) to enlist ethical principle when this seemed appropriate for the particular intrigue demanded by the occasion. The English might well have borne with him had he been only an effeminate man. Had he seemed only a pedantic Scot, they could easily have forgiven him. James, however, seemed to them a pedantic Scot with the mentality of a French harlot. No wonder it was whispered that King Elizabeth had been succeeded by Queen James.

At first the Puritan party in England had high hopes of him. Perhaps the thousand signatories of the Millenary Petition, presented to James on his way from Edinburgh to London and setting forth the grievances of that party, expected that because their new King came from Scotland he would be sympathetic to their cause. If so, they were grievously mistaken. Not only was English Puritanism alien to the outlook and tradition of the Scots, who were as little inclined to it as they were to the opposite party in the English Church; James was in any case the enemy of all democratic processes in both Church and State. In terms of his own kingcraft, he had thought he understood only too well the Scottish idea of Presbyterian government, noting as he did that it seemed to him to be as consonant with a monarchy as is God with the Devil. As for the English Puritans, he knew their views on monarchy were likely to be even worse for him, and he had determined to "make them conform." If they did not, he threatened he would "harry them out of the land, or yet do worse."

In James's eyes the Puritans were not, however, the greatest danger to his throne. In the Papists, whom all parties distrusted and disliked, he saw a graver potential peril because of their powerful political allies abroad. So when a conference was held at Hampton Court on January 14, 16, and 18, 1604, to hear about and judge upon "things pretended to be amiss in the Church," James astonished many by being rude to the Puritans while being relatively polite to the Papists, all the while seeming to regard himself as elevated above all parties and indeed above all principles in Christendom. There was, of course, no need for any such astonishment. Ought not a master of kingcraft to be able to play one party off against the other in the interest of his own absolute power? James, who was thought to have too many favorites at court, had really only one, as he had but one objective.

At the same time, he did have a bookish interest in the Bible. The idea of a new translation instinctively appealed to him. The Bishops' Bible had high authority behind it and satisfied some; but the Geneva Version was still being widely read, especially by those of Puritan sympathies. James fancied himself as a translator. When an eminent representative of the Puritan party, John Reynolds, President of Corpus Christi College, Oxford, "moved His Majesty that there might be a new translation of the Bible" that would satisfy all parties, Richard Bancroft, then Bishop of London, remarked caustically that "if everyman's humour should be followed, there would be no end of translating." James, however, was by no means inclined to reject the idea simply because of its source. He was disposed, on the contrary, to respect anyone who was interested in such matters. Here was a project in which he might have a hand. To direct a new Bible was a noble prospect.

Had James been in any sense the "canny Scot" of English mythology, he might well have demurred at the cost of a translation on the scale proposed. He was, on the contrary, a spendthrift. In any case, however, the project of translation was so much to his taste that he would have grudged it less than almost any other disbursement. In fact, thanks to his policies, there was unlikely to be anything in the treasury to disburse. An appeal for funds was therefore made to the bishops and clergy. This failed. So James proposed to reward the translators with ecclesiastical preferment. Provision was also made, however, for their free board and lodging while they would be actually engaged on the translation. The arrangements apparently worked quite well, and the vast undertaking was eventually completed with astonishing economy. No doubt James took full credit for this.

It is not difficult to see reasons for James's vast unpopularity. The qualities his subjects found so distasteful in him were largely unexpected. One might suppose it to be improbable that the list of the unexpected qualities that made him so unpopular could be extended. Yet there was one quality that took everyone perhaps more than ever by surprise. James had a horror of warfare. Some said that this was due to the fright he had received before birth at the violent scene in which his mother had been involved. Certainly James disliked war, and he really believed the pen could be mightier than the sword, especially, of course, if it were cleverly wielded by a king with the literary gifts he believed to be his. His fear of war with foreign powers allied to the papacy, such as Spain, led to his use of conciliatory methods towards his own Papist subjects. He sought to relax the restrictions imposed upon these under his illustrious predecessor. This proposed relaxation caused widespread panic in England, not least because it revealed that there were more people in England with loyalties to the papacy than had been generally believed likely.

James was prevented from carrying out his conciliatory program. Laws, stricter than ever, were enforced against Papists. Nevertheless, when his attitude was first manifested, it naturally raised Papist hopes. With the help of such a king, might not England be won back to Rome after all? Then, when the Papists saw that even under such a king most of England seemed still firm in its loyalty to the Reformation cause, their hope turned to fury.

No doubt it was this fury that led to the daring adventure commonly known as the Gunpowder Plot. It is no exaggeration to say that in a country such as England, which had in some ways seemed to be reluctant and ambivalent in its choice of the Reformation side, that event had the effect of ratifying forever England's choice. The Gunpowder Plot instilled in the common man such an ineradicable distrust of the papacy that two hundred years afterwards the average Englishman was still inclined to suspect a Papist's most innocent and casual word or action. An English Papist elicited from the vast majority of his compatriots the same kind of feeling that an American Communist is likely to evoke among his countrymen today. He was taken to be by definition intent upon the overthrow of the most precious political values. "English Papist" was almost a wordy way of saying "traitor."

I have called the Gunpowder Plot a daring adventure. It was that and much more. It is a commonplace of history that the defeat of the Spanish Armada by Elizabeth's England changed the course of world events to such an extent that but for it the whole pattern of the world today would have been radically different. It was only a decade and a half since that most decisive of England's victories against a dangerous hostile foreign power had been won. For good or ill, the sun had set forever upon the flag of Spain, and with it had sunk also Rome's grander hopes of temporal power. Yet the conspirators in the Gunpowder Plot were seeking, and knew they were seeking, to upturn human history with a few well-placed barrels of gunpowder.

There was no lack of professional skill in the preparations. They were made by men who had served as officers in the Spanish army in the Netherlands. In March, 1605, more than a ton and a half of gunpowder in thirty-six barrels, hidden under coal and faggots, had been secretly introduced into a vault immediately under the House of Lords. The immediate purpose was to kill both King and Parliament. Having accomplished this mass destruction of the whole government of England, the conspirators would have been ready to establish in its place something to wipe out every victory, naval and moral, that had raised England to whatever national greatness it had so far attained. There is no doubt of their intention, or of the care and skill they brought to their task. They were, with a single exception, Roman Catholic gentlemen of good family. The exception was the trusted servant of one of them. Nor is there any doubt of the immense significance of their purpose. The plot all but succeeded.

The principal instigator of the Gunpowder Plot was Robert Catesby (1573-1605). Educated at Gloucester Hall (now Worcester College). Oxford, Catesby had been among those arrested in 1596 as a political suspect. He was a participant in the rebellion of Essex in 1601, in which he was wounded. After imprisonment he was pardoned on payment of a huge fine, whereupon he was immediately involved in plots and schemes to bring about an invasion of England by Philip of Spain. Thwarted, he continued to look about for better methods. It is probable that he conceived the idea of the Gunpowder Plot in the late spring or early summer of 1603. He took one conspirator, his cousin, Thomas Winter, into his confidence, in January, 1604. At Catesby's instigation, Winter introduced himself to Guy Fawkes (1507-1606), whom he initiated into the plot. Fawkes, born into a good Yorkshire family, became, through his stepfather's influence, a zealous Papist. Having gone to

Flanders in 1593 to enlist in the Spanish army, he had acquired military experience by his assistance in the Spanish capture of Calais. Fawkes, courageous and fanatical, accredited as "a confident gentleman" and "best able for this business," also enjoyed the advantage of being quite unknown in London. He was therefore an excellent choice for the actual carrying out of the plans.

A house adjoining Parliament was hired, and Fawkes, assuming the name of Johnson, took charge of it as the tenant's servant. On the discovery of an adjoining cellar, immediately under the House of Lords, he placed the ammunition there, covering the barrels of gunpowder with faggots and coals, and arranging iron bars in such a way as to augment the force of the explosion. Leaving nothing to chance, Fawkes even brought fresh gunpowder to the scene in August, 1605, in case the barrels already placed there should have been affected by damp. A slow match was devised and prepared, to allow him fifteen minutes after lighting to make his escape to safety before the rulers of England should have been blown sky-high.

Catesby was firmly determined to keep the secret strictly within the conspirators' own trusted circle. He insisted on withholding it even from those peers who were believed to be sympathetic to the conspirators' aims. However regrettable it might seem, these noble sympathizers must be sacrificed for the certain accomplishment of the plot. In such a dangerous enterprise, no chances could be taken. Nevertheless, for the sake of financial assistance, the secret was shared with Francis Tresham, who is almost certainly the writer of a letter divulging it to Lord Monteagle, Tresham's brother-in-law. Monteagle had been at one time engaged in popish plots against the government, but had undergone a change of heart. The purpose of the letter was to give him friendly warning. He could avoid death by absenting himself from Parliament. The letter appealed to him to "devise some excuse to shift of your attendance of this Parliament, for God and man hath concurred to punish the wickedness of this time. And think not slightly of this advertisement, but retire yourself into your country, where you may expect the event in safety, for though there be no appearance of any stir, yet I say they shall receive a terrible blow, the Parliament, and yet they shall not see who hurts them. This counsel is not to be contemned, because it may do you good and can do you no harm, for the danger is past as soon as you have burnt this letter: and I hope God will give you the grace to make good use of it, to whose holy protection I commend you."

The prayer of this writer was that the recipient might make good use of the letter. Many have since thought the prayer was indeed abundantly answered, though not at all according to the intention of him who uttered it. The writer, apart from considerations of friendship, may have believed Lord Monteagle was still at heart a Papist and was only, out of weakness or under pressure of events beyond his control, riding with the Reformation tide. Though such a man could not be admitted to the inner circle of the conspirators, yet ought not he to be spared, since he could render useful service after the overthrow of King and Parliament and the final arrangement of English affairs according to a pattern more agreeable to the papacy and Spain?

At any rate, the writer was grievously mistaken. Lord Monteagle, whatever his past, had given up interest in murky plots and had become James's loyal subject. He therefore dutifully exhibited the letter to some of the King's ministers. At first there was puzzlement. What could the letter mean?

Meanwhile Catesby, apprised of the receipt of the letter and its disclosure in high places, refused to abandon the plans. Fawkes reported that, the letter notwithstanding, the gunpowder was untouched in the cellar below the House of Lords where it could still do the desired mischief. All it needed was the assembling of Parliament and the lighting of the slow match. Only a few days remained, and there seemed to be no evidence that the nature of the plot was known.

On November 4, 1605, however, the very eve of the day for which the dramatic spectacle was staged, a search was ordered. The hideous explanation of the letter came to light when, in the cellar above which Parliament was due to meet, the barrels of gunpowder were discovered.

The conspirators were rounded up within a few days. Some were killed in the process. Eight were executed. Tresham died in the Tower. Among the Jesuits known to have been implicated, one was executed, and others escaped. The arrests may have been facilitated by the fanatical zeal of one of the conspirators who, in a futile bid for an impossible victory, after he knew of the failure of the plot, lied to a fellow-conspirator that the King was dead.

Fawkes, on his arrest, behaved with characteristic coolness and courage, refusing at first to give information about his accomplices. James ordered his torture *per gradus ad ima.* There is evidence that it was applied with extreme severity. On November 9, Fawkes signed his Christian name, Guy, in a hand apparently too weak to do more. Tried with others on January 26, 1606, before a special commission in Westminster Hall, he was condemned to be drawn on a hurdle from the Tower to Parliament House. He was so weak from torture that, after making a brief penitent speech, he required assistance in order to mount the ladder at the scaffold. His infamy is commemorated to this day in England every year on November 5, in obedience to the old doggerel rhyme: "Remember, remember, the fifth of November." On that day, popularly called Guy Fawkes Day and so currently listed in *Whitaker's Almanack* and other such publications, firework displays are enjoyed, bonfires are lighted, and Guy Fawkes is burned in effigy. The celebrations have annually delighted generations of English schoolboys and others not always fully aware of the details or even of the historical importance of the event they commemorate.

If the feelings of England could be perpetuated to the present day in such demonstrations, what must it have been like at the time? Shakespeare's *Macbeth* may be dated shortly after the discovery of the Gunpowder Plot. In the porter's soliloquy in this play there is an allusion to it, and to the Jesuit complicity associated with it. "Knock, knock!" says the porter. "Who's there, i'th'name of Belzebub? . . . Knock, knock! Who's there, i'th'other devil's name? Faith, here's an equivocator that could swear in both the scales against either scale; who committed treason enough for God's sake, yet could not equivocate to heaven. O, come in, equivocator." [1]

The fear and suspicion, symbolized in the porter's thoughts on knocking that are immortalized by Shakespeare, haunted England for centuries. Through the Gunpowder Plot the Jesuits attained in England the height of their reputation as slippery equivocators whose word could never be trusted. They were to be counted among the agents of those powers whose hatching of the diabolical plot had come so near bringing England within their grasp. None but Papists seriously doubted that their fell purpose was the overthrow of every liberty and promise of liberty that made and would make England dear to her true sons bred on English soil.

In an adaptation of psalm 124, published in 1631 less than a generation after the event that had instilled such fears and suspicions into the English mind, we find an eloquent expression of them. The piece is described as a paraphrase of that psalm "By waye of thanksgiving for our great deliverances from the Papists Powder Plot." Apparently it was intended to be sung to a tune which, taken from a French Psalter of 1551, is now traditional in Scotland, where it is known as Old 124TH. The text of the adaptation of this psalm to the commemoration of the providential deliverance from the Gunpowder Plot is as follows:

> Now may England
> Confess and say surely;
> If that the Lord
> Had not our cause maintain'd,
> If that the Lord
> Had not our state sustain'd
> When Antichrist
> Against us furiouslie

[1] Act II, scene 3.

178

Made his proud Brags
And said, we should all die.

Not long ago
They had devoured us all:
 And swallowed quicke
 For ought that we could deeme:
Such was their rage
As we might well esteeme:
 And as proud floods
 With mighty force do fall;
So their mad-rage
Our lives had brought to thrall.

Our King and Queene
The Prince and princely race;
 Their Counsell grave,
 And chief Nobility;
The Judges wise
And prime tribe of Levi;
 With all the prudent
 Statesmen of the Land,
By Pouder fierce
Had perished out of hand.

The raging streames
Of Rome with roaring noise
 Had with great woe
 Ore-whelm'd us in the Deepe:
But, blessed Lord,
Thou didst us safely keep
 From bloodie teeth
 And their devouring jawes:
Which as a prey
Had griped us in their clawes.

But, as a bird,
Out of the fowler's grin,[2]
 Escapes away:
 Right so it far'd with us;
Broke were their nets
And Wee have scaped, Thus,
 God that made heaven
 And earth was our Helpe then
His mercy saved us
From these wicked men.

[2] gin

179

O let us therefore
With all thanks and praise
Sing joyfully
To Christ our heavenly King:
Whose wisedome high
This fact to light did bring:
Grant then o Lord
We doe thee humbly pray
We may accord
To praise thy name alway.
Amen.

At the time of the publication of the King James Version of the Bible in 1611, the memory was naturally still exceedingly fresh. The mood it generated is echoed in the Epistle Dedicatory still to be found prefixed to modern copies of the King James Version. This relatively short letter is to be distinguished from the lengthy one addressed to "the Reader," the text of which is included as an appendix in the present book.[3] The Epistle Dedicatory opens with the words:

To the most High and Mighty Prince, James, by the Grace of God, King of Great Britain, France, and Ireland, Defender of the Faith, &c. The Translators of the Bible wish Grace, Mercy, and Peace, through JESUS CHRIST our Lord. Great and manifold were the blessings, most dread Sovereign, which Almighty God, the Father of all mercies, bestowed upon us the people of England, when first he sent Your Majesty's Royal Person to rule and reign over us.

After reference, in the extravagantly flattering language of the period, to "the setting of that bright Occidental star, Queen Elizabeth," and to "the appearance of Your Majesty, as of the Sun in his strength," the address goes on to say:

If, on the one side, we shall be traduced by Popish persons at home or abroad, . . . we may rest secure, supported within by the truth and innocency of a good conscience, having walked the ways of simplicity and integrity, as before the Lord, and sustained without by the powerful protection of Your Majesty's grace and favour.

Such courtly flattery notwithstanding, the policies of James were already highly unpopular, and were to become even more so. The victories of the English navy over Spain, only a few years before, had astonished the world and raised the prestige of England everywhere. Now, in the face of continued Spanish schemes and intrigues, he let the

[3]See below, appendix to chapter 24, pp. 220-42.

navy decline to such an extent that pirates raided English ships with impunity even in the English Channel. When he sent forth pedantically diplomatic protests at such insults, Spaniards openly laughed. Sir Walter Raleigh, one of the greatest seafaring heroes at the zenith of England's glory, was beheaded for the sake of appeasing the pride of the Spanish ambassador. While England's naval power waned, the Dutch abundantly prospered at sea, ousting the English from the trade with Russia that had been opened up under Elizabeth. They even drove the English from their own fishing grounds. The Portuguese subjects of the Spanish King even tried to prevent the English from peacetime trading on the coasts of Africa and the East Indies, and but for the East India Company, which armed its ships for battle, they might have succeeded. In 1623 the Dutch, having expelled the Portuguese from Ceylon and the Spice Islands of the Molucca Sea, massacred the English there, while James remained powerless to do anything to stem the tide of England's shame. Papist Spain was allowed to recover not a little of the power of which Elizabeth's England had divested it.

James, who has been called "the wisest fool in Christendom," seemed so obstinately stupid in his policies of appeasement that not even the Gunpowder Plot could be expected to teach such a man. From the standpoint of the national welfare James might well be called a fool. From that of his own selfish interest he was perhaps as wise as he believed himself to be. No king less profoundly committed to his own vanity and dedicated to the foibles of such a curiously unfortunate temper could have pursued James's course with such singleness of miserable purpose. That he had made himself unpopular on both sides of the Scottish border did not trouble such a man. Was not this part of the hazards attending success in kingcraft?

Yet this was the monarch under whom were united the crowns of Scotland and England. His is the name given forever to the most influential translation of the Bible. Nor was his association with this mighty enterprise only an accidental one. Nothing was nearer whatever heart such a man could have. In his early days he had translated some thirty psalms into a metrical version characteristically called "The Psalmes of King David, Translated by King Iames." His interest in the project of translating the Bible was as genuine as could be. He delighted in it, and though he was unlikely to be much misled by the hyperbolic language used for flattering him, he was no doubt proud of the Epistle Dedicatory and glad to have been the monarch under whom such an enterprise had been fulfilled.

That the Bible, which has been transmitted throughout the ages in such curious, devious, and often very unexpected ways, should have influenced our language and culture so profoundly through a translation associated with such an unlikely king is not perhaps as wholly astonishing as might at first appear. After all, this incident in the story of the transmission of the Bible is not more strange than the whole story presented in the present book. Whether this story reflects the workings of a divine providence beyond human ken or but a complex pattern of the vagaries of chance is something the reader must judge for himself. Yet, remembering Boccaccio's saying that the Christian Church must be divine, since no purely human institution could have survived the corruption that has afflicted it, if one were to say the same of the Bible, at least the point would be by no means unintelligible. If we are thoughtful enough to pause for wonder at the Church that could survive the eighth Henry of England, surely we shall stop no less to wonder at the Bible that could survive King James.

Stone walls do not a prison make.
—Richard Lovelace

CHAPTER 21 *The King James Regulations*

The plans for the King James Version of the Bible were the most elaborate that had ever been devised for any such project. The panel of translators was the largest; the rules imposed upon them were the most detailed and the most restrictive; the aim was the production of a work of scholarship and literary accomplishment that would both satisfy the leaders of all ecclesiastical parties and evoke the universal affection of the people; the result, in terms of the knowledge of the day and of the available tools, was such a masterpiece that even those who had set their sights so high could hardly have foreseen the extent of its influence.

On July 22, 1604, the King, having received nominations of proposed translators, announced in a letter to Archbishop Bancroft that he had appointed "fifty-four learned men." He also drew up a list of instructions. Some of the translators actually began their work about this time. It was not till 1607 that it was formally undertaken. Forty-seven men were actually entrusted with the work, and several of these died before it was completed.

The plan was that the translators should be divided into six companies, each formally charged with a portion of the work. The six companies would meet, two at Oxford, two at Cambridge, and two at Westminster.

Each company was placed under the formal direction of a churchman whose official position imposed upon him a high degree of responsibility. The two companies that met at Westminster, for example, were put under the direction of the Dean of Westminster and the Dean of Chester. The Oxford companies were placed respectively under the Regius Professors of Hebrew and Greek of that University, and at Cambridge the two companies were likewise placed under the Cambridge counterparts of the holders of these distinguished academic positions.

Eventually, a committee was also formed consisting of twelve delegates, two from each of the six companies, to engage in the revision of the work. This committee met daily at Stationers' Hall, London, during a period of nine months. For this, each of its members received a fixed stipend of thirty shillings a week from the King's Printer. This was a more businesslike arrangement than was provided for the general body of the translators, who, we have already seen, were recompensed in vaguer ways. There was also another committee of two, consisting of Miles Smith and Thomas Bilson. The latter was appointed from outside the general body of translators; to the former, prominent among them, is generally attributed the lengthy Epistle to the Reader that has been included as an appendix in the present work.

The rules provided for the guidance of King James's panel of translators were as follows:

1. The ordinary Bible read in the Church, commonly called the Bishops' Bible, to be followed, and as little altered as the truth of the original will admit.

2. The names of the prophets and the holy writers, with the other names of the text, to be retained as nigh as may be, accordingly as they were vulgarly used.

3. The old ecclesiastical words to be kept, viz., the word *church* not to be translated *congregation,* &c.

4. When a word hath divers significations, that to be kept which hath been most commonly used by the most of the ancient fathers, being agreeable to the propriety of the place and the analogy of the faith.

5. The division of the chapters to be altered either not at all, or as little as may be, if necessity so require.

6. No marginal notes at all to be affixed, but only for the explanation of the Hebrew or Greek words which cannot, without some circumlocution, so briefly and fitly be expressed in the text.

7. Such quotations of places to be marginally set down as shall serve for the fit reference of one Scripture to another.

8. Every particular man of each company to take the same chapter or chapters; and having translated or amended them severally by himself where he thinketh good, all to meet together, confer what they have done, and agree for their parts what shall stand.

9. As any one company hath dispatched any one book in this manner, they shall send it to the rest to be considered of seriously and judiciously, for his Majesty is very careful in this point.

10. If any company, upon the review of the book so sent, doubt or differ upon any place, to send them word thereof, note the place, and withal send the reasons; to which if they consent not, the difference to be compounded at the general meeting, which is to be of the chief persons of each company at the end of the work.

11. When any place of special obscurity is doubted of, letters to be directed by authority to send to any learned man in the land for his judgement of such a place.

12. Letters to be sent from every bishop to the rest of his clergy, admonishing them of this translation in hand, and to move and charge as many as being skilful in the tongues, and having taken pains in that kind, to send his particular observations to the company either at Westminster, Cambridge, or Oxford.

13. The directors in each company to be the Deans of Westminster and Chester for that place, and the king's professors in the Hebrew or Greek in either university.

14. These translations to be used when they agree better with the text than the Bishops' Bible: Tindale's, Matthew's, Coverdale's, Whitchurch's, Geneva.

15. Besides the said directors before mentioned, three or four of the most ancient and grave divines in either of the universities, not employed in translating, to be assigned by the Vice-Chancellor upon conference with the rest of the Heads to be overseers of the translations, as well Hebrew as Greek, for the better observation of the fourth rule above specified.

These regulations were much more thoroughgoing and effectual than had been the provisions for the making of the Bishops' Bible. They were almost certainly drafted by Richard Bancroft, who had become Archbishop of Canterbury in the year of the Hampton Court Conference, at which the translation had been proposed. Bancroft, on account of the age and incapacity of his predecessor, John Whitgift, had been virtually acting as Archbishop of Canterbury for five years before taking office. He was a vigorous enemy of the Puritan party. His hand is reflected in the rules, which were designed chiefly to insure that the new translation of the Bible would be suitable to be authorized for the Church of England, not for partisan interests within it. After all, one of the chief pruposes behind the translation was to cause the version the Puritans liked, the Geneva Bible, to be superseded. But for the failure of the Bishops' Bible to achieve this, the version now undertaken could hardly have been proposed.

The provision that the new version should be based on the Bishops' Bible was at first sight very restrictive; but it did not mean that the translators were not free to alter that version wherever it stood in need of correction. The rule required only that the Bishops' Bible was to be taken as the point of departure. Changes were not to be made arbitrarily or for the sake of novelty. They were freely permitted, however, as long as any good reason could be shown.

Moreover, though the Bishops' Bible was the basis for the new work, the translators were not only free to turn to other, earlier versions; in some circumstances they were obliged to do so. Whenever one of these earlier versions agreed better with the text than did the Bishops' Bible, that earlier version was to be followed. And in fact the translators did not only this. They had before them a great many other translations of the Bible into various tongues—Luther's German Bible, of course, and the Vulgate; but they also referred to Italian, Spanish, and other accessible translations. Among their ancient sources were the Syriac New Testament and the Aramaic Targums. It goes without saying that they made diligent use of the best Hebrew and Greek manuscripts available.

Three of the most ancient and important biblical manuscripts, however, were not available. One of them, Codex Vaticanus, was hidden away at that time by the Vatican authorities. The Codex Sinaiticus was in the East, to be discovered more than two and a half centuries later by

Tischendorf and purchased in our own century from the Soviet government by the British Museum. The Codex Alexandrinus was to become known in the West shortly after the publication of the King James Bible;[1] but when the translators were engaged upon their work, this manuscript was unfortunately still not within their reach, nor did they even know of its existence. Nevertheless, they did use every tool they could lay their hands on, including every accessible manuscript.

In one respect, however, there was a distinct restriction connected with having the Bishops' Bible imposed as the basis of the new work. The rule that the old ecclesiastical terms should be kept was directed against the use of certain terms favored by the Puritans. Notably, their use of the word "Congregation" for "Church" was accounted a piece of party banner-waving and was not to be permitted. It was plain that arguments could be adduced in favor of one term or another; but in such cases the overriding principle was that when a word had "divers significations," that one was to be taken that "had been most commonly used by the most eminent Fathers." Naturally, such a rule was likely to give rise to argument concerning its interpretation. Bancroft found no difficulty in providing a decisive answer to all such questions about the application of the rule. He explained that it was His Majesty's pleasure that three or four of the most eminent divines of the university should supervise the translation to the extent of seeing that this rule was obeyed according to its intention. Since the intention was to prevent the Puritans from interpreting it according to their liking, there could be no doubt of the result of that arrangement. The wording of the Bishops' Bible would remain.

The rule prohibiting marginal notes was a good one. Such notes, as we have seen, had disfigured even the best of previous translations. They had provided scope for polemics. By eliminating notes the most obvious danger was removed of producing, through the introduction of these polemic asides, yet another party Bible. The only marginal comments to be permitted were those brief notes that might be necessary to explain Hebrew or Greek terms that could not well be expressed in the text of the translation, and also occasional cross-references that might be helpful to the biblical student.

Less universally acclaimed was the rule conserving the traditional division into chapter and verse. This, we have frequently seen already, was a comparative novelty in the history of setting forth the biblical text. The ancient Fathers had known nothing of any such arrangement. It had been devised as a scholarly convenience during a period in the Middle Ages in which an interest in the Bible had been revived. In

[1] More will be said about these very important codices in chapter 26.

terms of the needs of thirteenth-century biblical scholars at the University of Paris it had been an admirable invention. To scholars of the seventeenth century it seemed otiose. Some felt that the division into verses was particularly misleading to the reader. To these scholarly objections there seemed to be no effective answer except the appeal to custom. In effect, the old ecclesiastical principle was invoked, *nihil innovetur nisi quod traditum est:* novelties are forbidden except those that have been handed down! Many modern translators, as we shall see, eliminate these divisions that by the seventeenth century had long become customary and were long so to remain. There is no doubt that their elimination often helps to make passages more readily intelligible.

Nevertheless, there was more to be said for the seemingly stuffy conservatism of the rule on this question. For the first time in history the Bible was becoming everyman's book; and as the students at the Sorbonne had needed an easy means of referring to the text, so now, four hundred years later, ordinary folk who were taking to the study of the Bible had a similar need of a handy means of reference. In the life of the Church there is often more wisdom in custom than the brightest minds of the age are always able to see. If it were always good for the Church to follow the advice of its most advanced biblical scholars and to think the thoughts of its most subtle theologians, it would be a university or school, which is not what the Church is supposed to be. Cleverness is not part of the fundamental nature of the Church, though many individuals in it may have the responsibility, not always discharged, of avoiding stupidity.

The application of the rule requiring the original Hebrew and Greek proper names to be kept as near as possible to the original form was not always as happy as one might expect. The Douai-Reims translators had used hellenized forms such as "Isaias" and "Jeremias," which till recently remained customary in English-speaking Roman Catholic circles. The King James Version naturally adhered more closely to the Hebrew forms. Yet the New Testament itself had hellenized the Hebrew forms, and so the King James translators gave us, as their rules required of them, "Elijah" in the Old Testament and "Elias" in the New. Worse still, the oak under which Deborah was buried was no longer to be called, as older translators had called it in rendering Genesis 35:85, "the oak of lamentation." It must be as we now have it, both in the King James Version and also (apart from a slight change of spelling) in the Revised Standard, an oak that "was called Allon-bachuth."

If the reader knows enough Hebrew to know what Allon-bachuth means, he does not need an English translation at all. The Douai translators, for all their use of "azymes" and "holocausts" that is deprecated in the King James translators' Epistle to the Reader, and for all the "exinaniting" and other oddities for which they have been so much chided, surely did better for us in this passage by telling us simply that the name of the place was "the oak of weeping." (This translates the Vulgate, *Quercus fletus*.) In the following verse, moreover, where the King James Version informs us that Jacob came out of Padan-aram, the Douai says he came out of Mesopotamia of Syria. This may be less than perfect; but besides being more gentle to the reader it provides him with at least a rough idea of the former whereabouts of Jacob, instead of giving us the resonant Hebrew name of a place which, for all the reader could be expected to know, might be one of the lesser mountains on the moon.

The literary influence of the King James Version is well known. Not even Shakespeare has more profoundly affected our literature. The most godless of men, provided only that he has inherited English for his mother tongue, is confronted with the influence of the King James Version of the Bible almost wherever he turns. It has been injected into the stream of the language. It has invigorated and enriched all subsequent English prose. Even the most modern of modern English that has any literary merit still occasionally echoes its cadences and often reflects its turns of phrase. As it taught an itinerant tinker, John Bunyan, how to write vivid and striking English of enduring character and power, so it bequeathed to generations of writers, many of them far removed from Bunyan's religious interests, the liveliest stream of good English ever harnessed to a book.

The cause of this literary success is seldom adequately examined. It could not have been due solely to the intrinsic power of the Bible itself, for the Bible had already appeared in many guises, none of which resulted in a work that has played any comparable part in the history of our English language and literature. Nor was the success due to the mere technical ability of the translators or to any conspicuously creative gifts they might have severally enjoyed. The work could not have been done without able writers; yet but for one circumstance the ablest of them could not have produced the King James Version of the Bible.

The explanation, I would contend, lies in what would seem a paradox to those who imagine that complete literary freedom is the most important condition of good style. For the secret of the literary splendor and lasting success of the King James Version is that it was written by men hampered by exacting discipline and sometimes irritating restrictions. Far from being able to give free rein to their literary fancies, they had to be constantly referring to their rules. In such circumstances, all their ingenuity was strained in breaking them with impunity wherever they could. The literary power of their work springs like a fountain out of the desert of their regulations. In art and literature not only is it the case that, as Richard Lovelace was to write a generation afterwards,

"Stone walls do not a prison make, nor iron bars a cage;"[2] in art and literature stone walls and iron bars are the very stuff out of which artists and writers make literary masterpieces. The beauty and genius of our language and the vivacity of our literature proceed out of the prisons of history and grammar.

When the King James translators were prosecuting their labors, the rules of English orthography were still at a relatively primitive stage of their development. The language was to become, in a century or two, both more precise and much more complex. These translators showed, however, what genius could be already revealed in the English tongue when able men were called upon to adhere to structures and patterns and allowed only as much rein as able men need. To this example was due in no small measure the achievements of later ages in the history of English literature, in which poets and other writers could exhibit their skill in producing an infinite variety of riches out of increasingly restricted sets of rules.

The purity of English style for which the King James Version is justly celebrated is not without parallels today; but they are not common in an age in which technological preoccupations inevitably spawn curious forms of jargon. Theology, especially in its more unlearned contemporary forms, is by no means exempt. So luxurious is the crop of contemporary "theological" gobbledegook that in one of my earlier books I satirically suggested how the Bible might be updated in terms tomorrow's reader might be expected to understand. Instead of the King James rendering, "Ye are the light of the world. A city that is set on a hill cannot be hid," I proposed: "You, that is to say, the persons being hereby addressed, are, under the circumstances and having regard to the predications already made in the preceding paragraph concerning sodium chloride, the illumination of the terrestrial globe. An urban area organized to in some definitely outstanding degree be situated on a natural elevation of the terrestrial surface is one in which the use of camouflage is not within the bounds, considering the exigencies of the various factors in the situation concerned, and hereinbefore mentioned, of practical possibility."[3]

[2] A similar Stoic thought is expressed by one of Lovelace's French contemporaries, Paul Pellisson-Fontanier, who wrote on the walls of his cell in the Bastille:

> Doubles grilles, à gros cloux,
> Triples portes, forts verroux,
>   Aux âmes vraiment méchantes
> Vous représentez l'enfer:
>   Mais aux âmes innocentes
> Vous n'êtes que du bois, des pierres, du fer.

[3] *From a Christian Ghetto* (London: Longmans Green, 1954), p. 82.

Hayyim Nachman Bialik (1873-1934), perhaps the greatest of modern Jewish poets, has vividly expressed the inadequacy of all translation in his picturesque saying: "He who reads the Bible in translation is like a man who kisses his bride through a veil." Still, when a veil there must be, the translator's task is to make it as gossamer-fine a veil as may be. Indeed, the face of even the most beautiful of women may be enhanced by a veil, if only the veil be worthy of her beauty. The King James translators did not pretend to be providing a new veil. Their function was, rather, to let more light through the veils already in use. This fundamental principle is admirably exhibited in their explanation [4] that it was never their intention either to make an entirely new translation or even to turn a bad one into a good. Their purpose was, rather, to make, out of many good translations, one that would be better than all. After all, what is the purpose of any translation? It is to open windows and let in light, to remove the cover of the well so that the people may drink and not be, as were Jacob's children, thirsty for want of a bucket to draw the water that was at their feet.

Every member of the panel of translators was to work first of all individually on an assigned chapter or chapters. He was then to bring his work to his colleagues and go over it with them, so that after discussion of debatable points the company might eventually agree upon what should be left standing. Each company was similarly to take its book to another company for review. They were reminded that "His Majesty is very careful on this point." Should there remain difficulties that had not been resolved by this procedure, there was still a remedy. At the end of the proceedings, there would be a general meeting of the leaders of the companies, on which occasion the variant readings would come up for further discussion. Nor were the translators precluded from seeking the help of other scholars not of their number. Particularly difficult points were to be directed to such specialists as might be found able and willing to render aid.

The bishops were told to admonish their clergy to direct all persons skilled in the ancient tongues to send in their observations to the translation company concerned. No doubt this was not as unsafe an injunction then as it would be today, when so many people are so eager to proffer their advice in inverse proportion to their knowledge. One can imagine with what horror such a directive would be received today by the chairman of any translation committee! Nowadays persons engaged on such projects are obliged, even in the absence of such official encouragement of private individuals, to mask their doings with some measure of anonymity in order to obtain a modicum of the peace necessary for scholarly pursuits. Otherwise they might have to invoke police protection from

[4] See appendix to chapter 24, p. 237.

the crowds of self-appointed helpers, to say nothing of the "inquirers" who in any case would descend upon them in hope of finding out the latest discoveries about matters such as the wedding arrangements of Cain and Abel.

The translators did not forget the dignity and uniqueness of the book they were called upon to translate. They remind the reader that St. Basil had likened the Bible to a "physician's shop" containing "preservatives against poisoned heresies." It is "not only an armour, but also a whole armoury of weapons, both offensive and defensive; whereby we may save ourselves and put the enemy to flight. It is not an herb, but a tree, or rather a whole paradise of trees of life, which bring forth fruit every month, and the fruit thereof is for meat, and the leaves for medicine." [5]

[5] See appendix to chapter 24, p. 225.

CHAPTER 22 *The King James Translators*

The work of producing the King James Version was entrusted, as we have seen, to a larger body of translators than had ever before been engaged upon any translation of the Bible into English or any revision of the English Bible. For three reasons it is important as well as interesting to know something about their character, qualifications, and personal idiosyncracies. In the first place, their enterprise resulted in the greatest monument in English literature as well as the most influential contribution to the literary history of religion in the English-speaking world. In the second place, many of their names naturally tend to seem shadowy and remote even to the best informed reader, in comparison with those of the scholars who have undertaken such work nearer our own time. Finally, the very virtues of the King James Version that give it the timelessness it enjoys also obscure from us the flesh-and-blood qualities of the living men who made it. We have seen what sort of man it was who sponsored the project and gave his name to it forever. The actual work, we have seen, was entrusted to a panel of forty-seven men, some of whom died before its completion. We shall do well to look at some of the more interesting figures among them.

The names of the members of the six companies, with alternative spellings sometimes used for some of them, may be listed as follows:

First Company (*First Westminster Company*) [*Genesis–II Kings*]

Lancelot Andrewes	Robert Tighe (Teigh)
John Overall	Francis Burleigh (Burley)
Hadrian à Saravia	Geoffrey King
Richard Clarke (Clerke)	Richard Thompson
John Layfield	William Bedwell (Beadwell)

Second Company (*First Cambridge Company*)
[*I Chronicles–Ecclesiastes*]

Edward Lively	Thomas Harrison
John Richardson	Roger Andrewes
Lawrence Chatterton (Chaderton)	Robert Spalding
Francis Billingham	Andrew Byng

Third Company (First Oxford Company) [*Isaiah–Malachi*]

John Harding
John Reynolds (Rainolds)
Thomas Holland
Richard Kilbye

Miles Smith
Richard Brett
Richard Fairclough

Fourth Company (Second Oxford Company)
[*Gospels, Acts, Revelation*]

Thomas Ravis
George Abbot
Richard Edes
Giles Thompson (Thomson)

Henry Savile
John Peryn (Perrinne, Perne)
Ralph Ravens
John Harmer (Harmar)

Fifth Company (Second Westminster Company) [*Romans–Jude*]

William Barlow
Ralph Hutchinson
John Spencer (Spenser)
Roger Fenton

Michael Rabbett (Rabbet)
Thomas Sanderson
William Dakins

Sixth Company (Second Cambridge Company) [*Apocrypha*]

John Duport
William Branthwaite (Branthwait)
Jeremiah Radcliffe
Samuel Ward

Andrew Downes
John Bois
William Ward (Warde)

Lancelot Andrewes (1555-1626), who presided over the First Westminster Company, is one of the most eminent figures in English Church history and one of the principal influences in the formation in the seventeenth century of a distinctively Anglican theology. Disliking the extravagances of the English Puritans, he sought a theology that would be reasonable, humane, Catholic and, not least, based upon sound learning. He was closely associated with Richard Hooker, George Herbert, and other likeminded English divines, and he cultivated also the friendship of liberal scholars on the continent of Europe, including the Dutch jurist and theologian Hugo Grotius (1583-1645) who, though much influenced by Roman Catholic doctrine, remained outside the Roman fold, and Isaac Casaubon (1559-1614), a classicist and professor at the University of Geneva, who sought an alternative to an extreme Calvinism on the one hand and, on the other, the Roman way.

Andrewes, accounted by many Anglicans a pattern of English churchmanship at its best, expressed his deep and mature personal piety in one of the greatest devotional classics in the Christian Church, the *Preces Privatae*, published in 1648, which witnesses to the deep churchmanship and fine historical sense that lay behind the lyrical qualities in that manual of private prayer. Born in the parish of All Hallows, Barking, Andrewes went to Cambridge, where he became a Fellow and, in 1589, Master of Pembroke Hall. His preaching gifts attracted the attention of Elizabeth, who offered him in turn the bishoprics of Salisbury and Ely. These he declined, being unwilling to accept certain conditions imposed. In 1601 he became Dean of Westminster. James I, for all his shortcomings, recognized his merit, and under that monarch Andrewes became Bishop of Chichester in 1605, Bishop of Ely in 1609, succeeding eventually in 1619 to the See of Winchester, then the richest as well as one of the most ancient in England. James, at whose Hampton Court Conference Andrewes had played a leading part, had been attacked by the great Jesuit controversialist of the day, Robert Bellarmine. After the Gunpowder Plot, an Oath of Allegiance had been instituted, and James, in a tract published in 1608 under the title *Apology for the Oath,* had written a defence. When this was attacked by Bellarmine, under the pseudonym Matthaeus Tortus, Andrewes entered upon the defence of his sovereign the following year with a vigorous reply to the Italian Jesuit, entitled *Tortura Torti.*

Andrewes was indeed all sorts of a man. It is said he would spend a vacation by seeking out a master of a language he did not already know and devoting his temporary leisure to learning it. One of his contemporaries said he might have been "Interpreter General at Babel." Such scholarship enriched his sermons, which were elegantly adorned by Greek and Latin quotations in accordance with the fashion of the day. It is difficult to assess the depth of his knowledge of Hebrew; but there is no doubt that he had a good knowledge of its grammar and vocabulary. He also knew much about ordinary men. At Cambridge there was an alderman who, try as he would, could not keep awake at sermon in his parish church. He found it embarrassing to be roused from his slumbers and publicly rebuked from the pulpit. Such rebukes were customary in those days when sermons were accounted important moral events and spiritual instruments in the life of both Church and nation, rather than the timidly inspirational adventures upon the uninspired that they are too often nowadays expected to be. So he sought the advice of Andrewes. How could he conquer that intense inclination to sleep that overtook him at sermon? Andrewes apparently perceived at once an important factor in the case. The alderman ate too much. As another English divine once said, "It is hard work preaching to two pounds of beef and a pot of porter." The alderman took the good advice to dine more sparingly before sermon. The remedy did not work: the alderman's snores still disturbed the attentive hearers of the eloquence from the pulpit that had such a soporific effect on him. He again appealed to Andrewes who this time recommended him not only moderation in eating but a good nap before he approached the mysteries of the Word. The result, it is said, was eminently satisfactory. The story well expresses the more human side of Andrewes that was not least among his virtues.

John Overall (1560-1619) was also a Cambridge man, who became Fellow of Trinity and Regius Professor of Divinity at that university. Under James he became Bishop of Coventry and Lichfield in 1614, and four years later Bishop of Norwich. At the time of his work on the translation he was Dean of St. Paul's Cathedral, London. A brilliant Latinist, he also held the position of *praelector* in Greek in his earlier days at Cambridge. The extent of his Hebrew is not easy to determine.

With the Gunpowder Plot in view, Overall compiled what was known as his Convocation Book; but James prohibited its acceptance by Convocation, and publication of the book was actually delayed till 1690. James disliked the political theory he had defended. Overall's theory about the nature of kingship was grounded in the old principle of the medieval canonists, who had taught in effect that a revolution could be lawful where the prince flagrantly sinned against *aequitas,* justice. According to Overall, when a new government was firmly established in such circumstances, it could claim the obedience of the people as a duty to God. His teaching on this subject naturally could not but displease James, since it was plainly at variance with the specifically Tudor English conception of the Divine Right of Kings which James found congenial. It was not till the revolution in England actually occurred in 1688, bringing William and Mary to the throne, that Overall's doctrines came into favor in high places.

Saravia (1531-1613) was born of Hispano-Flemish parents at Hesdin, Artois, and became pastor at Antwerp, where he assisted in the drafting of the Calvinistic credal statement known as the Belgic Confession and drawn up in French for the Reformed Churches of Wallony and Flanders, principally by Guido de Brès (1522-1567). Based on the Gallican Confession adopted at Paris in 1559 by the First National Synod of the Reformed Church in France, it had been first drafted by Calvin himself. The religious disturbances in the Netherlands drove Saravia eventually to England for a time, after which he returned to Holland, becoming in 1582 Professor of Divinity at the University of Leyden. In 1585 he was again in England, and in 1560 we find him incorporated as a Doctor of Divinity in the University of Oxford, and acquiring fame as a prominent champion of episcopacy, which he expounded in his *De diversis gradibus ministrorum evangelii,* published in that year. This book is of more than ordinary interest to missionary-minded Christians: it was one of the first to press upon heirs of the Reformation the duty of preaching the Gospel in non-Christian lands. Like Andrewes, Saravia was a friend of Hooker and Casaubon. Since English was not his maternal tongue, he was presumably valued more for his general scholarship and linguistic skill than for any special contribution he could have made to the turning of the Bible into English.

Richard Clarke was a Fellow of Christ's College, Cambridge, and one of the six preachers at Canterbury. He died in 1634. Layfield, Fellow of Trinity College, Cambridge, from 1585 till 1603, and for some time Lecturer in Greek, was at the time of the work on the translation Rector of the parish of St. Clement Danes, London. Among his skills was a wide knowledge of architecture. He died in 1617. Robert Tighe, Archdeacon of Middlesex, was a Cambridge man who migrated to Oxford. He died in 1616. Burleigh was one of the early fellows of King James's College at Chelsea. Geoffrey King, Fellow of King's College, Cambridge, succeeded Robert Spalding in 1607 as Regius Professor of Hebrew in that university. Richard Thompson, another friend of Casaubon, was sometimes nicknamed "Dutch Thompson" from the land of his birth. He was apparently a good Hebraist.

Bedwell is of more than passing note. Born in 1561 or 1562, he devoted many years to compiling an Arabic lexicon, becoming the father of Arabic studies in England. He rightly drew attention to the importance of a knowledge of Arabic for the proper understanding of Hebrew. A pioneer in oriental studies, he also worked on a Persian dictionary. His interests included mathematics, and he promoted the use of a ruler invented by his uncle for geometric purposes. This came to be known as "Bedwell's Ruler."

Edward Lively, President of the First Cambridge Company, was a Fellow of Trinity College, Cambridge, from 1572 till 1578, and became Regius Professor of Hebrew in the University of Cambridge, probably in 1575. One of the greatest Hebraists in England, he died in 1605, amid the preliminaries of the translation, leaving his eleven children destitute.

John Richardson, Regius Professor of Divinity in the University of Cambridge from 1607 till 1617, became Master of Trinity in 1615.

Lawrence Chatterton was one of the four Puritan divines who took part in the Hampton Court Conference. He was from 1584 till 1622 the first Master of Emmanuel College, Cambridge. He adopted his Puritan views in his student days, to the distress of his father, who clung to Rome. His father wrote him that if he would renounce his opinions he would receive all the care an indulgent father could bestow; but in case young Lawrence might feel disinclined to change them, his father took the precaution of enclosing with his letter a shilling for the purpose of buying a beggar's wallet. Lawrence, far from being intimidated by his father's picturesquely expressed threat, not only persevered in his views but, in later life, foreseeing the possibility of his being succeeded by a man who did not hold similar opinions, resigned the Mastership of Emmanuel to make sure of the appointment of a successor after his own heart. Actually he survived not only that successor but two subsequent holders of the position, attaining, it is said, the age of 103 and enjoying such good health that in his last years he could still read Greek without spectacles and carry on conversation without even the repetitiousness that is common in even the least senile of very elderly people.

Dillingham, who became a Fellow of Christ's College, Cambridge, in 1581, was much admired for his Greek skills. He is said to have debated in Greek at the university disputations, instead of using the customary Latin. There is no evidence of the extent of his Hebrew. It would be unlikely to be as good as his Greek.

Harrison was Vice-Master of Trinity College, Cambridge, from 1611 till 1631. A Puritan, he was much loved for his meekness and charitable attitude towards those who held different opinions. It is said that when a report reached him that one of his students had abused him in a speech, Harrison inquired whether the student had actually named him, Thomas Harrison, as the object of his venom. When it was acknowledged that the student had not actually named him, Harrison remarked: "Then I do not believe he meant me." Surely such a remark betokens a delightful disposition! He also enjoyed a considerable contemporary reputation as a Hebraist.

Roger Andrewes was a brother of the celebrated Lancelot. He was Master of Jesus College, Cambridge, from 1618 till 1632. Spalding, who became a Fellow of St. John's College, Cambridge, in 1593, succeeded Edward Lively in 1605 as Regius Professor of Hebrew in the University of Cambridge. He died a few years later. Byng, of Peterhouse, Cambridge, became in 1608 Regius Professor of Hebrew in that university. A stall in the great cathedral church known as York Minster had been set aside for him about three years before that date. He died in 1651.

John Harding, President of the First Oxford Company, was Regius Professor of Hebrew in the University of Oxford from 1591 till 1598, and from 1604 till his death in 1610. In 1604 he became a Canon of Lincoln, and in 1607 President of Magdalen College, Oxford.

Special interest is naturally attached to John Reynolds (1549-1607), since it is to his remark at the Hampton Court Conference that the birth of the project of making the King James Version may be ascribed. A Devonshire man, born at Pinhoe, he became a Fellow of Corpus Christi College, Oxford, in 1568, acquiring much repute there as a Greek scholar and for his lectures on Aristotle. His Hebrew was probably equal to that of any of the translators. In 1586 he resigned his fellowship, probably as a result of a disagreement with the president of his college, William Coke.

Reynolds resided at the Queen's College from 1586 till 1595. In a modern history of Queen's by R. H. Hodgkin, there is an interesting note about him. "About the time that Rainolds joined Queen's he was appointed . . . to a university lectureship for the confutation of papal doctrines. There can be little doubt that he did much to establish both a strong anti-Roman sentiment and a strong tradition of learning in his adopted college. One of his pupils at Queen's maintained that Rainolds was really a moderate man, one who wore a surplice in the college chapel and knelt at the Sacrament. When we read the Authorized Translation of the Major Prophets, we may think that we are often hearing the sonorous and scholarly words of Rainolds."

His views as the leader of the Puritan party at the Hampton Court Conference are reflected in some observations he made while at Queen's on the subject of the place of recreation in the life of a student, which are quoted by Hodgkin in the same place: "You say," wrote Reynolds, "that there is a time for sports, playes, dances, a time for earnest studies: the man consisteth not of one part alone: he hath a body as well as a minde. Time of recreation is necessarie, I graunt: and thinke as necessarie for scholers that ar scholers in deede, I meane, good students, as it is for any. Yet in my opinion it were not fit for them to play at stoole ball among wenches; nor at Mum-chance and Maw with idle loose companions, nor at Trunkes in Guild-hals, not to danse about Maypoles, nor to rifle in alehouses, nor to carowse in tavernes, nor to robbe orchardes." [1]

He became Dean of Lincoln, and in 1598 he succeeded in exchanging positions with Coke, to the great satisfaction of the Fellows of Corpus, who disliked the latter's administration. A Calvinist and identified with the English Puritan party, being its principal champion at the Hampton Court Conference, he was able to command the respect even of opposing camps. He was the teacher of Hooker, one of the ablest Anglican divines of the period. Reynold's combination of noble character and great erudition, which elicited respect from his enemies, caused his friends to have a saying that it was hard to decide whether it was his scholarship or his piety that ought to command the greater admiration. Churchmen today do not often confront their friends with the necessity of making such a decision. Sometimes the decision has to be, rather, which is more forgivable, the lack of character or the deficiencies of learning.

Great indeed must have been the combination of qualities in Reynolds that enabled him to do so much to foster the new version, his known Puritan sympathies and James's distaste for them notwithstanding. As might be expected of such a man, he brought to his work an extreme devotion that was believed to have hastened his death. His colleagues met weekly at his lodgings even when he was ill, to go over their work

[1] R. H. Hodgkin, *Six Centuries of an Oxford College* (Oxford: Blackwell, 1949), pp. 80-81.

and compare notes. Some of his friends, seeing his emaciation from illness, begged him not to throw away his life for the cause of even so great a project as the translation of the Bible; but he greeted their well-meant concern for him with only wise words and a smile. He died at the age of fifty-eight, while the work was still in progress.

Holland became a Fellow of Balliol College, Oxford, in 1573. Appointed Regius Professor of Hebrew in the University of Oxford in 1589, he became Rector of Exeter College in 1592. He died in 1612, soon after the completion of the work.

Kilbye became Rector of Lincoln College in 1590, Prebendary of Lincoln Cathedral in 1601, and Regius Professor of Hebrew in the University of Oxford in 1610. He was a friend of the famed Isaac Walton, who relates an anecdote about him. A young Derbyshire preacher had treated his long-suffering congregation of simple country folk to a sermon that consisted chiefly of criticism of the new translation. Hoping, no doubt, to impress his people with his own learning, the young clergyman gave them three reasons why a certain word should have been otherwise translated. Kilbye sent for the youthful preacher afterwards and, telling him he might have fed his flock with more profitable nourishment, remarked that the three reasons he had mentioned had not gone unnoticed by the translators. On the contrary, they had well considered every one of them, but had in the long run reached the conclusion that they did not outweigh thirteen reasons to the contrary which led them to translate the word as they did. Kilbye died in 1620.

To Miles Smith is attributed the Translators' Preface.[2] To him also, along with Bishop Bilson (not one of the panel), was entrusted the final revision of the whole work. Associated at Oxford with Corpus Christi and Brasenose Colleges, he was a Canon of Exeter Cathedral from 1595 till 1599, and Bishop of Gloucester from 1612 till his death in 1624. Known for his Puritan views, he enjoyed a reputation for his knowledge of Semitic tongues. His sermons also attest this.

Richard Brett, who enjoyed very great repute among his contemporaries as a Hebrew, Aramaic, and Arabic scholar, became a Fellow of Lincoln College, Oxford, in 1586, and Rector of Quainton, Buckinghamshire, in 1595. He died in 1637.

The identity of Fairclough is obscure. It seems likely, however, that he is to be identified with a man of this name who migrated in 1581 from New College, Oxford, to Cambridge, and became Rector of Bucknell, Oxfordshire, in 1592.

The President of the Second Oxford Company, Thomas Ravis, was noted for his antipathy to the Puritans. Dean of Christ Church, Oxford,

---

[2] For the complete text, see the appendix to chapter 24, pp. 220-42.

from 1596 till his consecration as Bishop of Gloucester in 1605, he succeeded Bancroft in 1607 as Bishop of London, when the latter became Archbishop of Canterbury. His policy in the See of London closely followed Bancroft's. He swore to oust those whose Puritan leanings made them reluctant to conform. "By the help of Jesus," he declared, "I will not leave one preacher in my diocese who doth not subscribe and conform." This attitude was not as unimaginatively intransigent as it may sound to modern ears. Ravis felt, as did many others in the English Church, that the strength of the Reformation in England depended upon unity of practice as well as unity of principle. He saw the Puritans as threatening that unity. No doubt many Anglicans today would applaud his attitude, seeing in the celebrated comprehensiveness claimed for the modern Anglican Communion a source of weakness and danger as well as virtue and strength.

He died in December, 1609, before the work of translation was finished, and is buried in St. Paul's Cathedral.

Abbot (1562-1633) is an unusually interesting figure. Born in Guildford, Surrey, the son of a cloth worker, he was educated at Balliol and became Master of University College, Oxford, in 1597, serving as Vice-Chancellor of the university in 1600, 1603, and 1605. His marked Puritan sympathies brought him more and more into conflict with men of the opposite party such as William Laud. On the other hand, he defended, in 1606, political views more congenial to James than had been those of Overall, and in James's eyes this may have gone far to compensate for his Puritan opinions. In 1608 he undertook a mission to Scotland in hope of making episcopal government acceptable to the Scots.

Contrary to the belief of those who imagine Scotland to have been Presbyterian from Reformation times, the Scots had never opposed episcopacy in principle. John Knox and his associates, in planning the government of the Reformed Kirk, had expressly provided for a body of superintendents with episcopal functions. The word "superintendent" was not, of course, original with the Scottish Reformers. They intended, in using it, to convey the pastoral character of the episcopal function, rather than its *dominium*, which Wyclif had attacked in the fourteenth century. John Poynet, Bishop of Winchester, wrote: "Who knoweth not that the name *bishop* hath been so abused, that when it was spoken the people understood nothing else but a great lord, that went in a white rochet with a wide shaven crown. . . . Now to bring people from this abuse, what better means can be devised than to teach the people their error by another word out of Scripture of the same significance." The word Poynet proposed was "superintendent," which has roots in the writings of St. Augustine and St. Thomas Aquinas as well as in the practice of the church of Scotland after the Reformation. In the seventeenth century, bishops actually functioned in the Scottish Church along with presbyteries. Bishops operate elsewhere today within the presbyterian system, and their absence from the Church of Scotland has been dictated by unfortunate political circumstances rather than any fundamental objection on the part of historically minded Scottish Presbyterians. In the seventeenth century the Scottish clergy had received their ordination sometimes from bishops, sometimes from presbyteries. John Menzeis, in *Roma Mendax,* published in 1675, expressed the opinion that presbyterian orders were valid even where they had been derived from Rome.

At any rate, Abbot was fairly successful in his mission to the Scots. The way seemed open to the fulfilment of one of James's greatest desires, the union of the Church of England and the Church of Scotland. Not without reason, however, were the Scots suspicious of James, and resented even more the seeming interference in Scottish Church affairs of William Laud, who became Archbishop of Canterbury in 1633 under James's successor, Charles I.

From 1608 onwards, preferments came in swift succession to Abbot, culminating in his advancement in 1611 to the archiepiscopal See of Canterbury. In this office he proved fearless in expressing his Puritan sympathies, and because such views were becoming less and less fashionable among the upper classes in England, he found himself increasingly isolated. His fidelity to his principles, however, even to the point of opposing James himself, won him almost universal respect.

At the age of sixty a mishap befell him, the circumstances attending which vividly reflect the spirit of his times. One day, while out hunting, he aimed an arrow at a deer. The arrow glanced from a tree and killed a gamekeeper. The latter's death was of course entirely accidental, and morally no blame could be attached to Abbot, since the gamekeeper had been warned to keep out of the way. Abbot nevertheless took the occurrence so much to heart that he never forgave himself. Besides bestowing a liberal annuity on the gamekeeper's widow, he entered upon a self-imposed fast once every month for the rest of his life. According to Canon Law, moreover, he became technically a "man of blood" and therefore disqualified from the service of the Church. Suspended for a time, he was arraigned before a commission of six bishops, including Lancelot Andrewes, and four laymen. Opinion on the verdict was equally divided. James, however, decided in Abbot's favor, so dispensing him from the technical irregularity. Even this token of royal favor did not make Abbot less firm in resisting royal edicts that he disapproved. As unsparing to others as he was to himself, he was disliked by some of the clergy who resented his severity; yet he was said to have had a "very fatherly presence." It was he who, on James's death, crowned Charles I in 1625. He had much sentimental affection for his birthplace, and at his death in 1633 was taken thither for burial.

Richard Edes, who became Dean of Worcester in 1597, died in 1604 so that he could not have taken any significant part in the work. Some think he was replaced by his successor in that office, James Montague, while the name of John Aglionby, Principal of St. Edmund Hall, Oxford, who died in 1610, has also been mentioned in this connection. Giles Thompson, of University College, Oxford, became a Fellow of All Souls in 1580, Dean of Windsor in 1602, and Bishop of Gloucester in 1611, the year before his death. He was also Registrar of England's highest and most ancient order of chivalry, the Most Noble Order of the Garter. His work on the translation of the Bible is said to have been very diligent.

Sir Henry Savile (1549-1622) of Brasenose College, Oxford, became in 1565 a Fellow and, in 1585, Warden of Merton. He enjoyed a wide repute as a Greek scholar who was also a mathematician and historian. He travelled in Europe, collecting many valuable manuscripts and books which he later donated to the Bodleian Library. His services to Oxford also include the foundation of chairs in astronomy and geometry. On his return from Europe he was appointed Greek tutor to Queen Elizabeth I. It was rare in those days for women, even princesses, to have education of this kind. Savile's own wife had none of it. When he was engaged upon one of his most cherished and celebrated projects, a most scholarly edition of the works of St. Chrysostom in eight folio volumes, she expressed a little feminine jealousy at the enormous devotion he was lavishing upon his work.

"I wish I were a book," she said. "Then you would a little more respect me."

Distressed by an illness that overtook him, the cause of which she took to be overwork, she threatened to burn his Chrysostom.

"So to do were great pity," suggested a tactful scholar-friend of her husband.

"Why?" she asked. "Who was Chrysostom?"

"One of the sweetest preachers since the time of the Apostles," explained her husband's friend.

"Then I would not burn him," was the lady's generous reply.

When the magnificent edition was eventually issued from Sir Henry's private press at Eton, in type imported from Holland and at his own personal expense of about eight thousand pounds, it was, apart from the Bible, the most important grand-scale work ever published in England, and so scholarly that it is still even at the present day of some value in determining the true text of St. Chrysostom. It was very expensive. At a time when an English pound could have bought you six carcasses of mutton, it cost nine pounds. The death of his son at the time he was engaged upon the translation of the Bible had deeply grieved him, and it was this bereavement that stimulated his resolve to devote himself and his fortune more than ever to the cause of learning. He was knighted by James. One wonders whether Lady Savile ever really forgave the Christian Father she had taken to be her rival.

Peryn became a Fellow of St. John's College, Oxford, in 1575, and was from 1595 till his death in 1615 Regius Professor of Greek in the university, being also, from 1604, a Canon of Christ Church. There is some doubt about including in the list the name of Ralph Ravens, a Fellow of St. John's College, Oxford, and, from 1605, Rector of Great Easton, Essex, till his death in 1616. Some put in his stead the name of Leonard Hutton, Canon of Christ Church. Harmar, Fellow of New College, Oxford, was Regius Professor of Greek in the university from 1585 till 1590, Headmaster of Winchester from 1588 till 1595, and Warden of Winchester from 1596 till his death in 1613.

The Second Westminster Company was under the presidency of William Barlow, a member of the Hampton Court Conference and its historian. Having become a Fellow of Trinity Hall, Cambridge, in 1590, he was Dean of Chester from 1602 till 1605 and Bishop of Lincoln from 1608 till his death in 1613. Elizabeth is said to have admired him, remarking of one of his sermons that though his text was "taken from the cart," his talk was good instruction for her court.

Hutchinson, a Londoner by birth, became Archdeacon of St. Albans in 1581 and Prebendary of St. Paul's Cathedral in 1589. Spencer, one of James's chaplains, was President of Corpus Christi College, Oxford, till his death in 1614. Fenton, a Lancashire man, was one of the most popular preachers of the day. He became Fellow of Pembroke Hall, Cambridge, and, in 1609, Prebendary of St. Paul's Cathedral, London. He died in 1616. One of his admirers, in grieving at his death, refers to the "natural majesty of his style, like a master bee without a sting." Rabbett and Sanderson are more obscure figures. Rabbett is believed to be of Trinity College, Cambridge, and to have died in 1630, and Sanderson to have been a Fellow of Balliol College, Oxford, and, from 1606 till 1614, Archdeacon of Rochester, becoming a Canon of St. Paul's Cathedral in 1611. Dakins became a Fellow of Trinity College, Cambridge, in 1594. He died in 1607.

The Second Cambridge Company, charged with the translation of the Apocrypha, had as its president John Duport. Duport's family had come to Leicestershire from Caen, Normandy. In 1580 he became a Fellow, and in 1590, Master of Jesus College, Cambridge. Serving four times as Vice-Chancellor of the University, he became Prebendary of Ely in 1609. He died in 1617. Branthwaite became a Fellow of Emmanuel College,

Cambridge, and, in 1607, Master of Gonville and Caius College. He died in 1620. Radcliffe was a Fellow of Trinity College, Cambridge. Samuel Ward, associated with Christ's and Emmanuel Colleges, became in 1610 Master of Sidney Sussex College, Cambridge, which acquired a reputation as a breeding ground of Puritanism. Oliver Cromwell was an undergraduate there. Ward, who was one of the English representatives at the Synod of Dort, died in 1643. His namesake on the panel, William Ward, was a Fellow of King's College, Cambridge. Downes, who in 1571 became a Fellow of St. John's College, Cambridge, was Regius Professor of Greek in the university from 1585 till his death in 1628. He was another of Casaubon's friends. They corresponded in Greek.

John Bois, the last remaining member of the panel to be considered, was born at Nettlestead, Suffolk, in 1560. He is said to have been an extremely gifted child. The legends of his precocity, which relate that he could not only read the Hebrew Bible at the age of six but write the Hebrew alphabet with elegance, are matched by others concerning his extraordinary industry as an undergraduate later on. He is said to have worked from four o'clock in the morning till eight at night.

At the time of his election in 1580 as a Fellow of St. John's College, Bois had smallpox, and it is reported that he had to be carried thither in a blanket. It is also reported that about this time he thought of a medical career. The modern reader, learning of these arrangements for the transportation of a smallpox victim to college, may be inclined to feel that there was certainly no lack of need for the pursuit of medical studies. Medicine was indeed still relatively backward at that time. The physician lacked prestige in comparison with other learned professions; but he was soon to acquire much greater dignity. It must be remembered that at the time the translators worked on the King James Version even so elementary a medical fact as the circulation of the blood had not been established, though it was about to be the subject of William Harvey's celebrated treatise, published in 1628. At any rate, Bois decided against a medical career, and one of his reasons, that reading about diseases tends to induce hypochondria, is one that can command our sympathy. No doubt there were other more important reasons, however, and in any case he was probably better suited for the pursuit of those studies that led to his appointment as one of the King James translators.

When the work of the Second Cambridge company on the Apocrypha was finished, Bois joined the First Cambridge Company at their request. He and Andrew Downes also represented the Second Cambridge Company as delegates to the committee that met for nine months at Stationers Hall to conduct the final revision. Bois certainly did not shorten his life by industry. He lived to be eighty-three.

The English Bible—a book which if
everything else in our language should perish,
would alone suffice to show the whole extent of
its beauty and power.—Macaulay

CHAPTER 23 *The King James Version*

The labors of the translators of the King James Version resulted in a handsome volume in folio, printed in fine black letter. Published in 1611 and issued from the press of Robert Barker, it contained 1,500 pages and had a thickness of over three inches, excluding the binding. The type was set in double columns. Each page was enclosed in rules measuring 9 inches wide by 14½ inches long. Pages of the well-preserved copies prized by book collectors measure 10½ by 16½ inches.

The title of the first issue of the King James Bible reads as follows:

> The/Holy/Bible,/Conteyning the Old Testament,/and the New:/ Newly Translated out of the Originall/tongues, & with the former Translations/diligently compared and reuised, by his/Maiesties speciall cōmandement. *Appointed to be read in Churches.*/Imprinted at London by Robert/Barker, Printer to the Kings/most Excellent Maiestie./ Anno Dom. 1611.

Black letter is used for the text; but the chapter heads, the marginal references, and all words supplied by the translators in the text are in Roman type. Italic type is used for alternative readings.

This title is the center of an engraving showing the figures of Moses and Aaron, the former at the right, the latter at the left. The Four Evangelists fill the corners. At the top is the tetragrammaton, the name of God in Hebrew, below which appears the Sacred Dove, symbol of the Holy Spirit, and again below this is the Lamb, symbol of Christ. At the foot of a page is a traditional symbol of the redeeming work of Christ, especially in the Eucharist—a pelican "vulning" herself, that is, wounding herself with her beak to feed her young with her own blood. The artist's signature is: "C. Boel fecit in Richmont."

The New Testament title reads:

> The/Newe/Testament of/our Lord and Sauior Iesvs Christ./⁋ Newly Translated out of/the Originall Greeke: and with/the former Translations diligently/compared and reuised by his/Maiesties speciall Com/ mandement./Imprinted/at London by *Robert/Barker,*/Printer to the/ Kings most Excellent/Maiestie./Anno. Dom. 1611./cum Privilegio.

This title has a woodcut border representing along one side the badges of the Twelve Tribes of Israel and along the other the Twelve Apostles. The Four Evangelists appear again, represented by the traditional emblems, a man, a lion, an ox, and an eagle, for Matthew, Mark, Luke, and John respectively.

The version so produced under King James came to be known as the Authorized Version, and it is so designated in Britain to this day. The designation is misleading. The work was, as we have seen, initiated and planned by the highest authorities in Church and State. The intention, amply fulfilled, was that it should command, by reason of its intrinsic merit, universal acceptance throughout the land. The book therefore went forth with the fullest approval of the highest authorities. In this sense the version was certainly authorized for use in public worship and was described, indeed, as "Appointed to be read in Churches." No legal instrument, however, at any time conferred any legal authority upon it. There was no Act of Parliament, no Royal Proclamation, no Privy Council decision or decree. It made its own way, as had been intended, on its own merit. This universal acceptance eventually gave it greater authority than it could have acquired through any such formality. The authority it was to enjoy was greater than officialdom could have bestowed upon it. It sprang from the hearts of the people. It was authorized by popular acclamation. In the 1662 edition of the English Book of Common Prayer it was adopted as the text for the liturgical Epistles and Gospels, though the older version of the Psalter was retained and has been retained to this day.

The language and style of the King James Version were becoming just a little archaic even by the time it was published. The rules imposed upon the translators made this inevitable. One of the secrets of the beauty and enduring power of this version lay in the fact that it was neither couched in antiquated language nor yet dressed up in current linguistic novelties or colloquialisms. It was not in the latest, the most fashionable, or up-to-date kind of English that could be contrived. On the contrary, the translators, however they might interpret their rules, could not divest their work, even had they so wished, of the slightly archaic dignity that was transmitted to it by their following the older version. Even in its great modern American successor published in 1952 for public use, the Revised Standard Version, which is a thoroughgoing revision of the King James Bible in terms of modern scholarship, much of that traditional dignity is retained despite the clarification of the now more unintelligible archaisms. Modern versions such as the New English Bible, being intended for private reading and having therefore another function, are naturally in a different case.

This slight archaism in the language of the King James Bible was one of its greatest charms. The style was sufficiently modern to be plainly understood at the time, yet just old-fashioned enough to carry with it the dignity of the recent past. For this and many other reasons the King James Bible had both the appeal of a new version and the authority of the older version of which it was technically a revision.

The translators were, apart from the unfortunate exclusion of Hugh Broughton, to whom we must presently return, representative of the best Hebrew as well as of the best Greek scholarship of the day. Their knowledge of Hebrew that the King James Version reveals is accounted by modern Hebraists very remarkable indeed, considering the comparatively undeveloped state of Hebrew learning at that time. The materials available to the translators were considerable. The catalogue of Hebrew and related items assembled by Thomas James, Bodley's librarian, the year the King James Version was begun, illustrates this. It includes Aramaic materials as well as Hebrew dictionaries and grammars. There are also complete Talmudic texts and copies of Targums in the original as well as in Latin translation, besides the texts of the Targums in the various polyglot Bibles in the collection and a considerable number of commentaries on the Hebrew Bible. Though the great fourth-century Greek manuscripts of the Bible were not at that time available, the translators had access to the best materials of the day for the Septuagint and New Testament, and knew how to use them. Their work was in every way, therefore, well deserving of the acclamation it received.

Let no one suppose, however, that the King James Version received universal acclamation at once. True, it had no difficulty in superseding the Bishops' Bible of which it was a revision. There was, indeed, no issue of that Bible after 1606, apart from about half a dozen reprintings of the New Testament. The Geneva Bible was much less easily vanquished; yet vanquished it gradually was. Between 1611 and 1614, the King James went into seventeen editions, against six of the Geneva Bible. Between 1611 and 1644, there were 182 editions of the King James Bible to fifteen of the Geneva. Nevertheless, it continued to face competition from the Geneva Version, whose popularity was especially great among the English Puritans, and after the Geneva Bible ceased to be printed in England, many copies of this sturdy competitor of the King James Version were imported from Holland for use in English households.

The King James Bible did not merely face competition, however. It met vehement opposition, including attacks by prominent scholars of the time. Indeed it was bitterly attacked before it saw the light of day. One consultant to whom a copy had been sent before publication, with a request for his opinion, declared it to be "so ill done" that it would grieve him as long as he lived. "Tell His Majesty," he wrote, "that I had rather be rent in pieces with wild horses, than any such translation by my consent should be urged upon poor parishes."

The author of this curiously unrestrained attack upon the work of the King James translators was Hugh Broughton. Since he was one of the best scholars in England, his opinion cannot be ignored. Learning does not infallibly bestow impeccable judgement, however, and in estimating the value of his opinion one must bear in mind that Broughton had been trying to obtain support for a translation of the Bible he desired to undertake himself. He had explained his plans in a letter to Lord Burleigh, dated June 21, 1593. In 1597 he had further delineated his views on the subject. He even published some samples of the translation he sought to undertake. No one doubted his learning; but his attacks on the Bishops' Bible, thoughly largely justified, were too vehement, outspoken, and unrestrained. He is said to have been very sweet-tempered and lovable to his friends; but in controversy he was so waspish that instead of winning over his opponents he succeeded only in infuriating them. One of his contemporaries, Thomas Morton, who became Bishop of Durham, is said to have once greeted him with the request that the conversation *begin* with all the insulting epithets Broughton had in mind to bestow upon him, so that the conversation itself might then proceed without such frequent interruption by Broughton's cries of "dolt" and "dullard." Apparently Broughton took this in good part as a joke and continued to be as bellicose as ever.

His proposals were by no means unpractical. He had an excellent plan, which included the appointment of five associates to work with him. He ought certainly to have been included in James's panel of translators, and probably he would never have been excluded from it but for the violence of his disposition. In view of all this, his outburst when the finished work was presented to him is only what must have been expected. He counted the "idle" words in various passages for which, he said, the translators would have to render account on the Day of Judgement. It need hardly be said that the destination he prognosticated for His Grace the Lord Archbishop of Canterbury was hell.

No doubt Broughton, despite his insufferable conduct and his obvious prejudice against the work of the panel from which he had been excluded was by no means entirely unjustified in his criticisms. More than a generation after the publication of the new version, Dr. John Lightfoot, in a sermon preached on August 26, 1645, before the Long Parliament, argued for the necessity of a "review and survey of the translation of the Bible," so that the people "might come to understand the proper and genuine reading of the Scriptures by an exact, vigorous, and lively translation." Nothing much was done, however. A bill was drafted and proposed to be brought before Parliament in 1653. This bill would have authorized the appointment of a committee to examine the faults of the version that by that time had won such general acclaim. The bill was suspect, however, since it betrayed partisan interests, and so for this and probably other reasons, no action was ever taken.

This is not to say that a copy of the first edition of the King James Version reads exactly like a modern one. Not only were spelling and punctuation gradually modernized according to the orthographic principles developed through the scholarly tastes accompanying the later development of the language itself; there was also a gradual and thoroughgoing correction of a vast number of printers' errors that had crept into various editions. As we are about to see, the first edition itself contained many. As editions multiplied, so also did the list of errors. This was aggravated during the Civil War in England, during which period scholarly standards declined. Editions printed in Holland at this time were so full of printers' errors that in 1643 the Westminster Assembly of Divines was already complaining, in a report to Parliament, of the incorrectness of these foreign editions of the King James Bible. They gave three instances: at Genesis 36:24, instead of the correct text "found the mules" was an incorrect one reading "found her rulers"; at Ruth 4:13, instead of "the Lord gave her conception" appeared "the Lord gave her corruption"; and at Luke 21:28, for "your redemption" was found "your condemnation." In 1659 a tract was printed at Finsbury by William Kilburne entitled "Dangerous Errors in Severall Late Printed Bibles: to the great scandal and corruption of sound and true religion." The author claimed to have discovered many thousands of "pernicious erroneous and corrupt Erratas Escapes and Faults in several impressions of the Holy Bible and Testament within these late years commonly vended and dispersed," and pointed in particular to the Bibles printed by Henry Hills and John Field, printers to the University of Cambridge.

Since for one reason or another the authorities seemed unable to take any useful action in such matters, private individuals addressed themselves to the task. Various forms of biblical paraphrase appeared; eventually, new private translations were undertaken, which we shall consider in later chapters; and finally came the great revisions that belong to the modern period of our story.

Two separate kinds of defect must be distinguished in considering the shortcomings of the King James Version as it was transmitted in the seventeenth century. On the one hand, there was the multiplication of errors, aggravated by adverse circumstances but principally due to the carelessness of printers. On the other hand, there were the blemishes charged against the translation itself. While Broughton had probably much exaggerated these, there is no doubt that the work of the translators, for all its many virtues, was not by any means faultless.

There was also, however, a third kind of shortcoming in the King James Version that cannot be laid at the door either of the printers or of the translators. The latter cannot be held accountable for not using materials they did not possess.

Not only have the advances in biblical scholarship in the past fifty years made the work of translators and commentators at the end of the nineteenth century as out-of-date as a nineteenth-century scientist's account of the universe; even about the time the King James translators were at work at the beginning of the seventeenth century, discoveries were being made that were to render the King James Bible textually out-of-date a few years after it had appeared in 1611. Sixteen years after the publication of the first edition, a manuscript was to reach England that would have been of immense help to the King James translators, had it been available to them in time. The romantic story of the adventures of this manuscript, the Codex Alexandrinus, and of the discovery of other texts that have since revolutionized the biblical translator's work is better relegated to a later part of our study, where it can be told in greater detail than can be done here without excessive interruption of the sequence of the story of the King James Bible that is our present concern.

The gradual alteration of the King James Version, not only in respect of the numerous errors that crept in, but also of the text itself, might suggest that a copy of the first edition would be very different indeed from any modern edition of this version that one would purchase today in a bookstore. From certain points of view this is indeed the case; yet it would be easy to exaggerate the difference. Generally speaking, a copy of the 1611 edition reads, apart from the seventeenth-century spelling, very much as does a modern one, as the following example will illustrate. The text reproduced is that of the twenty-third psalm as it appeared in the edition of 1611:

The Lord *is* my shepheard, I shall not want.
2. He maketh me to lie downe in greene pastures: he leadeth mee beside the still waters.
3. He restoreth my soule: he leadeth me in the pathes of righteousness, for his names sake.
4. Yea, though I walke through the valley of the shadowe of death, I will fear no euill: for thou *art* with me, thy rod and thy staffe, they comfort me.
5. Thou preparest a table before me, in the presence of mine enemies: thou anointest my head with oyle, my cuppe runneth ouer.
6. Surely goodnes and mercie shall followe me all the daies of my life: and I will dwell in the house of the LORD for euer.

We shall have an opportunity later of considering examples of texts that read differently from those to which we are now accustomed in

210

modern editions of the King James Bible. First of all, however, we must attend to the fact that from the considerable incidence of printers' errors in the first edition were bred a host of others, apart from further errors that were independently introduced as editions multiplied.

Two issues of the first edition of the King James Bible, published in 1611, are called respectively "The He Bible" and "The She Bible." These designations refer to the most notable difference in their texts. In the He Bible, the verse Ruth 3:15, is correctly rendered: "Also he said, Bring the vaile that thou hast vpon thee, and holde it. And when she helde it, he measured sixe *measures* of barley, and laide it on her; and he went into the citie." The She Bible incorrectly reads, instead, "and she went into the citie." The two issues are also distinguished, however, by two separate sets of errors. A "pure" He Bible contains certain errata which include the following:

Genesis 10:16: Emorite *(for* Amorite)
Exodus 38:10: hoopes *(for* hooks)
Leviticus 13:56: the plaine be *(for* the plague be)
Leviticus 17:14: ye shall not eat *(for* ye shall eat)
I Esdras 4: Anocrynha *(for* Apocrypha)
Matthew 16:25: his his *(for* his)

A "pure" She Bible may be distinguished from a "pure" He Bible by the presence of certain errata which include the following:

Dedication, line 8: Chkist *(for* Christ)
Exodus 9:13: that they may serue thee *(for* that they may serue me)
Matthew 26:36: Judas *(for* Jesus)

Sheets from the two issues were often arbitrarily mixed together. It seems there was also another issue, the date of which is uncertain but probably 1613. Moreover, the sheets of the later folio editions of 1617, 1634, and 1640 were set up in such a way as to be interchangeable with each other and with the issues of the first edition, so that the technical problems of collation may sometimes exasperate the most patient and baffle the most diligent of bibliographers.

Before going on to consider, in the next chapter, some details about the more interesting and important editions of the King James Bible, it is convenient to notice the use of a device employed in the King James Version at the outset and familiar to us in modern editions. The purpose of the device was to enable the reader to distinguish between English words that actually translated words in the original Hebrew or Greek and words that were necessarily added only to make sense in English. In black-letter editions, the latter words were printed in "Roman small" type. Where the text of the Bible itself was printed in Roman type, another means had to be found for indicating the words that were added only to make good English sense. Italics were used for this purpose. For example, in the psalm set forth above, the word *"is"* in the first verse is italicized, because it has no counterpart in Hebrew but is needed to make an intelligible English sentence. This practice of italicizing such words has been perpetuated. It is a pity that not all readers of the King James Version understand its significance.

CHAPTER 24 *Corrections and Curiosities in the King James Editions*

Apart from the first issues of the King James Bible in folio, there was a duodecimo edition, followed by a quarto edition, of the New Testament, and there were quarto and octavo editions of the whole Bible in Roman type. As the new version quickly gained favor, editions followed in rapid succession. One is said to contain more than three hundred textual variations from the original issues of the first edition.

To correct these errors, a revised edition was prepared and came out in 1629, followed by another in 1638. The latter is the first Cambridge edition in folio. Generally speaking, this revision, which we are told was ordered by Charles I, was very well done. It was the work of a group of Cambridge scholars. They did, nevertheless, introduce a few new errors.

Among these was one of great theological importance to the Church —so much so that some people (probably without even the slightest foundation) alleged that Oliver Cromwell had bribed the printers a thousand pounds to introduce it! At Acts 6:3, where we read of the candidates for the ministry appointed to assist the apostles in the work of the Church ("seven men of honest report full of the Holy Ghost and wisdom"), the correct text makes the apostles say, "whom we may appoint over this business." The 1638 Cambridge text altered this to read, "whom ye may appoint over this business." This error, which falsely gives the appearance of biblical support here for the appointment of ministers by the people, represented a notion congenial to Oliver Cromwell's party, but abhorrent to Anglicans and Scottish Presbyterians alike.

Between 1611 and the end of the eighteenth century, nearly a thousand editions of the King James Bible were published, and some of the errors introduced have made certain editions bibliographical curiosities. Notable is the one nicknamed the Wicked Bible, published in 1631. This edition, by omitting the word "not" at Exodus 20:14, made the Bible say, "Thou shalt commit adultery." For this lively but textually unwarranted revision, the printers were fined three hundred pounds. Similarly, the unrighteous Bible, published in 1653, derives its nickname from its rendering, at I Corinthians 6:9: "the unrighteous shall inherit the kingdom of God." Cotton Mather in 1702 complained of the "Scandalous

213

Errors of the Presswork" through which "The Holy Bible itself . . . hath been affronted," and referred to an edition of the Bible, not identified, which for the text at psalm 119:161, "Princes have persecuted me," gave artistic expression to the truth of his complaint by putting "Printers have persecuted me."

Printing of the Bible at the University of Oxford did not begin till 1675. In that year was issued a quarto edition of the King James Bible with the words "At the theater in Oxon" on the base of a broken column depicted on the title page, which shows a representation of the Transfiguration of Christ, being also adorned by two female figures, one veiled and representing the Law, the other with a nimbus and representing the Gospel.

In this edition the spelling was revised by John Fell, Dean of Christ Church, Oxford, who is celebrated in the impromptu riposte of Thomas Brown (1663-1704). The Dean, having threatened the latter with expulsion from the House, promised to pardon him if he could translate at sight Martial's epigram,

> Non amo te, Sabidi, nec possum dicere quare;
> Hoc tantum possum dicere, non amo te.

Whereupon Thomas Brown offered the following very free translation:

> I do not love thee, Dr. Fell;
> The reason why I cannot tell;
> But this I know and know full well;
> I do not love thee, Dr. Fell.

Errors continued to appear. An Oxford edition of 1717 had as the heading of the twentieth chapter of Luke, which treats of the parable of the vineyard, "The Parable of the Vinegar." Known accordingly to bibliophiles as the Vinegar Bible, it was sumptuously produced, printed in large type and copiously illustrated with steel engravings. At least three copies were on vellum. Its looks were, however, the best of it. Printed by J. Baskett, it was so full of misprints that it was dubbed a "basketful of [printer's] errors."

The Bible edited by Thomas Paris of Trinity College, Cambridge, and printed for the University of Cambridge by Joseph Bentham in 1762 exhibited such diligent correction of the text, emendation and regularization of the spelling and punctuation, and elimination of printers' errors, that it came to be known as the Standard Edition. It is of great importance historically, since it provided what may be accounted the basis of modern editions of the King James Version. The language was modernized and the use of italics extended. It was published in folio and quarto. Most of the folio copies are said to have been destroyed in a bookseller's fire at Cambridge, so that they are very rare. The British Museum and the Library of Corpus Christi College, Cambridge, are among the few libraries that possess one.

The process of modernization was carried further in an edition published in 1769 at Oxford, also in folio and in quarto. This edition was prepared by Benjamin Blayney, Regius Professor of Hebrew in the University of Oxford. The volumes were larger and more handsome than the Cambridge Bible of 1762, and the text came to be known as "The Oxford Standard." It is the standard text used in the setting up of modern editions of the King James Version. The chapter headings provided in this Oxford edition of 1769 were prepared, Blayney tells us, "with a prodigious expense of time, and inexpressible fatigue," being elaborately conceived according to eighteenth-century taste. It became customary, therefore, in later editions to revert to the shorter chapter headings used in the first edition of 1611, which, with appropriate modernization of spelling, are used in modern editions.

Even all this did not wholly eliminate errors from future editions of the King James Bible. These persisted in editions published as late as the nineteenth century. In 1804 came an edition known as the Murderer's Bible. At Numbers 35:18, for "the murderer shall surely be put to death," it read "the murderer shall surely be put together." There is also an octavo of 1801 in which, at Jude 16, "murmurers" reads "murderers." An early American edition published by Jesper Harding at Philadelphia is known as the Dagger Bible because the printers had put, instead of the symbol †, the word "dagger" by which the symbol is known, so making the text read, at I Kings 1:21, "The king shall dagger sleep". A similar error found its way into a Cambridge Bible of 1805. The proofreader's marginal instruction "to remain" was incorporated in the text, so that Galatians 4:29 was made to read "him that was born after the Spirit to remain." This error was repeated in later editions published in 1806 and 1819 respectively. In an 1806 edition, for "the fishers shall stand upon it," at Ezekiel 47:10, was printed "the fishes shall stand upon it." This error was likewise repeated twice, in 1813 and in 1823. Perhaps the Cockney pronunciation of the printer is reflected in the mistake occurring in an Oxford edition of 1807, at Matthew 13:43, where there is an injunction to him who has "ears to ear." The same edition, at Hebrews 9:14, has "good works" for "dead works." An Oxford edition of 1810, at Luke 14:26, enjoined the aspirant to discipleship to hate "his own wife," so winning the designation, the Wife Hater's Bible. The Rebekah Bible is one printed at London in 1823, in which it is written that Rebekah arose with her "camels," not her "damsels."

Generally speaking, however, errors were gradually eliminated. The standard of accuracy achieved in the later decades of the eighteenth century represented an immense improvement over the faulty seventeenth-century editions. Moreover, before the time of the Oxford Standard, opportunity had already been taken of quietly introducing some other changes apart from the correction of printers' errors. Some of these were indeed the improvements they were intended to be.

For example, we may note the following from the Gospels alone. The reading of the first edition at Matthew 16:16 was "Thou art Christ." From 1762 this became "Thou art the Christ." From the same date "the words of Jesus," at Matthew 26:75, changed to "the word of Jesus." From 1743 the words "for press" at Mark 2:4 were changed to "for the press." The phrase at Mark 5:6, "he came and worshipped," was transformed in 1638 to "he ran and worshipped," and from this date, too, *"there is* no man good but one" became *"there is* none good but one." "Understanding of things" at Luke 1:3 became, from 1629, "understanding of all things." The familiar Gospel utterance at John 15:20, which in the 1611 edition had been rendered "the servant is not greater than the Lord," was altered in 1762 to read, as it now does, "the servant is not greater than his lord."

Among editions that are for other reasons interesting to bibliophiles may be mentioned a Bible produced at Aberdeen in 1670. This was a diminutive curiosity. Known as the Thumb Bible, it measured one inch square, and its thickness was half an inch. The use of India paper has given us more readable miniatures. A modern Oxford edition printed on such paper and in beryl type provides, for the pocket of all enjoying fairly good eyesight, the whole New Testament within the compass of a book measuring no more than a 3″ by 5″ index card and one eighth of an inch thick, including morocco binding.

The introduction of various apparatus has not always been attended by the happiest results. An edition superintended by Bishop Lloyd at Oxford, published in 1701, included in the margin the ingenious but very mistaken computation of the chronology of the Bible according to the reckoning of James Ussher (1581-1656), Archbishop of Armagh, Ireland. Ussher was not only a learned man in his day but also a man widely and deservedly respected both for his sincerity and for his tolerance. A Calvinist himself, he was on terms of friendship with many who differed from him both in his own Church, such as Archbishop Laud, and among the English Dissenters, and he labored for the reconciliation of ecclesiastical differences. After the Irish rebellion of 1641, he remained in England. On his death, Oliver Cromwell recognized his merits by giving him a state funeral in Westminster Abbey.

It is regrettable that such a great man should be so commonly known nowadays less for his noble character, vast erudition, and splendid efforts for reconciliation among conflicting parties than for the misconceived system of biblical chronology that is given in his *Annales Veteris et Novi Testamenti*, published in 1650-1654. His attempt to compute the chronology of the Bible seemed a reasonable enterprise in its day, however absurd it has since come to appear in terms of modern knowledge. Upon Ussher's calculations were based the marginal notes on chronology placed in Lloyd's edition of the Bible in 1701 and widely reproduced in other editions for long afterwards.[1] They included the year 4004 B.C. as the date alleged for the creation of the world. Those who smile at this would do well to bear in mind that in Ussher's day such a view was no less excusable and no more ridiculous than were the views about the universe held by eminent scientists fifty years ago that now already appear ludicrously antiquated to modern schoolchildren.

The first edition of the King James Bible published in Scotland was one in octavo printed at Edinburgh in 1633. The first to be printed in Ireland appeared in 1714. It is believed that an edition published in 1752 and bearing the imprint of Mark Baskett, London, was in fact printed surreptitiously in America. At any rate, the first edition of the Bible openly published in the United States appeared in 1782, six years after the Declaration of Independence. It was printed with an endorsement from Congress by Robert Aitken, an enterprising Scottish printer who had come to Philadelphia in 1769. Encouraged by Congressional discussion of the subject, he had already brought out four editions of the New Testament, in 1777, 1778, 1779, and 1781, respectively.

The edition of the King James Bible published by Aitken in 1782 was generally in two volumes, though a few copies were issued in a single one. Copies are now very rare. Only about thirty are known to survive. He sought to obtain exclusive right of publication of the Bible; but Congress, while encouraging the project, did not grant him this. Though the Presbyterian Synod of 1783 recommended the Bible he produced, he labored under great difficulties and lost money on the enterprise.

Other printers took up the work, including Isaiah Thomas, who provided his customers with an unusual arrangement for those undertaking to subscribe in advance. The price was to be forty-two shillings; but he announced that he was prepared to receive this sum in wheat, rye, corn, butter, or pork, to be delivered to his stores in Boston or Worcester on or before December 20, 1790. The balance of twenty-one shillings had to be paid to him in cash, and it would fall due for payment as soon as

---

[1] A similar reckoning is used in editions of the Douai Version published as late as the nineteenth century, where the year of the birth of Noe (Noah) is confidently stated as *Anno Mundi* 1056. The date of the creation of Adam and Eve is A.M. 1, and of their expulsion from Eden A.M. 2. Adam's firstborn, Cain, receives A.M. 130 as the year of his birth.

the product was available for delivery. Isaiah Thomas won considerable respect for his labors, receiving the commendation of George Washington and honorary degrees.

There was no lack of competition in the business of printing Bibles in the United States even before the end of the eighteenth century. Isaac Collins of New Jersey published a New Testament in 1788 and produced, also in 1791, a Bible the proofs for which he claimed had been read eleven times. This edition was so notable for the accuracy of its printing, according to the standards of that time in America, that the only errors found in it were a broken letter and a punctuation mark. The New Testament was also published at New York in 1790 by Hugh Gaine, and the Bible in 1792. There were at least three other American editions before the close of the century. One was issued by Hodge and Campbell in 1792; another known as Brown's Self-Interpreting Bible bore as its frontispiece an engraving by William Dunlap; and in 1794 there was an edition published at Philadelphia by William Young. In Philadelphia was also published, in 1806, the Cary Bible.

As we leave these byways in the history of the King James Version to turn to the eighteenth-century attempts of private individuals to provide alternative versions, we may pause for a brief reassessment of the significance of the King James Version upon the literature and life of the English-speaking world. The secret of its glory has already been considered. The nature and extent of its influence remain to be stated.

The service the King James translators rendered to the English language is different from that which Dante performed for his native Italian, and different again from what Luther did for German. It is no less significant than either. Not even Shakespeare has more deeply affected English literature. The King James Version is unique among the literary wonders of the world. We have seen that, moulded upon the best in the literary inheritance of the day, it exhibited that vitality that springs from awareness of the ceaseless flow of a living speech. We have seen, too, that its influence has bequeathed to us a noble standard and tradition of literary style, and that its cadences are echoed in thousands of now everyday turns of speech, even where their origin has been forgotten by many who use and delight in them.

Yet the King James Bible, though indeed the greatest literary monument of the English-speaking world, has never been merely a literature. It has guided through the path of life and the valley of death a billion hearts and minds that it has taught, consoled, and enlightened. It has much formed the characters of those who have led the English-speaking peoples in the development of such virtues as they may possess. Even those who have propounded religious and political idealisms far removed from the faith of the men and women for whom the King James Version was devised have owed more to it than they have always been ready to admit. No doubt often they have been unaware of the extent of their debt, as many who attribute to Karl Marx the dictum "Religion is the opium of the people" have forgotten, if they ever knew, that it was created in a very different context [2] a generation earlier by Charles Kingsley, an eminent English churchman.

The King James Bible has survived all hazards, from the astonishing vanity and weakness of the monarch who welcomed the project of the translation that bears his name to the endless catalogue of errors and defects that has afflicted the process of its transmission. Now that it has been in large measure inevitably supplanted as a result of the revisions of modern times, its influence endures. Its place in the life and language of all who claim English for their mother tongue is neither more nor less immortal than is the history of the English-speaking world.

To this English-speaking world the King James Version bestowed an inheritance that is unique. Of course the Bible belongs to all men, irrespective of the maternal tongue they happen to inherit. There is no reason to expect that the English-speaking peoples should have any particular share in it. It would be natural, indeed, to expect the contrary. Whatever value the message of the Bible has cannot depend upon a translation into English or any other tongue. Every language grows and fades like a flower. "The flower fadeth: but the word of our God shall stand for ever." Such was the genius of the King James Version, however, that it made that word speak so directly to those who heard it that they could and did forget it was only a translation. Never did translation speak with such lifegiving power. Not even the Vulgate was destined to have such immense influence over so many, even if it matched in a more austere way its extraordinary beauty and grace.

It is written that on the Day of Pentecost the apostles so spoke that their hearers "were confounded, because that every man heard them speak in his own language. And they were amazed and marvelled, saying one to another, Behold are not all these which speak Galileans? And how hear we every man in our own tongue, wherein we were born?" Such was the power of the King James Version that there was no such question to be asked. For good or ill, the Bible spoke to millions of men in a way it had never spoken before. It was to them as if God himself were speaking to them in English. And it was English so peerless as to seem almost worthy to be such an instrument. Well might the learned say, *non nobis, Domine*. And the peasant could now hear them say the

---

[2] Kingsley's use was as far removed from Marx's as, in our own century, is Bonhoeffer's plea for living "as if God did not exist" removed from Sartre's atheistic nihilism. For the literary and ideological influence of the Bible on skeptics, see below, p. 386.

same with no less splendid grace: "Not unto us, O Lord, not unto us, but unto thy name give glory."

Appendix to Chapter 24

The Preface to the King James Version

This preface is attributed to Miles Smith. Verbose by modern standards, it provided a useful explanation of the project. Moreover, reflecting the difficulties that beset the translators, and revealing their ideals and aims, as well as the circumstances of their time, it is of extraordinary historical and practical interest to the modern student of the history of the English Bible. Since it is not printed in modern editions of the King James Version and is not even otherwise readily available to the modern reader, it is reprinted here:

THE TRANSLATORS TO THE READER.

The best things have been calumniated.

Zeal to promote the common good, whether it be by devising any thing our selves, or revising that which hath been laboured by others, deserveth certainly much respect and esteem, but yet findeth but cold entertainment in the world. It is welcommed with suspicion in stead of love, and with emulation in stead of thanks: and if there be any hole left for cavill to enter, (and cavill, if it do not finde a hole, will make one) it is sure to be misconstrued, and in danger to be condemned. This will easily be granted by as many as know storie, or have any experience. For, was there ever any thing projected, that savoured any way of newnesse or renewing, but the same endured many a storm of gain-saying, or opposition? A man would think that Civility, wholesome laws, learning and eloquence, Synods, and Church-maintenance, (that we speak of no more things of this kinde) should be as safe as a Sanctuary, and out of the danger of the dart, as they say, that no man would lift up the heel, no, nor dogge moove his tongue against the motioners of them. For by the first, we are distinguished from bruit beasts led with sensualitie: By the second, we are bridled and restrained from outragious behaviour, and from doing of injuries, whether by fraud or by violence: by the third, we are enabled to inform and reform others, by the light and feeling that we have attained unto our selves: Briefly, by the fourth being brought together to a parle face to face, we sooner compose our differences then by writings, which are endlesse: And lastly, that the Church be sufficiently provided for, is so agreeable to good reason and conscience, that those mothers are holden to be lesse cruell, that kill their children assoon as they are born, then those nourcing fathers and mothers (wheresoever they be) that withdraw from them who hang upon their brests (and upon whose breasts again themselves do hang to receive the Spirituall and sincere milk of the word) livelihood and support fit for their estates. Thus it is apparent, that these things which we speak of, are of most necessarie use, and therefore, that none, either without absurdity can speak against them, or without note of wickednesse, can spurn against them.

Yet for all that, the learned know that certain worthy men have been brought to untimely death for none other fault, but for seeking to reduce their country-men to good order and discipline: and that in some Common-weals it was made a capitall crime, once to motion the making of a new Law for the abrogating of an old, though the same were most pernicious: And that certain, which would be counted pillars of the State, and paterns of Vertue and Prudence, could not be brought for a long time to give way to good Letters and refined speech, but bare themselves as averse from them, as from rocks, or boxes of poison: And fourthly, that he was no babe, but a great cleark, that gave forth (and in writing to remain to posteritie) in passion peradventure, but yet he gave forth, that he had not seen any profit to come by any Synode, or meeting of the Clergie, but rather the contrary: And lastly, against Church-maintenance and allowance, in such sort, as the Embassadours and messengers of the great King of kings should be furnished, it is not unknown what a fiction or fable (so it is esteemed, and for no better by the reporter himself, though superstitious) was devised: Namely, that at such time as the professours and teachers of Christianitie in the Church of Rome, then a true Church, were liberally endowed, a voyce forsooth was heard from heaven, saying; Now is poyson poured down into the Church, &c. Thus not onely as oft as we speak, as one saith, but also as oft as we do any thing of note or consequence, we subject our selves to every ones censure, and happy is he that is least tossed upon tongues: for utterly to escape the snatch of them it is impossible. If any man conceit, that this is the lot and portion of the meaner sort onely, and that Princes are priviledged by their high estate, he is deceived. As *the sword devoureth aswell one as the other,* as it is in *Samuel,* nay as the great Commander charged his souldiers in a certain battell, to strike at no part of the enemie, but at the face; And as the king of *Syria* commanded his chief captains *to fight neither with small nor great, save onely against the King of Israel:* so it is too true, that Envie striketh most spitefully at the fairest, and at the chiefest. *David* was a worthy Prince, and no man to be compared to him for his first deeds, and yet for as worthy an act as ever he did, (even for bringing back the Ark of God in solemnitie) he was scorned and scoffed at by his own wife. *Solomon* was greater then *David*, though not in vertue, yet in power: and by his power and wisdome he built a Temple to the LORD, such a one as was the glory of the land of Israel, and the wonder of the whole world. But was that his magnificence liked of by all? We doubt of it. Otherwise, why do they lay it in his sonnes dish, and call unto him for easing of the burden, *Make*, say they, *the grievous servitude of thy father, and his sore yoke, lighter.* Belike he had charged them with some levies, and troubled them with some cariages; Hereupon they raise up a Tragedie, and wish in their heart the Temple had never been built. So hard a thing it is to please all, even when we please God best, and do seek to approove ourselves to every ones conscience.

The highest personages have been calumniated.

If we will descend to latter times, we shall finde many the like examples of such kind, or rather unkind acceptance. The first Romane Emperour did never do a more pleasing deed to the learned, nor more profitable to posterity, for conserving the record of times in true supputation, then when he corrected the Calender, and ordered the yeer according to the course of the Sunne: and yet this was imputed to him for novelty, and arrogancy, and procured to him great obloquie. So the first Christened Emperour (at the leastwise that openly professed the faith himself, and allowed others to do the like) for strengthning the Empire at his great charges, and providing for the Church, as he did, got for his labour the name *Pupillus,* as one who would say, a wastefull Prince, that had need of a Guardian, or overseer. So the best Christened Emperour, for the love that he bare unto peace, thereby to enrich both himself and his subjects, and because he did not seek warre but finde it, was judged to be no man at arms (though indeed he excelled in feats of chivalry, and shewed so much when he was provoked) and condemned for giving himself to his ease, and to his pleasure. To be short, the most learned Emperour of former times, (at the least, the greatest polititian) what thanks had he for cutting off the superfluities of the laws, and digesting them into some order and method? This, that he hath been blotted by some to be an Epitomist, that is, one that extinguished worthy whole volumes, to bring his abridgements into request. This is the measure that hath been rendred to excellent Princes in former times, even *Cum benefacerent, male audire.* For their good deeds to be evill spoken of. Neither is there any likelihood, that envie and malignity died, and were buried with the ancient. No, no, the reproof of *Moses* taketh hold of most ages; *You are risen up in your fathers stead, an increase of sinfull men. What is that that hath been done? that which shall be done: and there is no new thing under the Sunne,* saith the wise man: and S. *Steven, As your fathers did, so do you.* This, and more to this purpose, His Majestie that now reigneth (and long, and long may he reign, and his off-spring for ever, *Himself, and children, and childrens children alwayes*) knew full well, according to the singular wisdome given unto him by God, and the rare learning and experience that he hath attained unto; namely, that whosoever attempteth any thing for the publike (specially if it pertain to Religion, and to the opening and clearing of the word of God) the same setteth himself upon a stage to be glouted upon by every evill eye, yea, he casteth himself headlong upon pikes, to be gored by every sharp tongue. For he that medleth with mens Religion in any part, medleth with their custome, nay, with their freehold; and though they finde no content in that which they have, yet they cannot abide to hear of altering. Notwithstanding his Royall heart was not daunted or discouraged for this or that colour, but stood resolute, *as a statue immoveable, and an anvile not easie to be beaten into plates,* as one saith; he knew who had chosen him to be a Souldier, or rather a Captain, and being assured that the course which he intended, made much for the glory of God, and the building up of his Church, he would not suffer it to be broken off for whatsoever speeches or practises. It doth certainly belong unto Kings, yea, it doth specially belong unto them, to have care of Religion, yea, to know it aright, yea, to professe it zealously, yea, to promote it to the uttermost of their power. This is their glory before all nations which mean well, and this will bring unto them a farre most excellent weight of glory in the day of the Lord Jesus. For the Scripture saith not in vain, *Them that honour me, I will honour,* neither was it a vain word that *Eusebius* delivered long ago, that piety towards God was the weapon, and the onely weapon that both preserved *Constantines* person, and avenged him of his enemies.

His Majesties constancie notwithstanding calumniation, for the survey of the English translations.

But now what piety without trueth? what trueth (what saving trueth) without the word of God? what word of God (whereof we may be sure) without the Scripture? The Scriptures we are commanded to search, Joh. 5. 39. Esa. 8. 20. They are commended that searched and studied them, Act. 17. 11. and 8. 28, 29. They are reproved that were unskilfull in them, or slow to beleeve them, Mat. 22. 29., Luk. 24. 25. They can make vs wise unto salvation, 2 Tim. 3. 15. If we be ignorant, they will instruct vs; if out of the way, they will bring us home; if out of order, they will reform us; if in heavinesse, comfort us; if dull, quicken

The praise of the holy Scriptures.

223

us; if cold, inflame us. *Tolle, lege; Tolle, lege,* Take up and read, take up and read the Scriptures, (for unto them was the direction) it was sayd unto S. *Augustine* by a supernaturall voyce, *Whatsoever is in the Scriptures, believe me,* saith the same S. *Augustine, is high and divine; there is verily trueth, and a doctrine most fit for the refreshing and renewing of mens mindes, and truely so tempered, that every one may draw from thence that which is sufficient for him, if he come to draw with a devout and pious minde, as true Religion requireth.* Thus S. *Augustine.* And S. *Hierome, Ama Scripturas, & amabit te sapientia, &c.* Love the Scriptures, and wisdome will love thee. And S. *Cyril* against *Julian; Even boyes that are bred up in the Scriptures, become most religious, &c.* But what mention we three or four uses of the Scripture, whereas whatsoever is to be beleeved or practised, or hoped for, is conteined in them? or three or four sentences of the Fathers, since whosoever is worthy the name of a Father, from Christs time downward, hath likewise written not onely of the riches, but also of the perfection of the Scripture? *I adore the fulnesse of the Scripture,* saith *Tertullian* against *Hermogenes.* And again, to *Apelles* an Heretike of the like stamp, he sayth, *I do not admit that which thou bringest in* (or concludest) *of thine own* (head or store, *de tuo*) without Scripture. So Saint *Justin Martyr* before him; *We must know by all means,* saith he, *that it is not lawfull* (or possible) *to learn* (any thing) *of God or of right pietie, save onely out of the Prophets, who teach us by divine inspiration.* So Saint *Basil* after *Tertullian, It is a manifest falling away from the Faith, and a fault of presumption, either to reject any of those things that are written, or to bring in* (upon the head of them, ἐπεισάγειν) *any of those things that* are not written. We omit to cite to the same effect, S. *Cyril* B. of *Hierusalem* in his 4. *Cataches.* S. *Hierome* against *Helvidius,* Saint *Augustine,* in his third book against the letters of *Petilian,* and in very many other places of his works. Also we forbear to descend to latter Fathers, because we will not weary the reader. The Scriptures then being acknowledged to be so full and so perfect, how can we excuse our selves of negligence, if we do not studie them, of curiosity, if we be not content with them? Men talk much of εἰρεσιώνη, how many sweet and goodly things it had hanging on it; of the Philosophers stone, that it turneth copper into gold: of *Cornucopia,* that it had all things necessary for food in it, of *Panaces* the herb, that it was good for all diseases: of *Catholicon* the drugge, that it is in stead of all purges: of *Vulcans* armour, that it was an armour of proof against all thrusts, and all blows, &c. Well, that which they falsely or vainly attributed to these things for bodily good, we may justly and with full measure ascribe unto the Scripture, for spirituall. It is not onely an armour, but also a whole armory of weapons, both offensive, and defensive; whereby we may save our selves, and put the enemy to flight. It is not an herb, but a tree, or rather a whole paradise of trees of life, which bring forth fruit every moneth, and the fruit thereof is for meat, and the leaves for medicine. It is not a pot of *Manna,* or a cruse of oyl, which were for memory onely, or for a meals meat or two, but as it were a showre of heavenly bread, sufficient for a whole host, be it never so great; and as it were a whole cellar full of oyl vessels, whereby all our necessities may be provided for, and our debts discharged. In a word, it is a Panary of wholesome food against fenowed traditions; a Physitions shop (Saint *Basil* calleth it) of preservatives against poysoned heresies; a Pandect of profitable Laws against rebellious spirits; a treasury of most costly jewels, against beggerly rudiments; Finally, a fountain of most pure water springing up unto everlasting life. And what marvell? The originall thereof being from heaven, not from earth; the author being God, not man; the enditer, the holy spirit, not the wit of the Apostles or Prophets; the Pen-men such as were sanctified from the womb, and endued with a principall portion of Gods spirit; the matter, verity, piety, purity, uprightnesse; the form, Gods word, Gods testimony, Gods oracles, the word of trueth, the word of salvation, &c. the effects, light of understanding, stablenesse of perswasion, repentance from dead works, newnesse of life, holinesse, peace, joy in the holy Ghost; lastly, the end and reward of the studie thereof, fellowship with the Saints, participation of the heavenly nature, fruition of an inheritance immortall, undefiled, and that never shall fade away: Happy is the man that delighteth in the Scripture, and thrice happy that meditateth in it day and night.

But how shall men meditate in that, which they cannot understand? How shall they understand that, which is kept close in an unknowen tongue? as it is written, *Except I know the power of the voyce, I shall be to him that speaketh, a Barbarian, and he that speaketh, shall be a Barbarian to me.* The Apostle excepteth no tongue; not Hebrew the ancientest, not Greek the most copious, not Latine the finest. Nature taught a naturall man to confesse, that all of us in those tongues which we do not understand, are plainly deaf; we may turn the deaf ear unto them. The *Scythian* counted the *Athenian,* whom he did not understand, barbarous: so the *Romane* did the *Syrian,* and the *Jew,* (even Saint *Hierome* himself calleth the Hebrew tongue barbarous, belike because it was strange to so many) so the Emperour of *Constantinople* called the *Latine* tongue, barbarous,

Translation necessary.

though Pope *Nicolai* do storm at it: so the *Jews* long before *Christ,* called all other nations, *Lognazim,* which is little better then barbarous. Therefore as one complaineth, that alwayes in the Senate of *Rome* there was one or other that called for an interpreter: so lest the Church be driven to the like exigent, it is necessary to have translations in a readinesse. Translation it is that openeth the window, to let in the light; that breaketh the shell, that we may eat the kernell; that putteth aside the curtain, that we may look into the most holy place; that removeth the cover of the well, that we may come by the water, even as *Jacob* rolled away the stone from the mouth of the well, by which means the flocks of *Laban* were watered. Indeed without translation into the vulgar tongue, the unlearned are but like children at *Jacobs* well (which was deep) without a bucket, or something to draw with: or as that person mentioned by *Esay,* to whom when a sealed book was delivered, with this motion, *Read this, I pray thee,* he was fain to make this answer, *I cannot, for it is sealed.*

The Translation of the old Testament out of the Hebrew into Greek

While God would be known onely in *Jacob,* and have his Name great in *Israel,* and in none other place, while the dew lay on *Gideons* fleece onely, and all the earth besides was dry; then for one and the same people, which spake all of them the language of *Canaan,* that is, *Hebrew,* one and the same originall in *Hebrew* was sufficient. But when the fulnesse of time drew neer that the Sunne of righteousnesse, the Sonne of God should come into the world, whom God ordained to be a reconciliation through faith in his blood, not of the *Jew* onely, but also of the *Greek,* yea, of all them that were scattered abroad; then lo, it pleased the Lord to stirre up the spirit of a *Greek* Prince, (*Greek* for descent and Language) even of *Ptolome Philadelph* King of *Egypt,* to procure the translating of the Book of God out of *Hebrew* into *Greek.* This is the translation of the *Seventy* Interpreters, commonly so called, which prepared the way for our Saviour among the Gentiles by written preaching, as Saint *John* Baptist did among the *Jews* by vocall. For the *Grecians* being desirous of learning, were not wont to suffer books of worth to lye moulding in Kings Libraries, but had many of their servants, ready scribes, to copie them out, and so they were dispersed and made common. Again, the *Greek* tongue was well known, and made familiar to most inhabitants in *Asia,* by reason of the conquests that there the *Grecians* had made, as also by the Colonies, which thither they had sent. For the same causes also it was well understood in many places of *Europe,* yea, and of *Afrike* too. Therefore the word of God being set forth in *Greek,* becometh hereby like a candle set upon a candlestick, which giveth light to all that are in the house, or like a proclamation sounded forth in the market place, which most men presently take knowledge of; and therefore that language was fittest to contain the Scriptures, both for the first Preachers of the Gospel to appeal unto for witnesse, and for the learners also of those times to make search and triall by. It is certain, that that Translation was not so sound and so perfect, but that it needed in many places correction; and who had been so sufficient for this work as the Apostles or Apostolike men? Yet it seemed good to the holy Ghost and to them, to take that which they found, (the same being for the greatest part true and sufficient) rather then by making a new, in that new world and green age of the Church, to expose themselves to many exceptions and cavillations, as though they made a Translation to serve their own turn, and therefore bearing witnesse to themselves, their witnesse not to be regarded. This may be supposed to be some cause, why the Translation of the *Seventy* was allowed to passe for currant. Notwithstanding, though it was commended generally, yet it did not fully content the learned, no not of the *Jews.* For not long after *Christ, Aquila* fell in hand with a new Translation, and after him *Theodotion,* and after him *Symmachus:* yea, there was a fift and a sixt edition, the Authours whereof were not known. These with the *Seventie* made up the *Hexapla,* and were worthily and to great purpose compiled together by *Origen.* Howbeit the Edition of the *Seventy* went away with the credit, and therefore not onely was placed in the midst by *Origen* (for the worth and excellency thereof above the rest, as *Epiphanius* gathereth) but also was used by the *Greek* Fathers for the ground and foundation of their Commentaries. Yea, *Epiphanius* above named doeth attribute so much unto it, that he holdeth the Authours thereof not onely for Interpreters, but also for Prophets in some respect: and *Justinian* the Emperour enjoyning the *Jews* his subjects to use specially the Translation of the *Seventie,* rendreth this reason thereof, because they were as it were enlightened with propheticall grace. Yet for all that, as the *Egyptians* are said of the Prophet to be men and not God, and their horses flesh and not spirit: so it is evident (and Saint *Hierome* affirmeth as much) that the *Seventy* were interpreters, they were not Prophets; they did many things well, as learned men; but yet as men they stumbled and fell, one while through oversight, another while through ignorance, yea, sometimes they may be noted to adde to the Originall, and sometimes to take from it; which made the Apostles to leave them many times, when they left the *Hebrew,* and to deliver the sence thereof according to the trueth of the word, as the Spirit gave them utterance. This may suffice touching the *Greek* Translations of the old Testament.

The translating of the Scripture into the vulgar tongues.

There were also within a few hundred yeers after CHRIST, Translations many into the Latine tongue: for this tongue also was very fit to convey the Law and the Gospel by, because in those times very many countreys of the West, yea, of the South, East, and North, spake or understood Latine, being made Provinces to the *Romanes*. But now the Latine Translations were too many to be all good, for they were infinite (*Latini Interpretes nullo modo numerari possunt,* saith Saint *Augustine.*) Again, they were not out of the *Hebrew* fountain (we speak of the *Latine* Translations of the Old Testament) but out of the *Greek* stream, therefore the *Greek* being not altogether clear, the *Latine* derived from it, must needs be muddie. This mooved S. *Hierome* a most learned father, and the best Linguist, without controversie, of his age, or of any that went before him, to undertake the translating of the Old Testament, out of the very fountains themselves, which he performed with that evidence of great learning, judgement, industry and faithfulnesse, that he hath for ever bound the Church unto him, in a debt of speciall remembrance and thankfulnesse.

Translation out of Hebrew and Greek into Latine.

Now though the Church were thus furnished with *Greek* and *Latine* Translations, even before the faith of CHRIST was generally embraced in the Empire: (for the learned know that even in S. *Hieroms* time, the Consull of *Rome* and his wife were both Ethnicks, and about the same time the greatest part of the Senate also) yet for all that the godly-learned were not content to have the Scriptures in the Language which themselves understood, *Greek* and *Latine,* (as the good Lepers were not content to fare well themselves, but acquainted their neighbours with the store that God had sent, that they also might provide for themselves) but also for the behoof and edifying of the unlearned, which hungred and thirsted after Righteousnesse, and had soules to be saved aswell as they, they provided Translations into the vulgar for their Countrymen, insomuch that most nations under heaven did shortly after their conversion, hear CHRIST speaking unto them in their mother tongue, not by the voice of their Minister onely, but also by the written word translated. If any doubt hereof, he may be satisfied by examples enough, if enough will serve the turn. First Saint *Hierome* saith, *Multarum gentium linguis Scriptura ante translata, docet falsa esse qua addita sunt, &c.* i. *The Scripture being translated before in the languages of many Nations, doeth shew that those things that were added* (by *Lucian* or *Hesychius*) *are false.* So S. *Hierome* in that place. The same S. *Hierome* elsewhere affirmeth, that he, the time was, had set forth the translation of the *Seventy, sua lingua hominibus* i. for his countreymen of *Dalmatia.* Which words not onely *Erasmus* doeth understand to purport, that Saint *Hierome* translated the Scripture into the *Dalmatian* Tongue, but also *Sixtus Senensis,* and *Alphonsus a Castro* (that we speak of no more) men not to be excepted against by them of *Rome,* do ingenuously confesse as much. So S. *Chrysostome* that lived in S. *Hieromes* time giveth evidence with him: *The doctrine of S. John* (saith he) *did not in such sort* (as the Philosophers did) *vanish away: but the Syrians, Egyptians, Indians, Persians, Ethiopians, and infinite other nations being barbarous people, translated it into their (mother) tongue, and have learned to be (true) Philosophers,* he meaneth Christians. To this may be added *Theodoret,* as next unto him, both for antiquity, and for learning. His words be these, *Every country that is under the Sunne, is full of these words,* (of the Apostles and Prophets) *and the Hebrew tongue* (he meaneth the Scriptures in the *Hebrew* tongue) *is turned not only into the Language of the Grecians, but also of the Romans, and Egyptians, and Persians, and Indians, and Armenians, and Scythians, and Sauromations, and briefly into all the Languages that any Nation useth.* So he in like manner, *Vlpilas* is reported by *Paulus Diaconus* and *Isidor* (and before them by *Sozomen*) to have translated the Scriptures into the *Gothicke* tongue: *John* Bishop of *Sivil* by *Vasseus,* to have turned them into *Arabick,* about the yeer of our Lord 717: *Beda* by *Cistertiensis,* to haue turned a great part of them into *Saxon: Ethnard* by *Trithemius,* to have abridged the French Psalter, as *Beda* had done the *Hebrew,* about the yeer 800: King *Alured* by the same *Cistertiensis,* to have turned the Psalter into *Saxon: Methodius* by *Aventinus* (printed at *Ingolstad*) to have turned the Scriptures into *Sclavonian: Valdo,* Bishop of *Frising* by *Beatus Rhenanus,* to have caused about that time, the Gospels to be translated into *Dutch*-rithme, yet extant in the library of *Corbinian: Valdus,* by divers to have turned them himself, or to have gotten them turned into *French,* about the yeere 1160: *Charles* the fift of that name, surnamed *The wise,* to have caused them to be turned into *French,* about 200 yeers after *Valdus* his time, of which translation there be many copies yet extant, as witnesseth *Beroaldus.* Much about that time, even in our King *Richard* the seconds dayes, *John Trevisa* translated them into *English,* and many *English* Bibles in written hand are yet to be seen with divers, translated, as it is very probable, in that age. So the *Syrian* translation of the New Testament is in most learned mens Libraries, of *Widminstodius* his setting forth; and the

Psalter in *Arabick* is with many, of *Augustinus Nebiensis* setting forth. So *Postel* affirmeth, that in his travail he saw the Gospels in the *Ethiopian* tongue. And *Ambrose Thesius* alledgeth the Psalter of the *Indians,* which he testifieth to have been set forth by *Potken* in *Syrian* Characters. So that, to have the Scriptures in the mother tongue, is not a quaint conceit lately taken up, either by the Lord *Cromwell* in *England,* or by the Lord *Radeuil* in *Polonie,* or by the Lord *Ungnadius* in the Emperours dominion, but hath been thought upon, and put in practise of old, even from the first times of the conversion or reformation of any Nation; no doubt, because it was esteemed most profitable to cause faith to grow in mens hearts the sooner, and to make them to be able to say with the words of the Psalm, *As we have heard, so we have seene.*

The unwillingness of our chief adversaries, that the Scriptures should be divulged in the mother tongue, &c.

Now the Church of Rome would seem at the length to bear a motherly affection towards her children, and to allow them the Scriptures in their mother tongue: but indeed it is a gift, not deserving to be called a gift, an unprofitable gift: they must first get a Licence in writing before they may use them, and to get that, they must approve themselves to their Confessor, that is, to be such as are, if not frozen in the dregs, yet sowred with the leaven of their superstition. Howbeit, it seemed too much to *Clement* the 8. that there should be any Licence granted to have them in the vulgar tongue, and therefore he overruleth and frustrateth the grant of *Pius* the fourth. So much are they afraid of the light of the Scripture, (*Lucifugæ Scriptuarum,* as *Tertullian* speaketh) that they wil not trust the people with it, no not as it is set forth by their own sworn men, no not with the Licence of their own Bishops and Inquisitors. Yea, so unwilling they are to communicate the Scriptures to the peoples understanding in any sort, that they are not ashamed to confesse, that wee forced them to translate it into English against their wills. This seemeth to argue a bad cause, or a bad conscience, or both. Sure we are, that it is not he that hath good gold, that is afraid to bring it to the touch-stone, but hee that hath the counterfeit; neither is it the true man that shunneth the light, but the malefactour, lest his deeds should be reproved: neither is it the plain-dealing Merchant that is unwilling to have the weights, or the meteyard brought in place, but he that vseth deceit. But we will let them alone for this fault, and return to translation.

Many mens mouthes haue been open a good while, (and yet are not stopped) with speeches about the Translation so long in hand, or rather perusals of Translations made before: and ask what may be the reason, what the necessitie of the employment: Hath the Church been deceived, say they, all this while? Hath her sweet bread been mingled with leaven, her silver with drosse, her wine with water, her milk with lime? (*Lacte gypsum malè miscetur,* saith S. *Ireney.*) We hoped that we had been in the right way, that we had had the Oracles of God delivered unto us, and that though all the world had cause to be offended and to complain, yet that we had none. Hath the nurse holden out the breast, and nothing but winde in it? Hath the bread been delivered by the Fathers of the Church, and the same proved to be *lapidosus,* as *Seneca* speaketh? What is it to handle the word of God deceitfully, if this be not? Thus certain brethren. Also the adversaries of *Judah* and *Hierusalem,* like *Sanballat* in *Nehemiah,* mock, as we hear, both at the work and workmen, saying; *What do these weak Jews, &c. will they make the stones whole again out of the heaps of dust which are burnt? although they build, yet if a fox go up, he shall even break down their stony wall.* Was their Translation good before? Why do they now mend it? Was it not good? Why then was it obtruded to the people? Yea, why did the Catholicks (meaning Popish *Romanists,*) always go in ieopardie, for refusing to go to heare it? Nay, if it must be translated into English, Catholickes are fittest to do it. They have learning, and they know when a thing is well, they can *manum de tabula.* We will answere them both briefly: and the former, being brethren, thus, with S. *Hierome, Damnamus veteres? minimé, sed post priorum studia in domo Domini, quod possumus laboramus.* That is, *Do we condemn the ancient? In no case: but after the endeuours of them that were before vs, we take the best paines we can in the house of God.* As if he said, Being provoked by the example of the learned that lived before my time, I have thought it my duetie, to assay whether my talent in the knowledge of the tongues, may be profitable in any measure to Gods Church, lest I should seeme to have laboured in them in vain, and lest I should be thought to glory in men, (although ancient,) above that which was in them. Thus S. *Hierome* may be thought to speak.

And to the same effect say we, that we are so farre off from condemning any of their labours that traveiled before us in this kinde, either in this land or beyond sea, either in King *Henries* time, or King *Edwards* (if there were any translation, or correction of a translation in his time) or Queen *Elizabeths* of ever-renouned memorie, that we acknowledge them to have been raised up of God, for the building and furnishing of his Church, and that they deserve to be had of us and of posteritie in everlasting remembrance. The judgement of *Aristotle* is worthy and well knowen: If *Timotheus had not beene, we had not had much sweet musicke; but if Phrynis (Timotheus his master) had not*

The speeches and reasons, both of our brethren, and of our Adversaries against this worke.

A satisfaction to our brethren.

231

been, we had not had Timotheus. Therefore blessed be they, and most honoured be their name, that breake the yce, and give the onset upon that which helpeth forward to the saving of souls. Now what can be more availeable thereto, then to deliver Gods book unto Gods people in a tongue which they understand? Since of an hidden treasure, and of a fountaine that is sealed, there is no profit, as *Ptolomee Philadelph* wrote to the Rabbines or masters of the Jews, as witnesseth *Epiphanius:* and as S. *Augustine* saith; *A man had rather be with his dogge then with a stranger* (whose tongue is strange unto him.) Yet for all that, as nothing is begun and perfited at the same time, and the later thoughts are thought to be the wiser: so if we building upon their foundation that went before us, and being holpen by their labours, do endeuour to make that better which they left so good; no man, we are sure, hath cause to mislike us; they, we perswade our selves, if they were alive, would thanke us. The vintage of *Abiezer,* that strake the stroake: yet the gleaning of grapes of *Ephraim* was not to be despised. Se *Judg. 8 verse 2. Joash* the king of *Israel* did not satisfie himself, till he had smitten the ground three times; and yet he offended the Prophet, for giving over then. *Aquila,* of whom we spake before, translated the Bible as carefully, and as skilfully as hee could; and yet he thought good to go ouer it again, and then it got the credit with the Jews, to be called κατ' ἀκρίβειαν, that is, acurately done, as Saint *Hierome* witnesseth. How many bookes of profane learning have been gone over again and again, by the same translators, by others? Of one and the same book of *Aristotles* Ethikes, there are exstant not so few as sixe or seven severall translations. Now if this cost may be bestowed upon the gourd, which affordeth us a little shade, and which to day flourisheth, but to morrow is cut downe; what may we bestow, nay, what ought we not to bestow vpon the Vine, the fruit whereof maketh glad the conscience of man, and the stemme whereof abideth for ever? And this is the word of God, which we translate. *What is the chaffe to the wheat, saith the Lord? Tanti vitreum, quanti verum Margaritum?* (saith *Tertullian*) if a toy of glasse be of that reckoning with us, how ought we to value the true pearl? Therefore let no mans eye be evill, because his Majesties is good; neither let any be grieved, that we have a Prince that seeketh the increase of the spirituall wealth of Israel (let *Sanballats* and *Tobiahs* do so, which therefore do bear their just reproof) but let us rather blesse God from the ground of our heart, for working this religious care in him, to have the translations of the Bible maturely considered of and examined. For by this means it cometh to passe, that whatsoever is sound already (and all is sound for substance, in one or other of our editions, and the worst of ours far better then their authentike vulgar) the same will shine as gold more brightly, being rubbed and polished; also, if any thing bee halting, or superfluous, or not so agreeable to the originall, the same may be corrected, and the trueth set in place. And what can the King commaund to be done, that will bring him more true honour then this? and wherein could they that have been set a worke, approve their duetie to the King, yea their obedience to God, and love to his Saints more, then by yeelding their service, and all that is within them, for the furnishing of the work? But besides all this, they were the principall motives of it, and therefore ought least to quarrell it: for the very Historicall trueth is, that upon the importunate petitions of the Puritans, at his Majesties comming to this Crown, the Conference at Hampton Court having been appointed for hearing their complaints: when by force of reason they were put from all other grounds, they had recourse at the last, to this shift, that they could not with good conscience subscribe to the Communion book, since it maintained the Bible as it was there translated, which was, as they sayd, a most corrupted translation. And although this was judged to be but a very poor and emptie shift; yet even here-upon did his Majestie begin to bethink himself of the good that might ensue by a new translation, and presently after gave order for this Translation which is now presented unto thee. Thus much to satisfie our scrupulous Brethren.

Now to the later we answer; that we do not denie, nay we affirm and avow, that the very meanest translation of the Bible in English, set forth by men of our profession (for we have seen none of theirs of the whole Bible as yet) containeth the word of God, nay, is the word of God. As the Kings speech which he uttered in Parliament, being translated into *French, Dutch, Italian* and *Latine*, is still the Kings Speech, though it be not interpreted by every Translator with the like grace, nor perad-venture so fitly for phrase, nor so expresly for sence, every where. For it is confessed, that things are to take their denomination of the greater part; and a naturall man could say, *Verum vbi multa nitent in carmine, non ego paucis offendor maculis, &c.* A man may be counted a vertuous man, though he have made many slips in his life, (else, there were none vertuous, for *in many things we offend all*) also a comely man and lovely, though he have some warts upon his hand, yea, not onely freakles upon his face, but also skarres. No cause therefore why the word translated should be denied to be the word, or forbidden to be currant, notwithstanding that some imperfections and blemishes may be noted in the setting forth of it. For what ever was perfect

An answer to the imputations of our Adversaries.

under the Sunne, where Apostles or Apostolike men, that is, men indued with an extraordinarie measure of Gods spirit, and priviledged with the priviledge of infallibilitie, had not their hand? The Romanists therefore in refusing to hear, and daring to burne the Word translated, did no lesse then despite the spirit of grace, from whom originally it proceeded, and whose sense and meaning, as well as mans weakenesse would enable, it did expresse. Judge by an example or two. *Plutarch* writeth, that after that *Rome* had been burnt by the *Galles,* they fell soon to build it again: but doing it in haste, they did not cast the streets, nor proportion the houses in such comely fashion, as had been most sightly and convenient; was *Catiline* therefore an honest man, or a good Patriot, that sought to bring it to a combustion? or *Nero* a good Prince, that did indeed set it on fire? So, by the story of *Ezra,* and the prophesie of *Haggai* it may be gathered, that the Temple built by *Zerubbabel* after the returne from *Babylon,* was by no meanes to be compared to the former built by *Solomon* (for they that remembred the former, wept when they considered the latter) notwithstanding, might this latter either have been abhorred and forsaken by the *Jews,* or prophaned by the *Greekes?* The like we are to think of Translations. The translation of the *Seventie* dissenteth from the Originall in many places, neither doeth it come neer it, for perspicuitie, gravitie, majestie; yet which of the Apostles did condemn it? Condemn it? Nay, they used it, (as it is apparant, and as Saint *Hierome* and most learned men do confesse) which they would not have done, nor by their example of using it, so grace and commend it to the Church, if it had been unworthy the appellation and name of the word of God. And whereas they urge for their second defence of their vilifying and abusing of the *English* Bibles, or some pieces thereof, which they meet with, for that heretikes (forsooth) were the authors of the translations, (heretikes they call us by the same right that they call themselves Catholikes, both being wrong) we marveile what divinitie taught them so. We are sure *Tertullian* was of another minde: *Ex personis probamus fidem, an ex fide personas?* Do we trie mens faith by their persons? we should trie their persons by their faith. Also S. *Augustine* was of an other minde: for he lighting upon certain rules made by *Tychonius* a *Donatist,* for the better understanding of the word, was not ashamed to make use of them, yea, to insert them into his own book, with giving commendation to them so farre forth as they were worthy to be commended, as is to be seen in Saint *Angustines* third book *de doctrina Christiana.* To be short, *Origen,* and the whole Church of God for certain hundred yeers, were of an other minde: for they were so farre from treading under foot, (much more from burning) the Translation of *Aquila* a Proselyte, that is, one that had turned *Jew;* of *Symmachus,* and *Theodotion,* both *Ebionites,* that is, most vile heretikes, that they joyned them together with the *Hebrew* Originall, and the Translation of the *Seuenty,* (as hath been before signified out of *Epiphanius*) and set them forth openly to be considered of and perused by all. But we weary the unlearned, who need not know so much, and trouble the learned, who know it already.

Yet before we end we must answere a third cavill and objection of theirs against us, for altering and amending our Translation so oft; wherein truely they deal hardly, and strangely with us. For to whom ever was it imputed for a fault (by such as were wise) to go over that which he had done, and to amend it where he saw cause? Saint *Augustine* was not afraid to exhort Saint *Hierome* to a *Palinodia* or recantation; the same S. *Augustine* was not ashamed to retractate, we might say, revoke, many things that had passed him, and doeth even glory that he seeth his infirmities. If we will be sonnes of the Trueth, we must consider what it speaketh, and trample upon our own credit, yea, and upon other mens too, if either be any way an hinderance to it. This to the cause: then to the persons we say, that of all men they ought to be most silent in this case. For what varieties have they, and what alterations have they made, not onely of their Service books, Portesses and Breviaries, but also of their *Latine* Translation? The Service Book supposed to be made by Saint *Ambrose* (*Officium Ambrosianum*) was a great while in speciall use and request: but Pope *Hadrian* calling a Council with the ayd of *Charles* the Emperour, abolished it, yea, burnt it, and commanded the Service Book of Saint *Gregory* universally to be used. Well, *Officium Gregorianum* gets by this means to be in credit, but doeth it continue without change or altering? No, the very *Romane* Service was of two fashions, the New fashion, and the Old, (the one used in one Church, the other in another) as is to be seen in *Pamelius* a Romanist, his Preface, before *Micrologus.* The same *Pamelius* reporteth out of *Radulphus de Rivo,* that about the yeer of our Lord, 1277, Pope *Nicolas* the third remooved out of the Churches of *Rome,* the more ancient books (of Service) and brought into use the Missals of the Friars Minorites, and commaunded them to be observed there; insomuch that about an hundred yeers after, when the above-named *Radulphus* happened to be at *Rome,* he found all the books to be new, (of the new stamp.) Neither was there this chopping and changing in the more ancient times onely, but also of late: *Pius Quintus* himself confesseth, that every Bishoprick almost had a peculiar kinde of service, most unlike to that which others had: which moved him to abolish all other Breviaries, though never so ancient, and priviledged, and published by Bishops in their Diocesses, and to establish and ratifie that onely which was of his own setting foorth, in the yeer 1568. Now, when the father of their Church, who gladly would heal the sore of the daughter of his people softly and sleightly, and make the best of it, findeth so great fault with them for their oddes and jarring; we hope the children have no great cause to vaunt of their uniformity. But the difference that appeareth between our Translations, and our often correcting of them, is the thing we are specially charged with; let vs see therefore whether they themselves be without fault this way, (if it be to be counted a fault, to correct) and whether they be fit men to throw stones at us: *O tandem major pareas insane minori:* they that are lesse sound themselves, ought not to object infirmities to others. If we should tell them that *Valla, Stapulensis, Erasmus,* and *Vives* found fault with their vulgar Translation, and consequently wished the same to be mended, or a new one to be made, they would answer peradventure, that we produced their enemies for witnesses against them; albeit, they were in no other sort enemies, then as Saint *Paul* was to the *Galatians,* for telling them the trueth: and it were to be wished, that they had dared to tell it them plainlier and oftner. But what will they say to this, that Pope *Leo* the tenth allowed *Erasmus* Translation of the New Testament, so much different from the vulgar, by his Apostolike Letter and Bull; That the same *Leo* exhorted *Pagnin* to translate the whole Bible, and bare whatsoeuer charges was necessary for the work? Surely, as the Apostle reasoneth to the *Hebrews,* that *if the former Law and Testament had been sufficient, there had been no need of the latter:* so we may say, that if the old vulgar had been at all points allowable, to small purpose had labour and charges been undergone, about framing of a new. If they say, it was one Popes private opinion, and that he consulted onely himself; then we are able to go further with them, and to averre, that more of their chief men of all sorts even their own *Trent*-champions *Paiva* and *Vega,* and their own Inquisitor *Hieronymus ab Oleastro,* and their own Bishop *Isidorus Clarius,* and their own Cardinall *Thomas a Vio Caietan,* do either make new Translations themselves, or follow new ones of other mens making, or note the vulgar Interpreter for halting; none of them fear to dissent from him, nor yet to except against him. And call they this an uniform tenour of text and judgement about the text, so many of their Worthies disclaiming the now received conceit? Nay, we will yet come neerer the quick: doth not their

236

Paris edition differ from the *Lovaine,* and *Hentenius* his from them both, and yet all of them allowed by authority? Nay, doth not *Sixtus Quintus* confesse, that certain Catholikes (he meaneth certain of his own side) were in such an humour of translating the Scriptures into *Latine,* that Satan taking occasion by them, though they thought of no such matter, did strive what he could, out of so uncertain and manifold a varietie of Translations, so to mingle all things, that nothing might seem to be left certain and firm in them, &c? Nay further, did not the same *Sixtus* ordain by an inviolable decree, and that with the counsell and consent of his Cardinals, that the *Latine* edition of the Old and New Testament, which the Councill of *Trent* would have to be authentike, is the same without controversie which he then set foorth, being diligently corrected and printed in the Printing house of *Vatican?* Thus *Sixtus* in his Preface before his Bible. And yet *Clement* the eight his immediate successour, to accompt of, publisheth another edition of the Bible, containing in it infinite differences from that of *Sixtus,* (and many of them weighty and materiall) and yet this must be authentike by all means. What is to have the faith of our glorious Lord JESUS CHRIST with Yea and Nay, if this be not? Again, what is sweet harmony and consent, if this be? Therefore as *Demaratus of Corinth* advised a great King, before he talked of the dissensions among the *Grecians,* to compose his domestick broils: (for at that time his Queen and his son and heir were at deadly fuid with him) so all the while that our adversaries do make so many and so various editions themselves, and do jarre so much about the worth and authority of them, they can with no shew of equity challenge us for changing and correcting.

But it is high time to leave them, and to shew in brief what we proposed to our selves, and what course we held in this our perusall and survey of the Bible. Truely (good Christian Reader) we never thought from the beginning, that we should need to make a new Translation, nor yet to make of a bad one a good one, (for then the imputation of *Sixtus* had been true in some sort, that our people had been fed with gall of Dragons in stead of wine, with whey in stead of milk;) but to make a good one better, or out of many good ones, one principall good one, not justly to be excepted against; that hath been our indeavour, that our mark. To that purpose there were many chosen, that were greater in other mens eyes then in their own, and that sought the trueth rather then their own prayse. Again, they came or were thought to come to the work, not *exercendi causa* (as one saith) but *exercitati,* that is, learned, not to learn: For the chief overseer and ἐργοδιώκτης under his Majestie, to whom not only we, but

The purpose of the Translators, with their number, furniture, care, &c.

also our whole Church was much bound, knew by his own wisdome, which thing also *Nazianzen* taught so long ago, that it is a preposterous order to teach first & to learn after, yea that τὸ ἐν πίθῳ κεραμίαν μανθάνειν, to learn and practise together, is neither commendable for the workman nor safe for the work. Therefore such were thought upon, as could say modestly with Saint *Hierome, Et Hebræum Sermonem ex parte didicimus, & in Latino pene ab ipsis incunabulis &c. detriti sumus. Both we have learned the Hebrew tongue in part, and in the Latine we have been exercised almost from our verie cradle.* Saint *Hierome* maketh no mention of the *Greek* tongue, wherein yet he did excell, because he translated not the old Testament out of *Greek,* but out of *Hebrew.* And in what sort did these assemble? in the trust of their own knowledge, or of their sharpnesse of wit, or deepnesse of judgement, as it were in an arm of flesh? At no hand. They trusted in him that hath the key of *David,* opening and no man shutting; they prayed to the Lord the Father of our Lord, to the effect that Saint *Augustine* did; *O let thy Scriptures be my pure delight, let me not be deceived in them, neither let me deceive by them.* In this confidence, and with this devotion did they assemble together; not too many, lest one should trouble another; and yet many, lest many things haply might escape them. If you ask what they had before them, truly it was the *Hebrew* text of the Old Testament, the *Greek* of the New. These are the two golden pipes, or rather conduits, wherethrough the olive branches emptie themselves into the gold. Saint *Augustine* calleth them precedent, or originall Tongues; Saint *Hierome,* fountains. The same S. *Hierome* affirmeth, and *Gratian* hath not spared to put it into his Decree, That *as the credite of the old Books* (he meaneth of the Old Testament) *is to be tried by the Hebrew Volumes, so of the New by the Greek tongue,* he meaneth by the originall *Greek.* If trueth be to be tried by these tongues, then whence should a translation be made, but out of them? These tongues therefore, the Scriptures we say in those tongues, we set before us to translate, being the tongues wherein God was pleased to speak to his Church by his Prophets and Apostles. Neither did we run over the work with that posting haste that the *Septuagint* did, if that be true which is reported of them, that they finished it in seventy two dayes; neither were we barred or hindred from going over it again, having once done it, like Saint *Hierome,* if that be true which himself reporteth, that he could no sooner write any thing, but presently it was caught from him, and published, and he could not have leave to mend it: neither, to be short, were we the first that fell in hand with translating the Scripture into English, and consequently distitute of former helps, as it is written of *Origen,* that he was the first in a manner, that put his hand to write Commentaries upon the Scriptures, and therefore no marveil, if he over-shot himself many times. None of these things: the work hath not been hudled up in seventy two dayes, but hath cost the workmen, as light as it seemeth, the pains of twise seven times seventie two dayes and more: matters of such weight and consequently destitute of former helps, as it is written of businesse of moment a man feareth not the blame of convenient slacknesse. Neither did we think much to consult the Translators or Commentators, *Chaldee, Hebrew, Syrian, Greek* or *Latine,* no nor the *Spanish, French, Italian,* or *Dutch;* neither did we disdain to revise that which we had done, and to bring back to the anvill that which we had hammered: but having and using as great helps as were needfull, and fearing no reproach for slownesse, nor coveting praise for expedition, we have at the length, through the good hand of the Lord upon us, brought the work to that passe that you see.

Some peradventure would have no varietie of sences to be set in the margine, lest the authoritie of the Scriptures for deciding of controversies by that shew of uncertainitie, should somewhat be shaken. But we hold their judgement not to be so sound in this point. For though, *whatsoever things are necessarie, are manifest,* as S. *Chrysostome* saith, and as S. *Augustine, In those things that are plainely set down in the Scriptures all such matters are found that concern Faith, Hope, and Charitie.* Yet for all that it cannot be dissembled, that partly to exercise and whet our wits, partly to wean the curious from loathing of them for their everywhere-plainnesse, partly also to stirre vp our devotion to crave the assistance of Gods Spirit by prayer, and lastly, that we might be forward to seek ayd of our brethren by conference, and never scorn those that be not in all respects so complete as they should be, being to seek in many things our selves, it hath pleased God in his divine providence, here and there to scatter words and sentences of that difficultie and doubtfulnesse, not in doctrinall points that concern salvation (for in such it hath been vouched that the Scriptures are plain) but in matters of lesse moment, that fearfulnesse would better beseem us then confidence, and if we will resolve, to resolve upon modestie with Saint *Augustine,* (though not in this same case altogether, yet upon the same ground) *Melius est dubitare de occultis, quam litigare de incertis,* it is better to make doubt of those things which are secret, then to strive about those things that are uncertain. There be many words in the Scriptures, which be never found there but once, (having neither brother nor

Reasons moving us to set diversity of sences in the margine, where there is great probability for each.

neighbour, as the *Hebrews* speak) so that we cannot be holpen by conference of places. Again, there be many rare names of certain birds, beasts and precious stones, &c. concerning which the *Hebrews* themselves are so divided among themselves for judgement, that they may seem to have defined this or that, rather because they would say something, then because they were sure of that which they sayd, as Saint *Hierome* somewhere saith of the *Septuagint*. Now in such a case, doeth not a margine do well to admonish the Reader to seek further, and not to conclude or dogmatize upon this or that peremptorily? For as it is a fault of incredulitie, to doubt of those things that are evident: so to determine of such things as the Spirit of God hath left (even in the judgement of the judicious) questionable, can be no lesse then presumption. Therefore as Saint *Augustine* saith, that varietie of Translations is profitable for the finding out of the sense of the Scriptures: so diversitie of signification and sence in the margine, where the text is not so clear, must needs do good, yea, is necessary as we are perswaded. We know that *Sixtus Quintus* expresly forbiddeth, that any varietie of readings of their vulgar edition, should be put in the margine (which though it be not altogether the same thing to that we have in hand, yet it looketh that way) but we think he hath not all of his own side his favourers, for this conceit. They that are wise, had rather have their judgements at libertie in differences of readings, then to be captivated to one, when it may be the other. If they were sure that their hie Priest had all laws shut up in his breast, as *Paul* the second bragged, and that he were as free from errour by speciall priviledge, as the Dictators of *Rome* were made by law inviolable, it were another matter; then his word were an Oracle, his opinion a decision. But the eyes of the world are now open, God be thanked, and have been a great while, they finde that he is subject to the same affections and infirmities that others be, that his body is subject to wounds, and therefore so much as he prooveth, not as much as he claimeth, they grant and imbrace.

Reasons inducing us not to stand curiously upon an identity of phrasing.

Another thing we think good to admonish thee of (gentle Reader) that we have not tyed our selves to an uniformitie of phrasing, or to an identitie of words, as some peradventure would wish that we had done, because they observe, that some learned men somewhere, have been as exact as they could that way. Truly, that we might not varie from the sense of that which we had translated before, if the word signified the same thing in both places (for, there be some words that be not of the same sense everywhere) we were especially carefull, and made a conscience, according to our dutie. But, that we should expresse the same notion in the same particular word; as for example, if we translate the *Hebrew* or *Greek* word once by *Purpose*, never to call it *Intent;* if one where *Journeying,* never *Travelling;* if one where *Think,* never *Suppose;* if one where *Pain,* never *Ache;* if one where *Joy,* never *Gladnesse,* &c. Thus to mince the matter, we thought to favour more of curiosity then wisedome, and that rather it would breed scorn in the Atheist, then bring profit to the godly Reader. For is the kingdome of God become words or syllables? why should we be in bondage to them if we may be free, use one precisely when we may use another no lesse fit, as commodiously? A godly Father in the Primitive time shewed himself greatly moved, that one of newfanglenes called κράββατον σκίμπους, though the difference be little or none; and another reporteth, that he was much abused for turning *Cucurbita* (to which reading the people had beene used) into *Hedera.* Now if this happen in better times, and upon so small occasions, we might justly feare hard censure, if generally we should make verball and unnecessary changings. We might also be charged (by scoffers) with some unequall dealing toward a great number of good English words. For as it is written of a certain great Philosopher, that he should say, that those logs were happie that were made images to be worshipped; for their fellowes, as good as they, lay for blocks behinde the fire; so if we should say, as it were, unto certain words, Stand up higher, have a place in the Bible alwaies, and, to others of like qualitie, Get ye hence, be banished for ever, we might be taxed peraduenture with S. *James* his words, namely, *To be partiall in our selves, and judges of evill thoughts.* Adde hereunto, that nicenesse in words was alwayes counted the next step to trifling, and so was to be curious about names too: also that we cannot follow a better pattern for elocution then God himself; therefore he using divers words, in his holy writ, and indifferently for one thing in nature: we, if we will not be superstitious, may use the same libertie in our English versions out of *Hebrew* and *Greek,* for that copie or store that he hath given us. Lastly, we have on the one side avoyded the scrupulositie of the Puritanes, who leave the old Ecclesiasticall words, and betake them to other, as when they put *washing* for *Baptisme,* and *Congregation* instead of *Church:* as also on the other side, we have shunned the obscuritie of the Papists, in their *Azymes, Tunike, Rationall, Holocausts, Præpuce, Pasche,* and a number of such like, whereof their late Translation is full, and that of purpose to darken the sense, that since they must needs translate the Bible, yet by the language thereof, it may be kept from being understood. But we desire that the Scripture may speak like it self, as in the language of *Canaan,* that it may be understood even of the very vulgar.

Many other things we might give thee warning of (gentle Reader) if we had not exceeded the measure of a Preface already. It remaineth, that we commend thee to God, and to the Spirit of his grace, which is able to build further then we can aske or think. He removeth the scales from our eyes, the vail from our hearts, opening our wits, that we may understand his word, enlarging our hearts, yea correcting our affections, that we may love it above gold and silver, yea that we may love it to the end. Ye are brought unto fountains of living water which ye digged not; doe not cast earth into them with the Philistines, neither preferre broken pits before them with the wicked Jews. Others have laboured, and you may enter into their labours; O receive not so great things in vain! O despise not so great salvation! Be not like swine to tread under foot so precious things, neither yet like dogs to tear and abuse holy things. Say not to our Saviour with the *Gergesites,* Depart out of our coasts, neither yet with *Esau,* Sell your birthright for a measse of pottage. If light be come into the world, love not darknesse more then light: if food, if clothing be offered, go not naked, starve not yourselves. Remember the advice of *Nazianzene, It is a grievous thing* (or dangerous) *to neglect a great faire, and to seeke to make markets afterwards:* Also the encouragement of S. *Chrysostome, It is altogether impossible, that he that is sober (and watchfull) should at any time be neglected:* Lastly, the admonition and menacing of S. *Augustine, They that despise Gods will inviting them, shall feel Gods will taking vengeance of them.* It is a fearful thing to fall into the hands of the living God: but a blessed thing it is, and will bring us to everlasting blessednesse in the end, when God speaketh unto us, to hearken; when he setteth his word before us, to read it; when he stretcheth out his hand and calleth, to answere, Here am I; here we are to do thy will, O God. The Lord worke a care and conscience in us to know him and serve him, that we may be acknowledged of him at the appearing of our Lord JESVS CHRIST, to whom with the holy Ghost, be all praise and thanksgiving. Amen.

*Oh, Sir! What a delectable residence
we might establish here.*—Edward Harwood,
translating Peter's words to Jesus on the
Mount of Transfiguration

CHAPTER 25 *English Translations Between the
King James and the Revised Version*

This chapter will treat, besides the Roman Catholic and Jewish use of vernacular translations in the English-speaking world, various entirely independent translations by private individuals between the appearance of the King James Version in 1611 and that of the Revised Version in 1885.

We have already seen how ill prepared had been the English-speaking Roman Catholic minority for the fruits of the labors undertaken on their behalf by the Douai-Reims translators. The circulation of even the few editions of the Reims New Testament was meager. As for the Douai Old Testament, it was reprinted only once, in 1635. In the eighteenth century, English Roman Catholics were under extreme political disabilities and suffered under severe penal laws. Apart from the few old families that had remained faithful to the Pope and a few respected priests, Roman Catholics in Britain were a small and despised minority. The penal laws against them were widely supported because most people believed, not without historical grounds, that Roman Catholics were highly capable of alliances with hostile foreign powers and were therefore all potential traitors.

The fear such suspicions engendered was combined with distaste for the backwardness of Ireland, which was accounted typical of the surviving bastions of waning papal power. There was nothing, therefore, to inspire Roman Catholics in the British Isles with any hope of influencing Protestants through a better translation of the Bible. There was no need for the revision of the Douai Bible that even their priests generally did not urge them to read. In these circumstances it is certainly very remarkable that there was nevertheless not only considerable dissatisfaction with the Douai Bible on the part of the more enlightened English-speaking Roman Catholics but a series of attempts by their more thoughtful priests to achieve its revision.

In 1718 a new version of the New Testament for the use of Roman Catholics appeared. It was the work of Dr. Cornelius Nary, who was dissatisfied with the English of "the Doway Bible and Rhemish New Testament." He expressed the prevalent opinion that the Douai Version was so literal and archaic that "in a number of Places it is unintelligible, and all over so grating to the Ears" that "most People will not be at the Pains of reading" copies of such a book. "Besides, they are so bulky, that they cannot conveniently be carried about for publick Devotion; and so scarce and so dear that the Generality of the People neither have, nor can procure them for their private use." In such statements Nary was plainly replying to the complaints of the "Protestants," among whom he was esteemed, and expressing his own determination to rectify matters as best he could. He excused himself for translating from the Vulgate rather than from the Greek on the ground that his purpose was limited to the practical one of providing the faithful with a means of understanding "the Scripture as it is read in the Catholick Church, and as they hear it in the publick service and at their private Devotions." For all that, Nary did know Greek and made use of his knowledge. He appended a few notes, and these were partly to show the sense of the Greek and partly to reconcile seeming contradictions in the New Testament itself. The following specimen, showing Nary's rendering of the first three verses of Luke 5, gives a fair indication of his good sense of English rhythm.

And it came to pass that as the multitudes pressed upon him to hear the word of God, he stood by the Lake of Genesareth, And saw two ships standing by the Lake; but the fishermen were gone down, and were washing their nets. And having gone aboard one of them, which was Simon's, he prayed him to put back a little from the land, and he sat down and taught the people from aboard the ship. And when he had done speaking, he said unto Simon: Launch out into the deep, and let loose your nets for a draught.

According to an obituary notice at the time of his death in Dublin in 1737, Nary, a doctor of the Faculty of Theology of Paris, was "a gentleman of great Charity, Piety and Learning, and very much esteemed by Protestants, as well as by those of his Religion." Nary was indeed an exceptional man. That his influence on his less enlightened brethren was limited is shown by the appearance in 1730 of another English version by Robert Witham, who thought Nary too ready to follow the "Protestant lead." He had much less sense of the importance of the Greek, and his version was much more reactionary and polemic in character.

In 1738 a new, revised edition of the Reims New Testament was published, the first to appear for over a hundred years. Known to bibliographers as the fifth edition of that version, it was an elegant production, a handsome folio edition, well printed and with woodcuts. The frontispiece consists of the crucifix, with the Virgin on the right, representing the Roman Church, and on the left the figure of Aaron, representing the synagogue. Some of the more notorious renderings of the earlier editions were improved, so that, for example, the young man who had been described as "clothed with sindon upon the bare" is now "cloathed with linnen cloath over his naked body." The revision is generally attributed to Richard Challoner and Francis Blyth. The latter was Vicar-Provincial of the Order of Carmelite Friars in England and was for some years attached to the Portuguese Embassy in London. Challoner (1691-1781) became Vice-President of Douai College and afterwards Vicar Apostolic of the London district, being also raised to the episcopate as a bishop *in partibus infidelium*.

It should be explained that in the days of the penal laws against Roman Catholics, and indeed till 1850, it was the practice of the Roman Church authorities to use a convenient constitutional device to signalize their claim on England and their hope of resubjugating it to Rome as soon as opportunity might arise. Since the law of the land at that time precluded the possibility of having any regular Roman Catholic hierarchy in England, Rome took the position that England was for the time being a missionary country. So vicars apostolic were appointed instead of bishops. Nevertheless, a vicar apostolic could be a bishop, though without a formal jurisdiction such as a bishop in Spain, for instance, would enjoy. Such ecclesiastics were charged with the oversight of "districts," not dioceses, because, on the Roman theory, England was for the time being an "infidel region" whose ecclesiastical overseers must therefore be accorded an inferior status. Encouraged by the most decisive of the Roman Catholic Relief Acts, the Roman Catholic Emancipation Act, 1829,[1] and the defection to Rome of a considerable number of Anglican clergy who followed the lead given by John Henry Newman (1801-1890), who was received into the Roman Church on October 9, 1845, Pius IX "restored" England to noninfidel status in 1850. Steps were taken by the English authorities to prevent the Roman bishops in England from assuming the names of the historic English episcopal sees; nevertheless, the principle was made to appear secure, and Roman Catholics in England looked forward confidently and devoutly to the time when the fruits of the Reformation in England would rot and die like every other plague upon the True Church. The Roman hierarchy was similarly "restored" in Scotland in 1872.

In the early nineteenth century there was a stream of other Roman Catholic versions in English. Besides the versions and editions already circulating, Coyne's Bible appeared in 1811, Haydock's in 1811-1814, the Newcastle New Testament in 1812, Syers' Bible in 1813, Wogan's in 1814, MacNamara's in 1813-1814, Began's New Testament in 1816, and Gib-

[1] 10 George IV, c. 7.

son's Bible in 1816-1817. After the Roman Catholic Emancipation Act, 1829, the stream developed into a flood. So vast is the number of Roman Catholic Bibles and New Testaments, so diverse their readings, and so complicated the story of their dissemination that it is very doubtful that it could ever be properly told. Practice was so anarchical that it would be extremely difficult and often impossible for a modern novelist, however good his historical sense, to recount exactly what text a particular priest would use for the Epistle or Gospel in a particular Roman Catholic parish in England or Ireland on any particular Sunday during the reign of Queen Victoria. Father Hugh Pope, a learned English Dominican expert on the subject, has written: "In Manchester the Epistle and Gospel might be read from Syers' Bible, adhering mostly to Challoner's earlier revisions, unless that huge folio proved too unwieldy in the pulpit. In Liverpool, Dr. Gibson's magnificent folio editions, 1817 and 1822, following Challoner's later revisions, might have been used, if any pulpit could accommodate them. Owing to their condemnation by Dr. Troy, Ireland probably never heard Coyne's edition, 1816, nor MacNamara's, 1818, though if they ever were used in the pulpit, people would have had the privilege of listening to the Epistle and Gospel as originally translated in 1582. Nor is it likely that the Dublin clergy would have tolerated Coyne's New Testament, 1820, in their pulpits, despite the prefixed Approbation by Dr. Troy; for it was published by the Protestants' Fund for the 'conversion' of the presumed ignorant Irish Catholics."

An interesting anonymous translation of the Gospels was published in London in 1836, purporting to be translated from the Greek with critical notes "by a Catholic." Since at that time the number of Roman Catholics in England capable of such scholarly work was quite limited, speculation about the author was rife. Who could it be? Cardinal Wiseman, in making cautious note of it in the *Dublin Review,* damned it with faint praise —a prudent move, since there was reason to suspect the work of a wicked wag bent upon poking fun at the Church which, at the biblical Renaissance three centuries earlier, had punished men for reading the Gospels in Greek. The translator turned out to be John Lingard, a scholarly Roman Catholic who had quietly undertaken the work without seeking ecclesiastical approbation. In many ways the translation was felicitous and vivacious. The seed that fell on rocky ground "sprouted quickly, because it had no depth of soil." For "do penance" was substituted "repent."

In the United States, Francis Patrick Kenrick, brother of Peter Kenrick, an American Roman Catholic prelate prominent in the Opposition party that was so notoriously ill treated by the Papalist party at the First Vatican Council in 1870, published in six volumes, between 1849 and 1860, a complete revision of the traditional English Roman Catholic version of the Bible. He claimed that his work, though done from the Vulgate, was the result of diligent comparison with the Hebrew and Greek. It was, indeed, a revision with many independent and sometimes admirable features. "Wary as serpents, guileless as doves" is one of his happiest turns of phrase. His solution in the embarrassing choice between the traditional Roman Catholic "do penance" and the obviously King James "repent" was to use these renderings alternately—surely not the best or the most needed sort of compromise. Still, Kenrick's was a most impressive piece of work to come out of the mid-nineteenth-century Roman Catholic community in the United States. Both he and his brother were indeed very remarkable men and a great credit to their Church.

Meanwhile, in England, in 1885, the Roman Catholic Synod of Westminster, with a view to ending the chaos, proposed a translation of the Bible to be undertaken by scholars chosen by Cardinal Wiseman himself. Two years later the future Cardinal Newman, then the greatest scholar available for the task, expressed his willingness to undertake it; yet nothing came of this laudable proposal. Translations continued to multiply, and no prospect of uniformity in the vernacular use of the Bible in English-speaking Roman Catholic parishes was coming into sight.

Very different is the story of Jewish translations during this period. In the eighteenth and nineteenth centuries, English-speaking Jews used the King James Version. It was by far the best English Bible available. Of course they were not entirely satisfied with it. Before the French Revolution, European Jewry was in many ways for long hampered by circumstances beyond its control. The Jews, hindered by the widespread sufferings that had come in the train of the Inquisition, had been too much thrown back upon the maze of Talmudic lore that so often before in the course of their history had obscured from them the text of their own sacred literature. Moreover, till 1861, when Seligman Baer and Franz Delitzsch published at Leipzig a portion of their cautious work on the Hebrew text, they were at the disadvantage of having no critical edition of that text upon which to base important new translations.

In Holland and England the eighteenth-century Jew did have better opportunities for contact with the Gentile world, and it was in such countries that the prospect of emancipation seemed brightest. In fact, however, it was in the unlikely climate of eighteenth-century German Jewry that Moses Mendelssohn (1729-1786), the great prophet of Reform Judaism, appeared. So famous is he in the annals of Jewry that he has been called the third Moses. (The second Moses, on this reckoning, is Moses Maimonides [1135-1204], the greatest Jewish philosopher of the Middle Ages, whose thought deeply influenced that of the great thirteenth-century Christian schoolman, Thomas Aquinas.) Moses Mendelssohn was born in Dessau, the son of a poor scribe. Being a delicate boy who suffered from curvature of the spine, he was educated at home by his father and the local rabbi. In his youth he bought, out of his very meager earnings, a Latin copy of the *Essay concerning Human Understanding* by the English philosopher John Locke. With the help of a Latin dictionary he was able to read this work, which exerted a considerable influence over his eager mind. He attained literary success and was granted by Frederick the Great, King of Prussia, the title of "Protected Jew" (*Schutze-Jude*), which afforded him unmolested residence in Berlin. Now devoting himself to the task of securing emancipation for all Jews, he translated the Pentateuch, issued in 1783, and some other parts of the Hebrew Bible into High German. The effect of this was incalculable. It opened up to German Jews the treasures of the German language and inspired in them an interest in the culture from which they had so long been barred. Moses Mendelssohn's progeny included the founder of the famous Mendelssohn banking house (his eldest son) as well as his grandson, Felix, the composer. His work on the translation of the Hebrew Bible into German was completed by David Friedländer (1750-1834) and other disciples and friends.

Among Jews in Italy and France similar translation work was undertaken. Isaac Samuel Reggio (1784-1855) published an Italian translation of the Pentateuch in 1821, and a very learned edition of the Bible in French, principally the work of S. Cahen, appeared between 1831 and 1851. Lazare Wogue produced a French translation of the Pentateuch which, appearing between 1860 and 1869, was the basis of a more popular French version made by the French rabbinate under the direction of Zadoc Kahn and published between 1899 and 1906. An Italian version of the Hebrew Bible begun by Samuel David Luzzato (1800-1865) was completed by his pupils and published between 1868 and 1875. There was an incomplete Dutch translation by S. Mulder published as early as between 1826 and 1838. The Pentateuch in Russian was printed in 1862 and the Psalter in 1864.

Challoner saw how desirable it would be for English-speaking Roman Catholics in his day to have a simpler and more readable version of the Bible than the traditional Douai-Reims Version seemed capable of affording them. He produced a version of his own that was, for its day and in the circumstances, a fairly good revision of the Douai Bible. The New Testament appeared in 1749 and the whole Bible the following year. Notes were few. Challoner's debt to the King James Version is striking. He was no great scholar; but he was a practical churchman with much common sense. So, for example, in place of the then traditional Roman Catholic wording "But when I was made a man, I did away with the things that belonged to a little one," Challoner echoed the King James

Version, "But when I became a man, I put away the things of a child."

Numerous errors in the Challoner Bible necessitated several revisions. A revised text of his New Testament was actually included in the Bible published in 1750, and in a third revision of the New Testament, published in 1752, there were more than two thousand changes besides considerable striving after drastic modernization of the English. A second revision of the Old Testament was published in 1763 and a fourth revision of the New Testament in 1764. In 1772 came a fifth edition, still containing many misprints besides those included in an appended list. For all the limitations of Challoner's Bible, there is no doubt of its value in the history of Roman Catholic versions in English. Not only did its position seem secure at the time of his death in 1781; till comparatively recent times Challoner's Bible continued to be widely used among those English-speaking Roman Catholics throughout the world who read the Bible at all. It is surprising to find, therefore, that two years after his death another version of the New Testament was issued at the suggestion of the Roman Catholic Archbishop of Dublin, Dr. Carpenter. This version, by Bernard MacMahon, was singularly unfortunate. He was apparently unqualified for the task. Not only did his New Testament incorporate numerous ill-advised alterations and corruptions; it was followed in 1791 by a version of the Bible which, instead of mending matters, simply perpetrated these evils on a more extensive scale. Yet because MacMahon's Bible had ecclesiastical approbation, it was assured of and obtained wide circulation. The Roman Catholic bishops in Ireland, to the extent that they recommended Bible reading at all, persisted in encouraging the sale of the MacMahon New Testament and Bible, though Challoner's work, for all its faults, was very much better.

In 1788, fifty years after the publication of the fifth edition of the Reims New Testament, a sixth edition was published in Liverpool. In 1790 a large quarto edition of the Douai Bible, the first Roman Catholic Bible to be published in the United States and the first *quarto* English Bible of any kind to be published there, was issued by Carey, Stewart and Company of Philadelphia. The text was a mixture of several editions of Challoner's. The New Testament generally follows the 1752 revision of this Bible. MacMahon's influence seems to be negligible. In 1792 there was published in Edinburgh a now exceedingly rare duodecimo New Testament whose text, though based on the 1752 edition of Challoner's, exhibits some interesting variations, including quaint phrases such as, at Matthew 26:69, "Peter sat without in the Cove." This anonymous edition, happily lacking the influence of MacMahon, apparently met with little success. The translations done by the heterodox Father Geddes were intended as the basis of his critical work on the Old Testament in which he was in advance of most scholars of his day. More will be said of his work in a later chapter.[2]

Feeling against Roman Catholics still ran very high in England at the beginning of the century. Their attitude towards the foundation in 1804 of the British and Foreign Bible Society, the first and still the largest of the constellation of such societies whose work in translating and disseminating the Bible throughout the world is now widely celebrated, served to confirm the general opinion that they were enemies of the Bible itself. The Church to which Pius IX was to address, sixty years later, the notorious *Syllabus of Errors,* therein condemning such Bible societies along with Communism and other "pests," was certainly by no means well disposed to them in 1804. There was nevertheless a group of zealous churchmen, including a few Roman Catholic laymen, who felt that if Roman Catholics were prohibited from reading the New Testament in any form not bearing the express approval of their Church, then funds should be raised to provide them with the New Testament in a form their Church did approve, so that they might share at least to this extent in the benefits it was the aim of the British and Foreign Bible Society to provide. A fund was launched, therefore, for the express purpose of "printing the Rhemish New Testament, and dispersing it gratuitously, or at a low price, among the Roman Catholics in the United Kingdom." There would be no notes or comments of any kind, "excepting that the letter of Pope Pius VI to the Archbishop of Florence, and the Approbation of the English Colleges of Rheims and Douai, always prefixed to this edition, will also be reprinted." The intention was, of course, to respect the conscience of the Roman Catholic minority in England and provide them, free if need be, with their own New Testament. It was hoped that, as far as possible, the work would be undertaken by the Roman Catholics themselves. In March, 1813, "The Roman Catholic Bible Society" was actually founded with a view to fulfilling these aims.

This project was, if not eminently generous, at least very fair. The violent reaction it elicited from the Roman Catholic bishop, Dr. Milner, is therefore astonishing. This prelate, who had denounced Father Geddes while admitting he had not read his work, called the Roman Catholic Bible Society "in its very title a departure from the Catholic Rule of Faith." By this he referred to the claims of his Church to be "the Catholic Church"—a claim that other Christians disallow, repudiating it with the Roman Church's practice (peculiarly odious to other Christians) of propagating the claim by calling other Christians "non-Catholics." Bishop Milner insisted that the notes (whose extremely anti-Protestant character

[2] See below, pp. 269 ff.

250

was notorious) were vital, being, he insisted, "precisely the part that is wanted at the present day, to render an English translation of the present text safe and profitable in the hands of the laity." This outburst took many Roman Catholic laymen, no less than others, by surprise, for they had not been accustomed to the notion that the ecclesiastical approbation given to the Reims New Testament was valid only when this version was accompanied by the offensive polemical notes. At length a compromise was effected. The fourteen most offensive notes were omitted; the other 226 were retained. Another Roman Catholic bishop, Dr. William Poynter, became president of the Roman Catholic Bible Society, and in 1815 the society issued the Reims New Testament for the use of Roman Catholics. There were two editions, an octavo and a duodecimo, and the text used was that of the comparatively rare 1740 Challoner revision, though with some pleasing modernizations, such as "said" for "saith." Free of the MacMahon influence, it was a good version of its kind and had considerable influence on the later history of Roman Catholic Bible translation in the English-speaking world, being reprinted in 1818 both by Sidney and Horrabin and by Keating and Brown, and also in 1823 by Bagster.

Meanwhile, as early as 1789, the year of the French Revolution that was to have such a decisive effect on the history of European Jewry, a version of the Pentateuch in English appeared. This version purported to be an emendation of the King James Version, departing from its model only where this "deviates from the genuine sense of the Hebrew expressions, or where it renders obscure the meaning of the text, or, lastly, when it occasions a seeming contradiction." So conceived, the work was dedicated to the Bishop of Salisbury, Dr. Barrington. There were other such attempts, followed by a translation of the whole Hebrew Bible into English by Benisch, which appeared between 1851 and 1856. In 1884, the year before the appearance of the Revised Version of the Bible, Michael Friedländer had offered English-speaking Jewry yet another attempt at the revision of the King James Version.

The version of the Hebrew Bible in English that was prepared by Isaac Leeser and published at Philadelphia in 1853 remained for long, however, the most widely used version in English-speaking Jewry. Based upon the King James Version, it borrowed considerably from German versions. It was not a notable piece of scholarship. Despite its popularity, its inadequacy was increasingly felt as Jewry in the United States expanded, and at length a project for its thorough revision was considered in 1892 at the second biennial convention of the Jewish Publication Society of America. By this time, however, the Revised Version of the Bible had appeared, and the outcome of this project belongs, therefore, to a later chapter of our story.[3]

[3] See below, pp. 314-15.

Meanwhile, both the intrinsic merit and the literary appeal of the King James Version won for it a general acceptance throughout the English-speaking world that made any official revision difficult. Between 1611 and 1881, at least seventy "private" versions appeared, however, not counting Roman Catholic ones. Several very interesting attempts were made in the eighteenth century by private individuals to provide independent translations.

One of these was by Daniel Mace, a Presbyterian with advanced ideas on the subject of biblical criticism. In 1729 he published a Greek text of the New Testament, based on his use of the more recently available manuscripts and offered as an improvement on the text then generally accepted. With this he brought out his own translation in English that accorded with the fashion of the day. A chain of error has caused Daniel Mace's work to be attributed to a William Mace who was a lecturer in Civil Law. Published anonymously, because of the advanced and therefore suspect ideas of the translator, it was so attributed by Cotton in his *Editions of the Bible,* a standard source and even in the British Museum Catalogue,[4] as well as by distinguished contemporary writers. William Whiston, Newton's successor in the Chair of Mathematics at Cambridge and widely known for his translation of the work of the Jewish historian Josephus, also published a translation of three Greek New Testament manuscripts.

The translation published in 1755 by John Wesley naturally attracted some attention, since the Methodist movement due to his influence was already a spreading spiritual force. Wesley's version was in fact a rather conservative private revision of the King James Version. It was entitled *The New Testament with Notes, for Plain Unlettered Men who know only their Mother Tongue.* The title is not one that would commend itself to any publishing house today!

In 1768 was published Edward Harwood's *A Liberal Translation of the New Testament,* which was as bold in its departure from the King James Version as Wesley's had been cautious. "Oh, Sir!" exclaims Peter at the Transfiguration. "What a delectable residence we might establish here." For more than a thousand years the cloisters of Europe had echoed at eventide with the simple, direct, and sonorous Latin of the *Nunc dimittis,* Simeon's canticle of joy that is so beautifully rendered in the English Prayer Book:

---

[4] In *The Bible in the Making,* I pointed out (p. 196 n.) the error in the British Museum Catalogue and was assured that eventually it would be corrected. Even so great a scholar as the late Norman Sykes repeated it in *The Cambridge History of the Bible: the West from the Reformation to the Present Day,* ed. S. L. Greenslade (Cambridge: Cambridge University Press, 1963), p. 189.

> Lord, now lettest thou thy servant depart in peace:
> according to thy word.
> For mine eyes have seen: thy salvation,
> Which thou hast prepared: before the face of all people;
> To be a light to lighten the Gentiles: and to be the
> glory of thy people Israel.

Harwood, claiming to replace "the bald and barbarous language of the old vulgar version with the elegance of modern English," was now offering instead: "O God, thy promise to me is amply fulfilled. I now quit the post of human life with satisfaction and joy, since thou hast indulged mine eyes with so divine a spectacle as the great Messiah."

Even a modern atheist with only a year of Latin behind him must surely stand in awe of the beauty, if nothing else, of the scene at Vespers in a well-ordered monastic church as the monks, making the sign of the cross, slowly chant the exquisitely simple words of joy attributed to the Virgin Mary: *Magnificat anima mea Dominum. Et exultavit spiritus meus: in Deo salutari meo.* For the opening words of the Magnificat, Harwood gave this rendering: "My soul with reverence adores my Creator, and all my faculties with transport join in celebrating the goodness of God my Saviour, who hath in so signal a manner condescended to regard my poor and humble station. Transcendent goodness! Every future age will now conjoin in celebrating my happiness!" Mary's prophetic faith might be said to have had its fulfilment with the aid of Latin and English renderings such as are provided in the Vulgate and the King James Versions. The promise, couched in Harwood's language, would have needed for its fulfilment an even greater miracle than Mary could have felt called upon to expect.

A similar spirit had lain behind the translation that Anthony Purver, a Quaker, had brought out in 1764. He called it "a new and literal" translation, and it came to be popularly known as "The Quaker Bible." In his version of the Lord's Prayer, "hallowed" becomes "sacredly reverenced," while "The flowers appear on the earth" (Song of Solomon 2:12) is transmogrified as "Earth's lap displays her infant flowers." The simplicity Quakers profess to love is difficult to discern here. Nor is it easy to see any other respect in which this version is an improvement over the King James Bible. Surely the style of such versions, florid and flamboyant when not prosy and dull, could have done nothing to diminish popular contentment with the King James Version or the prestige this had by now long won.

Nathaniel Scarlett's translation of the New Testament, published in 1798, substituted "immerse" for "baptize," divided the text into sections, and set forth dialogue as in a drama. After the organization of the American Bible Union in 1850, there were many attempts at "immersion" versions.

In considering twentieth-century discussions upon the rulings of the United States Supreme Court on the use of the Bible in our public schools, Americans should not forget the remarkably active interest taken by some of the greatest figures in the early history of this country in the matter of Bible translation. Thomas Jefferson and Benjamin Franklin were both very much interested in the subject, and Noah Webster actually undertook a revision of the King James Version.[5]

The first translation of the Septuagint into English was made in the United States by Charles Thomson, who was Secretary to Congress and a friend of Jefferson. The circumstances of his development of an interest in this project are remarkable. At an auction he had happened to pick up for a few cents a book that the auctioneer described as having "outlandish letters" and which turned out to be in fact part of the Septuagint. At this time the distinguished buyer of this item knew no Greek. The book fascinated him, however, and he set about learning Greek in order to read it. Encouraged by his friend Jefferson, he decided to devote his retirement, which took place in 1789, to an attempt at translating the Septuagint, and the result of his labors appeared in 1808. Omitting the Apocrypha, he included only the books of the Greek Septuagint that are contained in the Hebrew Bible. His was a remarkable accomplishment for a man who was professionally untrained. In England, Sir Lancelot Brenton brought out a translation of the Septuagint independently in 1844, also omitting the Apocrypha. Noah Webster's revision of the King James Version was published at New Haven in 1833, and though it has little importance, the fact that Webster undertook it is, of course, noteworthy.

Meanwhile, in England, independent versions continued to be made, such as one by Gilbert Wakefield. Wakefield seems to have been temperamentally given to dissent. He was a dissenter in theology, a dissenter in politics, and a dissenter in translation methods. He disliked Harwood's style and sought to follow the King James Version much more closely. Yet he felt impelled to make certain changes, substituting a new word for what he considered a "low, obsolete or obscure one," and a new phrase for one that he took to be "coarse or uncouth."

Archbishop William Newcome's translation of the New Testament was printed in 1796 and published in 1800. Newcome was an ardent advocate of the revision of the King James Version. He based his translation on

---

[5] On early American Bibles see John Wright, *Early Bibles of America* (New York: Thomas Whittaker, 1892).

the contemporary critical Greek text of Griesbach,[6] and in dialogue he used quotation marks—a striking novelty at that time.

As early as 1810, the Lady Margaret Professor of Divinity at the University of Cambridge, Dr. Herbert Marsh, later Bishop of Peterborough, recognizing the critical work that was already being done by European scholars on the biblical text, made an admirable pronouncement on the merits and shortcomings of the King James Version and the need for its revision. "It is probable," he said, "that our Authorized Version is as faithful a representation of the original Scriptures as *could* have been formed at *that period*. But when we consider the immense accession that has been made, both to our critical and philological apparatus; when we consider that the most important sources of intelligence for the *interpretation* of the original Scriptures were *likewise* opened after that period, we cannot possibly pretend that our Authorized Version does not require *amendment*." That the character of the critical revolution that was taking place should have been appreciated so early, by a contemporary of Griesbach, witnesses to the timely awareness among the English episcopate of the need for official revision. Dr. Marsh was making this pronouncement several years before even the birth of either Tischendorf or Westcott or Hort, and at a time when the revolution in New Testament studies was still in its infancy.

In 1818 a translation of the New Testament was published in London that was based upon three eighteenth-century attempts at New Testament translation. For the Gospels was used a translation made by George Campbell in 1789, for the Epistles one made by James MacKnight in 1795, and for the rest of the New Testament the work of another eighteenth-century translator, Philip Doddridge. It was this Campbell-MacKnight-Doddridge version that Alexander Campbell took (together with the critical Greek text of Griesbach) as the basis for the translation he issued in 1826. Alexander Campbell (1788-1866) was a seceding minister in Scotland who in 1809 had emigrated to the United States. In 1827 he founded a congregation called Campbellites or Disciples of Christ, now one of the larger American Protestant denominations. His translation, which ran into six editions, has often been reprinted. It was much marred by the unnatural English he inherited. To say, for example, that "a city situate on a mountain must be conspicuous" is to betray a misunderstanding of the genius of the English tongue at a point where the Tyndale and the King James Version still vigorously conserve and display that genius. Once again, the weakness of addiction to passing fads and fashions in language is vividly shown. The language of the earlier English versions not only remains singularly robust by compari-

[6] See below, pp. 264-65.

son; it now sounds distinctly modern where Campbell's is heavy and dated, displaying the typically eighteenth-century cumbersome Latinity bereft of the terseness that is Latin's principal strength.

Wise indeed had been the rules laid down by King James' translators. They were widely forgotten, however, by those who essayed new translations in Campbell's day. In 1833 appeared in Boston *A New and Corrected Version of the New Testament* by Rudolphus Dickinson, who aimed at replacing "the frequently rude and occasionally barbarous attire" of the King James Version by "a splendid and sweetly flowing diction" so that the ears of "accomplished and refined persons" might not be offended. The quality is what one would expect from the author of such aspirations. The translation is more literal than Harwood's, but the style is similar. "When Elizabeth heard the salutation of Mary," wrote Dickinson, "the embryo was joyfully agitated." [7]

The tendency among authors of independent versions at this time seems to have been towards literalism. Edward Barlee's very free rendering of the Epistles, which consisted mainly of the King James text with explanatory phrases and was published in 1837, was an exception. The more typical aim is often announced in the titles, as, for instance, in the version offered by William Heberden, who was physician-in-ordinary to George III: *A literal translation of the Apostolical Epistles and Revelation, with a concurrent commentary.* So also we have *A literal translation of the last eight books of the New Testament,* published at London in 1854. The author is said to be F. Parker. He used a pseudonym, Herman Heinfetter. Having also produced *An English Version of the New Testament from the text of the Vatican Manuscript,* he apparently hoped to complete a translation of the whole Bible but died before going very far with the Old Testament.

Robert Young, author of a celebrated Bible concordance, produced *The Holy Bible . . . translated according to the letter and idiom of the original languages,* which was published in 1862. This is a very remarkable piece of work. Critical of the King James translators, Young advanced his own theories about how translation from the Hebrew should be done. Pointing out peculiarities in the Hebrew use of tenses, such as the use of the present tense in Hebrew to indicate what would in other languages be expressed by past or future, he adopted the practice of using the present tense in English to translate such idiomatic Hebrew turns of phrase. So we have: "And Abram goeth up from Egypt. . . . and Abram is exceedingly wealthy in cattle, in silver, and in gold. . . . And also to Lot, who is going with Abram, there hath been sheep and oxen and tents, and the land hath not suffered them to dwell together, for their

---

[7] Luke 1:41.

substance hath been much, and they have not been able to dwell together, and there is strife between those feeding Abram's cattle and those feeding Lot's cattle, and the Canaanite and the Perizzite are then dwelling in the land."

In the United States, however, there were some nineteenth-century translations of a different sort that prefigured, rather, the great twentieth-century "everyday speech" translations such as those of Moffatt and Phillips. One of these was by Andrew Norton, *The Gospels, a new translation,* published at Boston in 1855. He replaced the archaic "thou" with the more modern "you," for instance. So also did Leicester Ambrose Sawyer, in *The New Testament, translated from the original Greek with chronological arrangement of books,* except that Sawyer did not go so far as to use the everyday form where the Deity was being addressed. In England in the mid-nineteenth century there were also some interesting attempts at revision, rather than translation. An English rector, T. J. Hussey for instance, produced such a revision of his own with the King James Version in parallel columns, which was published in 1844-1845. Another noteworthy work of this kind was H. Highton's *Revised Translation of the New Testament.*

The increasing critical sense that was developing among scholars in the nineteenth century is reflected in a translation of the Gospels by G. W. Brameld, published in 1870. He claimed that "the spurious passages are expunged; the doubtful bracketed; and the whole revised after the texts of Griesbach, Lachmann, Tischendorf,[8] Alford and Tregelles." In the same year John Bowes published a translation of the New Testament "from the purest Greek." Translations from the text of Tischendorf appeared in the seventies, for instance one by George Noyes [9] and another by Samuel Davidson. The striving after literalism that has already been noted is found once again in the New Testament produced by an English curate, William Crickmer, who provided the reader with exact indications of the disposition of the words and phrases of the original Greek. In 1869, just before the Revised Version was undertaken, one of the leading figures associated with it, Dean Alford, published *The New Testament, newly compared with the original Greek and revised.* By this time the need for a thorough revision that would have the full authority of the Church was widely felt among educated churchmen enjoying the Reformation heritage in the English-speaking world.

[8] See below, pp. 262-63.
[9] See below, p. 363.

*I saw a man who saw another man
who saw the sea.*—Portuguese proverb (*vi hum
homem que vio outro homem que vio o mar*)

CHAPTER 26 *Light from the East*

We must now turn our minds back again to the seventeenth century, for the need of a revision of the King James Version had been felt by some from the beginning. Hugh Broughton had expounded this need with learning and expressed it with spleen even before the first edition saw the light in 1611. Soon afterwards, however, the character of the need was seen to be more radical than the earliest critics could have recognized. Gradually this need came to be universally admitted by all informed readers of the English Bible. The reasons for this development now call for our attention.

The sixteenth-century biblical Renaissance had been inspired by an ardent desire, characteristic of the spirit of the age, for a return to the original sources. It had been accomplished, however, with very imperfect textual tools. Those who engaged in it were by no means unaware of the limitations under which they labored. As for their critics, the more reactionary ones in the Roman Church excused themselves for translating the New Testament from the Vulgate rather than the Greek on the ground that no satisfactory Greek text existed.

It is true that the existence of one of the great fourth-century Greek biblical manuscripts, the Codex Vaticanus, was known to scholars in Western Europe at the time the King James Version was being prepared, for it had been catalogued in the Vatican Library as early as 1475 [1] and had been used as the basis of an edition of the Septuagint published at Rome in 1587 under the authority of Pope Sixtus V. The manuscript was so closely guarded by the popes, however, who did not choose to make available to the scholarly world at large the precious text it contained, that it never became accessible to the scholarly world in even a limited way for two hundred years after the first publication of the King James Version. Indeed, it became available to scholars only through the fortunes of war, for it was Napoleon who carried it back from Rome as a prize of war to Paris, where it was studied before being returned to

---

[1] One British scholar, Sir Frederic Kenyon, has questioned this; but the evidence in favor of it appears decisive to most scholars. In any case, it is certain that Codex Vaticanus was in the Vatican Library in 1481. A fifth edition of Kenyon's *Our Bible and the Ancient Manuscripts*, first published in 1895, was published in 1958 by Eyre and Spottiswoode, London.

Rome in 1815. There is no reason to suppose that, but for Napoleon's military enterprise and other circumstances extraneous to the intentions of the Roman custodians of this codex, it would ever have been made accessible at all to any but the most trusted of Rome's sons. In fact, thanks to these extraneous circumstances and modern technological progress, photostatic reproductions of it are now available even to students who have never set foot in Italy.

There were also, of course, other important manuscripts that were known at the time the King James translators did their work. One of these was a Graeco-Latin manuscript, dating from probably the fifth century and including the Gospels, the Acts, and a small fragment of the Latin of the third Epistle of St. John. This manuscript had been taken in 1546 to the Council of Trent by the Bishop of Clermont.[2] Its text was used also in the *editio regia* of the New Testament published in Paris in 1550. The Calvinist theologian Thedore Beza, having obtained this manuscript about ten years after this time, from the convent of St. Irenaeus at Lyons, presented it in 1581 to the University of Cambridge. It is accordingly known to scholars as Codex Bezae. Great as is its importance to scholars it contained only a small portion of the biblical text, so that its value was limited in comparison with that of Codex Vaticanus. In any case, though there were two editions of Codex Bezae, the more serious critical study of this manuscript did not begin till after the publication of the Revised Version in 1885.[3]

Long before the text of Codex Vaticanus had come within the general ken of scholars, however, another similar and hardly less important manuscript reached England. This manuscript, Codex Alexandrinus, came sixteen years after the appearance of the first edition of the King James Bible, and its acquisition was due to a very remarkable set of circumstances.

In 1572 a man had been born in Crete who was destined to become Patriarch of Alexandria and the first theologian of any importance in the Greek Orthodox Church since the Fall of Constantinople in 1453. This man, Cyrillos Lucaris or Cyril Lucar (1572-1637), inherited the traditional Greek distaste for Rome. Nevertheless, he seems to have evinced for a time an attitude of interest in and even admiration for the Roman Church that was unusual, not to say eccentric, among the Greek Orthodox, whose outlook towards Rome was notoriously hostile,

---

[2] Kenyon has questioned this, too; but again the evidence appears sufficient.

[3] The extent to which it has since developed may be judged from the wealth of material dealt with in contemporary studies such as the monograph by Eldon Jay Epp, *The Theological Tendency of Codex Bezae Cantabrigiensis in Acts* (Society for New Testament Studies Monograph Series; Cambridge: Cambridge University Press, 1966).

for the Greeks have always felt a strong sense of independence of Rome and a disdain for it as an ecclesiastical parvenu and corruptor of the One Indivisible Catholic Church. The young Cyril Lucar had gone to Venice and Padua to pursue his studies. Apparently as a result of his firsthand observations and contacts with the Roman Church that he made in the course of his studies in Italy, he was disillusioned. Far from developing his temporary interest in the Roman Church, he was not only turned from it but underwent a change of attitude that led him to take a more and more sympathetic interest in the work of the Reformed Church in Western Europe. When he became. in 1602, Patriarch of Alexandria, and, in 1621, Patriarch of Constantinople, the Reformed Church in the West had an occasion for rejoicing.

His principal aim throughout his mature life was to reform the Eastern Church on lines similar to those so carefully and skilfully laid down by Calvin. It was for this reason that he sent many promising young Greek theologians to study at the universities of England, Switzerland, and the Netherlands. With the assistance of a Calvinist theologian, Antoine Léger, he caused a translation of the Bible into the vernacular to be undertaken for the use of his people, and in various other ways set the scene for the thoroughgoing reformation of the Greek Church on Calvinist lines. In 1629 he published a confessional statement, Calvinist in doctrine and temper, though accommodated, of course, to the spirit of the Greek Church and the genius of Greek thought and language. Though his authorship of this is disputed, there is no doubt that at least he endorsed it. Not unnaturally, his power and influence in the Eastern Church, welcome as it was among the heirs of the Reformation in the West, was not less bitterly resented and feared by the Jesuits, who used every means at their disposal to bring about his undoing. As a result of their co-operation with the more reactionary elements in the Greek Church itself, Lucar suffered much persecution, including banishment on several occasions. At last his enemies, by accusing him of a design to stir up the Cossacks against the Sultan Nurad, succeeded in persuading the latter, when he was about to set out on a war against Persia, to have the great Greek patriarch executed. At the order of the Sultan, he was cruelly strangled to death by janissaries.[4]

In 1625, when Cyril was Patriarch of Constantinople, he arranged through the British ambassador, Sir Thomas Roe, to present to King James a Greek manuscript of the Bible as a token of his affection for and interest in the Church of England and the Calvinist doctrines that he

---

[4] Cyril Lucar's was by no means an isolated case of Eastern Orthodox interest in Reformation influences in the West. There have been flirtations with Lutheran and Anglican authorities too; but his case, besides being intrinsically important, is peculiarly relevant to the literary history of the Bible.

probably believed this Church to be capable of expressing in a peculiarly effective way. The manuscript was sent about that time to George Abbot, Archbishop of Canterbury, whose Puritan sympathies, distasteful to James, have been noted in an earlier chapter, as well as the prominent role he played in the translation of the Bible. Through a delay, it was not received till 1627, by which time James was dead and had been succeeded by Charles I.

The early history of this great biblical manuscript is obscure. It is likely to have been written in Egypt, and it probably had become the property of the Athonite monks. Since the tenth century, these monks have inhabited Mount Athos on the peninsula that stretches from the coast of Macedonia to the Aegean Sea. They are now settled in more than twenty separate monasteries on that ancient and celebrated site, possessing great literary and artistic treasures. Their life is essentially as it was in, say, the age of Dante. Their rule still forbids the presence of any female, even a female animal, within the monastic properties.[5] At any rate, the precious manuscript that came to England through the interest and beneficence of Cyril Lucar is known to have been written early in the fifth century. The earliest manuscript of the Greek Bible to become generally available to scholars in the West after the sixteenth-century biblical Renaissance, it contains, besides much else of interest, the two so-called Epistles of Clement and what is perhaps still the best extant text of the Apocalypse. The manuscript was used by Brian Walton (*c.* 1600-1661), Bishop of Chester, in his *Biblia Sacra Polyglotta* which, begun in 1653 and completed in 1657, included the Old Testament, New Testament, and Apocrypha, being one of the first books in England to have been printed by subscription. Codex Alexandrinus passed in 1757, with the rest of the Royal Library, to the British Museum, where it is still housed.

Scholars quickly saw that even if the King James translators could have done twice as well as they had done, they would still have been laboring under the enormous disadvantage of lacking access to biblical manuscripts of such antiquity and importance as this Codex Alexandrinus most certainly was. Their work, no matter how good it might be, was already from a scholarly point of view outmoded.

Nor was the sense of a need for revision due to the sudden appearance of one manuscript only. There were others, and who could tell how many more there might be? The Codex Ephraemi, for instance, had been in Paris since the sixteenth century, having been brought thither by Catherine de Médicis. When the Codex Alexandrinus came to England,

---

[5] The purpose of this rule was less fanatical than it is popularly taken to be. The monks were to be discouraged from commercial enterprises such as the breeding of animals.

the existence of the Codex Ephraemi in Paris was well known. What was not known was that it contained a fifth century New Testament text. For by the twelfth century this manuscript had been converted into a palimpsest, with a new manuscript superimposed upon the original writing. Only in the eighteenth century was this precious original writing uncovered.

The proposals made in the Long Parliament in 1653 for a full revision of the King James Version came to nothing, though. As has been seen, certain unobtrusive alterations were made in various editions of the Bible that fast became, for all its known shortcomings, by far the most influential book in the English-speaking world. The greater this influence, which was felt in all classes of a then very socially stratified society, the more difficult it was, of course, to bring about any radical change. The King James Version of the English Bible had popularly acquired, within a comparatively short time, almost the status of an immutable oracle of God. It was not till the late nineteenth century that the accumulation of scholarly discoveries had mounted to the point where a revision of the King James Version could no longer be delayed.

By this time the Codex Vaticanus, a little older than Codex Alexandrinus and for five hundred years jealously guarded by the custodians of the Vatican Library, had become accessible, as we have seen, to the scholarly world. On vellum, said to be antelope skin, with three columns to the page, it contains one of the most ancient texts of the Bible, though it is unfortunately incomplete, lacking the New Testament from Hebrews 9:15 onwards. Another nineteenth-century biblical find, however, drew attention most dramatically to the need for revision of the English Bible. I recount once again the romantic, oft-told story of the discovery of Codex Sinaiticus.

In May, 1844, a German scholar, Constantin Tischendorf (1815-1874), was visiting the monastery of St. Catherine, on Mount Sinai, a great gaunt building, walled in like a Norman keep. His purpose was to unearth any manuscript fragments of any sort that he might chance to find, and that the monks might be willing to let him see. By extraordinarily good fortune—some might say providentially—he discovered 129 leaves of manuscript in a trash bin and was told by the monks that they were about to be burned, and that moreover two other similar bins of rubbish had already been so destroyed. It was not till a much later visit to the monastery that Tischendorf discovered enough of the manuscript to reveal its full value. At any rate, in 1867, after a series of very involved transactions, the assembled manuscript was presented to the Tsar of Russia and placed in the Imperial Library. The monks received from the Tsar the sum of nine thousand roubles, which was very roughly the equivalent, at that time, of seven thousand dollars. Through the Tsar's influence they also secured for their own nominee the Archbishopric of Sinai. The manuscript, which came to be known as Codex Sinaiticus, is written on vellum, with four columns to the page. Though in some respects defective, it contains the whole of the New Testament. Apparently three different scribes were engaged upon the work, and two of them were evidently bad spellers. Indeed, one of them was such a bad speller that modern scholars have wondered how he ever came to be entrusted with the work. Be that as it may, the manuscript was a discovery of the greatest importance for biblical scholarship, calling further attention to the urgent need for a revision of the King James Version by a team of scholars who would be able to take into account, as the King James translators could not, the important biblical discoveries that had been made since 1611. Within three years after the Codex Sinaiticus had been presented to the Tsar of Russia, definite action had been taken by the English Church authorities for the Revised Version of the English Bible, to which a separate chapter will be devoted later.

The subsequent history of Codex Sinaiticus is of remarkable interest. At the Bolshevik Revolution, it passed, of course, with other treasures, into the hands of the Soviet government. In 1933, however, the British government succeeded in purchasing it for the sum of £100,000 (about half a million dollars at that time), so that, having passed out of Soviet custody, it is now among the treasures of the British Museum, where it is exhibited to the general public alongside the Codex Alexandrinus.

The great manuscript discoveries were indeed important factors in the situation that eventually revealed the urgent need for revision of the King James Version. Yet in themselves they could not have led to the new sort of understanding of the Bible that made the fulfilment of that need inevitable. Manuscripts are only tools for the biblical scholar; what matters is the use he is able to make of them. How did the nineteenth-century scholars use their tools?

It was well known and very obvious to them that the Latin Version that had been handed down in the Western Church in the Middle Ages had a long history. Jerome, in a letter written to Pope Damasus in 384, had explained why he deemed it necessary to revise the Latin text of the Bible and on what principles such revision ought to be undertaken. At that early date there was already a great variety of Latin texts, and these differed much, not only among themselves but also from the Greek manuscripts then available. A particular Latin rendering at that date might be better or worse (that is nearer or farther from the original text) than a particular Greek rendering in a currently circulating manuscript. For the Latin, though a translation, might have been handed down more faithfully at that point than the Greek.

This is easily understood if we imagine Shakespeare's having been handed down to us only in manuscript copies after the earliest had been lost. It might then well be said that a French translation of, say, 1750 would be more faithful to Shakespeare (at any rate, in respect of a particular passage or line) than an English manuscript of the same date. The English scribe might have been careless and the French one more accurate; or else the English scribe might have been copying from the work of a careless scribe, while the French translator might have had the good fortune to have before him a better text to translate than the English scribe had to copy.

This principle had been recognized even at the time of the sixteenth-century biblical Renaissance, when it had been in fact much invoked by those who, on the Roman side, tried to belittle the value of going to the sources in the original languages rather than attending to the traditional Latin text. As the biblical Renaissance proceeded, however, other facts became no less apparent. Latin was not the only language into which the Bible had been translated in ancient times. There were also, for instance, Syriac and Coptic translations. As early as the beginning of the nineteenth century, the German scholars Johann Jakob Griesbach (1745-1812) and Johann Leonhard Hug (1765-1846) perceived that the Peshitta Version, which may be regarded as the Syriac counterpart of the Latin Vulgate, must have had a similar history. They postulated an Old Syriac Version lying behind the Peshitta. Unfortunately, however, they had at that time no adequate manuscript evidence to back up their theory.

They thought they knew what such a text might be; but they were somewhat in the position of John Couch Adams, the nineteenth-century Cambridge mathematician who worked out, from deviations detected in the planet Uranus, the orbit of the planet Neptune whose existence was still hypothetical and was to remain so till, through the efforts of the French astronomer Leverrier, Neptune was actually seen in 1846. So Griesbach and Hug could not prove their hypothesis; but they could and did formulate it. In 1858, however, William Cureton (1808-1864), an Englishman who between 1837 and 1849 was on the staff of the British Museum, published some fragments of a fifth-century Syriac manuscript of the Gospels. Another English scholar, Henry Tattam (1789-1868) had brought this back in 1842 from the Nitrian desert, with some other Syriac and Coptic discoveries, and it had been Cureton's task to catalogue it. The manuscript, now known as the Curetonian Syriac, contains large fragments of the Gospels. This was the kind of evidence Griesbach had needed when he had formulated his theory earlier in the century.

The fact that in the second century Tatian had composed a harmony of the Gospels, the Diatessaron, had for long been known. Eusebius (c. 260–c. 340), widely recognized as "the Father of Church History," had alluded to it in his history of the Church, an important source of information for scholars. In the time of Griesbach, however, scholars generally supposed it to have been lost. Of great importance, therefore, was the publication in 1836, by the Fathers of an Armenian community in Venice, of an Armenian version of the works of Ephraem of Syria, among which was a commentary on the Diatessaron. Unfortunately, few scholars knew Armenian, so that this was overlooked by many at the time, and indeed even when the Armenian Fathers put out a Latin translation of it in 1876, it did not receive adequate attention. Only in 1880, when Ezra Abbot, an American scholar, drew attention to it, did the discovery attract all the attention it deserved. There is an even more interesting sequel to this story; but its consideration must be postponed till we are able to review, later on, the still more exciting modern developments after the Revised Version was published. It is mentioned now only to help to indicate the kind of discoveries that were being made in the middle of the century, resulting in the important beginnings of a new era in the understanding of the Bible.

We have seen that such an era can be inaugurated only by the interplay of two forces: the light shed by newly discovered manuscripts, and the use scholars make of these by critical examination and analysis. Three centuries earlier, Cardinal Ximenes in the Greek text of the New Testament he had issued in 1514, in what came to be known as the Complutensian Polyglot Bible, must have used Greek manuscripts in order to determine his text. It is not known what manuscripts he did use; but at any rate the text he produced has since been shown to be of no great value. The Greek text offered by Erasmus, though not printed till 1516, was actually published earlier than the Complutensian. It was also apparently based on Greek manuscripts of no particular value.

Four editions of the Greek text based on the Complutensian and on the text of Erasmus were published by Estienne. The third of these editions, published in 1550, became the standard text in England. Beza also published several editions, some in folio and some in octavo. In 1624 and 1633 two editions of the Greek New Testament were published by Elzevir. The latter, on account of a phrase in the preface, came to be known as the Textus Receptus or "Received Text."

Gradually, critics such as Richard Bentley (1662-1742) in England and Johannes Albrecht Bengel (1687-1782) in Germany began to develop critical methods of arriving at the true text. They were badly hampered, however, by the lack of tools. Nevertheless, Bengel developed the theory that there were "families" of texts of the New Testament, and Griesbach took this theory farther, mapping out certain groups so well that his theories, though they have been modified, have never been fundamentally changed by subsequent scholarship. Other scholars such as Karl Lachmann (1793-1851), the first to produce a text in which Textus Receptus was abandoned, contributed to technical, methodological advances, as did Tischendorf himself and his remarkable contemporary, a Cornishman by birth, Samuel Prideaux Tregelles (1813-1875).

The work of Brooke Foss Westcott (1825-1901) and Fenton John Anthony Hort (1828-1892) provided, however, the foundation of modern textual criticism of the New Testament. These two English scholars, both eventually members of the committee that produced the Revised Version of the New Testament, developed a scholarly method of establishing the best text. They argued that evidence from the early Christian Fathers shows that the text of the New Testament had become stereotyped by the fourth century and that therefore all important changes in the text must have taken place before then. The task before the textual critic is the recovery of the history of the text before that period.

Since there are no earlier manuscripts, how is this to be done? Westcott and Hort proposed two scientific criteria for discerning the text to be preferred. Firstly, if one variation can be shown to be due to the mixture of two others, it is plainly later than the sources from which it was derived. Secondly, if the earliest Christian Fathers always use one of the alternatives rather than another, it is plain that the former represents a better text. Apart from the use of these criteria one may also, *faute de mieux*, resort to the cautious use of probabilities.

Here is how Westcott and Hort proposed to apply the method. Suppose (and there are many examples) that in a set of manuscript sources we find three alternatives: a short reading in Group A, a short reading in Group B, and a longer reading in Group C. It is to be taken as highly probable that the longer reading is composed of the combination of two shorter ones. By this means they decided that two groups of manuscripts that Westcott and Hort called Western and Neutral respectively are to be preferred over another group called Syrian.

At some point earlier than the fourth century (probably much earlier), there were two great families of New Testament text. Later was evolved, probably in Syria, a text indebted sometimes to one, sometimes to the other, sometimes to both. These Syrian revisers might have also used, of course, other sources. Westcott and Hort thought they probably had used another source, and that this represented a school of Alexandrian scholars working on manuscripts in the so-called Neutral textual family. Of these three pre-Syrian textual families, the Alexandrian, the so-called Western, and the so-called Neutral, the latter two go back to the earliest period of which we have any knowledge. The Old Latin and Old Syriac versions of the second century help to provide means for the reconstruction of the Western text, while from Origen, for instance, we can obtain evidence leading to a reconstruction of the so-called Neutral. From all this much can be deduced concerning the ancestry of the great manuscripts that had come to light: in Codex Vaticanus and Codex Sinaiticus, for example, was preserved to a great extent the so-called Neutral text, while Codex Bezae represented the so-called Western.

It is obvious that the theories of Westcott and Hort, and especially their application, were open to criticism. Criticism was forthcoming at the time. It was noted, for instance, that the theory of a Syrian revision was based on probabilities only. Nevertheless, the work of these two great English scholars was a turning point in the study of the New Testament and the basis of further investigation that was made necessary soon after the Revised Version appeared. These later developments were inspired and aided, as we shall see, by the discovery of very important materials that began to come to light soon after the publication of the Revised Version of the New Testament in 1881. At any rate, not only the manuscripts discovered but the critical work done up to the time of Westcott and Hort showed how outmoded were now the New Testament tools that had been available to the King James translators, and how great was the need for scholars of the new age to revise the version that had become an integral part of the life of the English-speaking world.

But what of the Old Testament? The history of its text and of critical reflection upon it had followed very different lines. Jewish study of the Old Testament had been based on a text fixed probably in the second century after Christ and very assiduously preserved and handed down with remarkable purity. On the other hand, the earliest extant manuscripts of the Hebrew Bible dated from as late as the tenth century. So while the earliest manuscripts of the Greek New Testament belong to a date about three hundred years after they were written—long enough to make it very difficult to reconstruct a pure original text—the earliest manuscripts of the Hebrew Bible pertain to a date about a thousand years after the *latest* parts of it had been written. If one were to try to estimate the gulf in time between them and the *earliest* writings that went into its composition, the period would be nearer two thousand years. Moreover, though it is true that from the second century after Christ the Hebrew Bible was handed down with extraordinarily scrupulous care, various kinds of evidence prove that by the second century B.C. the text itself was already corrupt, and the problem of reconstructing it is formidable. In the eighteenth century, Benjamin Kennicott (1718-1783) made collations of Hebrew manuscripts from many parts of Europe and published an important critical text of the Hebrew Bible in 1776-1780. Apart from a few studies of this kind, no extensive work on the Hebrew text was attempted till the nineteenth century, and even by that time critical study of the Hebrew text of the Old Testament was still, generally speaking, at a comparatively rudimentary level. Apart from a fuller understanding of the Hebrew language itself than had been available at the time of the King James Version, and the general improvement in Semitic studies that had taken place by the time the revisers went to work in 1870, these had fewer new tools for work on the Old Testament than they had for work on the New.

On the other hand, critical reflection about the composition and structure of the Old Testament had been going on even in the days of Tyndale. For instance, the Reformers had noticed the curious fact that Moses, in the last of the five books of the Pentateuch traditionally attributed to him, appears to recount his own death. Carlstadt, Luther's extremist contemporary, explicitly denied the Mosaic authorship for that reason. Luther seems to have been personally indifferent on the subject, deeming it of little importance whether Moses wrote the Pentateuch or not; but at any rate he was well aware of the problem.

Thomas Hobbes (1588-1679) discussed the Old Testament in *Leviathan,* a book now prescribed for schoolboys but accounted at the time so atheistic that the House of Commons censured it, and its author was later prohibited from publishing further works of the kind in England. Hobbes drew the conclusion that while the Pentateuch may have been composed out of materials attributed and perhaps rightly attributable to Moses, it had been actually written after his death. He also concluded that the historical books belong to a much later period than the history to which they relate, and that this conclusion could be reached through an examination of the Old Testament itself, even without any external evidence that might be provided in support.

The great philosopher Baruch or Benedict de Spinoza (1632-1677), a heterodox Jew, drew attention also, in his *Tractatus Theologico-Politicus,* written in 1671, to the curious mixture of law and narrative in the Pentateuch, and to various inconsistencies and duplications, all of which suggested its composite character. Richard Simon (1638-1712), a French Oratorian priest, published in 1678 his *Histoire critique du Vieux Testament* in which he argued that the Pentateuch contained duplicate accounts of the same incident and that Moses could not be its author. He was expelled from the Oratorian Congregation for his scholarly work.

In 1753 a French physician, Jean Astruc (1684-1766), the son of a Reformed Church pastor, who was received at an early age into the Roman Church, published an important work *Conjectures sur les Mémoires originaux dont il paroît que Moyse s'est servi pour composer le Livre de la Genèse.* Astruc, though he did not dispute the Mosaic authorship of Genesis, pointed to the duplication of narratives, and particularly to the use in that book of two distinct names for God. From this fact, which is now among the rudiments of modern Old Testament study, Astruc very properly drew the conclusion that there were at least two types of passage, Jahvistic and Elohistic, after the names they respectively give to God. He saw that this demonstrated the composite character of the book, which, as handed down, must have had literary antecedents. Astruc may be considered, on this account, perhaps the great pioneer in critical study of the Old Testament after the sixteenth-century biblical Renaissance. Later scholars found more distinctions to be made; but Astruc detected at least one fundamental one.

Of great importance also, however, is the work of Johann Gottfried Eichhorn (1752-1857), who became in 1775 professor of Oriental Languages at Jena. He is one of the first commentators to conduct any scientific comparison of the Old Testament with other Semitic writings. Accepting the distinction suggested by Astruc between the Elohistic and the Jahvistic documents in the Pentateuch, Eichhorn detected also the distinction between the popular code in Deuteronomy and the priestly law in Exodus, Leviticus, and Numbers. He did a great deal to promote modern Old Testament studies. In 1853 Hermann Hupfeld (1796-1866) distinguished for the first time two separate sources, both using the same name for God (Elohim). These came to be known respectively as P and E.

Interest in such studies was nevertheless to be for long limited to a narrow class of individualists and specialists. Though the observations of Hobbes and Spinoza and the analyses of Astruc and Eichhorn were consonant with the rationalist temper of the century of Enlightenment, other forces delayed progress. Both in the Roman Church and among heirs of the Reformation there was resistance to conclusions that seemed to many to undermine the authority of the Bible, which in both traditions was revered as the basic document of the Christian faith.

It is all the more remarkable, therefore, to find Alexander Geddes [6] (1737-1802), an otherwise rather obscure priest in the certainly very obscure Roman Catholic minority in eighteenth-century Scotland, promulgating similar views quite independently. Father Geddes, who was friendly to and much admired by Burns, was an eccentric and interesting figure. His work, often passed over, deserves, I think, a little attention. He rejected (and according to modern scholarship he was wrong in rejecting) the conclusions of Astruc and Eichhorn on the Elohistic and Jahvistic passages; yet he agreed that the Old Testament was composite in character, arguing that the Pentateuch had been compiled in Canaan, probably in the reign of Solomon, and that it rested on various, partly written, partly oral, sources. He published a translation of the Bible from Genesis to Chronicles, bringing out the Pentateuch in 1792 and the rest in 1797.

In 1800 Geddes followed this work with *Critical Remarks on the He-*

[6] See above, pp. 249-50.

brew Scriptures corresponding with a New Translation of the Bible, in which he endeavored to destroy many assumptions made by "Protestants" and "Papists" alike on the subject of the Bible. For instance, the Red Sea story was commonly taken to be a "miracle"; but Father Geddes pointed out that it could very well be accounted for in a purely naturalistic way. The fleeing Israelites could have used "shallows fordable at low water." Of course, this is a fairly obvious idea that could not possibly have escaped the notice of generations of thoughtful people from very early times; nor does it really affect, one way or the other, the basic interpretation given by the devout to the story, namely, that the hand of God intervened in history. To those who so believe, it cannot really matter much whether this divine intervention was accomplished by a supernatural "dividing" of the sea or by the no less convenient provision, at the crucial moment, of what Father Geddes called "shallows fordable at low water." If the enemy pursuing me is thwarted from his design through the commonplace occurrence of spraining his ankle, I am just as much and just as little likely to attribute to divine Providence my timely deliverance from his clutches as would have been the case had he been struck down instead by a mysterious thunderbolt or an unknown and inexplicable disease. Indeed, if my enemy's destruction were to be accomplished by a spectacularly unexpected phenomenon, such as a sudden and unprecedented flood in the middle of the Sahara, I should hardly be accounted particularly impious if I afterwards inquired how this could have been the work of an intelligent Deity, since such a Deity would surely use less grossly and lavishly uneconomical methods for achieving what must be to him a very simple end. Nevertheless, in the eighteenth century, not to mention our own, such obvious reflections did not seem to obtrude themselves acutely upon the consciousness of the vulgar, and it was the popular beliefs current among these that Father Geddes wished to quash, even to the point of laboriously supporting his contention by reference to certain geographical facts observable in his own day in the region of Suez.

He also casts doubts upon the Flood, a story which he suggested had some historical foundation but had been grossly exaggerated in the telling. The story of the Garden of Eden he relegated entirely to mythological lore. "I believe the narrative of Genesis to be a most beautiful mythos, or philosophical fiction, dressed up in the garb of real history," he wrote in the *Critical Remarks.* He can hardly have been the first to have thought of this, since anyone reading the first three chapters of Genesis must find there at least two distinct accounts of the creation of man. These accounts are startlingly different from each other, the one very lofty in tone and the other so primitive that God is depicted as making Adam out of dust, as a child makes models out of play dough, and then even turning into a divine dressmaker, providing Adam and Eve with aprons made out of sewn-up fig leaves. Yet once again there have always been many who have liked to think of every biblical story as an account of historical events.

At any rate, the ecclesiastical superiors of Father Geddes were singularly alarmed by his opinions, fearing that they would be repugnant to the masses. Bishop Milner, while formally undertaking to "enter upon the Doctor's translation without any prepossessions," expressed in advance his suspicion, based on a general acquaintance with Geddes' views, that he would find Geddes treating the text of Holy Writ "with as little ceremony" as he would treat the works of Homer or Shakespeare. For these reasons the Bishop felt confident in being unwilling "to trust the translator farther than I can see him." Geddes was always highly suspect by his ecclesiastical superiors, and at his death his bishop refused the customary requiem mass.

He was, indeed, very heterodox in his theological opinions as well as advanced in his biblical views. He minimized the difference between "Papist" and "Protestant." The former rests his faith on "the supposed infallibility of his Church; although he knows not where that infallibility is lodged, nor in what it properly consists." But he went on to say that the "case of the vulgar Protestant is even worse" since he grounds it in what "he believes to be the infallible word of God." His was a protest against biblical literalism. But though Geddes professed to dislike this in both its "Papist" and its "Protestant" forms, he considered himself a "Catholic." "I am," he declared, "a Catholic *absolute,* Roman Catholic *secundum quid* ... neither Papist nor Protestant: but both between, like good Erasmus, in an honest mean, a genuine Catholic." Over his tombstone in the churchyard at Paddington, stand the words:

Reverend Alexander Geddes, LL.D
Translator of the Historical Books
Of the Old Testament,
Died Feb. 26, 1802
Aged 65

Christian is my name, and Catholic my surname.
I grant, that you are a Christian, as well as I,
And embrace you as my fellow disciple in Jesus,
And if you are not a disciple of Jesus,
Still I would embrace you as my Fellow Man.
(Extracted from his Works)
Requiescat in Pace

The allusion to his surname calls for explanation. Geddes is the name of an old Roman Catholic family in Scotland.

Old Testament studies continued through the nineteenth century, much influenced by the work of Wilhelm Martin Leberecht De Wette (1780-1849), who in his youth was very radical in his analysis of the biblical documents, though in his later years, under the theological influence of Schleiermacher, he became more conservative in tone. De Wette, in a work published in 1806-1807,[7] went beyond literary analysis to a consideration of the value of the biblical documents themselves. He proved that Deuteronomy belongs to the seventh century B.C., that the history recorded in Judges, Samuel, and Kings is incompatible with the view that the institutions described in the Pentateuch could be Mosaic in origin, and that Chronicles is untrustworthy in historical details.

De Wette's work was continued by others, such as the historian and Orientalist Heinrich Georg August Ewald (1803-75). From Göttingen Ewald went to Tübingen, where he joined with other scholars in opposition to Ferdinand Christian Baur (1792-1860), with whose name is principally associated the views of a school of New Testament scholars named after that university. Ewald believed that the document known as P (priestly code) was the earliest component of the Pentateuch. This view was developed by other scholars, not without assistance from the philosophical critique of history provided by the celebrated and then exceedingly influential philosopher, Georg Wilhelm Friedrich Hegel (1770-1831). Another view was taken by some scholars, however, and in 1865 a presentation of their theory was made by Karl Heinrich Graf (1815-1869). Exponents of this theory in its final form maintained that the order of the component documents was: JE (the Jahvistic and Elohistic elements), D (the Deuteronomic code), and P (the priestly code), with the legislation found in Ezekiel 40–48 forming the bridge between D and P.

Julius Wellhausen (1844-1918), who had studied under Ewald at Göttingen and whose highly influential *Geschichte Israels* was first published in 1878, established the view, which with modifications is still accepted, that in the Old Testament may be traced the story of the development from the very primitive religion of a nomadic people to the highly ethical religion of the prophets, culminating finally in the religion of the Law. While Wellhausen came too late on the scene for his influence to be adequately reflected in the Revised Version, the general movement of Old Testament studies in the direction to which he eventually pointed was certainly among the factors the revisers had to take into account in their work.

By the time of the Revised Version, then, the main principles behind modern biblical schorlaship, both in Old and in New Testament studies,

---

[7] *Die Beträge zur Einleitung in das Alte Testament.*

had been gradually established. From the present cursory review of this early development, one fact emerges with great clarity. In both fields, though their development followed different lines, the process that led to the establishment of these principles was slow at first but latterly gained considerable momentum. The process, inspired by the humanist forces behind the sixteenth-century biblical Renaissance, was delayed at first by many hindrances. Its eventual success was nevertheless inevitable. In the case of the New Testament, the great manuscript discoveries provided no doubt indispensable tools; but the development depended even more on the use scholars made of these tools. Yet this in turn depended absolutely on the particular attitude of mind the scholars brought to bear upon their work. This attitude would have been unattainable but for the biblical Renaissance that had so much earlier preceded its full manifestation. In the case of Old Testament studies there was comparatively little in the way of equipment to assist the process of development. In both cases, whatever light came from the East had to be refracted through very analytical Western minds before its full glory could be seen, and even then it could be seen only by men who cared enough for the Bible to be willing to subject this unique literature to that honest and searching inquiry that the best minds of the day had lavished upon it.

CHAPTER 27 *The Revised Version*

The need for a full-scale revision of the King James Version had been felt for more than two centuries. Indeed, we have seen it had been voiced even when the version appeared. From the 1840's, however, when men such as F. D. Maurice and J. H. Newman were engaged in controversies representative of their parties within the English Church, the desire for a revision of the King James Version had become more urgent. The discovery in 1859 of the Codex Sinaiticus was among the circumstances that made the need more pressing than ever.

At last action was taken. When Canon Selwyn, who in 1856 and 1857 had raised the matter in the Lower House of Convocation, was preparing in 1870 to introduce into the Lower House of Convocation a motion concerning the needed revision, Samuel Wilberforce, Bishop of Winchester, anticipating him, moved in the Upper House on February 10, 1870, "that a Committee of both Houses be appointed, with power to confer with any Committee that may be appointed by the Convocation of the Northern Province [York], to report upon the desirableness of a revision of the Authorized Version of the New Testament, whether by marginal notes or otherwise, in all those passages where plain and clear errors, whether in the Hebrew or Greek text originally adopted by the translators, or in the translation made from the same, shall, on due investigation, be found to exist." The inclusion of Hebrew suggests that the motion had originally been intended to include the Old Testament also. At any rate, Alfred Ollivant, Bishop of Llandaff, moved an amendment, accepted and carried, to include the Old Testament. The motion, so amended and carried, was sent down to the Lower House where it was carried the following day without a division. A joint committee, consisting of eight members of the Upper and sixteen of the Lower House, was appointed. On March 24 they met and agreed to report that revision was desirable and should be undertaken. Meanwhile, the Convocation of the Northern Province, while expressing themselves in favor of the correction of existing errors, indicated that they would deplore the recasting of the text of the Authorized (King James) Version. The recommendation of the joint committee was eventually presented on May 3. As we shall see presently, there was an attempt in the Lower House to restrict the work of revision to Anglican scholars; but this was unsuccessful. The recommendation, as presented, was as follows:

274

1. That it is desirable that a revision of the Authorized Version of the Holy Scriptures be undertaken.
2. That the revision be so conducted as to comprise both marginal renderings and such emendations as it may be found necessary to insert in the text of the Authorized Version.
3. That in the above Resolutions we do not contemplate any new translation of the Bible, or any alteration of the language, except when in the judgement of the most competent scholars such change is necessary.
4. That in such necessary changes the style of the language employed in the existing version be closely followed.
5. That it is desirable that Convocation should nominate a body of its own members to undertake the work of revision, who shall be at liberty to invite the co-operation of any eminent for scholarship, to whatever nation or religious body they may belong.

The Upper House of Convocation unanimously adopted this report. Eight bishops were nominated to represent it on the joint committee. The Lower House of Convocation discussed it on May 5, when some opposition was raised to the last clause of the fifth resolution. The report was adopted, nevertheless, with two dissentients, and on May 6 the Lower House selected eight of its number to represent it on the joint committee. The first meeting of this new joint committee was held on May 25. The rules devised provided for the separation of the committee into two companies, for the Old Testament and the New Testament respectively; nine members were to devote themselves to the Old Testament, seven to the New; eighteen "scholars and divines" were to be invited to join the Old Testament company, and nineteen others to join the New; the work of each company was to be communicated, on completion, to the other, so as to insure uniformity of language, as far as possible. There were also certain "bye-rules" on the procedure to be adopted in making corrections. The general principles laid down for the work as a whole were as follows:

1. To introduce as few alterations as possible into the text of the Authorized Version, consistently with faithfulness.
2. To limit, as far as possible, the expressions of such alterations to the language of the Authorized and earlier English versions.
3. Each Company to go twice over the portion to be revised, once provisionally, the second time finally, and on principles of voting as hereinafter is provided.
4. That the Text to be adopted be that for which the evidence is decidedly preponderating; and that when the Text so adopted differs from that from which the Authorized Version was made, the alteration be indicated in the margin.
5. To make or retain no change in the Text on the second final revision

by each Company, except *two-thirds* of those present approve of the same, but on the first revision decide by simple majorities.

6. Cases in which voting may be deferred.
7. Headings of chapters, etc., to be revised.
8. Permission to consult learned men, "whether at home or abroad."

Among those who received invitations to join the committee were Canon F. C. Cook, Father (later Cardinal) Newman, Dr. Pusey and Dr. W. Wright of the British Museum, who all declined, though Dr. Wright subsequently joined the Old Testament Company. Dean Alford, an original member appointed by Convocation, died in 1871, as did also Professor McGill. Dr. Wordsworth, Bishop of Lincoln, and Dr. Jebb, Dean of Hereford, resigned at an early stage, as did also Dean Merivale, one of the substitutes, and Dr. Tregelles. The following is the list of members of the two companies as constituted, who began their work in June, 1870.

Old Testament Revision Company

The Rt. Rev. Connop Thirlwall, Bishop of St. David's (Chairman till 1871)

The Rt. Rev. E. H. Browne, Bishop of Ely; afterwards of Winchester (Chairman from 1871)

The Rt. Rev. Christopher Wordsworth, Bishop of Lincoln

The Rt. Rev. Lord Arthur C. Hervey, Bishop of Bath and Wells

The Rt. Rev. Alfred Ollivant, Bishop of Llandaff

The Very Rev. R. Payne Smith, Regius Professor of Divinity, University of Oxford; afterwards Dean of Canterbury

The Ven. Benjamin Harrison, Archdeacon of Maidstone

The Ven. H. J. Rose, Archdeacon of Bedford

Dr. W. L. Alexander, Professor of Theology, Congregational Church Hall, Edinburgh

Mr. R. L. Bensly, Fellow and Hebrew Lecturer of Gonville and Caius College, Cambridge

The Rev. John Birrell, Professor of Oriental Languages, University of St. Andrews

Dr. Frank Chance, Sydenham

Mr. T. Chenery, Lord Almoner's Professor of Arabic, University of Oxford

The Rev. T. K. Cheyne, Fellow and Hebrew Lecturer of Balliol College, Oxford; afterwards Oriel Professor of the Interpretation of Holy Scripture, University of Oxford

Dr. A. B. Davidson, Professor of Hebrew, Free Church College, Edinburgh

Dr. B. Davies, Professor of Hebrew, Baptist College, Regent's Park, London

Dr. George Douglas, Professor of Hebrew; afterwards Principal of Free Church College, Glasgow

Dr. S. R. Driver, Fellow and Tutor of New College, Oxford; afterwards Regius Professor of Hebrew, Oxford

The Rev. C. J. Elliott, Vicar of Winkfield, Windsor

Dr. P. Fairbairn, Principal of the Free Church College, Glasgow

The Rev. F. Field, author of *Otium Norvicense;* editor of Origen's *Hexapla*

The Rev. J. D. Geden, Professor of Hebrew, Wesleyan College, Didsbury

Dr. C. D. Ginsburg, editor of *Ecclesiastes,* etc.

Dr. F. W. Gotch, Principal of the Baptist College, Bristol

Dr. John Jebb, Dean of Hereford

Dr. W. Kay, late Principal of Bishop's College, Calcutta

The Rev. Stanley Leathes, Professor of Hebrew, King's College, London

The Rev. J. R. Lumby, Fellow of St. Catherine's College; afterwards Norrisian Professor of Divinity, Cambridge

Dr. J. M'Gill, Professor of Oriental Languages, University of St. Andrews

Dr. J. J. S. Perowne, Professor of Hebrew, St. David's College, Lampeter; afterwards Bishop of Worcester

Dr. E. H. Plumtre, Professor of NT Exegesis, King's College, London

The Rev. A. H. Sayce, Fellow and Tutor of the Queen's College; afterwards Professor of Assyriology, University of Oxford

Dr. W. Selwyn, Canon of Ely; Lady Margaret's Professor of Divinity, University of Cambridge

The Rev. W. Robertson Smith, Professor of Hebrew, Free Church College, Aberdeen; afterwards Lord Almoner's Professor of Arabic and Fellow of Christ's College, Cambridge

Dr. D. H. Weir, Professor of Oriental Languages, University of Glasgow

Dr. W. Wright, Professor of Arabic, University of Cambridge

Mr. W. Aldis Wright, Librarian, afterwards Bursar, of Trinity College, Cambridge

New Testament Revision Company

The Rt. Rev. C. J. Ellicott, Bishop of Gloucester and Bristol (Chairman)

The Rt. Rev. S. Wilberforce, Bishop of Winchester

The Rt. Rev. G. Moberly, Bishop of Salisbury

The Most Rev. R. C. Trench, Archbishop of Dublin

The Rt. Rev. Charles Wordsworth, Bishop of St. Andrews

The Very Rev. E. H. Bickersteth, Dean of Lichfield (Prolocutor of the Lower House of Convocation)

The Very Rev. Henry Alford, Dean of Canterbury

The Very Rev. A. P. Stanley, Dean of Westminster

The Very Rev. Robert Scott, Dean of Rochester

The Very Rev. J. W. Blackesley, Dean of Lincoln

The Very Rev. Charles Merivale, Dean of Ely

The Ven. William Lee, Archdeacon of Dublin

The Ven. Edwin Palmer, Archdeacon of Oxford

Dr. Joseph Angus, President of the Baptist College, Regent's Park, London

Dr. David Brown, Principal of Free Church College, Aberdeen

Dr. John Eadie, Professor of Biblical Literature in the United Presbyterian Church, Glasgow

Dr. F. J. A. Hort, afterwards Hulsean Professor of Divinity, University of Cambridge

The Rev. W. G. Humphry, Prebendary of St. Paul's Cathedral, London

Dr. B. H. Kennedy, Canon of Ely; Regius Professor of Greek, University of Cambridge

Dr. J. B. Lightfoot, Hulsean Professor of Divinity, Cambridge; afterwards Bishop of Durham

Dr. W. Milligan, Professor of Divinity, University of Aberdeen

Dr. W. F. Moulton, afterwards Master of The Leys School, Cambridge

Dr. S. Newth, Principal of New College, Hampstead

Dr. Alexander Roberts, Professor of Humani'/, University of St. Andrews

Dr. F. H. A. Scrivener, afterwards Vicar of Hendon

Dr. G. Vance Smith, afterwards Principal of the Presbyterian College, Carmarthen

Dr. C. J. Vaughan, Master of the Temple; Dean of Llandaff

Dr. B. F. Westcott, Canon of Peterborough; Regius Professor of Divinity, University of Cambridge; afterwards Bishop of Durham

In the course of the ten years of the revisers' labors, changes took place, as might be expected, in the joint committee. Eventually there were sixty-five British participants in the work. Of these, forty-one were from the Church of England and five from the Church of Scotland. The others were from the Church of Ireland (Episcopal), the Episcopal Church in Scotland, the Scottish Free Church, the Baptists, the Methodists, the Congregationalists, the United Presbyterians, and the Unitarians. The cooperation of American scholars was also sought. As early as July 7, 1870,

Lord Alwyne Compton had moved in the Lower House of Convocation that the Upper House be requested to invite the cooperation of American scholars, and the Upper House readily assented. There were some normal difficulties that delayed matters, and the arrangements for the association with the English companies of two American counterparts were not completed till December 7, 1871. The American companies then awaited the first revision from London of Matthew, Mark, and Luke, before beginning their work on October 4, 1872. The American Committee, under the presidency of Dr. Philip Schaff of Union Theological Seminary, New York City, was divided into two companies, as follows:

Old Testament Revision Company (American)

Dr. W. H. Green (Chairman), Princeton Theological Seminary, N.J.

Dr. G. E. Day (Secretary), Divinity School of Yale University, New Haven, Conn.

Dr. C. A. Aiken, Princeton Theological Seminary, N.J.

Dr. T. W. Chambers, Collegiate Reformed Dutch Church, N.Y.

Dr. T. J. Conant, Brooklyn, N.Y.

Dr. J. de Witt, Theological Seminary, New Brunswick, N.J.

Dr. G. E. Hare, Divinity School, Philadelphia

Dr. C. P. Krauth, Vice-Provost of the University of Pennsylvania, Philadelphia

Dr. T. Lewis, Professor Emeritus of Greek and Hebrew, Union College, Schenectady, N.Y. (d. 1877)

Dr. C. M. Mead, Theological Seminary, Andover, Mass.

Dr. H. Osgood, Theological Seminary, Rochester, N.Y.

Dr. J. Packard, Theological Seminary, Alexandria, Va.

Dr. C. E. Stowe, Hartford, Conn.

Dr. J. Strong, Theological Seminary, Madison, N.J.

Dr. C. V. A. Van Dyck, Beirut, Syria

New Testament Revision Company (American)

Dr. T. D. Woolsey (Chairman), New Haven, Conn.

Dr. J. H. Thayer (Secretary), Theological Seminary, Andover, Mass.

Dr. Ezra Abbot, Divinity School, Harvard University, Cambridge, Mass.

Dr. J. K. Burr, Trenton, N.J.

Dr. Thomas Chase, President of Haverford College, Pa.

Dr. Howard Crosby, Chancellor of New York University, N.Y.

Dr. Timothy Dwight, Divinity School of Yale University, New Haven, Conn.

Dr. H. B. Hackett, Theological Seminary, Rochester, N.Y. (d. 1876)

Dr. James Hadley, Professor of Greek, Yale University, New Haven, Conn. (d. 1872)

Dr. Charles Hodge, Princeton Theological Seminary, N.J. (d. 1878)

Dr. A. C. Kendrick, University of Rochester, N.Y.

The Rt. Rev. Alfred Lee, Bishop of Delaware

Dr. M. B. Riddle, Theological Seminary, Hartford, Conn.

Dr. Philip Schaff, Union Theological Seminary, N.Y.

Dr. Charles Short, Columbia College, N.Y.

Dr. E. A. Washburn, Calvary Church, N.Y. (d. Feb. 1881)

Dr. Van Dyck had been appointed a consultant on Arabic questions. We must return later to the contributions of the American Committee and their outcome. Meanwhile, let us look at the arrangements for the New Testament Company that assembled on Wednesday morning, June 22, 1870, in the Chapel of Henry VII within Westminster Abbey. After they had participated in the Eucharist, in preparation for the scholarly undertaking that was accounted also a sacred work, they formally entered upon their assignment. The place of their labors was the Jerusalem Chamber, set aside for them by the Dean of Westminster, Arthur Penrhyn Stanley.

Dean Stanley was a leading broad churchman of the day, whose tolerance and vision were much appreciated by many both in his own Church and elsewhere. He had always desired to make Westminster Abbey a national shrine for all. The invitation to Holy Communion that he extended to all the scholars engaged at the abbey upon the revision of the Bible was much resented by certain Anglicans, not least because one of the scholars was a Unitarian. One wonders what Dean Stanley would have replied to the prominent and beloved American rabbi of very liberal opinions and friendly disposition who once asked me at an Episcopal service in the United States, conducted in the presence of the Archbishop of Canterbury and telecast, whether any would take offence if he, the rabbi, did not go up for Communion. I whispered back my assurance that none would.

The choice of the Jerusalem Chamber was apposite. In those far-off days when the abbey had been a Benedictine foundation, this room had been the parlor of the abbot's house. In the seventeenth century, when the Assembly of Divines prepared the Confession of Faith and the catechisms that were to play a prominent part in the later history of Presbyterianism, they had originally met, on July 1, 1643, in the Chapel of Henry VII in the abbey; but when autumn came, this proved too cold, and they moved on October 2 of that year to the Jerusalem Chamber. Half a century later, in the days of William III, a Prayer Book commission had also met here.

In this room, on four consecutive days of each month except August and September, the New Testament Company pursued its work. Their meetings lasted from eleven in the morning till six at night, with half an hour's interval for lunch. The procedure was as follows. When they assembled in the late morning, prayer was offered, and any matters of business correspondence were then dealt with. These preliminaries over, the chairman would read a short passage from the King James Version of the New Testament and invite textual changes. When he had received these, he would call for proposals concerning the manner in which the revision should be rendered in the place in question. Discussion would follow, and then the vote would be taken.

It was found that this procedure was too slow for the taste of some. At the ninth meeting, the daily average had been only seventeen verses. Attempts to accelerate the speed by change of procedure were not approved. The pace quickened later, however, though it seems never to have exceeded thirty-five verses a day. The first revision of Matthew was completed on May 24, 1871, the thirty-sixth day of meeting. The first revision of the whole of the New Testament was not finished till April 20, 1877, when the Company had had two hundred and seventy-three meetings. The second revision of the New Testament took ninety-seven further meetings. Extending over a period of about two and a half years, it was completed on December 13, 1878. After that, suggestions from the American Committee further delayed publication. On November 11, 1880, however, the Feast of St. Martin, the New Testament Company assembled in St. Martin's-in-the-Fields, where they offered thanksgiving for the completion of their work in a spirit of brotherly love, and with the prayer that God might deign to use the fruit of their labors for the honor of his name and for the good of mankind.

The arrangements for the Old Testament Company, which had first assembled on June 30, 1870, were similar, but they worked as a rule for six hours a day, and for ten days at a time. Their work was completed on June 20, 1884. The eighty-five sessions occupied 792 days.

The American Committee met in the Bible House, New York. They received from time to time and considered portions of the first revision done in London, and then sent back their criticisms. These were in turn considered by the British scholars who then sent to New York their second revision, and so again for the final one. Certain preferences that the American scholars recorded were placed at the end of the finished volume of the Revised Version. It must be remembered that all this involved considerable time, since ships in those days took much longer to cross the Atlantic than they do now, and it need hardly be said there was no faster means of sending mail.

The entire work of the scholars who met so often and so long in the

Jerusalem Chamber was done without fee. Their travel expenses were eventually provided, however, by an agreement between the Committee and representatives of the Oxford and Cambridge University Presses. These presses, in acquiring the copyright in the work, stipulated that the revisers should include the Apocrypha. So, as soon as the work of the New Testament was finished, the members of this Company began work on the Apocrypha, forming themselves into three committees, charged respectively with the following portions: Sirach, I Maccabees (Tobit and Judith were added later), and Wisdom and II Maccabees. The remaining books of the Apocrypha were translated by the Old Testament Company, aided by several other scholars, after it had finished its primary task in 1884, and the Apocrypha eventually appeared in 1895.

We have seen that the New Testament was finished on November 11, 1880. Publication was delayed, however, for a few months. At last, on Tuesday, May 17, 1881, the New Testament, a special copy of which was presented to Queen Victoria, appeared in London. So eagerly had the Revised Version of the New Testament been awaited that on that day traffic in the streets of the booksellers' quarter in London was disrupted. Publication in New York took place three days later, on Friday, May 20. Not only was there similar disruption in the streets of the corresponding quarter in New York City; that weekend the *Chicago Tribune* and the *Chicago Times* both printed the entire New Testament in a supplement. For this Herculean achievement, the *Tribune* employed ninety-two compositors and five correctors. It is said that they set up the entire New Testament in twelve hours. Within a few days, two million copies of the Revised Version were sold in Britain and America, and about three million in the first year.

The new version was, and remains, of considerable scholarly value. It encountered severe criticism, however, not only from conservative churchmen attached to the familiar King James Version, but also in scholarly circles where one might have expected the greatest sympathy. The gravamen of the most responsible sort of complaint was that the new version, while often more accurate, was stilted and pedantic, being therefore unsuitable for its purpose, which was to provide a revision to supersede the King James Version. As Spurgeon, the most renowned preacher of the day, neatly put it, the new version was "strong in Greek, weak in English." After all, the revisers had been appointed to do more than provide a schoolboy's crib to the Greek New Testament. Even one of the most favorable and appreciative reviews of the work, which appeared in the *Edinburgh Review* in July, 1881, noted this shortcoming. On both sides of the Atlantic it met with similar criticism. Few parish churches in England adopted it for public use. The enormous sale reflected desire and interest rather than satisfaction, and in the end the version became a tool for the scholar's desk rather than a volume to be placed on the church lectern or even to be read privately by the devout.

When, in 1905, Samuel Lloyd, a Governor of the British and Foreign Bible Society, published as a memorial of his society's centenary *The Corrected New Testament,* which purported to be an independent revision of the King James Version, he echoed the widespread objection, saying that the revisers had been "undoubtedly strong in Greek," but that their work nevertheless "cannot be accepted as conform to the standards of the purest English." The Bishop of Durham, who wrote a preface for Lloyd, wrote with episcopal caution and gentlemanly politeness of the much criticized Revised Version, explaining that it was "not altogether easy" for him to speak out critically on that subject, since his "two eminently great predecessors" in the See of Durham had played a leading part in the work. Even so, the Bishop commendably did not absolve himself from candor. He went on to say: "But they would have been the first to wish every student to express an opinion absolutely free. . . . And I feel compelled, after years of use of the Revised Version of the New Testament, to own to the conviction that while it is beyond all praise as an aid to study, it seriously lacks that ENGLISH FELICITY, if I may use the phrase, which should entitle it to take the place of the Authorized Version in our national heart."

On the whole, the objections were only too well grounded. For instance, at Matthew 5:26, the change from "till thou hast paid the uttermost farthing," "till thou have paid the last farthing," can hardly be said to be either necessary or an improvement. It was one of the most sharply and generally criticized alterations. At Luke 5:5, the revisers justified the change from "we have toiled all the night, and have taken nothing," to "we toiled all night and took nothing," on the ground that in Greek the aorist tense is used; but this is a pedantic change if ever there was one. Even where the language of the revisers seemed more modern, the change effected was not always indisputably for the better. At I Corinthians 5:1, for example, they changed "It is reported commonly," to "It is actually reported," which not everybody accounted an improvement. And why change "Praise our God, all ye his servants," at Revelation 19:5, to "Give praise to our God, all ye his servants"? On the other hand, there were, of course, some definite improvements. At I Timothy 3:13, "gain to themselves a good standing," was surely a desirable modernization of the King James "purchase to themselves a good degree." Certainly "And casting off the anchors, they left them in the sea" was a most desirable improvement, at Acts 27:40, upon "And when they had taken up the anchors, they committed *themselves* unto the sea."

The King James Version reads: "For he that eateth and drinketh unworthily, eateth and drinketh damnation to himself, not discerning the Lord's body" (I Cor. 11:29). But the word "damn" had acquired by the nineteenth century a specific vigour that it did not have in the seventeenth, when it was a fitting translation of a Greek word that means no more than "judge." So for "damnation" the revisers put "judgement." Many such accommodations to changing language were made. "The secret of the Lord," for instance, was changed to "the friendship of the Lord," and "to ear" became "to plough." Some of the changes were less happy, notably the seeming preference for Latin and Greek derivatives rather than plain English words—"finished" for "ended," "epistle" for "letter," and the like. These examples will indicate the character of the revision.

The Old Testament Company were on the whole much more conservative. They kept as far as possible to the Masoretic text, so that much less often did they have to decide between rival texts and manuscripts of the original. For this reason, though probably also because there were fewer competent Hebrew scholars available to criticize their work than there were Greek scholars to criticize that of the New Testament Company, the Old Testament generally met with fewer and less vehement objections. This is not to say, however, that there were not many changes. There were over two thousand in the Psalms, nearly thirteen hundred in Jeremiah, and nearly fourteen hundred in Job, for example; but broadly speaking the changes seemed to be much less controversial in character. At any rate they evoked less controversy. The Old Testament revisers not infrequently changed archaic and almost unintelligible words such as "breaches," which they modernized as "creeks." There is no doubt that they made many obscurities plain. The work on the Apocrypha was also in some ways useful, though it has been also subjected to much criticism that is too technical to be considered here.

In setting forth the Psalms and other books of the Old Testament that were originally written as poetry, the revisers adopted the original structure. The rest of the text was arranged in paragraphs instead of verses, though apparatus was provided so that the verses might be distinguished for reference purposes.

The Revised Version of the Bible appeared on May 19, 1885, unattended by the extraordinary scenes that had marked the publication of the New Testament in London and in New York years earlier. The title is as follows:

> The/Holy Bible/containing the/Old and New Testaments/Translated out of the Original Tongues/Being the Version set forth A.D. 1611/ Compared with the most ancient Authorities and Revised./Printed for the Universities of/Oxford and Cambridge/Oxford [or Cambridge]/At the University Press 1885.

Some of the suggestions of the American Committee were adopted in the text of the Revised Version. Others were only noted in an appendix. For example, it seemed to the American Committee that "spirit" should be substituted for "ghost." The word "ghost" had undergone much change of meaning since the days of the earlier versions of the English Bible. It did not originally have the "spooky" connotation it was to acquire. "Ghostly counsel" meant "spiritual advice," and the phrase "the Holy Ghost" did not evoke the puzzlement it does today. The English revisers recognized all this, of course; but they felt a change of this kind was not warranted by the conservative rules to which they were committed. Their reluctance to make such changes ought not to be too lightly dismissed as a mere perverse attachment to bygone usage.

In any case, bygone usage itself is not always unfamiliar to the modern ear: sometimes it is much more understandable than are the formal literary phrases of more recent times. The eighteenth-century Quaker's rendering of "hallowed" in the Lord's Prayer as "sacredly reverenced" is not only tastelessly florid: it now sounds more antiquated than does "hallowed." On the other hand, there are phrases in Tyndale, written as early as about 1530, that sound more modern today than do their counterparts in even the more recent translations of the Bible. For instance, where the King James Version called Joseph (Gen. 39:2) "a prosperous man," Tyndale just called him "a luckie felowe"—a phrase which, though belonging to a more archaic version, is as familiar to a modern ear as the most relaxed everyday conversation. Again, the King James and other versions tell us that when Eve reflected upon God's warning that if she and Adam ate the fruit they would die, the Devil, tempting her, said (Gen. 3:4) : "Ye shall not surely die." The translation is correct; but the dialogue is pedantic for a devil. Once again, Tyndale's rendering makes the Devil sound much more realistic and convincing to our ears: "Tush, ye shall not dye." That is how we should expect the Devil to talk to Eve!

After the disbanding of the Committee that had pursued its work at Westminster Abbey, the American Committee continued to maintain its organization. As the years passed, it became evident that the Americans wanted an independent edition of the Revised Version in which the preferences they had indicated would be included in the text rather than consigned to an appendix. In the original agreement with the university presses in England, granting them copyright, there had been a stipulation that for fourteen years every copy issued should contain an appendix with the preferred readings of the American scholars, and that during this period the Americans would reciprocate by sanctioning no other edition of the Revised Version. From 1885 the American Committee worked on a new recension of the Revised Edition, as they were by this time free to do, publishing the New Testament in 1900 and the whole Bible on August 26, 1901. This recension came to be called (inaccurately, for it was only a recension or edition of a version), the American Standard Version of the Bible. It is to be distinguished, of course, from the extremely important and excellent American revision of the Bible known as the Revised Standard Version, published half a century later, the story of which remains to be told in a later chapter.

A few examples must suffice to indicate some of the American changes. The Revised Version reads, at Ecclesiastes 12:5, "the caper-berry shall fail." This is unintelligible without the explanation that caper-berries were eaten as appetizers before meals, and when they failed to have this effect, people might attribute the failure to the onset of old age. The American recension has "desire shall fail." For "the way of the treacherous is rugged," at Proverbs 13:15, the Americans wrote "the way of the transgressor is hard." The Revised Version makes St. Paul say in his celebrated speech to the Athenians (Acts 17:22), "ye are somewhat superstitious." The Americans changed this to "ye are very religious." This is an excellent change, for there was nothing offensive in what Paul said; he was much too skilful an orator to offend his audience at the outset of his speech. Nevertheless, the "very" of the American Standard is misleading, obscuring the comparative of the Greek, which would be better rendered by an expression to suggest, rather, "too religious," "somewhat religious," or "on the religious side." The Americans also used "maiden" for "virgin"; but the two words are identical in English, as by the state of maidenhood can be understood nothing other than the state of virginity.

Among the features most highly criticized in the so-called American Standard Version must be mentioned the use of the word "Sheol" for various expressions used in the King James Old Testament to indicate an unseen world vaguely alluded to in expressions such as "the pit" and "the grave," and the use of the word "Hades" for corresponding expressions in the King James New Testament, such as "Gehenna." There is no doubt that here is a difficult decision for any translator; but equally there is no doubt that few modern readers or listeners would be enlightened by renderings such as "Sheol" and "Hades." The use in the American Standard Version of "Jehovah" for "Lord" is peculiarly unfortunate. In the first place, the word "Jehovah" is a bad transliteration of a Hebrew word. In the second place, it produces a curiously heavy and un-English effect at the best, while at the worst, as in the psalms, its use is quite monstrous. So to the impression of a version by British pedants is added that of an American lack of familiarity with the genius of the English tongue—a most depressing combination. In some respects, however, the

American Standard Version incorporated welcome improvements. It had indisputable merits, though their extent is debatable.

Be its merits what they may, the American Standard Version certainly found more widespread acceptance in America than ever the Revised Version obtained in Britain. It has been used in many churches in America, while the use of the Revised Version in British churches has always been rare. The influence of the American Standard is reflected in the form of the opening words of the Lord's Prayer as this is recited in the United States: "Our Father, *who* art in heaven." This form is unknown in England, where "which" is used, except among Roman Catholics, who inherit the "who" form through the Douai Version.

It is generally admitted that the Revised Version, both in its original English form and in that of the American Standard Version, was a premature undertaking. So much was, as we shall see, about to be discovered. In retrospect, this seems true enough. But at the time the enterprise, far from seeming premature, seemed to many long overdue. And after all, had it never been undertaken, the task of replacing the King James Version by any other designed to have the authority of the Church behind it would have been far more difficult. For all its shortcomings, the Revised Version was not only a noble achievement in itself, but one that will be found to have played a vital part in the movement to keep the Bible in a language "understanded of the people."

And not by eastern windows only
When daylight comes, comes in the light;
In front, the sun climbs slow, how slowly,
But westward look, the land is bright.
—A. H. Clough, "Say Not the
Struggle Nought Availeth"

CHAPTER 28 *More Eastern Light Through Western Windows*

No sooner was the Revised Version of the New Testament put out than a spate of new evidences began coming to light. These were soon seen to be of such a character as to make the revisers' work out of date almost as soon as it had come off the press. Nor was it only that new and better readings here and there were found; the literary nature of the New Testament was discovered to be different from and much more exciting than earlier translators had supposed. Those who, like Spurgeon, had instinctively felt that the scholarly preoccupations of the revisers had impeded them from producing the readable version the English-speaking world had so expectantly awaited were vindicated indeed; but they were vindicated not only by the popular disappointment but also by developments in New Testament scholarship itself. For the papyri and other evidences that began to come to the attention of scholars brought to light far more than textual faults; they quickly led to a radical discovery that was to revolutionize the whole conception of the biblical translator's task.

The revisers, like their predecessors, had supposed that the Greek of the New Testament was in one way or another a special sort of Greek. It was obviously not at all the Greek of Pindar or Plato; yet neither was it modern Greek. It was, they thought, a peculiar, "biblical" Greek. What now became abundantly evident was that the Greek of the New Testament, though indeed neither classical nor modern, was not at all special. It was the everyday Greek of the first-century marketplace.

In 1895 Dr. (later Sir) Frederic Kenyon first published his excellent book, *Our Bible and the Ancient Manuscripts,* whose much deserved popularity reflected the widespread interest the subject was already able to command, as the book itself reflected the vitality of biblical scholarship in England. In the same year a great German scholar, Adolf Deissmann, drew attention to samples of a huge quantity of Greek papyri that were coming to light—not biblical papyri, but commonplace things such as bills, receipts, jottings, letters, and other very ordinary writings and scribblings. The significance of these for biblical scholars lay in the fact that they showed over and over again that there was nothing at all special or "sacred" about the Greek used in the New Testament. It was the international commercial tongue of the day that the New Testament writers had naturally chosen as their medium for communicating what they had to say about the good news of Christ. This kind of Greek, now known to scholars as *Koinē*, was the cosmopolitan vernacular of the first century A.D. throughout the Mediterranean area. It was anything other than a pedantic or academic language. It was the racy, fluid, living speech of the marketplace. The revolutionary importance of this discovery must not be overlooked. It is disastrous for a translator to treat an ordinary living language as though it were a special idiom.

Imagine a modern American or British colloquialism, such as one might hear in a play or read in a novel. Suppose it is a New Yorker speaking: "This guy sure knows how to make a fast buck but he got it coming to him." Or a Cockney: "Wot a nerve pinching that bike—you aint arf gonna catch it from old battle-axe." How should one translate this sort of thing into pedantic, Ciceronian Latin, with a scrupulous care to preserve as far as humanly possible every word of the original? The result would be comical. Now, the men who wrote the New Testament did not use slang; but they used a very ordinary sort of Greek. It was the kind of Greek that is to be found in letters of the period written by mothers to their sons in the army, for instance—letters full of gossip and chatter. New Testament Greek is never vulgar or cheap; but it is essentially colloquial, even chatty.

Everyone now saw that the way to go about translating the New Testament was radically different from that which the revisers had considered it to be. The prospect of seeing the everyday Greek of a bygone age turned into the equally commonplace English of the present day was one that naturally captured the imagination of many people, whether they had personal ambitions to take any part in the exciting work or not.

The case of the Old Testament was different; yet here too was seen the need for making a less pedantic translation. It had become a Bible translator's tradition to tamper with the Hebrew as little as possible. So the idiomatic Hebrew phrase "And it came to pass" was so rendered, though it was not an English way of expressing the idea at all. The phrase reflected, indeed, a habit of speech among the Hebrews rather than an idea. It said little if anything more than "It was like this, you see" or "Now here's what happened." It was a Semitic cliché. Of course, once translated into English, it had become familiar and associated with the Bible, the book that generations of English-speaking peoples have so deeply loved. To many people, phrases of this kind were so closely associated with Bible reading that a Bible that did not have them would be to them like an expatriate Londoner's return to a London that had given up changing the Guard. The Hebrew phrase "in the day that" meant simply "when"; but to translate it "when" seemed not only to be "playing fast and loose" with the Hebrew text but to deprive the Bible of that mysterious far-off quality that had come to be associated with its style.

Mystery has, indeed, a vital role in all deeply religious feelings, and nothing could be more decrepit and ridiculous than a religion with the sense of wonder taken out of it. It is no more a religion than a eunuch is a man. Through the influence of certain kinds of Puritanism in the English-speaking world, the Bible had become for many almost the only place where that sense of wonder and mystery remained. It was the last surviving stronghold of it. If the mysterious beauty and wonder of its phrases and cadences were taken away, what was there left?

Many who saw all this knew also, however, that there was another side to the question. To have the Bible become a mere treasure-house of antique phrases and haunting cadences was to turn it into a magical incantation. In the Middle Ages the Bible had become exceedingly re-mote to most people, as we have abundantly seen; yet we have also seen that it was highly venerated. Was not this happening all over again? If people were to be lulled into a tranquil ecstasy as they sat in their pews listening to the voice of a clergyman entrancing them with his mellifluous diction or stupefying them with his monotonous attempts to seem un-monotonous, while they really did not understand a tenth of anything he read them, nor would understand it much better even after he had gone on, in his sermon, to half an hour's explanation of the passage he had been reading, were they any better off than a medieval congregation? Might they not almost just as well be hearing the Bible chanted in Latin? Perhaps better, since then they would not have to pretend they under-stood when they did not.

Plainly, there were many controversial issues involved here. Of one thing, however, all responsible and scholarly churchmen were certain: whatever was done with the Bible publicly in church, there ought to be a Bible that people could read at home or use privately in their pews in church—a Bible that everybody could read and understand. Had not quite simple people understood Paul in his day? For them it had been no problem to understand his language. Thanks to the international medium of Greek, Gentiles could feel they had even learned to under-stand Moses. The Bible would never come alive for the modern American or Englishman till it was so translated into his everyday speech that he had that same feeling about it. It had been written neither as an incanta-tion nor as a model of literary style, but as very plain speech proclaiming truth that was meant to go straight to a man's heart and did. Now, at the dawn of the twentieth century, a translator's aim must be to make the words of the Bible leap at his modern English-speaking readers as they had leapt at those who had heard them nearly two thousand years ago.

The radical discovery about the literary character of the New Testament naturally fired the imagination of many gifted individuals, inspiring them to respond to the challenge to produce a modern English version in idiomatic everyday speech that would bring out the true nature of the Greek, not least of St. Paul's letters. In the next chapter we shall have an opportunity to see in what ways many with a flair for this sort of work addressed themselves to the task of producing it. The new approach to the problem of Bible translation led eventually, moreover, to a thoroughgoing revision of the Revised Version and of its transatlantic counterpart, the American Standard Version, and to the consequent appearance, in the mid-twentieth century, of the Revised Standard Version, which will be considered later. In the sixty-five years between the publication in 1881 of the Revised Version of the New Testament and the appearance in 1946 of the Revised Standard Version of the New Testament, a vast number of discoveries took place.

The first and one of the most decisive of these discoveries was made by two Cambridge ladies, Mrs. Lewis and Mrs. Gibson. In 1892, in the monastery on Mount Sinai where Tischendorf had found the extremely valuable manuscript that was to become known as Codex Sinaiticus, these two ladies discovered some palimpsest leaves of a Syriac manuscript. They photographed them and brought the photographs home to England, where they were examined by two English scholars, Professor Bensly and Mr. F. C. Burkitt. Under a late eighth-century treatise lay a fifth-century Syriac text of the Gospels. Bensly and Burkitt recognized the text as belonging to the same textual family as the Curetonian manuscript, which at that time had been regarded as the only extant representative of the Old Syriac Version. It was now seen that the Sinaitic manuscript, though of the same family as the Curetonian, represented an earlier form of the latter.

People tend to expect from such finds more than is actually provided. One of the unique and very remarkable variants the Sinaitic Syriac contained was in the passage (Matt. 1:16) about Joseph's relation to his betrothed, the Virgin Mary, and to Jesus. In contrast to other texts, which call Joseph the husband or the betrothed of Mary, the mother of Jesus, the Sinaitic Syriac was found to read: "Joseph, to whom was betrothed Mary the Virgin, begat Jesus." This would seem clearly to imply a denial of the Virgin Birth and to be interesting on that account; yet elsewhere in the same manuscript are other passages which no less plainly imply the contrary assertion of the miraculous nature of the Nativity. So in this text no new evidence was provided on the subject of the original readings of passages relating to this traditional miracle. It might still be argued that the word "begat" may not have been intended literally, but only by way of indicating a relationship. After all, when devotion to Mary caused her to be acclaimed the Mother of God, she was accorded this title, at first sight startling, only because she had borne in her womb him whom orthodox Christians acclaimed as God, not that she was God's female parent. So by a perhaps not entirely dissimilar sort of figurative language it might have been said that Joseph was the father of Jesus.

What the Sinaitic Syriac did show was a much more scholarly point. It provided evidence that, contrary to what scholars had tended to suppose, there was no clean-cut division between the so-called "Neutral" and "Western" textual families. Sometimes the Sinaitic Syriac agreed with the Codex Vaticanus, sometimes with Codex Sinaiticus, occasionally with Codex Bezae, and occasionally with the Old Latin. So the facts were seen to be more complicated than previous scholars had supposed. The theory of Westcott and Hort needed modification. Despite all this, however, the theory of Westcott and Hort has never been wholly discarded, and when modern scholars look at the Old Syriac as a whole, they are generally able to class it with the Old Latin and Codex Bezae.

The attention of scholars was being turned to two particular groups of manuscripts, now known as Family 1 and Family 13. Each of these groups includes a number of manuscripts having much in common, so that they must be respectively descended from common ancestors, and each contains readings that disagree with the Textus Receptus. In 1877 a book had been published at Dublin, *A Collation of Four Important Manuscripts of the Gospels,* by two scholars, W. H. Ferrar and T. K. Abbot. Ferrar had been the first to identify the group now known as Family 13, so that it is often called, after him, the Ferrar Group. After his death, Abbot completed the work. Three of the four manuscripts of this group belonged to the twelfth or thirteenth century and came from Calabria. The fourth was written in the fifteenth century, probably in England, by Emmanuel of Constantinople. The ancestor of this manuscript must therefore have been at Calabria when the three earlier of these four manuscripts were written. Other manuscripts belonging to this family have since come to light. All agree with the Curetonian Syriac at important points, for example, in the reading at Matthew 1:16: "Joseph, to whom was betrothed Mary the Virgin, who bare Jesus Christ." They omit the passages in Matthew and Luke relating to the appearance of the angel in Gethsemane and the phenomenon of the Bloody Sweat (Matt. 16:2-3 and Luke 22:43-44). The story of the woman taken in adultery, which is traditionally found in John, is transferred in these manuscripts to the end of Luke 21.

Kirsopp Lake, who was later to become, at Leyden and at Harvard, one of the most renowned scholars of his generation, was still in his twenties when he began the researches that led to his subsequent fame. In 1902, when he was still an assistant curate at St. Mary's, Oxford, he published an edition of a group of four manuscripts numbered 1, 118, 131, and 209, collectively designated Fam. 1. The first of these four manuscripts was among those Erasmus had used in preparing the Greek New Testament he published in 1516.

Lake noticed that the text of Mark differed from that of the other three Gospels in such a way as to suggest that since the other Gospels had been longer and more doctrinally interpretative, they had enjoyed greater popularity and had been naturally, therefore, more often copied. Their greater popularity would have caused them to be more frequently revised, leaving Mark a relatively purer text. This hypothesis was to be of great importance in the development of New Testament studies in the twentieth century.

Of much interest to biblical scholars was the group of four vellum manuscripts acquired in 1906 by Charles L. Freer of Detroit from a dealer in Cairo. The manuscripts were placed in the Freer collection in Washington and were edited by H. A. Sanders, becoming known to scholars as the Washington manuscripts. One of these, containing 102 leaves about $10\frac{1}{4}$ by $12\frac{1}{2}$ inches, contains a Greek text of Deuteronomy and Joshua and shows that originally the whole of the Hexateuch was included, perhaps more. Sanders believed this manuscript belonged to the earlier half of the fifth century; but it is more generally assigned to the sixth. One of the other manuscripts in the group is a badly damaged psalter, similarly dated by Sanders in the early fifth century but more commonly assigned to the sixth or even the seventh century. In the third manuscript are some fragments of Paul's letters in a predominantly Alexandrian text. The remaining manuscript is by far the most interesting of the group. It is a manuscript of the Gospels, at least as old as the fifth century and possibly older, and has 374 pages of $5\frac{5}{8}$ by $8\frac{1}{4}$ inches, with thirty lines to the page, single column.

The most immediately startling feature of this manuscript of the Gospels is the insertion after Mark 16:14 of a very distinctive passage recounting a complaint by the disciples that their generation was in the grip of Satan, uttering their prayer to Christ to make his righteousness manifest, and recording his reply that while the dominion of Satan is in fact ended, other terrible things are in store as a result of the sins of men, for which reason Christ is delivered over to death in order that they may return to the true way, sin no more, and attain incorruptible glory. There is no doubt that the passage is spurious; but it is of interest as a striking witness to the peculiar character of this manuscript. The scribe, in writing Luke and Mark, was evidently either working from a variety of differing copies, or else he was copying a manuscript that had been produced by an earlier scribe with such an assortment before him.

In 1906 von Soden had called attention to a manuscript in a monastery in the Caucasus which, after an edition of it had been published by Beermann and Gregory in 1913, came to be known as the Koridethi Codex or Θ. Being relatively late—possibly ninth century—it would seem prima facie of no special account; yet because of the studies of Lake and another scholar, R. P. Blake, whose special knowledge of Georgian manuscripts enabled him to show its association with Fam. 1 and Fam. 13, it proved of great importance to the development of early twentieth-century researches into the New Testament text, as we shall see. Many other manuscripts also came to light about the time which, though individually of no such great importance, were collectively useful as contributions to the growing mass of evidence upon which scholars could now work. Though a new manuscript be of no great interest in itself, it may not only shed light on earlier finds but enhance their importance for further studies.

The papyrus fragments that were coming to light in great numbers about this time included many that contained pieces of New Testament text. Some dated from the third century. One such papyrus fragment might contain only a verse or two. The largest, from Oxyrhynchus, and probably dating from the late fourth century, contains only a few chapters from Hebrews. Collectively, however, the earlier ones considerably enhanced the New Testament scholar's existing tools. From Oxyrhynchus alone came fifty papyri, including thirty pertaining to the New Testament. They helped to show, for instance, that in Egypt, towards the end of the third century, there were already texts plainly of the so-called "Western" type. They confirmed the known shortcomings of the Textus Receptus; yet they also showed that the scheme of Westcott and Hort, though not wrong, had been much too simple to explain the facts. The question that an intelligent inquirer in those days naturally asked was: Which of the earliest extant manuscripts represents the text closest to the original? The accumulating evidence strongly indicated that no answer could be given to such a question. The importance of this negative conclusion was great. It meant there was an early period when practice was too inchoate to provide texts susceptible to any neat classification of manuscripts into families and groups. On this view one rival claimant could have no definite superiority over another.

These manuscripts and fragments, together with some Coptic, Syriac, and Latin finds that came to light in the first decades of the present century, constitute the principal events in the first thirty years of our century. Then came the discovery of a group of papyri in Egypt that was purchased by Chester Beatty and announced in London on November

19, 1931, in *The Times*. It contained twelve Greek manuscripts, one consisting of noncanonical Christian literature, eight of portions of Old Testament books in Greek, and three of portions of the New Testament. The least ancient of these manuscripts is no later than the fifth century in date, and the earliest, a manuscript containing portions of Numbers and Deuteronomy, has been placed in the first half of the second century. The manuscript containing portions of the Gospels and of Acts belongs to the third century, perhaps the earlier part of that century. To the third century probably also belongs another containing portions of Paul's letters, and yet another containing a portion of the Apocalypse.

To consider in full detail all that the Chester Beatty papyri did for modern biblical scholarship would take us too far beyond our scope. We shall have the opportunity of seeing the fundamental character of their importance as we turn to consider the use scholars made of the new tools now at their disposal. One incidental consequence of this particular find is so dramatic, however, that I will refer to it here before further reviewing the development of scholarly methods in the period under consideration.

Everyone knew, of course, that the papyrus roll was the standard form of book in the Graeco-Roman world in the first century, and that books made up in pages such as the one now in the hand of the reader of the present one were then unknown. It was also recognized that though the codex, that is, the newer form of book, did not come into *general* use till the fourth century, there were examples of its use in the intervening period. How did the transition take place? Among the Jews the tradition of the Scroll of the Law persisted, and indeed its use for ceremonial purposes persists in the synagogue to this day. Moreover, it was known that for pagan literature the roll form had remained universal in the second century and was still very general in the third. An accumulation of evidence was pointing to the conclusion, however, that the novel book form may have had a Christian origin. Now the Chester Beatty papyri proved an actual example of a third-century codex containing all four Gospels and Acts as well.

The consequences of this line of thought are more interesting than they may appear at first sight to be. When the Gospels were written, it would have been impossible to include more than one of them in a single roll of papyrus, for it was impracticable to make such a roll much more than thirty-five feet long, which is about the length of a modern American standard roll of wallpaper. On such a papyrus roll there would be room for one book such as Matthew, but not for more than one, so that the Gospels must have circulated at first individually. They could not well have wholly escaped being looked upon as rivals rather than as a corporate witness. Moreover, there were other and much more extravagant documents circulating as accounts of the Gospel story, and churchmen wanted therefore to encourage the universal acceptance of the four Gospels as a whole and to the exclusion of the more fanciful narratives. When we find Irenaeus, in the later part of the second century, remarking upon the peculiarly fitting character of the number four as the number of Gospels the Church ought to possess, we might be naturally inclined to take this as a calculation based upon a mystical interpretation of the number four. The discovery of the Chester Beatty papyri provided important evidence that Irenaeus could have given a more practical explanation. The new sort of book form coming into fashion among Christians would be admirably adapted to the inclusion of four Gospels. These would make a neat, natural-sized volume of the new type, and such a volume would soon have acquired considerable authority as a bibliographical unit containing all four of the most generally accepted accounts of the good news the Church proclaimed.

That the modern book form was a Christian invention now seemed more highly probable than ever. At the same time, Lake's hypothesis about Mark had even more interesting consequences. Once the Gospels were customarily in codex form, they would be generally copied, of course, as a whole; but when, before that time, they had been copied separately, the most popular would suffer at the hands of the copyists. So it was now seen that any such process of corruption before the codex had supplanted the roll, affecting least the less popular Mark, would have occurred at a very early date.

We have now taken note of the major manuscript discoveries that had been made by the time work on the Revised Standard Version was begun. What did the scholars of the intervening generations do with the stream of new materials that was made available to them? How did it affect their thinking, and what new methods and theories did it help them to develop?

Already we have seen the enormously important effect of Deissmann's conclusive proof that the language of the New Testament was of a character other than had been supposed. The consequences of this for any subsequent Bible translation were bound to be immense. The discovery of new manuscripts and fragments also created, however, an urgent demand among scholars for a new critical edition of the New Testament and for an inventory of all the manuscript evidence that had come to light.

The Textus Receptus had fallen into great disrepute as a result of the work of Westcott and Hort. There had been no lack of scholars to oppose their theories. Burgon and Miller are examples; but with their death the views of Westcott and Hort triumphed so decisively for a time that for some years the opinion prevailed that the New Testament text was now established in its essentials. In 1891, however, Rendel Harris published an important study of Codex Bezae, following it a few years later with a further work on the same subject. Through these studies he drew attention to the fact that the great antiquity of the so-called Western text had been generally underestimated. Its use in the second and third centuries was universal. The filial piety of the disciples of Westcott and Hort tended to be shocked by such a suggestion, because they had liked to think that these two indubitably great scholars had said the last word on the subject of the New Testament text and had produced the definitive edition of it. Harris' work proved to be of great importance in beginning a new phase of development.

The discovery by the two Cambridge ladies, the story of which has already been told, was of incalculable help in the development of this new phase. It was seen that, apart from Tatian's harmony of the Gospels, the oldest Syriac text seemed to be "Western" in character and similar to the African Latin text. At Oxford, studies of the Old Latin manuscripts were going on under the direction of William Sanday, as early as the time F. C. Burkitt had made the Sinaitic Syriac manuscript available, though the result of these Oxford studies was not published till about thirty years later, when Wordsworth and White's great critical edition of the Vulgate appeared in 1923. The Oxford studies showed that the African Latin was of greater value than Westcott and Hort had supposed; but the force of such contentions was not generally seen till the facts about the Old Syriac were brought to bear upon the facts about the Old Latin. Then in 1899 F. C. Burkitt called attention to a study by P. M. Barnard of the text of the Gospels used by Clement of Alexandria, showing that this is more akin to the Old Latin than, as had been taken for granted, to the so-called Neutral text. Burkitt boldly inquired whether the combined evidence of Codex Vaticanus and Codex Sinaiticus was really superior to the combined evidence of the Old Syriac and Old Latin. With the renewed interest in the so-called "Western" text that had been stimulated by the work of Harris, a new era of controversy began. Scholars who contributed to it searched in the manuscripts for evidence in support of their various theories. H. C. Hoskier, for instance, ingeniously sought to prove that polyglottal texts existed at an early date and that variations in the extant Greek text could often be explained on the view that an attempt had been made to bring the Greek into line with the Latin or Syriac alongside it. From a study of Acts, another scholar, A. C. Clark, tried to show that the so-called Neutral text arose from accidental scribal omissions from the so-called Western text.

Towards the end of the nineteenth century, it became known that the German scholar, H. von Soden, had been enabled to undertake, on an unprecedented scale, a critical edition of the text of the Greek New

Testament. Having been provided with large funds for the purpose, he was able to work with an abundance of expert assistance. So much was awaited from this work that the expectation of its appearance probably caused many scholars to mark time for some years, for it was widely believed that all previous editions, including Tischendorf's and Westcott and Hort's, would be completely outmoded by it. At last the result of the stupendous enterprise directed by von Soden appeared in separate volumes published between the years 1902 and 1913.

It was no less grand in conception and design than had been expected; but it proved a great disappointment, revealing many shortcomings. The use of an entirely new system of designating the manuscripts was particularly unfortunate. In preference to the haphazard but familiar and convenient system in general use among scholars, von Soden had devised, in a fashion not uncharacteristic of German scholarship, a new one designed to be more orderly and rational. The new system, however, was found to be not only cumbersome but of almost no practical advantage. Indeed, it looked as though its disadvantages would far outweigh its advantages. Happily, the generally accepted designation was, by the efforts of other scholars, preserved.

The basic theory of von Soden was presented in a very difficult and heavy fashion, demanding much study, which it duly received. While it has not stood the test of time, it is of some importance for an understanding of the development of textual studies, so it should be briefly stated here. As we saw earlier, four main types of text had been isolated through the work of Westcott and Hort, namely, those called Neutral, Alexandrian, Western, and Syrian. Von Soden classified all manuscripts as K (Koinē), H (Hesychian), or I (Ierousalem or Jerusalem). K included the principal later manuscript that Hort called Syrian, H what had been known as the "Neutral" group, consisting of about fifty manuscripts whose most celebrated exemplar is Codex Vaticanus, and in I were placed Codex Bezae, the Old Latin, the Old Syriac, Fam. 1, Fam. 13, and the like. K would have come originally from Syria, H from Egypt, being the text used by Cyril of Alexandria, and I represented the text used by Cyril of Jerusalem, hence its designation. There must have been a common ancestor, and its date would have to be placed no later than the end of the second century.

Such was, in barest outline, the theory advanced by von Soden. All known manuscripts, he thought, belong to one or other of these categories, and there was, he believed, a common ancestor, I-H-K, which was used by Origen, probably also by Justin and Marcion, and probably Tatian's Diatessaron was based upon it.

The reasons that have led scholars generally to set aside von Soden's theory are too complicated to be considered in detail here. Kirsopp Lake provided some very telling criticisms of it as early as 1908 in a pamphlet entitled *Professor H. von Soden's Treatment of the Text of the Gospels.* As manuscript evidence accumulated, methods of examining it improved. The discovery of the Freer manuscripts and the Koridethi Gospels was of considerable importance here. Such manuscripts could be shown to present a text which, apart from certain easily explicable variations, was common, yet agreed with neither the so-called Neutral type as represented by Codex Vaticanus nor the so-called Western type as represented by Codex Bezae. R. P. Blake, Kirsopp Lake's collaborator, who was, we have seen, expert in Georgian manuscripts, offered the view that the script of the Koridethi Gospels suggested a Georgian origin. A Georgian colony at Sinai could have been affected by both Egypt and Jerusalem. Then in 1924 came a very important and influential study by B. H. Streeter, *The Four Gospels.* Streeter was able to show that Origen, though he had a "Neutral" type of text at his disposal at Alexandria, had access also at Caesarea to another type which is represented by such manuscripts as the Koridethi Gospels. The text of manuscripts of the latter type could be called Caesarean.

The reconstruction of this Caesarean text was a challenging enterprise to Kirsopp Lake, who had already earlier hinted at such a possibility, and he undertook to reconstruct a text of Mark. Moreover, on the subject of the texts used by Origen, Lake was able to go further than Streeter. He pointed out that Origen, in writing certain works *at Caesarea,* had used a "Neutral" (Alexandrian) text; then, later, he had used a "Neutral" text for the earlier part of Mark but a Caesarean one for the rest of it; and finally he had reverted to the use of a Caesarean text exclusively. Lake showed that either the Caesarean text originated in Alexandria, or else Origen brought it to Caesarea himself. Moreover, Streeter had denied that Eusebius of Caesarea had used the Caesarean text, and Lake was able to give reasons against this. At any rate, Streeter and Lake between them made it seem clear that von Soden's classification would not do. The existence of the Caesarean textual family could be definitely upheld, and it must be separated altogether from the Western family.

The Chester Beatty papyri provided an example of a text of Mark that would seem to be very clearly of the Caesarean type. They also furnished scholars for the first time with irrefragable proof that not only the Gospels were circulating *as a collection* as early as the third century, but so also were Paul's letters.

One of the now best-known developments in New Testament scholarship during the period under review concerned the problem of the interdependence of the first three Gospels, called the Synoptics. That they were interrelated was recognized by some scholars at an early stage and is now almost universally admitted, though the precise nature of the literary interdependence is still by no means entirely settled. On the basis of critical studies made at the end of the nineteenth century in England by Sir John Hawkins and in Germany by Adolf Harnack, a theory was developed that posited a common ancestor, which was designated Q. Streeter, who put this theory into the form in which it came to be very generally accepted, held that behind the Synoptics lay not merely an oral tradition but a written Greek document, now lost. Though according to Streeter the *order* of Luke reflects this hypothetical Q more than does Matthew, the whole content of Q has gone into either Luke or Matthew or both. Streeter was cautious enough to concede that the existence of Q could not be accounted absolutely certain; but he regarded it as practically certain, and except among Roman Catholics (who have had a special ecclesiastical reason for not admitting the Q theory), almost all modern scholars have accepted it. One notable exception is Austin Farrer, who in his brilliant essays in criticism of the theory has evoked more interest among biblical scholars than he has won converts. The Q theory, though not impregnable, still commands general acceptance. Nevertheless, the biblical theories of Austin Farrer merit the closest scrutiny, for a mind of his extremely rare quality is often not merely brilliant but right.

Generally speaking, and with some deviations on points of detail, modern scholars during the period under review also reached agreement that Mark, earliest of the Gospels, was used by Matthew and Luke as a general framework into which they worked materials derived from Q, adding other materials from further written sources available to them and now also lost.

The period was a critical one, marking a turning point in understanding of the Bible, and therefore in biblical translation, not least in the translation of the New Testament. The new mood is reflected first in the avalanche of independent translations issued during this period, and secondly in the work of the scholars who eventually produced the Revised Standard Version. To these expressions of the new mood two further chapters will be devoted. As we shall see, those who undertook to translate the New Testament had to take into account both the exciting finds that were being made and the development of improved methods of scholarship in using these finds. The most practical concern now affecting the work of a New Testament translator, however, was the production of a version that would exhibit the all-important discovery about the nature of New Testament language itself.

As for the New Testament the work of Westcott and Hort, despite the radical critique it suffered, remained a foundation for further investigations, so for the Old Testament the Graf-Wellhausen hypothesis, that there are four major sources in the Pentateuch, continued to be a basis for all later studies. Wellhausen did not confine himself, however, to literary and historical studies of the Old Testament. He went on to interpret the whole history and literature of Israel in the light of the current scientific theories of his day, as Adolf Harnack (1851-1930) interpreted the New Testament to his generation in terms of nineteenth-century moral ideals and hopes. For these reasons both Wellhausen and Harnack have deserved and received much criticism by twentieth-century thinkers; but Wellhausen's basic literary discoveries about the Old Testament remain important, though they have been modified, as we shall see.

In 1881 William Robertson Smith was deprived of his chair in Old Testament studies in the Free Church College, Aberdeen. The persecution he had suffered for openly teaching views to which Wellhausen was about to give classical form in his *Prolegomena* had culminated in his trial for heresy. The immediate occasion of the Free Church proceedings against Robertson Smith was the article he had written for the ninth edition of the Encyclopaedia Britannica. He was able to defend himself against the charge of heresy by showing that his methods of biblical study were compatible with an orthodox position in his Church; yet his opponents, afraid of his influence on the rising generation of preachers, secured his deprivation [1] after a trial that lasted five years. His trial did much to make known among educated people in the English-speaking world the meaning of the new approach to biblical studies, and to allay their fears about it. Later, men such as S. R. Driver and Sir George Adam Smith were able to win public confidence more easily. Twenty years after Robertson Smith's deprivation, an obscurantist attempt to discredit George Adam Smith met with total failure.

The climate had changed radically from mid-Victorian times. In 1865, when Sir J. R. Seeley's *Ecce Homo,* an anonymously published life of Jesus, persuasively written but unevangelical and reminiscent of Renan, had been published, it was denounced by Lord Shaftesbury in language whose violence almost matched that of the sixteenth century. It was, he said, "the most pestilential volume ever vomited forth from the jaws of Hell." A popular preacher such as Joseph Parker (1830-1902), who built the City Temple, London, in 1874, had thundered from that influential Free Church pulpit against what he took to be the menace of biblical interpretation by the learned. "Have we to await a communication from Tübingen," he asked, "or a telegram from Oxford, before we can read the Bible?" [2] By the beginning of the twentieth century such outbursts in prominent places were becoming rare.

---

[1] As the occupant of a Free Church College chair, he did not enjoy the tenure attached to a chair in any of the university faculties of divinity. His removal from one of these would have been much more difficult, if not impossible.

[2] Quoted by W. B. Glover, *Evangelical Nonconformists and Higher Criticism in the Nineteenth Century* (London: Independent Press, Ltd., 1955), p. 163.

Old Testament studies have abundantly profited from the vast archaeological discoveries that have been made in Palestine, Egypt, and Mesopotamia. Egyptian hieroglyphics and Babylonian cuneiform have been deciphered, yielding information of great value to the Old Testament scholar. Before the end of the nineteenth century the Tell el Amarna tablets and the Elephantiné papyri had given scholars needed evidence about Egypt's relations with her neighbors. From 1929 onwards, another generation was to see, through the discovery of cuneiform tablets at Ras Shamra (anciently Ugarit), how in very early times a primitive Canaanite nature worship had for centuries imperilled the developing cult of Yahweh. Numerous and extensive excavations at ancient historic sites such as Nineveh and Jericho have brought to twentieth-century Old Testament scholars a wealth of information that would have astonished their forerunners.

Twenty years later, great popular excitement attended the finding of the Dead Sea Scrolls. The importance of these is not to be underestimated. It is great indeed, and the discovery is one of the most important ever made. Yet the nature of the importance is not what was popularly expected. Many people insufficiently familiar with the results of modern biblical studies looked for more from these particular discoveries than even the most sanguine scholar would think of expecting. The Qumran manuscripts began to come to light just after the publication of the Revised Standard Version of the New Testament in 1946 and before the appearance of that version of the Bible in 1952. In the latter, thirteen readings from the Dead Sea Scroll of Isaiah were used; yet Professor Millar Burrows of Yale, a member of the committee that prepared the Revised Standard Version and an authority on the Dead Sea Scrolls, wrote afterwards that he regretted their use in some cases, even where he voted for it at the time. His second thoughts on the subject favored the Masoretic reading. Generally speaking, what was striking about the text of the Dead Sea manuscript of Isaiah (many centuries older than the oldest hitherto known manuscript of any Old Testament book) was its similarity to, rather than its difference from, the text of existing manuscripts. The greatest value of the Qumran discoveries lies elsewhere, not least in showing the vast possibilities that are opened up for the future of biblical research. Even these valuable finds are probably only a token of what may be disgorged, perhaps in similarly unlikely circumstances, in the future.

The Graf-Wellhausen hypothesis that there are four major sources in the Pentateuch has remained, meanwhile, the starting point of modern literary and critical studies of the Old Testament; but it has been carried much further. In our own day, the greatest contemporary scholars have continued to use similar analytical methods with the finer tools at their disposal. That these methods have their limitations was recognized by

Herman Gunkel (1862-1932) at an early date within the period under discussion. Gunkel held that more was needed than an examination of the biblical documents themselves and an analysis of their literary history. The documents must be read in the light of their own setting. It was just this need for an appreciation of the nature of the Hebrew oral tradition of myth and legend that even the obscure Father Geddes had recognized in his own way as early as the eighteenth century. In the eighteenth century also, Johann Gottfried Herder (1744-1803) had seen, through his studies of Hebrew poetry, that the spirit of this poetry must have expressed itself in distinctive forms before these were later crystallized in writing. This was the idea that Gunkel and others now closely examined in the light of newer discoveries. Their new methods enabled them to identify certain literary "types" or "forms" in the Old Testament.

Out of this sort of approach has also been developed the work of Engnell, Haldar, and other representatives of the Uppsala School. These Swedish scholars have tried to show that while the Wellhausen scheme of four documents underlying the Pentateuch points to the truth, it must not be pressed too far. Since one is dealing with oral tradition, one can no longer, on this view, regard Wellhausen's J, E, D, and P as in any sense strictly datable units. It is useless to look for or speculate about the biblical editors, for the process was a gradual one in which pieces of oral tradition were very slowly assimilated and eventually given written form.

This school has also stressed the importance of liturgy in the construction of the Old Testament, and so the role of the prophet, a preoccupation for long characteristic of Old Testament scholars, has been diminished. Mowinckel, a Norwegian scholar, has gone so far in this direction as to see the Babylonian New Year festival as one of the basic clues to an understanding of the Psalms. In modern studies of the Christian Epistles and Gospels the liturgical approach has yielded many important insights, though here as elsewhere there is always, of course, the danger of exaggeration. Gunkel's concern for the *Sitz im Leben* caught the imagination of New Testament scholars, and his methods have influenced many, such as Karl Ludwig Schmidt, Martin Dibelius, and Rudolf Bultmann. The difference it has made to scholarly understanding of the Bible is incalculable. Perhaps one might get a very rough notion of its import by considering what it means to see contemporary streets and markets in Antwerp and Venice in the light of Flemish and Venetian cultural traditions respectively, and as functions of the contemporary economies of Belgium and Italy, instead of seeing them, in the manner of the more unenlightened tourist, as though they were displaced extensions of Lexington Avenue or picturesque adjuncts to Greenwich Village.

*Any new translation starts under a
special handicap. It appears to challenge in
every line the rhythm and diction of an English
classic, and this irritates many who have no
knowledge of the original.*—James Moffatt

CHAPTER 29 *Independent Modern English Versions*

The dramatic effect of Deissmann's discoveries and the new sort of approach that was being undertaken in England by such scholars as Kenyon showed how inevitably ill conceived had been the work of the patient and faithful men who had labored to give the English-speaking world the Revised Version. That version, so long awaited, had come too early after all, for it had appeared just before the discoveries that were to make it look radically out of date long before people could have had time to become accustomed to it. It was wholly unsuccessful, therefore, in replacing the familiar King James Version for general use, public or private, and it became at best an adjunct for the desk of scholarly preachers, rather than what it had been designed to be—the new Bible for the whole Church in the English-speaking world. Instead, the King James Version held the field.

Yet what greater challenge was there to a writer at the beginning of the twentieth century than to try his hand at a translation in the light of the new discoveries, lack of access to which had doomed the Revised Version to failure? To any young writer who had an acquaintance with the facts, a flair for writing clear, slightly racy English, and a classical education such as was common among educated men in the early part of this century, the challenge of writing a new translation of the New Testament might well have seemed irresistible.

As early as 1895 an English businessman, Ferrar Fenton, published *The New Testament in Modern English,* which was followed in 1903 by *The Bible in Modern English.* The interest of this work lies in its pioneering character and early date rather than in its merits as a translation. It contained some oddities, such as the use of "Ever-living" for "the Lord," and in other ways reflects something of the new aims without achieving the success that attended the efforts of later independent translators. Nevertheless, Fenton does herald the spirit of the new translation fever, and some of his efforts are very striking, for example his rendering of the opening of Psalm 100:

> Hurrah to the LORD all the Earth;
> Serve the LORD with delight;
> Come into His Presence with cheering.

Of much more importance, however, was the work of a company of some twenty scholars who, between 1898 and 1901, brought out, in three parts, *The Twentieth Century New Testament*. In 1904 there was a revised edition of this. The new aim was expressly declared in the preface, which explained that the translators wished to try to present to English readers the New Testament in a form as lively as that in which it had originally appeared many centuries before in Greek. The old measures of time and space that had been so puzzling to many readers of the Bible were modernized in twentieth-century English style as far as possible. The latest results of scholarship (for example, the chronological order that scholars were now giving to the four Gospels—Mark, Matthew, Luke, John) was followed. Paragraphs were used to make the New Testament read as much as possible like any other book, and dialogue was for the same reason put within quotation marks.

In 1903 a most interesting translation appeared, the work of a Londoner, Richard F. Weymouth, who published it under the attractive title *The New Testament in Modern Speech*. Wisely, Weymouth disavowed all intention of replacing the "standard" or "authorized" versions. He wished only to provide people with a translation that would supplement these, being written for home use in English that was always modern and sometimes even a little colloquial, yet never in the least offensively lacking in the dignity most readers tended to expect in the Bible. Being in idiomatic modern English, it was immediately intelligible as no then existing version was; yet there was nothing cheap or vulgar in the style. Here is a typical example at Acts 10:18-21:

"Is Simon, surnamed Peter, staying here?"

Peter was still pondering over the vision, when the Spirit said to him, "Three men are now inquiring for you. Rise, go down, and go with them without any misgivings; for it is I who have sent them to you."

So Peter went down and said to the men,

"I am the man you are inquiring for. What is the reason of your coming?"

Such unpedantic language differed little from that which a good London journalist reporting an event at the turn of the century would have used. There was nothing tawdry about it. It could offend no intelligent reader. It seemed to echo the dignity of the past while being couched in almost the language of the present.

The style used in the Gospels possessed the same attractive combination of qualities. For instance, at Matthew 9:12: "It is not men in good health who require a doctor, but those who are ill." And again, at Mark 10:14: "Let the little children come to me: do not hinder them; for to those who are childlike the Kingdom of God belongs." Yet again, the famous passage at I Corinthians 13 reveals the same qualities: "Love never fails. But if there are prophecies, they will come to an end; if there are tongues, they will cease; if there is knowledge, it will come to an end. For our knowledge is partial, and so is our prophesying." And take as a final example a passage on glossolalia or "speaking with tongues," at I Corinthians 14:7-9: "If inanimate things—flutes or harps, for instance—though they yield a sound, yet make no distinction in the notes, how shall the tune which is played on the flute or the harp be known? If the bugle, again, gives an uncertain sound, who will prepare for battle? And so with you; if with the tongue you fail to utter intelligible words, how will people know what you are saying? You will be talking to the winds."

Weymouth was not only a pleasantly gifted writer; he was a good scholar, using an up-to-date critical Greek text. His work deserved more than the modest success it attained, considerable though that was. An American edition of his New Testament was published long afterwards, in 1943.

The next translation was bolder and was destined for much greater fame. It was the work of James Moffatt, a Scotsman who, having taught in Scotland, came to Union Theological Seminary, New York City. In 1901 he published a scholarly introduction to the New Testament incorporating a fresh translation based, as was Weymouth's, on a critical Greek text. Twelve years later, as we shall see, was published the first edition of the translation of the New Testament that he offered to the general public.

Meanwhile a book appeared which, though not so much a translation as a modern aid, ought to be noted here since it has enjoyed a wide influence. In 1907 *The Modern Reader's Bible,* by Richard G. Moulton, a Chicago University professor, made its first appearance in book form, having already come out in a series of twenty-one separate publications. Moulton offered no translation novelties; indeed, his work was based largely on the Revised Version. The novelty lay in the methods he offered to people who wanted to study the Bible seriously. He greatly helped many readers for whom the antiquated structure of the Bible was a greater impediment to understanding than was the archaic English style of the then prevailing standard versions.

When Moffatt, in 1913, issued at Edinburgh *The New Testament, a New Translation,* the intention announced in the preface was fulfilled in his text. His declared aim was to translate the New Testament as one would translate any other piece of Greek literature of the period. Let its message speak for itself. If it be the Word of God, why should it need to be buttressed by a special "holy" style created by man's ingenuity? Why should a modern idiomatic style be draped, so to speak, with a supernatural coverlet? After all, what was the New Testament? It was the testimony of very human men filled with joyful excitement at the Good News of which they were writing. As scholars now saw, these men had been writing in the ordinary language of their day, as one would write a letter to a friend about an extraordinary event. The event was believed to be both unique and indescribably joyful. Yet in writing about it they would let that uniqueness speak for itself while they raced on with their story in the language of daily life.

The inner meaning of Moffatt's intention may be made clearer to some if they will but think of one of the most dramatic tragedies of modern times, the assassination of President John F. Kennedy. All the ordinary media of mass communication were at once put into action to keep the world abreast of news relating to the shocking event. Millions of people were profoundly moved. There was a sense not only of great tragedy but of participation in one of the most dramatic moments in human history. Every newsman knew he was uttering words that would become part of the historical record and go down to his hearers' children's children. Yet every newsman used the same style of language he would have used in reporting any other sad event. He might quote a line of poetry or a "great saying"; but he did not try to adopt any unusual or exalted tone as he breathlessly told the terrible tale. The momentous implications of the national tragedy were too great to need any special kind of language, or any but the simplest and most familiar sort of speech. If such an event did not speak for itself in everyday language, a "lofty" style would certainly do nothing for it. The men and women all over the world who poured forth many anguished words about it knew the effect of it did not depend upon anything anyone might say. They knew they were witnessing a great event in the political history of mankind. So they spoke naturally, excitedly, in everyday speech. So too, then, spoke those men who two thousand years ago proclaimed the event they believed to be the supreme event in human history, the event they proclaimed as the transformation of all human history.

Moffatt captured the significance of this fact about New Testament speech and gave it expression with unprecedented skill. He made Paul enjoin Titus to give "a hearty send-off" to Zenas the jurist (Titus 3:13). The high priests "made fun" of Jesus on the cross (Matt. 27:41). No longer was Paul made to say (I Cor. 13:1) that without charity he was "as sounding brass, or a tinkling cymbal"; now Paul was saying that without love, "I am a noisy gong or a clanging cymbal." The wise and the foolish virgins (Matthew 25) were now respectively sensible and stupid maidens. Nor did the former tell the latter to go "to them that sell, and buy for yourselves"; they said: "Better go to the dealers and buy for yourselves." The injunctions against "fornication, and all uncleanness or covetousness" (Eph. 5:3) became more intelligible denunciations of "sexual vice" and "impurity" and "lust." When the disciples were fishing without success (John 21), Jesus, in the now odd and cryptic language of the King James Version, had asked them: "Children, have ye any meat?" For this Moffatt wrote instead: " 'Lads,' said Jesus, 'have you got anything?' "

In 1924 the Old Testament appeared, in 1926 the first edition of the complete Moffatt Bible, and in 1935 what was called a "revised and final edition." Some of the Old Testament phrases were no less strikingly natural. Solomon (II Chron. 5:2) called together the sheikhs of Israel and the chiefs of the clans. Noah's ark (Genesis 6:14), familiar in imagery to every child yet shrouded in a mysterious "biblical English" name, now became simply a barge.

The Riverside New Testament, published in 1923, was the work of William G. Ballantine. The translator, a former President of Oberlin College, acknowledged his debt to various predecessors already mentioned in this chapter. He produced a very readable translation without verse numbers and with an index such as one would expect in any ordinary historical work.

Moffatt's translation had been in British rather than American idiom. In 1923 Edgar J. Goodspeed, a distinguished American biblical scholar, brought out, at the invitation of the University of Chicago Press, a translation whose English seemed more natural to American ears. It was suitably entitled *The New Testament, An American Translation.* Goodspeed used "you" rather than "thou" even in address to God. At Matthew 1:18 he said of the Virgin Mary that she was "about to become a mother under the influence of the holy Spirit." In 1927 the same press issued a companion volume, *The Old Testament, An American Translation,* which was the work of four scholars, T. J. Meek of the University of Toronto, Leroy Waterman of the University of Michigan, A. R. Gordon of McGill University, Montreal, and J. M. P. Smith of the University of Chicago. The variety of style not unnaturally reflected in a work of such composite authorship was mitigated in later editions. In 1931 appeared *The Bible, An American Translation,* and in 1939 came *The Complete Bible, An American Translation.* The latter included a translation of the Apocrypha by Goodspeed.

The American Baptist Publication Society published in 1924 *The Centenary Translation of the New Testament.* The aim of this translation, by Mrs. Helen Barrett Montgomery, a Wellesley graduate, was the characteristic one of the period: to make the language of the New Testament live for readers in the English-speaking world as it had lived in Greek for its original readers.

In such an epidemic of translation fever it was inevitable that more eccentrically motivated translations should appear. Two were published in California about this time. One, *The People's New Covenant (New Testament) Scriptural Writings,* published in 1925 by Arthur E. Overbury, of Monrovia, California, claimed to be "a revision unhampered by so-called ecclesiastical authority," which interpreted Scripture from a "meta-physical standpoint, and recognizes *healing* as well as *teaching* as a component part of true Christianity." The following year saw the appearance of the *Concordant Version of the Sacred Scripture, "New Testament," An Idiomatic, Consistent Emphasized Version.* This translation claimed to be "safe, sane, and scientific," and conformable "to the basic laws of language, in that, as far as feasible, each expression selected constantly represents its closest Greek equivalent, and each Greek word is given one, exclusive English rendering." The copious notes included an assurance to the effect that punctuation does not form part of the inspired Word of God.

There is even a translation into "basic English." This is a language invented on the principle of simplifying English by limiting the vocabulary. In general, only 850 words are used, but since it was apparently found impracticable to produce an English version within the compass of such a limited vocabulary, this was extended to a thousand words for the special case of the Bible. Under the direction of S. H. Hooke, Professor Emeritus of Old Testament in the University of London, a committee undertook the work of rendering the Bible into basic English. The results of their labors were reviewed by a committee formed by the Syndics of the Cambridge University Press, which published *The New Testament in Basic English* in 1941 and *The Basic Bible* in 1950.

In 1940 George Lamsa's translation "from original Aramaic sources" appeared under the title *The New Testament according to the Eastern Text.* This was followed, in 1957, by his version of the whole Bible. While Lamsa's work is not without merit, the claims he makes are generally questioned. Contrary to scholarly opinion, and working on a superficially fascinating but entirely unproven, not to say untenable, theory of his own, he maintains that the Peshitta (Aramaic-Syriac) Version represents the "original Eastern text of both the New and Old Testaments." Lamsa, who was born in Kurdistan, can claim an Aramaic dialect as his mother tongue, and it is well known that Christ spoke Palestinian Aramaic, which, though different from the Aramaic-Syriac of the Peshitta, is nevertheless akin to it. There are, however, complicated reasons which have for long convinced scholars that the Peshitta is a comparatively late translation of the Bible and by no means an original text itself,

Lamsa's renderings are often not without interest. He has been much influenced by the King James Version. Here are some passages to illustrate how he departs from it:

(a) JOHN 20:22
   King James Version: And when he had said this, he breathed on *them.*
   Lamsa: And when he had said these things, he gave them courage.

(b) I CORINTHIANS 7:5
   King James Version: Defraud ye not one the other, except *it be* with consent for a time, that ye may give yourselves to fasting and prayer; and come together again, that Satan tempt you not for your incontinency.
   Lamsa: Therefore do not deprive one another except when both of you consent to do so, especially at the time when you devote yourselves to fasting and prayer; and then come together again, so that Satan may not tempt you because of your physical passion.

(c) I CORINTHIANS 9:27
   King James Version: But I keep under my body, and bring *it* into subjection: lest that by any means, when I have preached to others, I myself should be a castaway.
   Lamsa: But I conquer and subdue my body so that, by no chance, when I have preached to others, will I despise myself.

That public attention is easily aroused may be seen from the widespread attention given to the Yonan Codex, a manuscript of the New Testament in Aramaic-Syriac which was exhibited in the Great Hall of the Library of Congress, at an "unveiling" ceremony on April 5th, 1955. According to the report of an art historian, Professor John Shapley of the Catholic University of America, it is a vellum manuscript consisting of 227 leaves (folios) measuring about 7 by 9 inches. The writing is in black ink, now somewhat brownish in part, and is in one column of twenty-eight to thirty-one lines to the page. The handwriting, uniform and very skilful, seems to be the work of one scribe, who, Professor Shapley says, "probably took serious account of his materials, for he gives a wide berth on folio 207 to a hole in the vellum—perhaps from the slaughter of the animal." The binding, though not contemporary with the manuscript, is old. Professor Shapley estimates the date of the manuscript itself (from palaeographical evidence) to be in or about the fifth century. On March 28th, 1955, the *Christian Science Monitor* published a picture of President Eisenhower scanning the pages of the codex as it was held out to him by the owner, Mr. Norman Yonan. For its brief journey from a bank vault to the White House and thence to the Library of Congress, the manuscript was insured for $1,500,000 and later permanently insured for that sum. A resolution adopted by the Society of Biblical Literature on December 30th, 1955, at its annual meeting in New York City, however, as a result of careful study of the manuscript by a company of experts who devoted part of the Christmas vacation to the task, was to the effect of deploring the publicity attending efforts "to raise by popular subscription $1,500,000 for the purchase of the so-called Yonan Codex." The society's report continues as follows:

According to members of our Society who have examined the manuscript, the Yonan Codex is a copy of the Syriac Peshitta, a version which was made from the Greek New Testament at about the beginning of the fifth century and which contains twenty-two of the twenty-seven books of the New Testament. Edessene Syriac, the language of this version, differs considerably from the Palestinian Aramaic used by Jesus more than four centuries earlier. About three hundred manuscripts of the Peshitta version are known to exist in the libraries of this country and Europe. Several of these are older than the Yonan Codex, which some of our members who are expert in Syriac paleography date in the seventh or eighth century. According to certain members of the Society who have frequently arranged for the purchase of Biblical manuscripts, a fair estimate of the value of a manuscript like the Yonan Codex is about $5,000.

It is to be remembered that the Society of Biblical Literature reports only the scholarly opinion of those of its members who conducted the investigation. Every scholar must be free to express the views to which his scholarly research leads him. It is to be clearly understood that no reflection is cast either by the society or by the present writer on the integrity of the motives of Mr. Yonan, who expressly disclaimed the intention of making personal profit out of the codex, and whose foundation proclaimed its resolve to devote the proceeds, when expenses should have been met, to the establishment of chairs in Aramaic in theological schools.[1]

The spate of Roman Catholic versions continued during this period as before. Most of them contained peculiarities of a not particularly interesting sort, and all of them either introduced new errors or at least perpetuated old ones. In 1901, however, a remarkable version of the Gospels, translated "from the Greek text direct, with reference to the Vulgate and ancient Syriac Version," made its appearance in New York. It was the work of Francis Spencer, a Dominican Father who in his youth had renounced his Anglican heritage in order to be received into the Roman Church. For some time a Paulist, he had, after ordination, joined the Dominicans. Before his death in 1913 he had completed the New Testament, and this was eventually published by The Macmillan

---

[1] To the best of my knowledge no such chairs have been established.

Company, New York, in 1937. Not undeservedly popular, it has been several times reprinted. The presentation is modern: the text is set forth in paragraphs, each under a heading. The words of Christ are printed in italics—a bold idea, since it is not always by any means clear whether the evangelist is attributing words to Christ or is making a comment of his own. Spencer provided notes such as one at Luke 24:30: "it would seem that Our Lord here performed the Eucharistic Sacrifice." At John 5:7-8, a passage known to modern scholars to be a very late interpolation, he provided a note admitting that most "Catholic critics today hold that" the passage is not part of the original text; nevertheless, he contended that the arguments for authenticity "have such weight that it would not be safe to regard non-authenticity as established." He is careful to refer to a decree of the Holy Office, January 15, 1897.

A very different sort of book was *The Layman's New Testament,* first published in London in 1928. Designed for the field work of the Catholic Evidence Guild, a society of zealous English laymen whose mission included polemics in the out-of-doors, it simply set forth, on the left, a Challoner text, and on the right, provided ammunition for the use of the Church Militant in dealing with Hyde Park hecklers and the like. The stock of ammunition was extended in a second edition published in 1934. Both editions are said to have been destroyed by the Germans in a less ecclesiastical Battle of Britain. A third was issued.

The Westminster Version is a much more scholarly enterprise. Edited by a Jesuit, Cuthbert Lattey, it was begun before the War of 1914-1918. Both British and American scholars contributed. To each translator was entrusted a particular book or number of books, with full personal responsibility for the assignment. Fascicles were issued until the New Testament was at last completed in 1935. By this time work on the Old Testament had been begun: its first fruit was the issue of the book of the prophet Malachi. Publication was planned in two recensions, a long one in large octavo and a short one, in a pocket edition. By 1936 the longer recension of the New Testament was completed in four handsome and finely printed volumes. The pocket edition appeared in 1948. An example of the style of this version is: "Ye are the salt of the earth; but if the salt become insipid, wherewith shall it be salted?" One of the notes argues for Indulgences, from I Corinthians 2:7. The Old Testament, though parts of it have been issued, is so far uncompleted. In view of the personal responsibility given to the various contributors in terms of the scheme for the work, it was hardly to be expected that there should be uniformity in the character and style of the translation as a whole; yet the result is very pleasantly readable and reveals much scholarly care and skill.

In the United States, the fully Americanized edition of the New Testament, edited by scholars under the patronage of the Roman Catholic

Bishops' Committee of the Confraternity of Christian Doctrine, published in 1941 and widely known as the Confraternity Edition, superseded previous versions to a very great extent. Because of its use among the armed forces in the War of 1939-1945, it also became well known to English-speaking Roman Catholics elsewhere. Despite the now-customary arrangement in paragraph form, the American spelling, the use of quotation marks, and the modernization of many turns of speech, e.g., "Do not be afraid" for "Fear not," it retains many curiously antique phrases, such as "And it came to pass." The notes are very restrained in comparison with those of the earlier Roman Catholic versions. When the text seems to demand explanation in terms of modern Roman Catholic practice, a brief explanation is given. For instance, where we read that a bishop must be "married but once" (I Tim. 3:2), a footnote explains that "priestly celibacy as a law is of later ecclesiastical institution." The use of the term "immorality" as a synonym for "fornication" occurs in both this edition and the Revised Standard. It enhances neither. "Immorality" as a synonym for "fornication" is not only a "genteelism" of the present day; it is highly misleading, for, of course, murder, bribery, theft, and all other unethical behaviour are immoral, as well as sexual misconduct. On the other hand, "we carry this treasure in vessels of clay" (II Cor. 4:7) is an example of the translation at its best. The Confraternity Version was conceived as a revision of the Challoner-Reims Version and a translation from the Vulgate. The Old Testament, however, was undertaken as a translation "from the original languages, with the critical use of all the ancient sources," into a thoroughly twentieth-century American English. So we have, for instance, the phrase, "whether or not the Lord had made his trip successful" (Gen. 24:21).

In 1939 the Roman Catholic hierarchy in England asked Ronald Knox to undertake a translation of the New Testament from the Vulgate. Knox's translation turned out to be, as expected, highly independent, reflecting his literary wit, which, being of a strikingly English sort, was something of an oddity in the Roman Catholic Church of his day. A draft edition, printed by subscription and for private circulation only, was issued in London in 1944. It was followed in 1945 by a final edition having the official approval of the Roman Catholic hierarchy in England. An example of the few changes made is the alteration of "lads" to "friends" in one place (John 21:5). A larger edition was published in 1948, and in 1949 the Old Testament was issued in two volumes of the same format, so completing the Bible in three volumes.

The American edition of Knox's translation of the New Testament followed the draft rather than the final British edition. Published in New York in 1944, it bore the imprimatur of Francis (now Cardinal) Spellman, which, however, is omitted from subsequent impressions. These impressions have continued, moreover, to be printed even since the issue in this country in 1946 of an illustrated edition which follows the final British edition, not the draft.

A version of the Psalms by Mary Perkins Regan, called the Fides Translation, was published in Chicago in 1955 by the Fides Publishers Association. An example from the *Miserere* is as follows:

> Have mercy on me, O God, because of Your goodness,
> because of Your deeds of mercy,
> blot out my injustice:
> Wash me from my guilt.
> cleanse me of my sin.

An interesting example of an independent modern American Roman Catholic translation is provided by James A. Kleist, S.J., and Joseph L. Lilly, C.M., in *The New Testament Rendered from the Original Greek with Explanatory Notes,* published by the Bruce Publishing Company, Milwaukee, in 1956. The *Hail Mary* verse (Luke 1:28) is rendered: "Greetings! child of grace! The Lord is your helper! You are blessed beyond all women!"

It was noted in an earlier chapter that the Jewish Publication Society, at its second biennial convention in 1892, had considered a project for the thorough revision of the English Version of the Hebrew Bible that had been prepared by Isaac Leeser and published in Philadelphia in 1853. A committee to undertake the work was duly appointed, and a portion was assigned to each member.

The plan was that the result of their labors would be eventually presented to an editorial committee under the presidency of Marcus Jastrow, for final review; but as the work proceeded, it was felt that this plan should be reconsidered, since it seemed that the work being done would result in an entirely new translation rather than a revision. In 1903, the Psalms, which had been the portion assigned to K. Kohler, was published. Dr. Jastrow died shortly afterwards and was succeeded in the presidency by S. Schlechter, head of the Jewish Theological Seminary of America. In order to expedite the work, the editorial committee was reconstituted in 1908, under an agreement that provided for seven members, S. Schlechter, Cyrus Adler, and Joseph Jacobs, representing the Jewish Publication Society, and K. Kohler, David Philipson, and Samuel Schulman, representing the Central Conference of American Rabbis, with Max L. Margolis as editor-in-chief. In December, 1908, the latter reported upon his progress and described the principles by which he had been guided in preparing a draft of the translation of the Pentateuch, a copy of which draft had been by this time submitted to the members of the editorial committee. The principles were slightly modified, and the scholars, now under the chairmanship of Cyrus Adler, proceeded with the work according to the revised program. This provided that propositions embodied in the manuscript draft remained unless challenged, in which case the suggested amendment, if seconded, was discussed, put to the vote, and, if carried by a simple majority, adopted. After the first proofs of the manuscript so amended had been seen by the seven members of the editorial committee, a great number of corrections were made and further improvements devised. By this time the scholars had sat for sixteen sessions of at least ten days each over a period of more than six years. At a seventeenth session, held in the fall of 1915, some queried points— between two and three hundred—that called for further discussion, were considered, and voted upon.

In 1917 the Jewish Publication Society's version of the Hebrew Bible was published. Essentially, it was little more than a modest revision of the Old Testament in the Revised Version of 1885. It served its purpose in the Jewish community between the two great wars; but Jewish scholars were no more satisfied with it than were Christian scholars with the Revised Version upon which it was so largely based. The need for a new version was increasingly felt, and in 1955 the Jewish Publication Society appointed a committee of seven scholars to undertake the new translation. These were:

Harry M. Orlinsky, Hebrew Union College (editor-in-chief)
H. L. Ginsberg, Jewish Theological Seminary (associate editor)
E. A. Speiser, University of Pennsylvania (associate editor)
M. Arzt, Rabbinical Assembly [Conservative]
B. J. Bamberger, Central Conference of American Rabbis [Reform]
H. Freedman, Rabbinical Council of America [Orthodox]
S. Graysel, Jewish Publication Society of America

The firstfruits of their labors, consisting of the Torah (the Pentateuch), appeared in 1962. The type and format, both in the more expensive and the more popularly priced bindings, are particularly pleasant, reflecting alike the robust vigor and the forward-looking confidence of the modern Jewish community in the United States.

The version, which is a translation from the Masoretic or traditional Hebrew text, exhibits singular vitality. The editor-in-chief, Professor Orlinsky, in a contribution to *The Journal of Biblical Literature*, has given an indication of the principles upon which the translators worked and the general direction towards which he sees modern biblical translation to be moving.[2]

---

[2] H. M. Orlinsky, "The New Jewish Version of the Torah: Toward a New Philosophy of Bible Translation" in *Journal of Biblical Literature*, LXXXII, 249-64.

Before leaving our inspection of independent modern English versions of the Bible, we must take note of an especially grand-scale venture published by Doubleday as the Anchor Bible. It is a scholarly project under the general editorship of Professors W. F. Albright and David Noel Freedman, and consists of translations and commentaries contributed by Jewish, Protestant, and Roman Catholic scholars in a multivolume work. The first volume, *Genesis,* was the work of E. A. Speiser, one of the editors of the new Jewish translation just mentioned, and appeared in 1964. Several other volumes have since come out. Though judgement must obviously be withheld till the completion of the work, the quality of the translations that have so far appeared augurs well for this ambitious enterprise.

Biblical style is a unique creation.
It can be parodied but it cannot be paralleled.
—Howard Mumford Jones

CHAPTER 30 *The Twentieth-Century Biblical Renaissance*

At the beginning of the present century, the future of the Bible looked singularly unpromising to the average person not committed to a particular kind of religious faith about it. The rapid progress that was already being made in the physical and biological sciences and the new vistas of knowledge that were opening up in anthropology and other sciences were of course among the reasons that led many to look upon the Bible as a book destined to pass more and more out of sight among thoughtful and progressive people.

It seemed plain to those who so reflected at that time on the future of the Bible that it would be fairly soon relegated to two classes only: on the one hand, the ignorant obscurantists who would go on for some time thumping it till universal enlightenment on the subject eventually overtook the human race, and on the other the small band of scholars of antiquarian tastes who are in every age by nature and temperament inclined to seek out and study those curiosities of the past that have least interest either for the present affairs of the day or for the future of mankind. Nor was such a view based only upon an increasing preoccupation with the sciences. It seemed to many that those from whom a championship of the Bible was to be expected were in the forefront of the movement that was bringing about its decline. Were not the leading divines in England and Germany engaged in undermining its authority as the infallible rule of faith, much as the sixteenth-century Reformers had been engaged in undermining the authority of the medieval papacy as the infallible mouthpiece of God?

At the beginning of the nineteenth century the prospects of both "Protestantism" and "Catholicism" had looked dim. It was true that in the course of that century both had astonishingly prospered. Yet one could not but wonder about the future. It seemed as though "Protestantism" had saved itself by unprecedented missionary expansion among remote and primitive peoples, while "Catholicism," quick to take advantage of the romantic revival, had saved itself by a reactionary revival of medieval superstitions (such as what "Protestants" take to be the quasi-pagan preoccupation with Mary) and an exercise of the most extreme form of ecclesiastical autocracy, through the suppression, at the Vatican Council in 1870, of the last vestiges of conciliarist opinion in the Church.[1] It was not easy to see a bright future for the Bible among "Protestants," who were now bent, it seemed, on quietly destroying the book their forefathers had so highly prized. Among "Catholics" the Bible had never played a comparable role. The Roman Catholic Church was the last place, it seemed, to look for any future the Bible might have.

In the course of the present century, all this has been dramatically changed in curiously unexpected ways. Interest in the Bible, far from receding, has enormously increased, not least in what were once accounted the least likely places. The changing mood of the Roman Catholic Church seemed to find striking expression during the pontificate of John XXIII. So conspicuous has been the twentieth-century biblical Renaissance in that Church that it calls for explanation in some detail. The changes are enormous. One has only to look at even the more popular Roman Catholic literature today to see already reflected the vast change of climate that seems to have taken place in theological circles. The Bible has "come out" at Rome. The encyclical of Pius XII, *Divino afflante,* issued on September 30, 1943, was an earnest of the new interest, not its measure. To understand the nature of this change and the cause of the new trends in modern Roman Catholic attitudes to the Bible it is necessary to look first not only within the history of that Church but also at the influences brought to bear upon her from the rest of Christendom, which are much more powerful than is commonly understood and certainly much greater than Roman theologians in the past were willing publicly to admit.

We have seen at a much earlier stage that the medieval Church took for granted that the Bible was the basic document that had been committed to the Church. As such it was diligently studied. There were, as we have also seen, conflicting views and tendencies in the Middle Ages on the question of its interpretation; but its authority was unquestioned. There were also, however, other sources of revelation for the medieval Christian—a body of traditional teaching. From the twin sources of Scripture and tradition had been developed a great mass of doctrine that theologians had to treat and systematize. Overriding all was the doctrine that in disputes about such matters God had provided, in the Church, an infallible teacher. The Church's infallible teaching was expressed in the official utterances of Pope and Council. By the time of the sixteenth-century Reformation, and a principal cause in bringing it about, was a fundamental and unresolved doubt about the relative func-

[1] I have treated this question in *The Vatican Revolution* (Boston: Beacon Press, 1957).

tions of Pope and Council in this expression of the Church's infallible teaching. Richard Baxter has robustly expressed the nature of the situation facing the medieval Church a century before the Reformation:

> When Popes damn Popes, and Councils damn them all,
> And Popes damn Councils, what must Christians do?

The Reformers saw, however, that there was an even more radical ill in the medieval Church they knew. The Church had never wavered, indeed, in her reverence for the Bible; but she had claimed to be mistress of the Holy Book she revered. Not least among their insights was this: the True Church always stands "under" the Bible, that is, under its judgement. The consequences of this insight were immense. The Church, the living Body of Christ, is not only the custodian of the Bible; the Bible is the sole norm of her faith.

Sola scriptura! This Reformation battle cry was not in itself *entirely* novel. In the thirteenth century St. Thomas had said: *sola canonica scriptura est regula fidei:* only canonical Scripture is the [a?] rule of faith. The Reformers, far from questioning this, sought to solve the late medieval ecclesiastical predicament by reforming the Church as standing "under" rather than "over" the Bible. If the Church was, as all agreed, the Bride of Christ, ought not she to listen first and above all to the Bible as the voice of her own Bridegroom and Lord? True, the Bible, as the written word, could not strictly take the place of the Word as spoken; yet, it was contended, God himself will speak through the Bible to those who humbly seek to hear his voice there. The learned could help to clarify points; but no man, be he pope or bishop or even the most learned scholar alive, can stand in any relation to the Bible that is *fundamentally* different from that in which stands the simplest peasant. If the Bible is God's Word *to* his Church, all are "under" the Bible.

Those who declined to accept the Reformation in its sixteenth-century form had to state an alternative position. The Council of Trent did this, and as expected in such circumstances, the alternative was stated in an extreme form. The Roman Church is alone the infallible teacher. In particular she is alone the authoritative interpreter of the Bible. It is for her alone to judge and determine, from the twin repositories of revelation (Bible and tradition), what the true revelation is and to guide the faithful accordingly.

The judgement of the Church in such matters is expressed in papal and/or conciliar pronouncements. The two channels of revelation were to be received and honored *pari pietatis affectu ac reverentia:* with equal devotion and reverence. A minority of the theologians at Trent had wanted this expressed differently. The Council, in drafting the decree, had rejected a form that would have expressed the view that divine revelation was transmitted partly in the Bible and partly in tradition. The Council preferred to avoid *saying* there were some doctrines that depended on tradition and others that depended on the Bible, though in fact it seems to have followed this view in some of its decrees, and of course the decision about which books are canonical and which are not must surely depend upon tradition. The Reformers had recognized this. The Reformers appealed over and over again to tradition, invoking the Fathers and other such "authorities" in the ancient Church. What the Reformers had insisted upon was that the Church could never be Mistress of the Bible, doling it out to the people and superintending the dole as a mother superintends the diet of a teething infant, today giving this and withholding that, tomorrow withholding that and giving this. The Reformers had more reliance on the digestion of Christians, since they believed such digestion was aided by God who surely would not suffer his children to choke to death on his own food.

This radical difference between the attitude of the Reformed Church and that of Rome came out conspicuously at Trent when that Council debated the question of vernacular translations. Though for Rome the Vulgate edition contained what was accounted the only authentic text, there was in principle no objection to translations into the vernacular. We have seen that such translations were made and disseminated with the Church's approval before Luther was born. In practice, however, objections were many and fierce. Cardinal Pacheco, supported by his theological advisor Alfonso de Castro, expressed in an extreme and Spanish form a growing fear of vernacular translations, calling them the "mothers of heresy." There were other much more moderate opinions on this subject at Trent. The point is that neither extremist nor moderate was in doubt about the right of the Church to provide the faithful with the Bible or to withhold it from them. The Bible was looked upon as the basic medicine in the Church's storehouse. In giving it to the people, the Church had the right and the duty to determine the dosage and to specify how the dose should be taken. A compromise was achieved between the moderates and the extremists who discussed such matters: vernacular translations were to be allowed, provided that they carried notes to protect the faithful from error.

Dismayed by the successes of the Reformation, Rome soon felt obliged to take much more seriously the question of the purity of the Vulgate text itself. Under the orders of Sixtus V, an edition of the Septuagint was produced at Rome in 1587. Sixtus thought he could establish no less easily a revised edition of the Vulgate text that could be held to be authentic and authoritative. The disastrously embarrassing consequences of this enterprise have been noted in a previous chapter.

The official attitude toward the Bible, developed at Rome in the sixteenth century, remained largely unchanged till modern times. It governed the work of scholars and commentators, and generally succeeded in keeping the Bible very subordinate in the thinking of average Roman Catholic layfolk. In contrast to the program of priestly studies in the older, contemplative orders, where the Bible continued to be read "with a surplice on," Jesuit universities sometimes encouraged trilingual biblical studies. The aim, however, was chiefly to defend the Church's insistence on the unique authority of the Vulgate. Commentaries of an extremely conventional character abounded and were used in such institutions. At the same time, however, there was also a tendency in some circles to move away from the old, uncritical, rigorist view that the Bible is verbally inspired by God so that its contents are of an entirely different order from all other literature.

In 1658 an English priest, Henry Holden, canvassed the view that the divine assistance granted to the writers of the Bible extended only to doctrinal matters. This meant that the Bible might err in historical and geographical matters, for instance, which did not affect the substance of the faith. To such a distinction Newman was to appeal in the nineteenth century. Meanwhile, in seventeenth-century France, the Jansenists had sought to make the Bible open to every man. They taught, indeed, that to withhold the Bible from anyone was a sort of excommunication from the Church. The French Gallicans at the Synod of Pistoia in 1786, which also condemned the use of Latin in Church services and the cult of the Sacred Heart in popular devotions, held that only incapability of reading the Bible excused a man from sin if he neglected it. Pius VI, in condemning eighty-five of the Pistoian articles, pronounced this estimate of the importance of Bible reading, though not heretical, nevertheless false, provocative, and rash. The extreme antipathy of Rome to the Bible societies, when these were founded at the beginning of the nineteenth century, has already been considered in a previous chapter.

Small wonder is it, then, that Roman Catholics won for themselves the reputation of having very little real affection for the Bible or concern about it beyond guarding it as a rich lady guards a diamond necklace she may seldom wear or wear only to ill advantage. It was a point upon which Newman, after his defection from the Church of England, was particularly sensitive. In 1884 he set forth the view that the Bible was not inspired in respect of its *obiter dicta* about historical facts and the like. Whether Paul really left his cloak at Troas with Carpus, for example, was not a matter that affected the biblical message. In such matters the Bible might err. Leo XIII, in his encyclical, *Munificentissimus Deus*, published November 18, 1893, claimed, however, that it was wrong to limit inspiration to matters of faith and morals, or to suggest that any of the biblical authors might be at any point guilty of error. No one outside the Roman Church could conceivably be in any doubt that this was a condemnation of Newman; yet so desperately were some Roman Catholic scholars seeking a way out of their difficulties without abandoning their subjection to Rome that there were some ingenious attempts to explain otherwise the circumstances leading to this papal pronouncement. At any rate, any obscurity left by Leo XIII was surely removed by Pius XII who in his comparatively enlightened encyclical *Divino afflante* expressly called the theory about *obiter dicta* an erroneous one and declared that its erroneous character had already been condemned in Leo XIII's encyclical. Newman's theory had been, indeed, a futile attempt, in the year the Revised Version was to appear, to make the Tridentine teaching about the Bible less unpalatable to educated Englishmen. Had it been approved by Rome, it would have encouraged opinions that were being advanced about that time by such a distinguished layman as Baron von Hügel, and would have paved the way for those French and other Modernists in the Roman Church whose views were to bring about one of the most serious crises therein before their eventual condemnation.

During the controversy that raged in the Roman Church in the last decade of the nineteenth and first decade of the twentieth century, under the name of Modernism, more serious attention was given at Rome to the question of the Bible than had ever been bestowed upon this question in that quarter since Trent. On October 30, 1902, Leo XIII set up a Biblical Commission to encourage Roman Catholic scholars in biblical studies. Yet the practical dangers attending such studies were only too well known to these scholars. Modernism had gravely alarmed Rome because, representing such well-informed opinion and thoughtful study by eminent scholars within her own fold, it was indeed a serious threat to a Church whose people were for the most part intellectually less prepared than any other in Christendom to understand and cope with such a movement in the context of the Church's faith. Despite the Tridentine expressions of reverence for the sacrosanctity of the Bible, not only were lay people generally unaccustomed to Bible reading; the majority of priests were untrained to deal with even the simpler biblical questions in terms of the standard of scholarship current in academic circles at the time.

The Roman Church was now encouraging priests to study the Bible and was guaranteeing them a new freedom in doing so, provided, of course, that they subjected the outcome of their freedom to ecclesiastical authority. With this purpose in view, Pius X, on February 23, 1904, empowered the Biblical Commission to confer degrees in Sacred Scripture by examination. The Biblical Institute was founded at Rome and placed under Jesuit control. Soon it was granting its own degrees and training men to teach in Roman Catholic seminaries for the priesthood, where after a papal decree in 1924 professors could no longer teach in the field of biblical studies unless they possessed a degree granted by the Biblical Institute or the Biblical Commission.

The strenuous resistance at Rome to the Modernism that threatened the life of the Church, and the effective persecution of scholars such as the Abbé Loisy, naturally inspired great caution on the part of all but the boldest and most independent minds among the clergy. Most saw only too plainly that biblical studies involved great professional danger. So in such matters discretion was to them the better part of speech. The faithful were generally unaffected by the Church's efforts to promote among the clergy at least a kind of attention to biblical questions. Modernism duly went underground as a result of the determined and effective persecution of those who openly dared to espouse it, and by the time the Church emerged from World War I, it was no longer overt. It had already been among the causes, however, of considerable losses to the Roman fold, not least in France, upon which so much of the intellectual life of the Church depended and still depends. The French Modernism that was forced underground earlier in the present century is at last bearing fruit. One must not overlook the fact, however, that Rome continues, of course, to control her own fruits. One of the most notable features of her organizational machinery is its capacity to go into reverse.

Benedict XV, in his encyclical *Spiritus Paraclitus*, issued on September 15, 1920, commanded daily Bible reading, within certain limits, to the faithful. Yet how cautiously one had to tread! Two random examples from the ecclesiastical proceedings of the twenties will illustrate the low level at which the battle for scholarly freedom had to be waged. The Biblical Commission, having been asked whether it was permissible to add, in footnotes to the Vulgate text, variant readings and other such aids to the student, replied in the affirmative.[2] This decision was a victory for scholars, no doubt, but a very modest one. The Code Commission was then asked whether, in the ecclesiastical canon [3] that provides that vernacular translations must either have the approval of Rome or else be published "under the vigilance of the bishops and with annotations," the word "and" (*et*) was to be interpreted "copulatively or disjunctively"! The reply was that it must be interpreted copulatively.[4] This decision was a brake upon scholarly enterprise.

As a natural result of the persecution of Modernism, most of the biblical work being turned out by biblical scholars within the Roman Church was of a very conservative sort. Rome's attitude could not have failed to foster this. Yet there was uneasiness. Something had to be done

[2] *Acta Apostolicae Sedis* 14-27, Biblical Commission, November 17, 1921.
[3] *Codex Iuris Canonici*, c. 1391.
[4] *Acta Apostolicae Sedis* 16-15, Code Commission, May 20, 1923, VIII.

to show the Church in a light that would not entirely discredit her in intellectual circles. So when an extremely conservative scholar wrote a series of biblical commentaries in thirteen volumes, they were placed on the Index, and when he later wrote arguing against the study of biblical tongues and in favor of reading the Bible only in the Latin of the authentic Vulgate, and circulated this very reactionary tract in Rome, the authorities there took advantage of the occasion by bringing about the publication of the now celebrated encyclical of Pius XII, *Divino afflante*. This encyclical encouraged an attitude to the study of the Bible that was novel to most Roman Catholic scholars. It enabled them at last to discuss, with a candor that formerly only a few had dared to exhibit, such questions as the precise relation of the Bible to tradition.

To anyone who remembers or can imagine the situation a generation earlier, the climate of debate after Vatican II seems changed almost beyond recognition. The establishment of biblical associations, together with numerous injunctions and counsels to engage in Bible reading, have affected the attitude of the laity, at least in the more enlightened lands. Yet there has been no fundamental change in the claim of the Roman Church to be Mistress of the Scriptures. The climate, so carefully created, seems promising indeed; yet it could be changed for the worse tomorrow, unless a much more radical critique of the Church's attitude to the Bible be admitted, and it is not easy to see how this can be done in such a way as to give Rome's biblical Renaissance anything of the character necessary to bring about ecumenical understanding at a thoroughly effective level. One cannot well forget that it was the need to "answer" Modernism that created the impulse for the impressive work begun at Jerusalem in 1890 by the great French Dominican scholar, Père Lagrange. The aim was to set up a Roman Catholic school of biblical scholars whose work would show that Rome's conservative reaction to Modernism was supported by biblical study of a caliber that could match and even excel that of the Modernists. Since then, the appearance, book by book, of the Jerusalem Bible, a French Version that is the result of the labors of that school of biblical scholars, witnesses to the high quality of their work.[5]

There are also other good modern French Roman Catholic translations. The Benedictines of Maredsous, Belgium, for instance, have produced a colloquial French version with fine scholarship behind it. In the more enlightened places in France, under the influence of the Benedictines and other orders, there is no doubt that the Bible is gradually coming to be read more and more in place of the traditional popular devotional manuals.

[5] An English translation of the Jerusalem Bible was published in 1966. For a specimen, see below, p. 372.

The issue in 1965 of an edition of the Revised Standard Version of the New Testament approved by authorities of the Roman Catholic Church was an event of great ecumenical importance—in some ways perhaps more important than any of the other remarkable improvements in the ecumenical climate that found expression in Vatican II. It was followed on July 15, 1966, by a similarly approved edition of that version of the complete Bible. The edition is called "The Revised Standard Version of the Bible—Catholic Edition," and has the authorization of the National Council of the Churches of Christ, a body that has ecumenical interests. The nature of the edition and the circumstances that led to the event will be considered in the next chapter, since they fall within the story of the Revised Standard Version, to which that chapter will be devoted.

It would be easy, however, to overrate the significance of the biblical Renaissance in the Roman Catholic Church, and easier still to exaggerate its extent. One's impressions depend so much on the company one keeps. When as recently as 1963 I visited the magnificent baroque cathedral in Mexico City, for example, thronged with mothers on Saturday morning, carrying almost newly baptized infants to the Bishop for confirmation, in accordance with new ecclesiastical laws encouraging this practice, a very different atmosphere prevailed. As I entered the cathedral, a priest at one of the altars was just beginning to rattle through a requiem Mass; by the time I had slowly walked round the cathedral, he had been replaced by another no less expeditious priest who, in a second requiem Mass, had already reached the Consecration. In a finely carved confessional, a priest sat snoring in full view of the public, and was periodically roused for long enough to shrive a penitent in less than half the time it takes a Mexican shoeblack to shine a shoe.

Meanwhile, a line of the faithful so long that I could not even see the end of it, stood approaching, one by one, a priest who, from a holy water stoup, sprinkled each supplicant with the asperges stick in his right hand, while with his left he pocketed the pesetas that were technically not simony because the holy water blessing is technically not a sacrament. So great was the demand for this ministration that he ran out of holy water. Curious to ascertain the procedure in such a case, I waited to see what he would do. For a moment the line stood still. The priest raised his hand, snapped his fingers, like a girl at the cash register of the five-and-ten, whereupon yet another priest came haring towards him. This priest, as he approached, zipped open his cassock, from the inside of which he withdrew a small green soft plastic perfume spray filled with holy water, with which he succeeded in diminishing the congestion by squirting the faithful individually till his colleague was able to obtain reinforcements.

In the bookrack of the great cathedral were only meager, ill-printed pamphlets bearing titles such as "Why I should not be a Protestant." Yet when I asked a debonair Dominican Father the following week, at the French Embassy, how the biblical Renaissance was affecting the multitudes I had seen that day, he laughed gaily, parrying my question by inquiring in a discreetly subdued voice how many of them I supposed could read even a newspaper. Not thus are ecumenical concerns advanced.

Within the Reformation heritage the twentieth-century biblical Renaissance has been of a different order and has performed a very different function. Biblical scholarship had been highly developed in the nineteenth century, by the closing years of which came its fruits in an era of great biblical dictionaries, encyclopaedias, and commentaries. Among ordinary people, the older, conservative ways of thinking about the Bible had been modified as a result of this scholarly enterprise. Nevertheless, the biblical researches of the nineteenth century had been generally conducted in an academic atmosphere far from the life of the Church. In Germany the dichotomy between biblical research and the life of the Church was particularly sharp. While here and there laymen of exceptional intelligence and piety might succeed in illuminating their Christian faith by following the course of the investigations that biblical scholars were making, the average person who tried to do so with earnestness and good will often felt like the lady who, after a lecture, was asked if the lecturer had clarified the subject for her and replied, "No; but I feel confused at a higher level." Even without the biblical scholars, people would have been feeling inevitably perplexed by the difficulty of relating the Bible to the thought of the day. Too often, the great achievements of biblical scholarship that had been conducted in a highly rarified intellectual atmosphere puzzled them more than ever. Some tried to ignore it or tuck it away in a separate compartment of their minds; others lost their faith altogether. It seemed plain to many that, whatever might be the intellectual merits of biblical scholarship, it was not ministering to the Church's life. On the contrary, some contended, it was killing the Church.

The work of the great nineteenth-century pioneers in modern biblical study had been conducted by men who regarded themselves as detached from partisan controversies in the Church. Their aim was analytical. They sought to do for the Bible what literary scholars were expected to do for Homer and Shakespeare. They felt they had no axe to grind. They were often, however, more committed than they knew to attitudes of mind inherited from the eighteenth-century Enlightenment. They accounted themselves liberal and in some respects amply justified their claim. Yet their religious liberalism was too often more narrow-minded than they knew.

The dogmatism of nineteenth-century liberalism came to a head in the early decades of the twentieth century, inevitably producing a reaction.

One turning point was the publication in Germany in 1918 of Karl Barth's commentary on Romans. It was different from the fashionable commentaries of the day, not least in its emphasis upon the need for an interpretation of the Bible according to its own peculiar categories. This important work, translated into English fourteen years later, was eventually to be repudiated to a great extent by its author, as he developed his theological enterprise. From the time of its appearance, however, one thing was made clear: not only had the study of the Bible in the nineteenth century become too analytical and specialized; consciously or otherwise, its leading exponents had fallen into the service of a particular way of thought. What was wrong with this way of thought was not that it was modern. What was wrong with it was that too often it had fallen into the trap of modernizing the thought of the Bible in such a way as to misunderstand its meaning. The need was now seen to be an approach to the Bible that would be faithful to the categories of thought proper to the biblical writers.

Here the influence of Barth's first important work, his commentary on Romans, is incalculable. There were other writers, however, who, not necessarily dependent upon him, took part in the same general movement. In Denmark, for instance, Johannes Pedersen's great work, eventually translated into English under the title *Israel: Its Life and Culture,* showed a vivid awareness of the problem. Pedersen provided scholarly tools for criticizing a great many of the basic, often hidden, presuppositions characteristic of nineteenth-century German scholarship. Pedersen led biblical scholars to pose in a new way the question of what the biblical writers meant when they used the terms they did use. It became clear that there were certain root metaphors, an understanding of which helped to show how the ancient Hebrew mind worked. When a Hebrew writer used terms such as "soul," for instance, he did not mean what the average person at the beginning of the twentieth century had in mind. The latter, influenced by a nineteenth-century idealism whose roots could be traced back to Greek philosophy, tended to think of the "soul" as having in some way a separate existence from the body. Was this what the psalmist meant? Surely not: the psalmist's whole system of presuppositions was different. To understand what an Old Testament writer meant, critical analysis of the text and historical research into events were not enough. To understand an Old Testament prophet, one must go much deeper. One must first understand the workings of his mind in terms of the categories in which his mind moved. As Norman Snaith emphasized in his work *The Distinctive Ideas of the Old Testament,* published in 1944, too much had been assumed about the patterns of thought that Israel had held in common with her neighbors, and it was now time to consider much more what were the distinctive modes of ancient Hebrew thought.

From such a way of looking at the Old Testament, another step followed naturally. The means of taking this step was provided in a most important and influential work published in 1935, *The Bible and the Greeks,* by C. H. Dodd. Dodd showed very convincingly how biblical ideas changed within the Bible itself. Through translation from the Hebrew to the Greek of the Septuagint a word could become invested with new possibilities of meaning. Literary and philological analyses by themselves tend to kill understanding of what Paul, for instance, really had in mind when he used a word. It is not enough to work our way back to Paul's day and note that when he spoke of demons, he meant something very different from what would be meant today. We must also note how the history of ideas before Paul's time affected his use of the word and the meanings with which he was able to invest it. In G. and F. G. Kittel's grand-scale theological dictionary of the New Testament,[6] which began its appearance in Germany as early as 1933 and is now well into English translation, an attempt is made, through a thoroughgoing examination of the semantic as well as the philological study of key words in the New Testament (e.g., "kingdom" and "sin") to provide means for an interpretation of the documents leading to a genuine understanding of what the New Testament writers meant by such words in terms of the ideologies that affected their concepts.

In short, the orientation of biblical scholars in the twentieth century has become much more theological than it commonly was in the nineteenth. For this very reason there has been considerable suspicion of it in academic circles. How can a scholar with particular theological concerns treat the Bible without attending to the particular theological axe he wishes to grind? For it would seem that unless he *has* such a theological axe, he cannot even enter into biblical researches of the kind that has been made fashionable. Not only the disciples of Barth, but others with very different and perhaps wider theological interests, have been particularly open to such suspicions. Indeed, almost all the old avenues have been reexplored in subtler ways. The old allegorizing methods of the Middle Ages, for instance, have found a modern expression in what is called typology. This is a method used by its proponents in hope of showing, through the realities of history, that there are correspondences between certain events in the Old Testament and certain events in the New. Not all subjects lend themselves to this treatment, and even where they do, the danger of axe-grinding is peculiarly obvious. It was obvious even in the Middle Ages that a prototype of this sort of approach, used by the Fathers and later Christian exegetes, could lead to the most extravagant fancies. Even if we allow for the safeguards with which any

---

[6] *Theologisches Wörterbuch zum Neuen Testament* (Stuttgart: Kohlhammer, 1933) .

reputable modern scholar would provide himself, the danger remains, modern methodological subtleties notwithstanding.

Another and highly influential mode of interpretation has been developed by Rudolf Bultmann and others. Every age has its own mythologies which affect the mould of its thought. Bultmann, impressed by the obvious fact that the biblical modes of thought depended upon mythological ideas that are difficult for people in the twentieth century to grasp, sought to "demythologize" the Bible. This he attempted to do with the aid of ideas borrowed from modern existentialist philosophy, leaning heavily and sometimes not altogether explicably on Heidegger. It is claimed that Heidegger provides the structures, the "existentials," for talking more adequately about man's being. Out of the dialogue engendered by this sort of approach has emerged a form of hermeneutics whose proponents claim for it a considerable degree of novelty. Others, however, think such "demythologizing" is but "remythologizing," and the question then arises whether all remythologizing is an improvement.

In post-Bultmannian German thought a special interest emerged in the idea of what has come to be called a New Hermeneutic. One of the central aspects of this is the thesis that language itself says what invisibly takes place in the life of a culture. Around such theses considerable discussion has taken place, reflecting the great concern among twentieth-century heirs of the Reformation for an understanding of the Bible that will take the fullest possible account of the results of modern biblical scholarship while doing no less than full justice to the meaning of the Bible itself.

Meanwhile, not least in the United States, there is a growing sense of disquiet among reflective people at the gulf that lies between those modes of conceptualizing ideas about the Bible that are characteristic of "liberal" theologians and those others that prevail among "conservative" laymen. The latter have found supporters eager to offer determined criticism of fashionable theological trends. Yet the gulf shows no sign of being effectively bridged. The heirs of the Reformation, unlike their Roman counterparts, have no adequate machinery for welding the thought and the life of the Church together. Nor in any case would they be willing to pay the price Rome pays for her accomplishment, even apart from the fact that her accomplishment seems to have proved less expedient today than it was when the Modernist Abbé Dimnet was able to define the Papal Index as a convenient device designed to enable the learned to write without fear of offending pious ears.

The gulf between "conservatives" and "liberals," no less than the chasm between "Catholics" and "Protestants," is formidable; yet ecumenists may take courage in the wise reminder given by the Jesuit Father Daniélou: "The Bible is the meeting place of Christians."

329

TRANSLATED FROM THE ORIGINAL TONGUES
BEING THE VERSION SET FORTH A.D. 1611
REVISED A.D. 1881-1885 AND A.D. 1901
COMPARED WITH THE MOST ANCIENT AUTHORITIES
AND REVISED A.D. 1952

—from the title page of the
Revised Standard Version

CHAPTER 31 *The Revised Standard Version*

The Revised Standard Version is a revision of the American Standard Version. The New Testament was published in 1945 and the Bible in 1952. By 1962 twelve million copies of the latter had been sold, and five million copies of the New Testament.

We have seen how much needed was the work of revision undertaken in the latter part of the nineteenth century, of which the American Standard Version was the outcome. We have seen, too, that no sooner was the revisers' work done than new discoveries were made that rendered the American Standard Version distinctly out of date even before it was published. It was the best available, however, and to safeguard the text till further revision could be done, copyright was taken out in the name of the publishers, Thomas Nelson and Sons. Hence the story recounted at the time by Luther Weigle of Yale of a man who objected to the "new" Bible.

"Who is this Tom Nelson who has written a new Bible?" he asked angrily. "I don't want Tom Nelson's Bible. I want the Bible the way the apostle James wrote it."

Nelson's copyright was transferred in 1928 to an organization known at that time as the International Council of Religious Education. Consisting of representatives of forty denominations in the United States and Canada, it established the American Standard Bible Committee, later known as the Standard Bible Committee, to which was entrusted not only the custodianship of the text of the American Standard Version but also the authority to consider a further revision when this should seem practicable. In 1937 the committee, which had already met several times in the course of the intervening years, began work on a new revision. Their mandate was to produce a "revision of the present American Standard Edition of the Bible in the light of the results of modern scholarship, this revision to be designed for use in public and private worship, and to be in the direction of the simple, classic English style of the King James Version.

The following principles were laid down by the revisers on the subject of the text of the New Testament from which the revised translation was to be made:

(1) No one type of text is infallible, or to be preferred by virtue of its generally superior authority. (2) Each reading must be examined on its merits, and preference must be given to those readings which are demonstrably in the style of the author under consideration. (3) Readings which explained other variants, but are not contrariwise themselves to be explained by the others, merit our preference. . . . Each variant reading must be studied on its merits and cannot be adopted or rejected by some rule of thumb, or by adherence to such a theory as that of the "Neutral Test." It is this eclectic principle that has guided us in the present Revision. The Greek text of this Revision is not that of Westcott-Hort, Nestle, or Souter; though the readings we have adopted will, as a rule, be found either in the text or the margin of the new (17th) edition of Nestle (Stuttgart, 1941).[1]

The correct Hebrew and Aramaic text of the Old Testament presented a different problem. As noted before, the oldest manuscripts of the Hebrew Bible are of a later date than the great New Testament manuscripts available, and much farther removed in time from the original writings they represented. By the time the Revised Standard Version was published in 1952, older manuscripts of Isaiah and Habakkuk had recently become available through the discoveries in the region of the Dead Sea; but these, though they were used, as we have seen, did not in any fundamental way change the nature of the problem or the technique of its solution, which was eventually expressed as follows in the preface to the Revised Standard Version:

The present revision is based on the consonantal Hebrew and Aramaic text as fixed early in the Christian era and revised by Jewish scholars (the "Masoretes") of the sixth to ninth centuries. The vowel-signs, which were added by the Masoretes, are accepted also in the main, but where a more probable and convincing reading can be obtained by assuming different vowels, this has been done. No notes are given in such cases, because the vowel points are less ancient and reliable than the consonants.

Departures from the consonantal text of the best manuscripts have been made only where it seems clear that errors in copying had been made before the text was standardized. Most of the corrections adopted are based on the ancient versions (translations into Greek, Aramaic, Syriac, and Latin), which were made before the time of the Masoretic revision and therefore reflect earlier forms of the text. In every such instance a footnote specifies the version or versions from which the correction has been derived, and also gives a translation of the Masoretic Text.

Sometimes it is evident that the text has suffered in transmission, but none

---

[1] Frederick C. Grant in *An Introduction to the Revised Standard Version of the New Testament* (International Council of Religious Education, 1946), p. 41.

of the versions provides a satisfactory restoration. Here we can only follow the best judgment of competent scholars as to the most probable reconstruction of the original text. Such corrections are indicated in the footnotes by the abbreviation *Cn*, and a translation of the Masoretic Text is added.

The Committee, as originally planned, was to have fifteen members, of whom not fewer than ten nor more than twelve were to be chosen for their biblical scholarship. The remainder were to be selected, rather, for their literary and practical qualifications. The Committee was, however, extended. Dr. James Moffatt served it as executive secretary from 1937 till his death on June 27, 1944, bringing to it his unusual combination of long practical experience as a translator of a celebrated independent translation of the Bible and exceptionally fine scholarly judgement.

In such a group of men there was inevitably a difference between those who wanted a textually conservative revision and those who, like Professor Edgar J. Goodspeed, desired a radical departure from the tradition of English Bible revision and the production of a more colloquial version. Moffatt represented a moderate position on this question, seeking to modernize the English thoroughly, yet always bearing in mind the principle that the Committee's task was to continue the revision of the King James Version, not to supplant this with a radically new translation. He helped much to guide the Committee toward the production of a version whose language, though brought up to date in all respects, would nevertheless conserve the dignity of the beloved King James Version, not unnecessarily offending the ears of those who were accustomed to the use of this in public worship. He saw and helped others to see that only in this way could the Revised Standard Version truly acquire its place in history as the lineal descendant and successor of the version that had given the English Bible its unique place in the literary as well as the devotional life of the English-speaking peoples. It is related of Moffatt that on one occasion a rendering of a passage was proposed which he resisted, whereupon the proposer triumphantly pointed out that what he had suggested was from Moffatt's own words in his independently produced version. To this Moffatt replied unhesitatingly that such colloquialism was all right in a private, independent translation but was out of place in the revision of the English Bible upon which they were now engaged.

The Committee was divided into two sections, one for the Old Testament and one for the New, as in previous similar undertakings, though some members served in both sections. The sections of the Committee eventually included the following:[2]

[2] Only when death occurred during the period of the Committee's work is the fact indicated. It should also be noted that the Graduate School of Theology, Oberlin, Ohio, no longer exists.

Old Testament Section

President Frederick C. Eiselen, Garrett Biblical Institute (d. May 5, 1937)

President John R. Sampey, Southern Baptist Theological Seminary

Dean Luther A. Weigle, Yale University

Professor Julius A. Bewer, Union Theological Seminary

Professor Alexander R. Gordon, United Theological College, Montreal

Professor James Moffatt, Union Theological Seminary (d. June 27, 1944)

Professor James A. Montgomery, University of Pennsylvania

Professor J. M. Powis Smith, University of Chicago (d. September 26, 1932)

Professor Charles C. Torrey, Yale University

Professor William R. Taylor, University of Toronto

Professor George Dahl, Yale University

Professor William A. Irwin, University of Chicago

Dean Willard L. Sperry, Harvard University

Professor Leroy Waterman, University of Michigan

Professor Millar Burrows, Yale University

Professor Kyle M. Yates, Southern Baptist Theological Seminary

Professor William F. Albright, Johns Hopkins University

Professor J. Philip Hyatt, Vanderbilt University

Professor Herbert G. May, Oberlin Graduate School of Theology

Professor James Muilenburg, Union Theological Seminary (later at San Francisco Theological Seminary)

Professor Harry M. Orlinsky, Jewish Institute of Religion

Dean Fleming James, University of the South

New Testament Section

Dean Luther A. Weigle, Yale University

Professor William P. Armstrong, Princeton Theological Seminary

Professor Henry J. Cadbury, Harvard University

Professor Edgar J. Goodspeed, University of Chicago

Professor James Moffatt, Union Theological Seminary (d. June 27, 1944)

Professor Archibald T. Robertson, Southern Baptist Theological Seminary (d. September 24, 1934)

Professor James Hardy Ropes, Harvard University

Professor Andrew Sledd, Emory University

Reverend Walter Russell Bowie, Grace Church, New York

President Frederick C. Grant, Seabury-Western Theological Seminary

Professor Millar Burrows, Yale University

Professor Clarence T. Craig, Oberlin Graduate School of Theology
President Abdel R. Wentz, Lutheran Theological Seminary, Gettysburg

The Chairman and the General Secretary of the International Council of Religious Education also served ex officiis, without being assigned to sections. They were concerned mainly with matters of finance, public relations, and general policy. The following served in this category:

Dr. Robert M. Hopkins, Chairman, International Council of Religious Education; General Secretary, World's Sunday School Association, New York

Dr. Hugh S. Magill, General Secretary, International Council of Religious Education, Chicago

Dr. Harold McAfee Robinson, Chairman, International Council of Religious Education; General Secretary, Presbyterian Board of Christian Education, Philadelphia

Dr. Roy G. Ross, General Secretary, International Council of Religious Education, Chicago

Dr. Walter D. Howell, Chairman, International Council of Religious Education; Secretary, Presbyterian Board of Christian Education, Philadelphia

President Arlo A. Brown, Chairman, International Council of Religious Education, Drew University, Madison, N.J.

Dr. Paul C. Payne, Chairman, International Council of Religious Education; General Secretary, Presbyterian Board of Christian Education

In order to have representatives from a wide variety of ecclesiastical denominations, an advisory board was formed. Associated with the Committee charged with the revision, the members of this board reviewed drafts and made suggestions in an advisory capacity. The denominations represented and their representatives serving in this capacity were as follows:

Advent Christian Church: President O. R. Jenks, Aurora College, Aurora, Ill.

African Methodist Episcopal Church: The Rev. Charles W. Abington, Philadelphia, Pa.

African Methodist Episcopal Zion Church: Bishop John W. Martin, Chicago, Ill.

Associate Reformed Presbyterian Church: Professor G. G. Parkinson, Due West, S.C.

Augustana Evangelical Lutheran Synod of North America: The Rev. J. Vincent Nordgren, Minneapolis, Minn.

Baptist Convention of Ontario and Quebec: Professor H. L. MacNeill, McMaster University, Hamilton, Ontario

Church of the Brethren: The Rev. E. G. Hoff, Elgin, Ill.

Church of God: The Rev. Otto F. Linn, Dundalk, Md.

Church of the Nazarene: Dr. Olive M. Winchester, Pasadena College, Pasadena, Calif.

Churches of Christ: The Rev. H. Leo Boles, Nashville, Tenn.

Churches of God in North America: The Rev. F. D. Rayle, Harrisburg, Pa.

Colored Methodist Church: Bishop William Y. Bell, Cordele, Ga.

Congregational and Christian Churches: Dr. Sidney A. Weston, Boston, Mass.

Disciples of Christ: Dean Stephen J. England, Phillips University, Enid, Okla.; Professor W. C. Morro, Texas Christian University, Fort Worth, Tex.; Professor Henry Barton Robison, Culver-Stockton College, Canton, Mo.

Evangelical Church: Bishop John S. Stamm, Harrisburg, Pa.

Evangelical and Reformed Church: Professor Allen G. Wehrli, Eden Seminary, Webster Groves, Mo.

Five Years Meeting of Friends in America: Professor William E. Berry, Earlham College, Richmond, Ind.

Mennonite Brethren in Christ: Dean J. A. Huffman, Taylor University, Upland, Ind.

The Methodist Church: Dean B. Harvie Branscomb, Duke University Divinity School, Durham, N.C.; The Rev. Lucius Bugbee, Cincinnati, Ohio; President F. G. Holloway, Western Maryland College, Westminster, Md.

Missouri Lutheran Synod: Dr. George V. Schick, Concordia Seminary, St. Louis, Mo.

Moravian Church in America: Professor Raymond S. Haupert, Bethlehem, Pa.

National Baptist Convention of America: The Rev. C. J. Gresham, Atlanta, Ga.

National Baptist Convention, U.S.A.: Dr. Marshall A. Talley, Nashville, Tenn.

Northern Baptist Convention: Professor Charles N. Arbuckle, Andover-Newton Theological Seminary, Newton Center, Mass.

Presbyterian Church in U.S.A.: Professor John W. Bowman, Western Theological Seminary, Pittsburgh, Pa.; The Rev. Park Hays Miller, Philadelphia, Pa.

Presbyterian Church in U.S.: Professor Donald W. Richardson, Union Theological Seminary, Richmond, Va.

Protestant Episcopal Church: The Rev. Cuthbert A. Simpson, 6 Chelsea Square, New York, N.Y. (later Dean of Christ Church, Oxford)

Reformed Church in America: President John W. Beardslee, Jr., New Brunswick Seminary, New Brunswick, N.J.

Southern Baptist Convention: Dr. T. L. Holcomb, Nashville, Tenn.; Dr. Hugh C. Moore, Nashville, Tenn.; Dr. Clifton J. Allen, Nashville, Tenn.

United Baptists of the Maritime Provinces: Professor W. N. Hutchins, Wolfville, Nova Scotia

United Brethren in Christ: The Rev. J. Gordon Howard, Dayton, Ohio

United Brethren in Christ (Old Constitution): The Rev. J. Ralph Pfister, Huntington, Ind.

United Church of Canada: The Rev. Frank Langford, Toronto, Ontario; The Rev. C. A. Myers, Toronto, Ontario

United Lutheran Church in America: Dean E. E. Flack, Hamma Divinity School, Springfield, Ohio

United Presbyterian Church in North America: President John McNaugher, Pittsburgh-Xenia Theological Seminary, Pittsburgh, Pa.; Professor James L. Kelso, Pittsburgh-Xenia Theological Seminary, Pittsburgh, Pa.

While the panels appointed for work on the Revised Standard Version consisted of men possessing the highest qualifications for their task, it is not to be supposed, of course, that the choice was so perfect as to be beyond dispute. No such choice ever leaves all eyebrows unraised. It will be remembered that no place was given, in the companies of the King James translators, for the name of Hugh Broughton, for instance, whose scholarship was universally recognized among his seventeenth-century contemporaries. So in the twentieth century were excluded from the Revised Standard panels the names of scholars whom many expected to be invited. The reason for their exclusion, however, was not usually hard to find. As Broughton, three centuries earlier, had been excluded because of his intolerably querulous disposition, so nearer our own day there were some who, renowned and admired biblical scholars though they were, were accounted for one reason or another temperamentally unsuited for team work. Not all scholars can work well, as did Moffatt, both independently and in committee. Some who can work brilliantly on their own do not contribute to the harmony needed in a scholarly team. One great scholar of the day, still living at the time of this writing, was so certain he must be included in the project that he actually wrote to inquire about his duties, so imposing upon the unfortunate recipient of his letter the singularly unpleasant duty of informing him that he had not been invited to participate in it!

Work on the Revised Standard Version was done for the most part in the Speech Room of Yale Divinity School (adorned by the original of Edwin White's picture of the signing of the Compact on the *Mayflower*), at Union Theological Seminary, New York City, and at the Hotel Northfield, East Northfield, Massachusetts. After some experimentation, the procedure adopted was as follows. One book of the Bible would be entrusted, in the first instance, to an individual member of the appropriate section of the Committee. When this individual had finished his work, copies were to be sent to all members of the section, and would form the basis of the first draft. It would then be considered phrase by phrase by the members of the section. Every member of the section had the right to propose alteration at any point, and decision to adopt such variations was made by vote. When the first draft so amended had been finished, it was mimeographed with a view to further study along with the other books. Further suggestions were invited, and to the making of these both the advisory committee and certain British consultants contributed. The result, for the Old Testament work, was the collection of nearly a thousand single-spaced typewritten pages of suggestions for the emendation of the first draft. The Old Testament section considered major questions relating to the final revision, and relegated to a subcommittee the minor questions that could be dealt with on general principles laid down by the section as a whole. Since work on the New Testament was done for the most part in wartime, it was difficult to get such cooperation from the British scholars; but, on the other hand, the draft of each New Testament book was revised twice before arriving at the final text.

What were the general principles employed in making the Revised Standard Version? The revisers had to take into account not only the discoveries made since the appearance of the Revised Version, but also the development among scholars of a more profound understanding of the Bible itself. The purpose to be kept in view was easily ascertained: to produce, in terms of the best scholarship of the day, a version designed for use in public worship as well as in private devotion. The difficulty lay in the practical implementation. For instance, Hebrew has a very common conjunction, whose primary meaning is easily enough translated into English as "and." In Hebrew, however, sentences are linked together by this conjunction to an extent that would be intolerable in any decent English prose composition. Moreover, the Hebrew conjunction also carries a great many other meanings not present in the English conjunction "and." So it is an even commoner word in Hebrew than is "and" in English. It can be translated as "when," "so," or "then"; sometimes punctuation translates it; sometimes it is better omitted. The revisers had to decide each case on its merits, bearing in mind the principle of preserving as far as possible the flavor of the older English versions.

The use in the older versions of the sonorous but largely meaningless "and it came to pass" was omitted, since this could be done without any direct shock to the average reader. On the other hand, while the revisers generally changed the phrase "shadow of death" into a phrase such as "deep darkness" or "gloom," so as better to represent the Hebrew, they boggled at doing this in the case of the twenty-third psalm because of the special place this beautiful psalm so rightly has in the hearts of so many people. So the less exact but time-hallowed phrase was retained in that case. This is only one example of innumerable difficulties confronting the revisers in balancing the sharp edge of accuracy on the soft moss of tradition. Another example of the revisers' difficulties is to be found in the Hebrew phrase that is literally translatable "sons of Israel," which the older English versions rendered "children of Israel." Faced with a variety of considerations, the revisers, in most places in the Old Testament and Apocrypha, adopted "people of Israel" as the best solution to the formidable array of minor problems connected with this one phrase.

Then there was the inevitable question of how to translate expressions referring to the excretory functions and the physical aspects of sexual life. How should one render expressions which, natural to an earthy people like the Hebrews, tend to seem indelicate to the ears of the average person in modern civilized society, that is, to those among us who would be accounted neither remarkably prudish nor startlingly blunt? One wishes to avoid absurd euphemisms; yet one has to bear in mind that the Bible is to be read in church in the presence of people of both sexes and all ages. Generally speaking, the revisers wisely kept the earthiness as far as possible. Sometimes they introduced a modern expression, as where we read (I Sam. 24:3) that "Saul went in to relieve himself," which is plain yet inoffensive, and certainly more intelligible than the rendering of the King James and other versions: "Saul went in to cover his feet," which is an old Hebrew euphemism. The Revised Version of the New Testament (1881) had followed the King James in rendering Paul's injunctions to married couples on the subject of their mutual responsibilities in the sexual relation (I Cor. 7:5): "Defraud ye not one the other." The Revised Standard Version is once again plain without indelicacy: "Do not refuse one another."

These were among the less important problems to be dealt with by the revisers. The greatest puzzles confronting them were in the rendering of words and phrases representing religious ideas. Where the King James Version had translated a certain Hebrew word by "mercy," the American Standard had put "loving kindness." The Hebrew word is not well translated by either. One is too particular, the other too vague. There is no single word in English that will do. The Hebrew carries a notion of fidelity, loyalty, devotion, and love that goes far beyond "mercy," which is too specific, and "loving kindness" which is too sugary. Eventually the revisers adopted, in most cases, "steadfast love." For more than one reason this is a major improvement.

While it is true that, as we have abundantly seen, the King James Version was an artistic accomplishment of the highest order, it often achieved a new artistry rather than the artistry of the original. The Vulgate likewise has a great beauty of its own; but it is not the beauty of the original. Hebrew poetry is of a peculiar kind. The language has relatively few abstractions. It expresses ideas immediately and in vivid imagery, conformable to Milton's requirement that poetry should be simple, sensuous, and passionate. It has been called "a language of verbs," and it is true that it consists largely of verbs and nouns, having comparatively few adjectives, for instance. Hebrew poetry is essentially lyrical. Sentences often consist of only two or three words, and the whole poem has a literary economy impossible in translation. The twenty-third psalm in Hebrew comprises only fifty-five words, and in even the best translations is likely to run to twice that number. Moreover, there is a formal feature in Hebrew poetry, the parallelism, which the older English versions made no attempt to represent visually, so that one can catch only echoes of it and then only if the translation is being read aloud by a very good reader. In the Revised Standard Version the parallelisms are clearly exhibited, as may be seen in the following passage from a familiar psalm (Psalm 121):

> I lift up my eyes to the hills.
>   From whence does my help come?
> My help comes from the Lord,
>   who made heaven and earth.

And again (Psalm 29):

> The voice of the Lord breaks the cedars,
>   the Lord breaks the cedars of Lebanon.
> He makes Lebanon to skip like a calf,
>   and Sirion like a young wild ox.

Of course everyone knows that the psalms are poetry, however they may be written. The parallelism is not entirely obscured for us even in the older English versions, and in the traditional singing of the Psalter it is preserved, after a fashion, through the old monastic choir rule requiring a pause equal in length to the time needed for a clear enunciation of the Latin word "Ave." In other books, however, it is so obscured that the average person accustomed to a version such as the King James may never even suspect that the original is not just lyrical prose but formal poetry. Take the book of Jeremiah. Some of it is pure poetry, and in the Revised Standard Version one cannot help seeing this. So we have the prophetic challenge (Jer. 5:30-31) :

> An appalling and horrible thing
>   has happened in the land:
> the prophets prophesy falsely,
>   and the priests rule at their direction;
> my people love to have it so,
>   but what will you do when the end comes?

And again the lament (Jer. 8:7) :

> Even the stork in the heavens
>   knows her times;
> and the turtledove, swallow, and crane
>   keep the time of their coming;
> but my people know not
>   the ordinance of the LORD.

The other celebrated versions such as the Latin Vulgate and the English King James have their own distinctive flavor; but in the Revised Standard Version is brought out more than in any of the earlier classic translations the authentic flavor of the original Hebrew.

In the New Testament the reforms are in some ways even more striking. The Revised Version of 1881 had not only been stilted. The English revisers had needlessly introduced a *fresh* crop of archaisms, reproduction antiques such as "howbeit," "would fain," and "must needs." Where the King James Version had given us the still acceptable "This is the will of God in Christ Jesus concerning you," the Revised Version had put, "This is the will of God in Christ Jesus to you-ward." In the Revised Standard this becomes, happily, "This is the will of God in Christ Jesus for you." The more authentic archaisms of the King James Version are also eliminated where modern usage and taste plainly calls for this. So "because that" and "for that" become "because" and "for," and for "compass around" we now have "surround."

Paul, in an English translation, has to be represented as though he were writing English. The English must therefore be as robust and direct as was his Greek. It must give the English reader, as far as possible, the same tone and general impression as it would have given to Paul's contemporaries. Otherwise we are making him sound somewhat as a popular modern American magazine article would sound when translated, not into slick, modern colloquial French, but into the seventeenth-century academic French of Richelieu. This is not, of course, an exact parallel; but it gives some idea of one of the problems of the New Testament translator. The word "epistle," for instance, has no possible place in a modern translation. It is now not merely antiquated; it has in it, for us, both a flavor of the grandiose, like "encyclical," and even a tinge of the ridiculous, since the word "epistle" has come to be occasionally used for "letter" in order to achieve a vaguely comic effect. It is only when we are making a feeble attempt to be funny that we speak nowadays of having received an epistle from a friend. It is letters that we write and receive. So the Revised Standard calls Paul's communications to the churches letters. This is what they would be called today in circumstances similar to those he knew. "The Acts of the Apostles" becomes, more correctly, "Acts of the Apostles," so eliminating the implication—which is not in the Greek—that a complete list is provided. One of the most inexcusable manifestations of conservatism in the English Revised Version had been the retention of Paul's name in the title of Hebrews. We have seen that the objection to this was long ago recognized. By the time of that revision there was very widespread recognition of what is now universally acknowledged, namely, that whoever wrote that letter, Paul did not. It is as unlike his style as any writing could be. The Revised Standard Version accordingly omits his name from the title.

By the summer of 1943, mimeographed copies of the final manuscript of the New Testament had been sent to the Old Testament section to secure the approval of the required two-thirds majority of the whole Committee. A final meeting of the New Testament section met at Northfield, Massachusetts, which confided the manuscript to a small editorial committee whose duty it was to prepare it for the press. Then at an impressive ceremony in Columbus, Ohio, on February 11, 1946, the Revised Standard Version of the New Testament was officially published. Dean Weigle presented the first copy to the International Council of Religious Education. A member of the New Testament section, Professor Clarence T. Craig, was granted leave of absence from his regular academic duties in order to devote himself to interpreting the significance of the project to congregations throughout the country.

The manuscript of the Old Testament, submitted likewise to the New Testament section, was completed by the early summer of 1951, and the Old Testament section held its last meeting during June 12-26 that year. An editorial subcommittee of four worked through July and August on the last stages of preparing the Old Testament for the printers, and on September 30, 1952, the Revised Standard Version of the Bible was at last published. The work had taken more than fourteen years. The first printing consisted of about a million copies. It has been estimated that in the first run were used a thousand tons of paper, two thousand gallons of ink, over seventy miles of cloth, and almost enough thread to go half-way round the world. By this time enough thread must surely have been used to go nearly to the moon. More importantly, the new version, by its widespread and increasing popularity among the English-speaking peoples, has burnished and strengthened the bond, so long forged by the English Bible, that binds these peoples together in a very troubled world.

It must not be supposed, however, that the Revised Standard Version of the Bible has evoked no hostility. Its rapid and extensive recognition does not mean that it has not been attacked. Clarence Craig's work in interpreting the New Testament to congregations throughout the United States was followed by efforts on a grander scale when the whole Bible was published in 1952. The publication was accompanied by more than three thousand "observances" in congregations, to introduce it and explain its significance. A Committee on the Use and Understanding of the Bible was appointed for a period of five years to engage in work similar to that of Craig but on a scale such as no single individual could have attempted. These efforts indubitably helped much to break down prejudice. Nevertheless, bitter attacks on the Revised Standard Version continued, reminiscent of the hostility that had been elicited by the appearance of the King James Version more than three centuries ago. In spite of the widespread recognition of its merits and the extensive acceptance of it for public as well as private use, it cannot be said to have universally supplanted the King James Version; but has gone far in that direction.

To the Standard Bible Committee were added, in 1960, the following new members: Francis W. Beare, Trinity College, Toronto; Raymond A. Bowman, University of Chicago; Frank Moore Cross, Harvard University; Robert C. Dentan, General Theological Seminary, New York City; Sherman E. Johnson, Church Divinity School of the Pacific, Berkeley, California; John Knox, Union Theological Seminary, New York City; Marvin H. Pope, Yale University; Alfred von Rohr Sauer, Concordia Seminary, St. Louis; Theodore O. Wedel, College of Preachers, Washington, D.C.; Amos M. Wilder, Harvard University.

Reference has already been made to the great ecumenical concern that found expression in 1965 in the issue of a Roman Catholic edition of the Revised Standard Version of the New Testament and in the following year of the complete Bible.[3] The circumstances that led to the event are as follows.

In spite of the long-standing prejudices evinced by the Roman Catholic Church authorities against the collaboration in versions not initiated and controlled by them, opinions began to be voiced, though perhaps a little timidly, even during the pontificate of Pius XII, to the effect that a common version for all Christians would greatly improve ecumenical under-

---

[3] On the subject of this edition see the article by A. Fox in *Theology*, LXIX (1966), 164-70.

standing and might not be a practical impossibility after all. With the election in 1958 of Cardinal Roncalli to the papacy as John XXIII, and the openness of discussion that he fostered, sometimes to the extreme embarrassment of the more conservative members of the Roman Curia, voices became bolder. In October, 1959, for instance, Father Walter M. Abbott, S.J., publicly expressed in the Jesuit journal *America* the opinion that such a common version "would be a great achievement in the history of Christianity." He made clear that of course he had no illusions that doctrinal differences would immediately disappear on account of it; but he saw, among other things, certain practical advantages in not perpetuating anomalous differences such as the different method of enumerating the Ten Commandments. Many church people in all traditions are notoriously disposed to magnify trivia, to be fascinated by them, and to fasten upon them as means of perpetuating exclusiveness and prejudice. The substance of the Ten Commandments, for instance, does not differ; but the Greek, Reformed, and Anglican Churches reckon the prohibition against false worship at the beginning of the Ten Commandments as two, while the Lutherans and Roman Catholics account them one. The former group then reckon the forbidding of covetousness at the end as one commandment, while the latter group accounts it two, so that the number always works out to ten. Nevertheless, this means that the sixth commandment is understood by Anglicans and Methodists, for instance, to be the one against murder, while Roman Catholics account it the one against adultery. The seventh is, for the former group the one against adultery, but for the latter the one against theft, so that a convert who, in the confessional, alluded to his sins in terms of the numbering of the commandments to which he had been previously accustomed, as might very well happen, would be likely to be puzzled, if not disturbed, at the advice his confessor proposed. At any rate, Father Abbott took the opportunity to remark that a group of Roman Catholic scholars in Britain had been recently making an examination of the Revised Standard Version and had reached the conclusion that very little needed to be altered to make it entirely acceptable for the use of Roman Catholics. Perhaps a score of alterations might be all that was needed.

At the Triennial Assembly of the National Council of the Churches of Christ held in 1963, Dr. Luther A. Weigle reported approval of a Catholic Edition of the Revised Standard Version for the use of British Roman Catholics. It would be edited by a committee of the Catholic Biblical Association of Great Britain. To Dr. Weigle's cooperation, and that of Dr. Gerald Knoff, were largely due the success of the efforts that had been made by Dr. Reginald Fuller, Secretary of the Catholic Biblical Association of Great Britain, Dr. Peter Morrison of Thomas Nelson and Sons, and Dom Bernard Orchard, Editor of *The Catholic Biblical Commentary,* to achieve a Roman Catholic edition of the Revised Standard Version that could lead the way to a common Bible for all Christians. The introduction to the New Testament in this edition sets forth in clear language and in an irenic spirit the background and the motivations:

> With the improvement in inter-denominational relations and the advance of Biblical knowledge, the possibility of producing a Bible common to all Christians was mooted as far back as 1953. It was felt that if such a thing could be achieved, it would be of incalculable benefit in wiping away remaining misconceptions and prejudices and in fostering still further good relations between the churches. The Word of God would then be our common heritage and a unifying link not only in theory but also in fact, and those engaged in theological discussion could appeal to the same authoritative text. This objective could be achieved in the quickest and most practical way by editing the Revised Standard Version for Catholic use. It would also provide Catholics with a complete version of the Bible from the original languages.
>
> A small committee of members of the Catholic Biblical Association was formed and permission obtained to examine this translation and suggest any changes that might be required to make it acceptable to Catholics. The Standard Bible Committee of the U.S.A. was then approached and they gave a warm welcome to the proposal. Here was a wonderful opportunity to make a real step forward in the field of ecumenical relations. However, ideas of this kind take time to penetrate all levels and many difficulties and delays ensued. But a change of mind has taken place and what seemed to many in 1953 to be a novel idea of doubtful value or even of no value at all, is now generally recognized to be a legitimate and desirable goal.

The aim was to make as few changes as possible and to make them only when they seemed to be "absolutely necessary in the light of Catholic tradition." Notes pointing out alternative interpretations would be provided apart from the text. The difference between the Roman and the Reformation tradition on the question of the books that are accounted within the latter as the Old Testament Apocrypha but among the former as canonical or deuterocanonical presented a more serious difficulty. It was not, however, an insuperable one, since the translation of the Old Testament Apocrypha had already been done and its publication by Nelson had taken place on September 30, 1957. [4]

Cardinal Cushing declared that the RSV-CE, as it is now commonly designated, would "do much to promote a greater bond of unity and a more fraternal climate between Protestants and Catholics. The very fact that we have adopted their text is a high tribute to Protestant scholar-

---

[4] The translation panel consisted of Luther A. Weigle, who was chairman, Millar Burrows, Henry J. Cadbury, Clarence T. Craig, Floyd V. Filson, Frederick C. Grant, Bruce M. Metzger, Robert H. Pfeiffer, and Allen P. Wikgren. J. Carter Swaim was added to it in place of Clarence Craig when the latter's death had occurred.

ship; their willing consent is a tribute to their Christian concern. The adoption of this text is also a sign of the advance of Biblical science and of the improved relations of Catholic and Protestant scholars. I pray that this edition will do much good for the advancement of the spirit of Christian charity and mutual understanding between the Churches." [5] These are indeed generous words and befitting an American prince of the Roman Church.

The importance of the approbation of the Revised Standard Version by authorities of the Roman Catholic Church can hardly be exaggerated. Not only does it have all the ecumenical advantages seen by so many churchmen who have hoped and prayed for what is sometimes called the Coming Great Church; it gives the Revised Standard Version a place in our present story that otherwise it might not have so manifestly enjoyed. For the original purpose envisaged by those who fostered and those who undertook the making of this version was to provide an up-to-date revision of the Bible *for Church use.* It was conceived, primarily, not as a literary monument or a scholarly triumph, though it was hoped to be both, but as a revision of the English Bible as this had been traditionally used, mainly in the King James Version, in public worship among all those who shared the Reformation heritage. The very duty imposed by the Standard Bible Committee upon itself and the corresponding mandate it gave to the translation panels inevitably cast upon the Revised Standard Version, irrespective of its scholarly accomplishments and its literary tours de force, the stigma of sectarianism. In spite of the presence on the Old Testament translation panel of a Jewish scholar, Dr. Orlinsky, everyone knew that the primary intent behind the version and its acknowledged principal function was that of a "Protestant Bible," that is, it was to be a version that would eventually enjoy, as far as possible, a quasi-official status in all Churches acknowledging their debt to the Reformation. Whatever popularity it might attain among private readers, either as a devotional book or as a literary masterstroke or as an exemplar of the translator's art, would have to be in some sense supererogatory. It was as essentially a "Protestant Bible" as the Roman Missal is essentially a Roman Catholic liturgical book, notwithstanding the fact that some people do use it for scholarly and other purposes. The publication of the Roman Catholic edition of this version has changed all that. The Revised Standard Version is no longer merely a "Protestant Bible" in the Tyndale-King James tradition that happens to have literary and scholarly qualities worthy of its antecedents; it may now be accounted, rather, a monument of literature and scholarship that enjoys also the approbation of the Churches.

[5] Quoted by the publishers, Thomas Nelson and Sons, New York, in a news release, June 4, 1965.

In doing our work, we have constantly
striven to . . . render the Greek . . . into the
natural vocabulary, constructions, and rhythms
of contemporary speech.—Introduction to
the New English Bible

CHAPTER 32 *The New English Bible*

The New English Bible, a translation into the English in colloquial use in mid-twentieth-century Britain, is one of the most interesting expressions of the contemporary biblical Renaissance. The project, which obtained the backing of the principal non-Roman Churches in Britain, established and non-established, had quiet beginnings.

In England, even before World War II, proposals had been made for a fresh revision of the Revised Version of the Bible. Professors G. R. Driver of Oxford and J. M. Creed of Cambridge had actually submitted specimens for consideration. Because of wartime conditions, nothing could be done, and in the form for which they were designed nothing ever was done with them.

Meanwhile, the Revised Standard Version of the New Testament appeared in the United States in February, 1946. About this time a Church of Scotland minister, Dr. George S. Hendry,[1] who was among those who felt there was a need in Scotland for a different sort of translation, having a function not served by the Revised Standard Version, sought to interest the authorities of his own Church in the project of such a new translation. For an understanding of the manner in which this project originated in the Church of Scotland, a few observations here about that Church may be useful, since the nature of its place in British life and its relation to other Churches are frequently and in various ways misunderstood.

The Church of Scotland claims continuity not only with the medieval Roman Church in Scotland in pre-Reformation times, but with the ancient Keltic Church of St. Columba whose celebrated foundation on the Isle of Iona did not submit to Roman customs till 714. The Columban Church gave place to the Pictish Church and the Scoto-Pictish Church; but at last, with the coming of Queen Margaret to the Scottish throne in 1070, Scotland was thoroughly romanized.[2] After the Reformation in 1560, the Scottish Church (*ecclesia scoticana,* as it was called by the chronicler of a period as early as that of King Girig [Giric], who

---

[1] Then a parish minister at Bridge of Allan; he later came to the United States as Professor of Systematic Theology, Princeton Theological Seminary.

[2] Before her coming, the crucifix, for example, was unknown in Scotland. The now familiar Keltic cross was much used, of course.

reigned from 878 to 889) went through several stages, being sometimes presbyterian, sometimes episcopalian in its government, till as recently as 1689, when its presbyterian form of government was established by law. It was secured at the time of the union with England in 1707, by the subscription of the British sovereign to an oath taken immediately after accession to the throne, to secure the presbyterian government of the Church of Scotland. All subsequent monarchs of Great Britain have taken this oath, which corresponds to the declaration to secure the Protestant succession, which is also required of them and is made later, at the coronation, for the protection of the Church of England. The ecclesiastical courts of Scotland are legally recognized as forms of public jurisdiction. Among these, the General Assembly is supreme, while the Presbyteries (over sixty in number) exercize corporate functions corresponding to those of a bishop in Churches whose form of government is episcopalian. There is *also*, indeed, in Scotland, another Church, non-established, episcopalian in government, and representing about three percent of the population.

Dr. Hendry, at the time the new translation was proposed, was a member of the Presbytery of Stirling and Dunblane. On March 12, 1946, he therefore gave notice of a motion he would propose at the next meeting of Presbytery, that the Presbytery should "overture" the General Assembly (that is, present to the supreme ecclesiastical court a motion for its consideration) in the following terms:

That whereas the language of the authorised version of the Bible is now antiquated and has become largely incomprehensible to the people; and whereas the work of preaching the gospel and instructing the young is gravely impeded thereby; the General Assembly appoint a Commission to prepare a translation of the Bible into the language of the present day, which translation shall be submitted to the General Assembly for its approval, and thereafter authorised for use in public worship and instruction.[3]

At the next meeting of Presbytery, held April 9, 1946, the Presbytery approved, and the Overture was received by the General Assembly of the Church of Scotland held at Edinburgh the following month. The General Assembly appointed a special committee to inquire into the matter and subsequently make such recommendations as might seem fitting. This special committee, after considering the merits of the proposal, felt that the object would be best achieved if the cooperation of other Churches could be obtained. Approaches were therefore made accordingly.

[3] This extract from the minutes of the Presbytery has been kindly provided by the Clerk of Presbytery, Mr. William Turner.

In October, 1946, as a result of these approaches made by the Church of Scotland Assembly Committee, delegates of the Church of England, the Church of Scotland, and the Methodist, Baptist, and Congregationalist Churches in Britain met in conference at the Central Hall, Westminster, London, and recommended that the proposed new translation be undertaken. At a second conference, held in the same place in January, 1947, representatives of the University Presses of Oxford and Cambridge were present, and at the suggestion of this second conference, representatives of the Churches already mentioned were appointed to form a joint committee, to be known as the Joint Committee on the New Translation of the Bible. This committee met for the first time in July, 1947, and by the time of its third meeting in January, 1948, invitations to be represented on the Joint Committee had been sent to and accepted by the following bodies: the Welsh Churches, the Irish Churches, the Presbyterian Church of England, the Society of Friends, the British and Foreign Bible Society, and the National Bible Society of Scotland. Dr. J. W. Hunkin, Bishop of Truro, acted as chairman till his death in 1950, when he was succeeded by Dr. A. T. P. Williams, then Bishop of Durham and later Bishop of Winchester. Four panels of translators were appointed, and the whole work was placed under the care of Professor C. H. Dodd of Cambridge, a leading British biblical scholar. Regular meetings of the Joint Committee have taken place since January, 1948, usually in the Jerusalem Chamber, Westminster Abbey, to receive progress reports from the conveners of the translation panels, and to make such suggestions and take such decisions as seemed necessary.

Strictly speaking, the actual work of translation was assigned to three panels, responsible respectively for the Old Testament, the New Testament, and the Apocrypha. Since the Revised Version of late Victorian days had been particularly attacked for its stylistic defects, those who sponsored the new translation felt it desirable to have a fourth panel whose function would be to consider questions of English style.

Professor C. H. Dodd, besides being in charge of the entire project, was appointed convener of the New Testament panel of translators, which included also the following members: G. S. Duncan, W. F. Howard, G. D. Kilpatrick, T. W. Manson, C. F. Moule, J. A. T. Robinson (who later, as Bishop of Woolwich, was to attract popular attention for his provocative theological excursus, *Honest to God*), G. Styler, and R. V. G. Tasker. Howard and Manson both died before the new translation of the New Testament appeared.

The New Testament panel often met in a first floor [4] room at Clare College, Cambridge. The procedure was as follows. A member of the

---

[4] That is, second floor by American reckoning.

panel first prepared a draft of a book of the New Testament and circulated it to the other members who, having carefully studied it, met to discuss it. The literary panel would then study the revised draft that had been prepared, and after agreement had been reached between the two panels, the draft went to the Joint Committee for final revision.

Considerable freedom was allowed the translators in respect of the Greek text to be used. Generally speaking, they followed two editions, those respectively of Nestle and of the British and Foreign Bible Society, and the text from which they worked was therefore in the general tradition of Westcott and Hort. Nor was there any radical lexicographical criticism. A few matters prompted more special researches; but on the whole standard works of reference such as Bauer's dictionary were found sufficient for the translators' purposes. In the use made of such works, moreover, the translators sought to steer a middle course between a slavish adherence to dictionaries and the freedom that is put to such good effect by several independent modern translators.

In such a work the translators had to consider a great many questions. They had to consider, for instance, the audiences to be reached. The translation was to be in colloquial English; but what kind of colloquial English? There is a great difference between English as spoken by, say, university dons and the crowd at an English football match, between that of farmers in Hampshire and that of miners in County Durham. How can one write the New Testament in English that will sound quite natural and colloquial to both Liverpool dockworkers and London bankers? Generally speaking, the translators, when they had to make a choice, chose the more dignified sort of colloquialism. On the other hand, the theological ideas of the New Testament are often as strange to the bankers as to the dockworkers, and the translators no doubt felt that the more pressing problem they had to face was how to convey to anyone, in a highly secularized society such as modern England, theological concepts implicit in the New Testament and far from the average modern Englishman's everyday concerns. The everyday language of one of the better British newspapers would be readily intelligible and fairly natural to all, though it might not be exactly the language all would be actually using. The real difficulty was, rather, how to bring out the meaning of the New Testament in such language so that all would get roughly the same sort of impression it was intended to convey to those who long ago had read it in the colloquial Greek in which it was written. If one bears in mind the magnitude of this difficulty, one must surely admire the result.

Dr. Theodore H. Robinson provided some interesting sidelights on the work of the translators during the earlier years of their labors. Addressing the English Baptist Assembly in 1957, he said:

Our method is as follows. A draft is prepared by a single scholar, who need not be a member of the relevant panel. Old Testament drafts are first submitted to a scholar who is, perhaps, the greatest Semitic philologist living, to whom I handed over the convenership of the panel at the beginning of this year. His suggestions often include meanings which are as yet to be found in no dictionary or lexicon. Then the panel as a whole discusses and modifies the draft, and it is sent to the literary advisers. Their recommendations are most valuable, and are always accepted unless, in the judgement of the translating panel, they fail to give the real sense of the original. When agreement has been reached between the two panels, the result is presented to the Joint Committee in the form of a Pink Book, and filed till the whole work is completed when it will be subjected to final revision.

We may now look at various kinds of problems which the translator has to face. Some of these, of course, are common to all translators, whatever be the languages with which they are concerned. In the first place we have to decide what we are to translate. It is not enough to have any one text before us; the writer's original words have been copied again and again, and it may safely be said that there are few cases . . . in which changes have not been made by accident or design.

For the New Testament we have a very large number of ancient MSS, and the translator has to decide for himself which of them is to be followed, in practically every verse. With the Old Testament the problem is different. The newly discovered Jordan scrolls show that from the beginning of the Christian era the utmost care has been taken by copyists to secure accuracy, and differences between MSS are rare and commonly quite unimportant. But we know that the Jewish community settled in Egypt by Alexander the Great in the fourth century B.C. had copies of the books included in our Hebrew Bibles. No Hebrew examples have survived, and this form of text is known to us only through the famous Greek translation which we call the Septuagint. . . . This was, as a matter of fact, the Bible of the New Testament writers and the early Christian Church; it was not until the fourth century that it was superseded in the Western Church by the Palestinian form of text.

But even when we have got all the help we can from the Septuagint and other ancient versions, there remain a great many places where the common Hebrew text is unintelligible. Sometimes our failure to find a meaning may be due to ignorance, but in a large proportion the Hebrew words are simply nonsense. This cannot have been original, and we are forced to guess what the writer actually set down. All translators have done this, generally without saying anything about it, but the modern conscience requires that we should state the facts in a marginal note.

Then begins the real work of translation. For this task I, personally, can claim only one qualification, though that is absolutely indispensable: I know that the task is impossible. This is true of every translation from one language into another. The best known sentence in all Latin literature is quite untranslatable: Julius Caesar never thought or said that all Gaul was divided into three parts. We know what he did say and mean, and we can explain and paraphrase it, but explanation and paraphrase are not translation. It is only rarely that a word in one language exactly covers a single word in another. There are nearly always overtones and undertones, delicate shades of meaning which cannot be expressly rendered in any other language by a single word. We are dealing with minds which do not think in our ways, with languages whose very structure is different from that of English, with writers whose political, social and moral background is often startlingly different from ours. . . .

Then again how are we to avoid one of the serious defects of the familiar versions and show how different are the styles of the various Biblical writers? . . . No one with any sense of style could possibly confuse the poetry of Ezekiel with that of Isaiah. Prose styles, too, vary considerably in both parts of the Bible. Each evangelist has his own, and all are widely different from that of St. Paul. In the Old Testament we have simple stories such as might be told to small children, formal accounts of historical events, biography, legal codes, vivid and powerful rhetoric, even little scientific and philosophical treatises. Any conscious and deliberate attempt to reproduce these styles would be fatal; it could result only in stiff and artificial English. The translator must be so steeped in the original that he unconsciously reproduces for his readers the kind of impression made on him by the Hebrew and Greek—if he can.[5]

Dr. Robinson concluded by indicating the policy of the translators in the difficult matter of steering between excessively traditional and excessively colloquial English. For example, Leviticus refers to certain diseases that render a person ceremonially "unclean," and such a person had to observe certain customs designed to prevent his coming into contact with other people during a prescribed period. It would be very tempting to a modern translator to say that "the patient must be placed in quarantine for eight days," or the like. Yet this would hardly do because there is really no strict parallel between modern sanitary conditions and the ceremonial regulations of biblical times. There would be no such serious objection, on the other hand, to saying that Jonah "went down into the hold" of the ship, or, as one would say in modern nautical speech, that he "went below."[6]

Professor C. H. Dodd stated the intention behind the translation as follows: "It is to be genuinely English in idiom, such as will not awaken a sense of strangeness or remoteness. Ideally, we aim at a 'timeless' English, avoiding equally both archaisms and transient modernisms. The version should be plain enough to convey its meaning to any reasonably intelligent person (so far as verbal expression goes), yet not bald or pedestrian. It should *not* aim at preserving 'hallowed associations'; it *should* aim at conveying a sense of reality. It should be as accurate as

[5] As reported in the English *Baptist Times*, May 16 and 23, 1957, by whose kind permission the report is here reproduced.

[6] On the more fundamental difficulties attending all translation work, however, see chapter 34.

may be without pedantry." He expressed also the hope that it would above all remove in some measure the barrier between the Bible and "a large porportion of our fellow-countrymen." [7]

The last meeting of the New Testament panel took place in February, 1960, and the New Testament was published in 1961 by the Oxford and Cambridge University Presses. As expected, it was in a distinctly colloquial English. The text is set forth in paragraphs, and quotation marks are used for dialogue; but for purposes of reference the conventional verse numbers are placed in the margins. The style is generally pleasant to the ear of any English-speaking reader and also to American ears, though the American reader finds himself reminded from time to time that the idiom is more British than American. Many familiar passages exhibit a delightfully new vitality, and the whole has a distinctive flavor. Here are some specimens from the Sermon on the Mount:

When he saw the crowds he went up the hill. . . . And this is the teaching he gave:
> 'How blest are those who know that they are poor;
> the kingdom of Heaven is theirs. . . .

'You are the salt to the world. And if salt becomes tasteless, how is its saltness to be restored? . . . Do not suppose that I have come to abolish the Law and the prophets; I did not come to abolish, but to complete. I tell you this: so long as heaven and earth endure, not a letter, not a stroke, will disappear from the Law until all that must happen has happened.[8] . . . I tell you, unless you show yourselves far better men than the Pharisees and the doctors of the law, you can never enter the kingdom of Heaven. . . . But what I tell you is this: Anyone who nurses anger against his brother must be brought to judgement. . . . If a man wants to sue you for your shirt, let him have your coat as well. . . . In your prayers do not go babbling on like the heathen, who imagine that the more they say the more likely they are to be heard. Do not imitate them. . . . This is how you should pray:

> "Our Father in heaven,
> Thy name be hallowed;
> Thy kingdom come,
> Thy will be done,
> On earth as in heaven.
> Give us today our daily bread.
> Forgive us the wrong we have done,
> As we have forgiven those who have wronged us.

[7] As quoted by T. H. Robinson, "A New Translation of the English Bible" in *The Bible Translator*, II (1951), 167-68.

[8] In a footnote, an alternative reading is provided: "Before all that it stands for is achieved."

And do not bring us to the test,
But save us from the evil one."

'For if you forgive others the wrongs they have done, your heavenly Father will also forgive you; but if you do not forgive others, then the wrongs you have done will not be forgiven by your Father. . . . Do not store up for yourselves treasure on earth, where it grows rusty and moth-eaten. . . . You cannot serve God and Money.'

The modern reader may sometimes feel he is hearing St. Paul for the first time when he reads injunctions such as these (I Cor. 5) :

I actually hear reports of sexual immorality among you, immorality such as even pagans do not tolerate: the union of a man with his father's wife. And you can still be proud of yourselves! You ought to have gone into mourning. . . . Your self-satisfaction ill becomes you. . . . In my letter I wrote that you must have nothing to do with loose livers. I was not, of course, referring to pagans who lead loose lives or are grabbers and swindlers or idolaters. . . . What business of mine is it to judge outsiders? God is their judge. You are judges within the fellowship. Root out the evil-doer from your community.

There is a racy quality in chatty asides such as: "You will want to know about my affairs, and how I am; Tychicus will give you all the news" (Eph. 6:21) .

According to the King James Version (Acts 21:33-37) , when Paul was arrested at Jerusalem, "the chief captain came near." Then, "when he could not know the certainty for the tumult, he commanded him to be carried to the castle." Paul "said unto the chief captain, May I speak to thee? Who said, Canst thou speak Greek?" The American Standard Version changed this very little except that the "tumult" becomes an "uproar" and Paul is "to be brought into the castle." In the Revised Standard Version, the "chief captain" is a "tribune," and he "could not learn the facts because of the uproar." So he orders Paul "to be brought into the barracks."

The New English Bible is surely more easily intelligible than any of these. Here we read: "The commandant stepped forward." When "he could not get at the truth because of the hubbub, he ordered him to be taken into barracks." Then Paul "said to the commandant, 'May I say something to you?' The commandant said, 'So you speak Greek, do you?' "

"The publicans," according to the King James Version, were told: "Exact no more than that which is appointed you" (Luke 3:13) . Soldiers were told: "Do violence to no man, neither accuse any falsely; and be content with your wages" (Luke 3:14) . According to the New English Bible "the tax-gatherers" were told: " 'Exact no more than the assessment.' " To the soldiers Jesus says: " 'No bullying; no blackmail; make do with your pay!' "

Surely not even the most reactionary opponent of change could deny that these are very patent improvements. The rendering of poetry such as the *Magnificat* and *Nunc dimittis* is impressive, too. In contrast to Harwood's grandiloquence, for instance, they are presented in vivid language that is truly English in its genius. Nor is it fair to compare them to the canticles made familiar in Christian liturgies, for the function of the New English Bible is different from that of such versions. It has a private reading function, not a liturgical one. Yet it is interesting to note that such is the power of long liturgical usage in making even obscure meanings plain in a way that many who have for long been steeped in a tradition in which the liturgical use of such canticles plays an important part will find that the "colloquial" renderings do lose something.

To read that God "has torn imperial powers from their thrones, but the humble have been lifted high" (Luke 1:52) is all right and indeed vigorous in its way; but the language of the Vulgate (*Deposuit potentes de sede et exaltavit humiles*) is more telling and terse, while the Book of Common Prayer ("He hath put down the mighty from their seat, and hath exalted the humble and meek"), though lacking the seven-word neatness of the Latin, continues to convey the images in a most striking way. We see tyrants' scepters crashing to the ground and a vast sea of a thousand generations of oppressed peoples rising to their feet, their faces all radiant with gratitude and awed by the triumph of the justice they have so long awaited. And in the midst of all we see Mary, symbol of God's unique and decisive manifestation of the "downing" of the strong and the "upping" of the weak. A young minority-group woman in the Roman Empire has become the focus of the most radical revolution of all time, so from now on it's down with boastful, bloodthirsty tyrants and up with the gentle and good of all classes. Those who have been hearing the *Magnificat* since childhood in the older versions may have seen all that in scores of ways already, so that there is hardly anything left for a new translation to do for them.

When all that is said, however, the New English Bible renderings of the *Magnificat* and *Nunc dimittis* may still be called masterpieces:

> Tell out, my soul, the greatness of the Lord,
> rejoice, rejoice, my spirit, in God my saviour;
> so tenderly has he looked upon his servant,
>   humble as she is.
> For, from this day forth,
> all generations will count me blessed,
> so wonderfully has he dealt with me,
>   the Lord, the Mighty One.

His name is Holy;
his mercy sure from generation to generation
    toward those who fear him;
the deeds his own right arm has done
    disclose his might:
the arrogant of heart and mind he has put to rout,
he has torn imperial powers from their thrones,
    but the humble have been lifted high.
The hungry he has satisfied with good things,
    the rich sent empty away.

He has ranged himself at the side of Israel his servant;
    firm in his promise to our forefathers,
he has not forgotten to show mercy to Abraham
    and his children's children, for ever. (Luke 1:46-55.)

This day, Master, thou givest thy servant his discharge in peace;
    now thy promise is fulfilled.
For I have seen with my own eyes
the deliverance which thou hast made ready in full view of all the
    nations:
A light that will be a revelation to the heathen,
    and glory to thy people Israel. (Luke 2:29-32.)

On the whole, the style of this version of the New Testament is less colloquial than some had expected. Though the English is always as intelligible as Dodd hoped it would be, the tendency seems to be more toward a somewhat elegant than toward a truly everyday speech. There is occasionally even a donnishness that makes dialogue sound especially a little incredible. "Still sleeping?" is an admirable opening for Jesus' rebuke to his disciples in Gethsemane; but "Up, let us go forward; the traitor is upon us" (Matt. 26:45-46) is not convincing. Even the most old-fashioned professor would not talk like that today, though a young one conceivably might do so in offhanded jest. To those who expect colloquialism of this version and whose ears are therefore attuned to the prospect of hearing living voices, the effect is disconcerting. Jesus sounds too much like a character on a stage, and almost a Shakespearian stage at that. Instances of this kind are by no means common, however, and of course a precise and fairly elevated style is in any case much less noticeable in letters and rapportage, where educated readers would expect it, than in dialogue. Here the modern novelist's technique accustoms us all to expect a close approximation to what the character depicted would actually say, and certainly to find unacceptable any phrases that nobody would actually use in speech.

It is to be remembered that the New English Bible, like the Revised

Standard Version and unlike independent versions, such as that of Goodspeed or that of Moffatt, is the work of a body of several translators. The consequent disadvantage is that one must not expect to find in it a characteristic style—the hand of a Phillips or of a Ronald Knox. It enjoys, however, advantages that in some ways may outweigh this. The New Testament translators' panel sent their drafts, as these were completed, to the literary panel. When the members of the latter panel had read one of these drafts, they made suggestions for improvement in English style. These were then considered by the translators' panel, and only when agreement was eventually reached, was the draft then sent to the Churches' Joint Committee for approval. The result was that not only did the New Testament have behind it a very high quality of biblical scholarship, enhanced by the criticism of literary artists; it also carried a very wide measure of ecclesiastical approval.

A million copies of the New Testament were printed when it appeared in 1961, and the demand was such that reprinting began almost as soon as they were off the press. The Old Testament is expected soon; but at the time of this writing it has not yet been published.

Variety's the very spice of life,
That gives it all its flavour.
—William Cowper, "The Task"

CHAPTER 33 *Conspectus of a Passage in Various English Versions*

An account of the principal versions of the English Bible has been given in previous chapters, and notice has been taken of representatives of the more important and interesting among the vast number of private or independent English versions in the course of many centuries. Occasionally, by way of exhibiting the flavor or illustrating the nature of a particular version, a brief specimen has been provided of a word or two, a few verses, or even a chapter from its text.

Some readers may wish to make a systematic examination of particular passages, and may be fortunate enough to have time for such research and access to an important library likely to contain the materials they need. Most readers, however, are likely to lack either the time for such a tedious task, or the opportunity, or both. For these a brief passage has been selected here and is set forth as it is rendered in more than fifty versions from the time of Wyclif down to the present day. The passage selected is not one of the easiest for a translator, and so is an interesting one to look at in a conspectus such as the one set forth in the present chapter. In the chapter that follows will be considered some of the problems of translation, both problems in general and the special problems connected with the translation of the Bible.

The passage is Hebrews 1:1-4:

An Early Middle English Version, late fourteenth century

God hath y-spoken in many maneres sumtyme in prophetes to oure fadres, bote al-ther last in these dayes he hath y-spoken to ous in his sone, whom he hath y-ordeyned to ben eyr of alle thinges, by whom also he made the worldes; and he is the brytnesse of his blisse, and the fygure of his substaunce, berynge alle thinges thorogh the word of his vertu, and makynge the purgacyoun of synnes, he syt on the ryght syde of the mageste an hygh in hefne; so muche y-maad betur than aungeles, in as muche as he hath anheryted a different name to-foren hem.

Wyclif Version (early), 1382

Manyfold and many maners sum tyme God spekinge to fadris in prophetis, at the laste in thes daies spak to us in the sone: whom he ordeynede eyr of alle thingis, by whom he made and the worldis. The which whanne he is the schynynge of glorie and figure of his substaunce, and berynge alle thingis bi word of his vertu, makyng purgacioun of synnes, sittith on the righthalf of mageste in high thingis; so moche maad betere than aungelis, by how moche he hath inherited a more different, *or excellent,* name bifore hem.

Wyclif Version (later), 1395-1408

God, that spak sum tyme bi prophetis in many maneres to oure fadris, at the laste in these daies he hath spoke to us bi the sone; whom he hath ordeyned eir of alle thingis, and bi whom he made the worldis. Which whanne also he is the brightnesse of glorie, and figure of his substaunce and berith all thingis bi word of his vertu, he makyth purgacioun of synnes and syttith on the righthalf of the maiestie in heuenes; and so much is maad betere than aungels, bi hou myche he hath enerited a more dyuerse name bifor hem.

Wyclif Version in Scots (Nisbet), *c.* 1520

God, that spak sum tyme be prophetis in mony maneris to our fadris, at the last 2 In thir dayis he has spokin to vs be the sonn; quham he has ordanit aire of all thingis, and be quham he made the warldis. 3 Quhilk quhen alsa he is the brichtnes of glorie, and figure of his substance, and beris althingis be word of his virtue, he makis purgatioun of synnis, and sittis on the richthalf of his maiestee in huenis; 4 And sa mekile is made bettir than angelis, be how mekil he has inheritit a mare dyuerse name before thame.

Tyndale Version, 1525

God in tyme past dyuersly and many wayes, spake vnto yᵉ fathers by prophets: but in these last dayes he hath spoken vnto vs by hys sonne, whom he hath made heyre of all thyngs: by whom also he made the worlde. Which sonne beynge the brightnes of his glory, and very ymage off his substance, bearynge vppe all thyngs with the worde of his power, hath in his awne person pourged oure synnes, and is sytten on the right honde of the maiestie an hye, and is more excellent then the angels in as moche as he hath by inheritaunce obteyned an excellenter name then have they.

Coverdale Version, 1535

God in tyme past dyuersly and many wayes, spake vnto y° fathers by prophetes, but in these last dayes, he hath spoken vnto vs by his sonne, whom he hath made heyre of all thinges, by whom also he made the worlde. Which (sonne) beynge the brightnes of his glory, and the very ymage of his substaunce, bearinge vp all thinges with the worde of his power, hath in his owne personne pourged oure synnes, and is set on the righte hande of the maiestie on hye: beynge even as moch more excellent than y° angels, as he hath obtayned a more excellent name then they.

Matthew Version, 1537

God in tyme past dyuersly and many wayes, spake vnto the father's b y° Prophetes but in these last dayes he hath spoken vnto vs by hys sonne, whom he hath made heyre of all thinges: by whom also he made y° worlde. Which sonne beynge the brightnes of his glory, and very ymage of hys substance, bearynge vp all thynges wyth the worde of hys power, hath in hys awne person purged oure synnes, and is sytten on the righte hande of the maiestye on hye, and is more excellent then the angels, in as moche as he hath by inherytaunce obteyned an excellenter name then haue they.

Great Bible, 1539

God in tyme past diuersly and many ways, spake vnto the fathers by Prophetes: but in these last dayes he hath spoken vnto vs by hys awne soone, whom he hath made heyre of all thinges, by whom also he made the worlde. Whych (sonne) beinge the brightnes of hys glory, and the very ymage of hys substance rulynge all thynges wyth the worde of hys power, hath by hys awne person pourged oure synnes, and sytteth on the righte hande of the maiestye on hye: beynge so moch more excellent then the angels, as he hath by inherytaunce obteyned a more excellent name then they.

Geneva Bible, 1560

1. At sondri times and in diuers maners God spake in ye olde time to *our* fathers by the Prophetes: 2. In these last dayes he hathe spoken vnto us by his Sonne, whome he hathe made heir of all things, by whome also he made the worldes, 3. Who being the brightnes of the glorie, and the ingraued forme of his persone, and bearing vp all things by his mightie worde, hath by him self purged our sinnes, and sitteth at the right hand of the maiestie in the highest places, 4. And is made so

much more excellent then the Angels in as muche as he hath obteined a more excellent name then thei.

Bishops' Bible, 1568

1. God which in tyme past, at sundrie tymes, and in diuers maners, spake vnto the fathers in the prophetes: 2. Hath in these last dayes, spoken vnto vs in the sonne, whom he hath appoynted heyre of all thynges, by whom also he made the worldes. 3. Who beyng the bryght-nesse of the glorie, and the very image of his substaunce, vpholding all thynges with the worde of his power, hauing by himselfe pourged our sinnes hath syt on the ryght hande of the maiestie on hye: 4. Beyng so much more excellent then the Angels, as he hath by inheritaunce ob-tayned a more excellent name then they.

Reims New Testament, 1582

1 Diversely and many vvaies in times past God speaking to the fathers
2 in the prophets: last of al in these daies hath spoken to vs in his Sonne, vvhome he hath appointed heire of al, by vvhome he made also the vvorldes.
3 VVho being the brightnesse of his glorie, and the figure of his sub-staunce, and carying al things by the vvorde of his povver, making
4 purgation of sinnes, sitteth on the right hand of the Maiestie in the high places: being made so much better then Angels, as he hath inherited a more excellent name aboue them.

King James Version, 1611

1 God who at sundry times, and in diuers manners, spake in time past vnto the Fathers by the Prophets,
2 Hath in these last dayes spoken vnto vs by *his* Sonne, whom he hath appointed heire of all things, by whom also he made the worlds,
3 Who being the brightness of his glory, and the expresse image of his person, and vpholding all things by the word of his power, when hee had by himself purged our sinnes, sate down on ye right hand of the Maiestie on high,
4 Being made so much better than the Angels, as hee hath by in-heritance obtained a more excellent Name then they.

King James Version (Present-day wording)

God, who at sundry times and in divers manners spake in time past unto the fathers by the prophets,

2 Hath in these last days spoken unto us by *his* Son, whom he hath appointed heir of all things, by whom also he made the worlds;

3 Who being the brightness of *his* glory, and the express image of his person, and upholding all things by the word of his power, when he had by himself purged our sins, sat down on the right hand of the Majesty on high;

4 Being made so much better than the angels, as he hath by inheritance obtained a more excellent name than they.

Mr. Whiston's Primitive New Testament, 1745

God, who at sundry times, and in divers manners, spake in time past unto the fathers by the prophets, 2 Hath in these last days spoken unto us by *his* Son, whom he hath appointed heir of all things, by whom also he made the ages. 3 Who being a beam of his glory, and the express image of his substance, and upholding all things by the word of his power, when he had by himself purged sins, sat down on the right hand of the Majesty on high: 4 Being made so much better than the angels, as he hath by inheritance obtained a more excellent name than they.

A New and Literal Translation of All the Books of the Old and New Testaments (Anthony Purver, "Quaker Bible"), 1764

GOD having spoken many times and many ways of old, to the Forefathers by the Prophets;

2. In these last Days has spoken to us by the Son, whom he put the Heir of all things, by whom also he made the Worlds.

3. Who being the Brightness of the Glory, the Mark of his Substance, and supporting all things with his powerful Word; when he had made a Cleansing of our Sins by himself, sate down at the right Hand of the Majesty on high:

4. And became so much better than the Angels, as he inherited a more excellent Name than they.

The New Testament with an Analysis (John Wesley), 1790

God, who at sundry times, and in divers manners, spake of old to the fathers by the prophets, hath in these last days spoken to us by his Son; Whom he hath appointed heir of all things, by whom he also made the worlds: Who being the brightness of his glory, and the express image of his person, and sustaining all things by the word of his power, when he had by himself purged our sins, sat down on the right hand of the Majesty on high, Being so much higher than the angels, as he hath by inheritance a more excellent name than they.

The Holy Bible . . . Translated from the Greek (Charles Thomson, Late Secretary to the Congress of the United States) , 1808

GOD, who in sundry parcels and in divers manners spake in time
2 past to the fathers by the prophets, hath in these last days, spoken to us by a son whom he hath constituted heir of all things, by
3 whom also he made the ages; who being an effulgence of the glory, and an impress of his substance, and upholding all things by the word of his power, having by himself made a purification
4 of our sins, sat down on the right hand of the majesty on high, being made as much superior to the heavenly messengers as the name he hath inherited is more excellent than theirs.

The Sacred Writings of the Apostles and Evangelists of Jesus Christ, Commonly Styled the New Testament (Campbell, MacKnight, and Doddridge) , 1826

God, who in sundry parcels and in divers manners, anciently spake to the fathers by the prophets,—hath in these last days spoken to us by a Son, whom he constituted heir of all things; (through whom also he made the worlds) , who, (being an effulgence of his glory, and an exact image of his substance, and upholding all things by the word of his power) , when he had made purification of our sins by himself, sat down at the right hand of the majesty in high places. He is by so much better than the heavenly messengers, by how much he hath inherited a more excellent name than they.

The Syriac New Testament Translation into English from the Peshitta Version (James Murdock) , 1852.[1]

In many ways, and many forms, God anciently conversed with our fathers, by the prophets: (2) But in these latter days, he hath conversed with us, by his Son; whom he hath constituted heir of all things, and by whom he made the worlds; (3) who is the splendor of his glory, and the image of himself, and upholdeth all by the energy of his word; and by himself he made a purgation of sins, and sat down at the right hand of the Majesty on high. (4) And he is altogether superior to the angels, as he hath also a name which excelleth theirs.

[1] Dr. Murdock (1776-1856) is described on the title page as "late Professor of Learned Languages in the University of Vermont," etc. The translation was published by the Scriptural Tract Repository, Boston and London.

The Holy Bible . . . Translated According to the Letter and Idiom of the Original Languages (Robert Young), 1862

1 In many parts and many ways, God of old having spoken to the fathers in the prophets, 2 in these last days did speak to us in a Son, whom He appointed heir of all things, through whom also He did make the ages; 3 who being the brightness of the glory, and the impress of His subsistence, bearing up also the all things by the saying of his might— through himself having made a cleansing of our sins, sat down at the right hand of the greatness in the highest, 4 having become so much better than the messengers, as he did inherit a more excellent name than they.

The New Testament Translated from the Greek Text of Tischendorf (George R. Noyes), 1873 [2]

1 God, who at different times and in different ways spoke of old to the
2 fathers by the prophets, hath at the end of these days spoken to us by his Son, whom he appointed heir of all things, by whom he also
3 made the worlds, who being a brightness from his glory and an image of his being, and upholding all things by the rod of his power, when he had by himself accomplished a cleansing of sins, sat
4 down on the right hand of the Majesty on high: having become so much superior to the angels, as he hath inherited a more excellent name than they.

Revised Version, 1881, and American Standard Version, 1901

1 God, having of old time spoken unto the fathers in the prophets by
2 divers portions and in divers manners, hath at the end of these days spoken unto us in *his* Son, whom he appointed heir of all things,
3 through whom also he made the worlds; who being the effulgence of his glory, and the very image of his substance, and upholding all
4 things by the word of his power, when he had made purification of sins, sat down on the right hand of the Majesty on high; having become so much better than the angels, as he hath inherited a more excellent name than they.

The Twentieth Century New Testament (First Edition), 1898-1901

God, who in the old days spoke to our ancestors, through the Prophets, at many different times and in many different ways, has in these latter

[2] This translation was published in Boston by the American Unitarian Association.

days spoken to us through the Son, whom he had appointed heir to everything, and through whom he had made the universe. He is the reflection of God's Glory and the embodiment of the divine nature, and upholds all creation by the power of his word. He made an expiation for the sins of men, and then *took his seat at the right hand* of God's Majesty on high, having shown himself as much greater than the angels as the Name that he has inherited surpasses theirs.

The New Testament in Modern Speech (Weymouth), 1903

God, who of old spoke to our forefathers in many fragments and by various methods through the Prophets, has at the end of these days spoken to us through a Son, who is the predestined Lord of the universe, and through whom He made the world. He brightly reflects God's glory and is the exact representation of His being, and upholds the universe by His all-powerful word. After securing man's purification from sin He took His seat at the right hand of the Majesty on high, having become as far superior to the angels as the Name He possesses by inheritance is more excellent than theirs.

The Twentieth Century New Testament (Revised edition), 1905

God, who, of old, at many times and in many ways, spoke to our ancestors, by the Prophets, has in these latter days spoken to us by the Son, whom he appointed the heir of all things, and through whom he made the universe. For he is the radiance of the Glory of God and the very expression of his Being, upholding all creation by the power of his Word; and when he had made an expiation for the sins of men, he "took his seat at the right hand" of God's Majesty on high, having shown himself as much greater than the angels as the Name that he has inherited surpasses theirs.

The Corrected English New Testament (Lloyd), 1905

God, having spoken in the prophets in time past, in many portions and in many ways, to the fathers, hath at the end of these days spoken to us by a Son, whom He appointed heir of all things; through whom also he made the world; who, being the effulgence of His glory, and the very image of His Being, and upholding all things by the word of his power, when he had made purification of sins, sat down at the right hand of the Majesty on high; being exalted so much above the angels, as he hath inherited a more excellent name than they.

The Modern Reader's Bible (Moulton), 1907

God, having of old time spoken unto the fathers in the prophets by divers portions and in divers manners, hath at the end of these days spoken unto us in a Son, whom he appointed heir of all things, through whom also he made the worlds; who, being the effulgence of his glory, and the very image of his substance, and upholding all things by the word of his power, when he had made purification of sins, sat down on the right hand of the Majesty on high; having become by so much better than the angels, as he hath inherited a more excellent name than they.

The New Testament, an American Translation (Goodspeed), 1923

It was little by little and in different ways that God spoke in old times to our forefathers through the prophets, but in these latter days he has spoken to us in a Son, whom he had destined to possess everything and through whom he had made the world. He is the reflection of God's glory, and the representation of his being, and bears up the universe by his mighty word. He has effected man's purification from sin, and has taken his seat on high at the right hand of God's Majesty, showing himself to be as much greater than the angels as his title is superior to theirs.

The Centenary Translation of the New Testament (Helen Montgomery), 1924

1. *The Son, God's Word to Man*
   God, who in ancient days spoke to our ancestors in the prophets, at many different times and by various methods, has at the end of these days spoken to us in a Son whom he appointed heir of all things; through whom also he made the universe. He, being an emanation of God's glory and stamp of his substance, and upholding the universe by the utterance of his power, after by himself making purification of our sins, has taken his seat on the right hand of the Majesty on High.
1. *The Son Superior to Angels*
   He is as much superior to the angels as the name that he has inherited surpasses theirs.

The People's New Covenant (New Testament) Scriptural Writings (Overbury), 1925

God, who at sundry times and divers manners, spake in times past unto our forefathers through the prophets, 2 hath in these latter days spoken unto us through a Son, whom He appointed an heir of all things; and for whom also He created the universe; 3 who, being a radiant reflection of His glory, and a complete expression of His being, and upholding all spiritual creation by the power of his word, having exemplified the possible demonstration of the nullification of evil on our behalf, sat down on the right hand of the majesty of God on high, 4 having proved himself superior to the angels, inasmuch as he hath inherited a more excellent name than they.

Concordant Version of the Sacred Scriptures, "New Testament," an Idiomatic, Consistent, Emphasized Version (Concordant Publishing Concern), 1926

By many portions and many modes, of old, God, speaking to the fathers in the prophets, in the last of these days speaks to us in a Son, Whom He appoints enjoyer of the allotment of all, through Whom He also makes the eons; Who, being the Effulgence of His glory and Emblem of His assumption, besides carrying on all by His powerful declaration, making a cleansing of sins, is seated at the right hand of the Majesty in the heights; becoming so much better than the messengers as He enjoys the allotment of a more excellent name than they.

A New Translation of the Bible (Moffatt, final edition), 1935

Many were the forms and fashions in which God spoke of old to our fathers by the prophets, but in these days at the end he has spoken to us by a Son—a Son whom he has appointed heir of the universe, as it was by him that he created the world. He, reflecting God's bright glory and stamped with God's own character, sustains the universe with his word of power; when he had secured our purification from sins, he sat down at the right hand of the Majesty on high; and thus he is superior to the angels, as he has inherited a Name superior to theirs.

The New Testament of Our Lord and Saviour Jesus Christ. Translated into English from the Original Greek (Francis Aloysius Spencer, O.P.), 1937

God, having spoken of old to our forefathers through the prophets, by many degrees and in many ways, has at the last in these days spoken to us by His Son, whom He appointed Heir of all things, and through whom He made the worlds. He being the effulgence of God's glory and the very image of his substance, upholds the universe by God's powerful mandate.

The New Testament: A New Translation and Explanation Based on the Oldest Manuscripts (Johannes Greber), 1937 [3]

1. On many occasions and in various ways God in times past spoke to our fathers through the prophets. Finally in our own day He has spoken to us through a son whom He appointed to rule over the universe and by whom He also caused the ages to be determined. In him is reflected God's glory, and he is the image of God's true being. He accomplishes everything in obedience to God's word of power. Through him God effected our purification from the sin of apostasy and then seated him at His right hand in the kingdom of heaven. He is as far above the angels as the name that he inherited is superior to theirs.

The New Testament. A Translation in the Language of the People (Charles B. Williams), 1937 [4]

It was bit by bit and in many different ways that God in olden times spoke to our forefathers through the prophets, but in these last days He has spoken to us through a Son, whom He had appointed lawful owner of everything, and through whom He had made the worlds. He is the reflection of God's glory and the perfect representation of His being, and continues to uphold the universe by His mighty word. After he had procured man's purification from sins, He took His seat at the right hand of God's majesty, thus proving Himself to be as much superior to angels as the title He has inherited is superior to theirs.

The New Testament According to the Eastern Text Translated from Original Aramaic Sources (George M. Lamsa), 1940

From of old God spoke to our fathers by the prophets in every manner and in all ways; and in these latter days, he has spoken to us by his Son;
2 Whom he has appointed heir of all things, and by whom also he made the worlds;
3 For he is the brightness of his glory and the express image of his being, upholding all things by the power of his word; and when he had through his person, cleansed our sins, then he sat down on the right hand of the Majesty on high;
4 And he is altogether greater than the angels, just as the name he has inherited is a more excellent name than theirs.

[3] The author, a former Roman Catholic priest, claims to have been in communication with the spirit world. In prefatory remarks he states that he finds that Codex Bezae most nearly approximates the truth. Published by the Johannes Greber Memorial Foundation, Teaneck, N.J.

[4] This translation, not to be confused with the one by Charles Kingsley Williams, below, aims at conveying the exact shade of meaning of the Greek verb tenses.

The New Testament in Basic English, 1941

In times past the word of God came to our fathers through the prophets, in different parts and in different ways; but now, at the end of these days, it has come to us through his Son, to whom he has given all things for a heritage, and through whom he made the order of the generations; who, being the outshining of his glory, the true image of his substance, supporting all things by the word of his power, having given himself as an offering making clean from sins, took his seat at the right hand of God in heaven; having become by so much better than the angels, as the name which is his heritage is more noble than theirs.

The New Testament . . . Translated from the Latin Vulgate (Confraternity Revision of the Challoner-Reims Version), 1941

God, who at sundry times and in divers manners spoke in times past to the fathers by the prophets, last of all in these days has spoken to us by his Son, whom he appointed heir of all things, by whom also he made the world; who, being the brightness of his glory and the image of his substance, and upholding all things by the word of his power, has effected man's purgation from sin and taken his seat at the right hand of the Majesty on high, having become so much superior to the angels as he has inherited a more excellent name than they.

The Holy Scriptures Containing the Old and New Testament. An Inspired Revision of the Authorized Version (By Joseph Smith, Junior), A New Corrected Edition, 1944

God, who at sundry times and in divers manners spake in time past unto the fathers by the prophets,
2 Hath in these last days spoken unto us by his Son, whom he hath appointed heir of all things, by whom also he made the worlds;
3 Who being the brightness of his glory, and the express image of his person, and upholding all things by the word of his power, when he had by himself purged our sins, sat down on the right hand of the Majesty on high;
4 Being made so much better than the angels, as he hath by inheritance obtained a more excellent name than they.

The New Testament in the Translation of Ronald Knox, 1944

In old days, God spoke to our fathers in many ways and by many means, through the prophets; now at last in these times he has spoken to us, with a Son to speak for him; a Son, whom he has appointed to inherit

all things, just as it was through him that he created this world of time;
a Son, who is the radiance of his Father's splendour, and the full expression of his being; all creation depends, for its support, on his enabling
word. Now, making atonement for our sins, he has taken his place on
high, at the right hand of God's majesty, superior to the angels in that
measure in which the name he has inherited is more excellent than theirs.

Berkeley Version of the New Testament from the Original Greek with Brief Footnotes (Gerrit Verkuyl), 1945

After God had of old spoken to our fathers at various times and in
many ways by means of the prophets, He has at the end of these days
spoken to us in his Son, whom He has appointed Heir to all things and
through whom He made the worlds. As the reflection of God's glory
and the true expression of His being, He sustains the universe by His
almighty word. And when He had effected our cleansing from sin, He
took His seat at the right hand of the Majesty on high.
He became as much mightier than the angels as the name He inherited
was superior to theirs.

The New Testament from the Greek Text as Established by Bible Numerics (Ivan Panin), 1945 [5]

1 God, having spoken of old to the fathers in the prophets by divers
2 portions and in divers manners, hath at *the* end of these : days spoken
to us in a Son, whom he appointed heir of all, through whom also he
3 made the ages; who being the Glory's effulgence, and *the* very image
of his : substance, and upholding : all *things* by the word of his :
power, when he had made purification of : sins, sat down on *the* right
4 of the Majesty on high; having become by so much better than the
angels, as he hath inherited a more superior name than they.

Revised Standard Version, 1946 [6]

In many and various ways God spoke of old to our fathers by the
prophets; but in these last days he has spoken to us by a Son, whom he
appointed the heir of all things, through whom also he created the
world. He reflects the glory of God and bears the very stamp of his
nature, upholding the universe by his word of power. When he had

[5] Panin claims that his translation is literal, with no redundant words. All words
not in the Greek are italicized. A colon is used to indicate the use of the article in
Greek where this is omitted in translation.

[6] The text of the Revised Standard Version—Catholic Edition is identical. An
asterisk guides the reader to a footnote that provides a theological interpretation of
the passage.

made purification for sins, he sat down at the right hand of the Majesty on high, having become as much superior to angels as the name he has obtained is more excellent than theirs.

The New Testament in the Westminster Version of the Sacred Scriptures (Cuthbert Lattey, S.J.), 1948

God, having spoken of old to the fathers through the prophets by many partial revelations and in various ways, in these last days hath spoken to us by one who is Son, whom he hath set up as heir of all things; by whom also he created the ages. He, being the flashing-forth of his glory, and the very expression of his being, sustaineth all things by God's word of power; and having made a cleansing from sin, "hath taken his seat at the right hand" of Majesty on high, having become as much greater than the angels as the name which he hath inherited surpasseth theirs.

The New Testament of Our Lord and Saviour Jesus Christ: The Letchworth Version in Modern English (T. F. Ford and R. E. Ford), 1948

God, who of old spoke at various times and in many ways to our fathers by the prophets, 2 Has in these last days spoken to us by his Son, whom he has appointed heir of all things, by whom also he made the worlds; 3 Who, being the brightness of his glory, and the very impress of his substance, and upholding all things by the word of his power, when he had by himself made purification of our sins, sat down at the right hand of the Majesty on high; 4 Having become as much better than the angels, as he has by inheritance obtained a more excellent name than they.

New World Translation of the Christian Greek Scriptures, Rendered from the Original Language by the New World Bible Translation Committee, A.D. 1950 (Watchtower Bible and Tract Society), 1950 [7]

1 God, who long ago spoke on many occasions and in many ways to our forefathers by means of the prophets, 2 has at the end of these days spoken to us by means of a Son, whom he appointed heir of all things, and through whom he made the systems of things. 3 He is the reflection of his glory and the exact representation of his very being, and he sustains all things by the word of his power, and after he had made a purification for our sins he sat down in the right hand of the majesty

[7] The complete Bible was published in this translation in 1961: first printing, 2,000,000; second printing, 1,500,000.

in lofty places. 4 So he has become better than the angels to the extent that he has inherited a name more excellent than theirs.

The New Testament, a New Translation in Plain English (Charles Kingsley Williams), 1952 [8]

1 In old times God spoke to our fathers by the prophets in many different ways; 2 in these last days he has spoken to us by a Son; he appointed him the heir of all the world; he created the world through him; 3 he is the reflection of God's glory and the living image of his being; he holds up the world by his word of power; when he had made purification from sin, he took his seat at the right hand of the majesty on high; 4 and so is seen to be as much better than the angels, as the name which he has come to possess is a better name than theirs.

The Authentic New Testament Edited and Translated from the Greek for the General Reader (Hugh J. Schonfield), 1955 [9]

At varying intervals and in varied fashions God spoke of old to our fathers by the Prophets; but at the close of these times he has spoken to us by a Son, whom he appointed heir to everything. By him also he instituted the Aeons. He, being the reflection of God's glory and the exact expression of his nature, bringing everything into being by the exercise of God's power, when he had effected an expiation for sins, sat down at the right hand of the Majesty in the heavenly heights. In this respect he is superior to the angels, in so far as he has obtained a more exalted status than theirs.

Expanded Translation of the Greek New Testament (Kenneth S. Wuest), 3 vols., 1956-1959 [10]

In many parts and in different ways God in former times having spoken to the fathers by means of the prophets, in the last of these days spoke to us in One who by nature is [His] Son, whom He appointed heir of

---

[8] This translation is not to be confused with that of Charles B. Williams, above. Charles Kingsley Williams was Assistant Vice-Principal of Achimota College, Ghana. The "Plain English" referred to in the title is based on a list of 1,500 "fundamental and common words that make up ordinary English speech." Mr. Williams actually uses about 160 or more words not included in the list, on the ground that these are special, doctrinal terms.

[9] Dr. Schonfield is a London-born, Glasgow-educated Jewish scholar. He believes the New Testament atmosphere is so Jewish that even the most imaginative Gentile can hardly grasp it.

[10] Wuest purports, in his translation, to do for all parts of speech what C. B. Williams, above, does for the verb.

all things, through whom also He constituted the ages; who, being the out-raying [effulgence] of His glory, and the exact reproduction of His essence, and sustaining, guiding, and propelling all things by the word of His power, having made purification of sins, sat down on the right hand of the Majesty on high; having become by so much superior to the angels as He has inherited a more excellent name than they.

The New Testament in Modern English (J. B. Phillips), 1958

God, Who gave to our forefathers many different glimpses of the truth in the words of the prophets, has now, at the end of the present age, given us the Truth in the Son. Through the Son God made the whole universe, and to the Son He has ordained that all creation shall ultimately belong. This Son, Radiance of the glory of God, flawless Expression of the nature of God, Himself the Upholding Principle of all that is, effected in person the reconciliation between God and Man and then took His seat at the right hand of the Majesty on high—thus proving Himself, by the more glorious Name that He has won, far greater than all the angels of God.

The New English Bible. New Testament, 1961

1 WHEN IN FORMER TIMES God spoke to our forefathers, he spoke
2 in fragmentary and varied fashion through the prophets. But in this final age he has spoken to us in the Son whom he has made heir to the
3 whole universe, and through whom he created all orders of existence: the Son who is the effulgence of God's splendour and the stamp of God's very being, and sustains the universe by his word of power.
4 When he had brought about the purgation of sins, he took his seat at the right hand of Majesty on high, raised as far above the angels, as the title he has inherited is superior to theirs.

The Jerusalem Bible, 1966

At various times in the past and in various different ways, God spoke to our ancestors through the prophets; but in our own time, the last days, he has spoken to us through his Son, the Son that he has appointed to inherit everything and through whom he made everything there is. He is the radiant light of God's glory and the perfect copy of his nature, sustaining the universe by his powerful command; and now that he has destroyed the defilement of sin, he has gone to take his place in heaven at the right hand of divine Majesty. So he is now as far above the angels as the title which he has inherited is higher than their own name.

Some hold translations not unlike to be
The wrong side of a Turkey tapestry.
—James Howell, "On Translations"

CHAPTER 34 *Is Translation Possible?*

The introduction to the New English Bible New Testament recognizes that "every intelligent translation is in a sense a paraphrase." The difficulty of translation from one language into another is far greater than is widely understood. The translator who is sensitive to this difficulty finds himself specially confronted by it, of course, in translating literary material such as the passage in the foregoing chapter, where the original mode of conceptualizing is remote from ours and was a special one even in its day. The translation difficulty is present, however, even in material that seems entirely pedestrian.

The word "dog" covers a variety of species varying from, say, a Chihuahua to a Saint Bernard. Finding a formal dictionary equivalent in another language is very easy. Suppose, however, that I am trying to tell an Eskimo who has seen only one kind of dog about my various neighbors, one of whom has a Chihuahua and another a Saint Bernard. Assume, even, that my knowledge of the Eskimo language is perfect and that my fluency in it leaves nothing to be desired: it does not follow I shall be able to communicate to the Eskimo a convincing, let alone an adequate account of the canine state of affairs in my neighborhood. I would begin with size, of course, and it would not be difficult to get an imaginative Eskimo to take in the notion that in my part of the world there are some curiously little and some astonishingly large dogs; but size constitutes only a very small part of the difference in the canine scenery.

Even the most everyday language, moreover, is concerned with much more than the mere naming of objects. It is concerned with relations and functions, and these introduce a much more grave translation difficulty. Even the word "mother," than which there is surely no more fundamental word in any language on earth, can convey different overtones in the minds of many New Yorkers today from those it would always create in the minds of medieval English villagers. The biological function of a mother has not changed but the modern mother in New York, whose children may see her returning home each evening, smartly dressed for her day's work as a stenographer in Manhattan, might not at all easily reproduce in their minds the image of a mother that the medieval villagers would conjure up, a presence so much associated with home and hearth that the latter would be all but inconceivable to them apart from it.

For a novelist today to note that a woman applied lipstick in public would mean no more than if he were to mention that she combed her hair in private; but in some Victorian settings the same observation might well be an obvious literary device, a neat shorthand euphemism for explaining that the woman was a prostitute engaged in the act of advertizing her trade. Indeed, even today, in England, to say of a woman that you had seen her the previous day on the street could mean only the worst, while in the United States it would be as inconsequential as if you were to say, in England, that you had seen her in the street.

Most people think they understand well enough what it means to talk of an Arab's fourth wife. They note that the custom in our culture is to have one wife and that in other cultures the number of wives is apparently different. They may even call to mind that in Spain the possession of a car is still something of a social distinction, and that a Volkswagen may be driven by a liveried chauffeur, while in California even the possession of four large cars by a middle class family would not be accounted particularly remarkable. There is no satisfactory analogy, however, between polygamy and monogamy on the one hand and, on the other, a Californian's four cars and a Spaniard's single one. The relation between an Arab's fourth wife and her husband may be in some respects and in some cases like the relation between a Californian's fourth car and himself; but if so, there the resemblance ends, and the difference begins. *All* domestic relationships in a polygamous society are affected by the fact that the society is polygamous, and to understand the full consequences of such differences requires more imagination, to say nothing of more information, than most of us can hope to possess. So our picture of the situation is likely to be wrong all the way through.

Or again, take an apparently simple question of transportation. In 1964, on the Athonite peninsula of Greece, I lodged at the monastery at Karies and inquired that night how I could get the following day to Vatopedi, a monastery a few miles distant, on the northern shore, and how long it would take. My monastic host replied that it would not take long, being only a morning's journey; but he insisted, rather severely, I thought, that I rise early—five o'clock—so as to have breakfast and be ready for the mule that would be provided for me. There was no *formal* difficulty in communication. My questions were quite clear to him and his answers to me. There was apparently, however, much misunderstanding, for I rose at five sharp, was given a demitasse of coffee called breakfast, and awaited the mule, which arrived at ten sharp and carried me to the monastery at one o'clock in the afternoon. The difference is not merely that if I had told the monk that I had taken the whole morning to get from Mexico City to New York, he might well have supposed the distance to be about ten miles; the difference must include the fact that I took a more literalistic view of time than he did, as well as a host of other facts that make "a morning's journey" a very different experience in that still extremely medieval part of rural Greece where the transportation alternatives are foot and mule, from what it is in the United States where the more obvious alternatives would be bus and plane. If, ignorant of this, I were called upon to improve upon a seventeenth-century English Bible translation, I might well be tempted to update "a day's journey" by rendering it "a day's trip"; but my attempt, far from thereby clarifying the meaning, would actually obscure it. With "a day's journey" there might be just sufficient hint of archaism to suggest to the reader that he must not think of modern transportation. He might perhaps think of a mule trip in the High Sierras. True, he would still be far from having in his mind an image either of the tedium of a muleback journey in the Middle East or of its charm. Still less could he imagine the difficulty of coaxing anyone native to that region of the world to begin any action whatsoever at any set time. Nevertheless, he would not be on notice from the translator that he was free to equate a journey in biblical times with a modern trip anywhere in the United States, even by mule or husky.

Attitude is so bound up with language as to present the translator with another curiously intricate problem. An Anglophile American might even say, "God save the Queen"; but no one who said, "God save our Queen" could be American. Everyone who has had any experience of writing English for both sides of the Atlantic knows that the correct translation into British English of the phrase "modern democracies such as the United States and Britain" is "modern democracies such as Great Britain and the United States."

That old German university phenomenon, the *ewige Student,* is literally translated "eternal student"; but since that *might* be interpreted by some Americans as an encomium rather than a reproach, the translator may resort to a more specific turn of phrase. I used, in a book published in the United States, the phrase "perpetual sophomore" to designate a certain type of person who matures intellectually up to a point and then never seems to get beyond it. When I came to revise the book for a British edition, however, I found I had to "translate" my own American English phrase because not only is there no category in English universities to correspond to the American sophomore; there could not well be one, since the normal undergraduate course is three years, not four, and the first year undergraduate is called, as in America, a freshman. To say "perpetual freshman," however, would introduce a new idea not intended at all, namely, one who never gets beyond his first year at college, which is not meant. Since at the English universities there is no particular designation used for undergraduates in their second or middle year, and since at Oxford and Cambridge the word "student" is not customarily applied to undergraduates and is even applied in another and technical sense to what Americans would call "faculty members" at one of the societies [1] of which the University of Oxford is composed, the best "translation" I could devise was "academic Peter Pan."

When a modern American reader finds the word "rabbi" in the story of a medieval Jewish ghetto in Europe, he may instinctively think of his friend, the man who is in charge of affairs at the local Reform temple or synagogue and whose function both in the community and among his people is not radically different from that of an Anglican rector or Presbyterian pastor in the same community and among his people. The function of the medieval rabbi in a Jewish ghetto in Europe, however, was so fundamentally different that the use of the same word to designate him is, however inevitable a choice for the translator, extremely misleading, to say the least. Again, when the date of Aristotle's birth is stated as 384 B.C., and that of Maimonides as A.D. 1135, a Jew cannot strictly allow the former,[2] and he cannot possibly allow the latter at all, since hidden in it is a specifically Christian confessional attitude: *anno domini,* "in the year of [our] Lord [Jesus Christ]."

"It is only to a very limited extent that linguistic signs can be exchanged without alteration of meaning," wrote Professor A. D. Ritchie in the early days of the philosophical movement called logical positivism.[3] True as this has been seen to be even in everyday language, the difficulty of translating intricate biblical concepts is peculiarly great. The story is told of a Scottish Presbyterian missionary to China in the old days who, not having acquired a mastery of the language, had to use the services of an interpreter. "The Lord God Almighty," he enunciated, "is Omnipotent, Omniscient, Omnipresent, and Infinite in Mercy and Compassion." He awaited the interpreter's rendering of his catechetical instruction. The interpreter, however, knowing there was no Chinese equivalent for the word "God," let alone for the highly theological concepts attached to it by the Scottish catechist, paused for a moment. Then he announced his

---

[1] These are mostly called colleges; yet in this particular case the term "college" cannot be used because it is officially *Aedes Christi,* Christ's House, usually called Christ Church and colloquially called "The House," and those dons who at colleges would be called Fellows cannot be so called, because their counterparts are partly nonecclesiastics and partly ecclesiastics who are canons of the Cathedral which, at Oxford, Christ Church happens also to be. "Translation" difficulties are formidable even within the same language!

[2] The modern Jewish convention is the use of the letters B.C.E., that is, "before the Christian era."

[3] A. D. Ritchie, *Essays in Philosophy* (London: Longmans Green, 1948), p. 72.

translation into Chinese, which might have been rendered back into English as follows: "Reverend gentleman says you are very well." Not a very adequate translation, perhaps; but better, no doubt, than any attempt at a literal rendering. There is really no strict literal translation of anything. Even "bread and wine" does not translate straightforwardly from a Latin language into English, for in Latin countries bread and wine constitute the very basis of life, while in the United States the latter is a luxury, and the former, being little more than the negative pole of a sandwich, does not have the fundamental function it has in, say, Italy or France, where it is still recognizably "the staff of life."

When we come to look at a biblical passage such as the one in the preceding chapter which, even for the Bible, is a very special one, we find enormous difficulties besetting the translator's path. For instance, literally, the Greek warrants only "in son," without even the peculiarity of a capital S. The translator cannot possibly write that, for it is not even idiomatic English. He must decide what sort of article he is to use. If he wishes, he can use an indefinite article; but this could suggest that the writer to the Hebrews was talking about one of many avatars of deity of which this happened to be one that constituted a distinguished case. The translator may feel he dare not do this, since he thinks he knows very well for many reasons that the writer did not mean anything of the sort. He may think the writer to have been wicked or mistaken for not thinking along such lines; but if he knows the writer would have said that the son to whom he referred was Very God, the Logos, the Unique Son, the Only Son, the Full and Final and Perfect Revelation of God, the Deity Incarnate who shows that all previous notions of deification and incarnation have been mere dreams, then he must translate to take account of this intention. So he may say "his (i.e., God's) Son," capitalizing the noun, since to be the only earthly son of God is surely a distinction that warrants an initial capital letter, if ever it is warranted. The translator, wishing neither to go so far as to introduce a "his" where there is none, nor yet merely to copy the solution of a classical English version, may put "the Son," preserving the notion of uniqueness that is inseparable from the context. Some translators may feel, on the other hand, that they have no right to put more than an indefinite article; yet the indefinite article is no more warranted than the definite. An ingenious rendering is the Westminster Version's: "who is Son"; but while the context abundantly justifies this, the translator must ask himself whether the text justifies it at all.

Those portions of the Bible that treat of philosophical ideas or raise theological questions are more than ordinarily troublesome. To understand them, not only must one know the antecedent history of ideas behind the word to be translated; one must also know of their subsequent history. Take, for instance, the word "sin." In the Middle Ages was developed a penitential system entailing a sort of calculus of offenses and the penalties attached to them. Certain offenses were accounted mortal, for they were said to kill the soul, while others were called venial, since they, though they injured the soul, did not destroy it. Within such a system, offenses varied in gravity, and each offense was a *peccatum*, a sin. One could therefore admit to having committed two mortal and seventeen venial sins, the former consisting of certain grave acts and the latter of acts accounted less grave, for example, two thefts of a substantial amount each, and seventeen minor pilferings. Modern theologians deplore the fact that most people, when they think of sin, think of it as one of a number of specifiable acts like adultery or theft. That this is not the conception of the biblical writers is easily shown. These writers mean by "sin" a more radical state of mind or attitude.

At first sight, then, it might seem that there ought to be a fairly easy way of expressing this in English so as to eliminate altogether the notion of a catalogue of crimes and peccadilloes, together with all other possible misunderstandings. Suppose we were to say "moral cancer" or else "alienation" instead of "sin." We would then be avoiding the particular mistake into which we are apt to be plunged by the word "sin"; but we should be in danger of falling into other and possibly even worse confusion. For the idea of a "moral cancer" is in several ways too sophisticated to express the biblical writers' mind. The supreme difficulty in trying to get back into the minds of the writers of antiquity lies in divesting ourselves of later cultural sophistications and entering into the simplicity of a more primitive stage of development and thought. The term "alienation," for instance, provides a striking example of the difficulty. Modern religious writers, not least the unlearned ones who pour forth theological verbiage unstintingly almost as though they had invented it, delighting in every new coinage as a child delights in an animal it has never seen before at the zoo, are exceedingly fond of words of this kind. If, instead of writing "now ye say, We see; therefore your sin remaineth," [4] we were to write "now you say, We see; therefore your alienation remaineth," the overtones of modern theological chitchat would get in the way of an understanding of the Bible. The Revised Standard Version has "guilt," which has many advantages yet is not unassailable. It is used, for example, in a highly technical sense in the Roman penitential system as well as in another and very different sense by some modern psychologists. The truth is: no word can really convey the writer's intent without the peril of betraying it. We have seen that even the simple phrase "bread and wine" betrays a contemporary Italian writer's intent. How, then, can a

---

[4] John 9:41 (KJV).

Bible translator avoid, when he is dealing with ideological terms, the betrayal of the original?

We easily appreciate the difficulty of translating English ideas into the language of the Eskimos, whose thought is very unlike ours. Rendering the word "write" into the language of a wholly illiterate African tribe has taxed missionary ingenuity. We less readily see that rendering the thought of a relatively simple society into the language of our highly complex one may be even more difficult. Our language is older, with roots in the past and successive layers of development. For instance, we use the word "heart" both to designate the organ that is the proper subject of cardiological research and also in a primitive way as though the heart were the seat of the affections. Children are taught to place their hands over the approximate site of their hearts in pledging allegiance to the American flag because this is the traditional way of symbolizing loyalty and affection, somewhat as is done in the Latin Mass at the recitation of the *Confiteor* and the *Domine, non sum dignus.* Such picturesque symbolism and the representational and linguistic use of hearts on St. Valentine's Day are hangovers from a time when the heart was really believed to be the seat of human love and affection. We have abandoned, however, other similar ways of locating the human passions. The Hebrews, for instance, located some of them in the kidneys, to which they attributed knowledge, joy, pain, and pleasure. The psalmist says, according to the King James Version, that "the righteous God trieth the hearts and reins," [5] and, according to the Revised Standard, he tries "the minds and hearts." "Reins" won't do for the modern reader; but "heart" will! If we were fully emancipated from long-established tradition (which happily is not so), hailing God as a cardiologist would seem to us just as ridiculous as does acclaiming him as a urologist. In discarding the one and not the other, the newer version is well adapted to modern ears; but this means that we assimilate a greater range of cultural development than we may always acknowledge, retaining much that is very primitive, sometimes side by side with language designed to express the most recent technological advance.

Ideas develop and are associated with other ideas historically in ways that are much more arbitrary than is commonly understood. For example, you can trace the course of the plague in medieval Europe from the churches dedicated to St. Sebastian and St. Roque.[6] St. Sebastian is believed to have been martyred in the Diocletian persecution at the beginning of the fourth century. He had nothing to do with the plague, and of course he had nothing to do with St. Roque, who lived a thousand

---

[5] Psalms 7:9.
[6] Also Roch (French), Rocco (Italian), and Rochus (Latin).

years later; but according to tradition he was shot with arrows and is usually depicted as a young man so martyred. In ancient times the plague was believed to have been caused by Apollo's arrows. When the plague decimated Europe in the fifteenth century, the plague-stricken did not need to go a thousand years back to classical mythology, however, in order to discover a reason for invoking St. Sebastian as their special patron. They saw him, in paintings and statuary, transfixed with arrows, which immediately and dramatically provided what they took to be evidence of his efficacy as a healer of the plague-stricken: the pain was, as we might say, "like a knife sticking into you," and who better than St. Sebastian knew the meaning of that torment and, in view of his acknowledged sanctity, could be relied upon to be expert in its cure?

St. Roque, according to tradition, was born in Montpellier, France, about 1295. Little is known of his life; but he is said to have stopped, in the course of a journey, at the plague-stricken town of Aquapendente, where he cured many by the sign of the cross, a sign which, according to tradition, he bore on his body as a birthmark, a circumstance that had suggested to him his vocation to a religious life. He went about nursing and healing. Having contracted the disease at Piacenza, he was expelled from the town and withdrew to the forest where he would have died but for a dog who daily brought him a loaf of bread. In art he came to be customarily represented with a dog. His life is so mixed up with legend, however, that his association with the dog probably had much to do with the spread of his cult, for if the sufferers could feel an affinity with the arrows of Sebastian, might not they also see in the emblem of a dog, of whose tooth-marks the nodules produced by the plague would remind them, a sure sign of the presence of yet another saint skilled in the healing art?

The primitive mind works by such associations to an extent we do not easily appreciate, and this creates for us a great barrier in understanding the intent of the biblical writers and a formidable obstacle to translation. A modern example illustrative of the point I am making came to my notice some years ago in Belgium, in the Flemish Premonstratensian Abbey of Tongerloo, where I was shown a statue of the Madonna and Child. Its history is of some interest. Of considerable antiquity, and believed lost at the time of the French Revolution, it turned up in private hands a few decades ago and was restored to its approximate place in the abbey grounds, where a cult soon developed among the local peasantry. The style of the sculpture is Romanesque, with a Byzantine stiffness and formalism. The Child on his Mother's lap is face down and leaning forward to an extent that seems odd to most people. The learned theological doctors of nearby Louvain have an explanation: the statue is intended to exhibit the redemption of the world over and into which the Christ

Child is leaning. The local Flemish peasantry, however, when their children have stomachache, bring them to the Madonna because it seems obvious to them that the reason the Baby Jesus is so placed is because he has that commonest of all infant ills, wind. The rich bankers from Brussels laugh or are shocked at this, thinking it very unseemly for the Divine Infant to be so afflicted; but in fact, of course, the whole idea accords particularly well with biblical ways of thought. In Hebrew *ruach* expresses both wind and spirit, both the breath that is inhaled and exhaled by our lungs and the Spirit of God that is called by the same name because it behaves like wind, blowing "where it listeth." This notion accords with one of the Genesis stories, which relates that the Lord God breathed into man's nostrils "the breath of life; and man became a living soul." [7] So the symbolism in the Madonna and Child statue might be accounted peculiarly fitting, since in traditional Christian theology the principle is well established that God sends forth the Holy Spirit, and that Holy Spirit proceeds, according to the tradition of the Latin Church, from the Father *and* the Son. The Flemish peasantry are closer to the Bible than either the learned doctors of Louvain or the rich bankers from Brussels!

By the same token, it may be argued that, admirable as are the great literary skill, immense scholarship, and extreme care that are put into the translation of the Bible, they do not necessarily result in an improvement in popular understanding of the Bible commensurate with the labor the translators lavish upon their literary achievement. To bring biblical ideas from ancient Palestine into the cottages of today's peasants, the palaces of today's kings, or even the offices of today's professors, is not really within the power of any man's literary art. Herein lies a profound truth in the characteristic doctrine of the Reformation that the Bible is not everyman's book in the sense that it can be read as we today would read the neighborhood paper; even less is it a book to be rabbinically dissected according to this or that exegetical school.[8] It is everyman's book in the sense that through it the Spirit of God may blow the elusive Wind that bears the insights of antiquity through the clouds of the ages; kindle the ensconced Light that quickens the mind with sudden comprehension of what matters and what matters not; and ignite the mysterious Fire that spreads the biblical message in all its intimacy and inwardness from loving heart to loving heart to the infinite enrichment of our human condition and (as Christians think) the attainment of eternal life.

The perfecting of the translator's art and the sharpening of the biblical

---

[7] Genesis 2:7 (KJV).

[8] Against such notions stands the Reformation doctrine of the *testimonium Spiritus Sancti.*

scholar's critical tools are indispensable. Truly religious men and women will always applaud them as well as use them, for they are surely the very instruments of grasping the literature such men and women revere above all other human utterance. Yet even the faultier renderings may carry, in their own way, the Breath, the Light, and the Fire that the Bible sees as the Spirit of God and so, though remote from the original, re-create in a new idiom the meaning and truth that the original, in its own way, once expressed. So it is that the English Bible as it has developed through various forms has acquired a power peculiar to itself and unknown beyond the borders of the English-speaking world. So it is, too, that the Latin Version, with which our story began, carried and carries still, notwithstanding both contemporary vernacularizing fashions and the distance of Latin from the Hebrew original, a power that has enabled it, after transforming the face of Europe, to continue to utter even in our own day, in sonorous simplicity, the Breath of Life, the Light of Understanding, and the Fire of Love: *Emittes Spiritum tuum, et creabuntur; et renovabis faciem terrae.*[9]

---

[9] Psalms 104:30 (Vulg.) ; 105:30 (KJV).

All that is literature seeks to
communicate power: all that is not literature
seeks to communicate knowledge.—Thomas De Quincey,
"Letters to a Young Man"

CHAPTER 35 *Biblical Literature and Creative Power*

The Bible, though it has evoked the boundless reverence and affection of many, elicits from others antagonism and contempt. Nor should anyone suppose the latter to be confined to the present day. On a shelf in my office in the School of Philosophy building in the University of Southern California, which also houses the Rare Book Collection of that school, and where some of the present work has been written, is a fine thick folio edition of St. Augustine's *De Civitate Dei,* published in 1505. It bears the signature of its owner, the celebrated German philosopher Arthur Schopenhauer, and extensive marginal notes in his hand. Schopenhauer takes the great Latin Church Father to have been grievously misguided in having exchanged his love of Cicero and the other pagan writers of antiquity for the Bible. He thinks the saint's judgement has been warped by the exchange and that in his thought he is "tortured miserably and only for the purpose of saving Jewish mythology." [1] Such an antipathy to the Bible is by no means rare. "For St. Augustine all true starting points define the first principles of Christian revelation; for Schopenhauer the same starting points make the validity of Christian revelation inconceivable." [2]

The precise extent of the literary and other influence of the Bible is incalculable and therefore unverifiable. There is nevertheless abundant evidence that it has been immense. Whether we rate the Bible high, accounting it either for literary or for theological reasons of paramount importance in the education of mankind, or rate it very low, even deploring it as a pernicious influence, we cannot escape the fact that, for good or ill, it has determined to an astounding degree the literary development of the Western world. It has also affected, to a far greater extent than is generally grasped, the literary fortunes of the East. Not

[1] "Scilicet ut salva sit mythologica Judaica, Noster misere torquetur." For a description of the book and comments on Schopenhauer's marginalia, see Martin Woods, "The *Folio Augustini* of Schopenhauer" in *Coranto* (Los Angeles: University of Southern California), IV (Fall, 1966), 17-23.
[2] *Ibid.*

only in modern times and among underdeveloped societies has it been the means whereby languages have been committed to writing; it has been long ago the occasion of the birth of written languages, without which no literature could have begun at all. For instance, the desire for a vernacular Bible brought about the reduction to writing of the Armenian, Ethiopic, Georgian, and Slavonic tongues. In other cases, though the part played by the desire for the vernacular Bible was not quite so radical as to be the very cause of the existence of the written language, the advent of the Bible was nevertheless the means of injecting such new life into the language as to stimulate the literature in spectacular ways. When the Bible came to Egypt and Syria, for example, the Coptic and Syrian languages had ceased to have any literary existence since the days of Alexander the Great. With the Bible they took a new lease on life and a new kind of life. From a purely literary standpoint they were reborn.

Of course the Bible has inspired literary as well as other follies and vulgarities. Nothing can be deduced from that reflection. For there is no power in the world, literary or otherwise, that has not been abused. The creative power of the Bible, like the creative power of all literature, can be put to evil purposes, as the most beautiful love lyric on earth can be turned into pornography: all you need is a dirty enough mind or a sufficiently unscrupulous will. The Bible has been indeed sheep's clothing to many a wolf. The question is, rather: Why have the most ravening, ruthless, and dangerous wolves chosen it as their disguise? Those who are closest to the Church know only too well that there is no need to go to the age of the Borgias to find ecclesiastical turpitude. By far the wickedest men I have ever known have been churchmen, and for the most part well-accepted churchmen at that. The power of the Bible has indubitably helped them in their evil as it has advanced others in good. Perhaps it is the awareness of this that makes the greatest, wisest, and holiest of men, when they seek to create great art, go obliquely rather than directly to the Bible for their themes. Milton's *Paradise Lost* is one of the few very great works of literature that successfully takes the Bible as its direct source of inspiration and here we must not forget how conspicuously and notoriously its sequel, *Paradise Regained,* fails by the same method. Dante's Commedia, though it could not have been written without the background of the Bible, makes much more subtle use of it. Spenser and Bunyan, each in his own way, can be called biblical allegorists, of course; but they use the Bible as a fount of the creative power that enables them to produce a new kind of literature. They do not in any sense copy the structure of the Bible or of a part of it, except in very limited ways. The Bible is, indeed, so uncannily close to life that the literary artist who slavishly took it as his model would court failure as surely as would the novelist who took his characters straight from life without benefit of the literary techniques that are necessary to make them credible. The literary shortcomings of the Bible, indeed, are due to its artlessness with which so much of it moves between God and the clod. The Bible is a literature; but it is less a literature than a fount of literature.

In the course of our study we have had many opportunities to see manifestations of the obvious and close connection of the Bible with the Synagogue and the Church.[3] We have seen, too, that the Bible, though it may be accounted more than anything else the undoubted charter of all Christians, emerged in the sixteenth-century biblical Renaissance as a peculiar Reformation heritage. Indeed, such is the traditional affection for the Bible in the hearts of heirs of the Reformation that, despite their obvious confessional bond with all their fellow Christians, Roman and Eastern Orthodox, they have also a curious affinity with their Jewish brethren that transcends the radical theological differences between Judaism and Christianity. As the Jews are appositely called "the People of the Book," since the Tanak is their classic national literature as well as their Sacred Writings, so to those Christians who share in the Reformation heritage might properly be accorded a similar designation which in their case would include, of course, the New besides the Old Testament, as well as a different understanding of the meaning of both.

The role of the Bible in Church and Synagogue, however, does not by any means exhaust its influence. The Bible has also a function far removed from that associated with the corporate life of any community. It is, if not everyman's book, certainly at least the book of every pilgrim. For no one can read the Bible intelligently without seeing that, whatever function may be attributed to it in the corporate worship of this or that religious body, it is nothing if not also, and perhaps preeminently, a literature that speaks to the individual in his existential loneliness. It speaks, above all, to the needy spirit of the pilgrim whose feet are weary with life's road yet who is acutely aware of the preciousness of its every inch. Not least does it speak to those who are tired of the follies of the world and, disgusted at the turpitudes of the Church and of organized religion, are become aware of the power and freedom of the individual human spirit to listen to and commune with the Eternal:

> O Lord, open thou my lips
> and my mouth shall show forth thy praise.
> For thou hast no delight in sacrifice;
> were I to give a burnt offering, thou wouldst not be pleased.

[3] For a brief account of some aspects of this subject from one important standpoint, see Robert M. Grant, *The Bible in the Church* (New York: The Macmillan Company, 1958).

> The sacrifice acceptable to God is a broken spirit;
> a broken and contrite heart, O God, thou wilt not despise.[4]

Without the Bible neither Church nor Synagogue could survive. They would be shorn of all the meaning with which they have been invested throughout the ages. They would be deprived of their very life. Yet though neither Church nor Synagogue can do without the Bible, the Bible does have a life apart from them.

Indeed, the influence of the Bible among the most profound skeptics may be as great as, perhaps even greater than, it is among believing Christians and observant Jews. Professor Fairchild reminds us that Rudyard Kipling was anything other than an orthodox or even a believing Christian, for having more sympathy with Indian mysticism, he did not even account the Christian faith more "true" than other faiths. Kipling, for all his flag-waving and disparaging observations about "lesser breeds without the law," recognized that the latter could sometimes, somehow or other, as Professor Fairchild puts it, "behave like Englishmen." "So fuzzy-wuzzy is 'a pore benighted 'eathen but a first class fightin' man.' "[5] Through all the attitude attributed to him as "an admirer of Emersonian self-reliance," however, run strong currents of biblical language, more especially that of the Old Testament. He talks of a "Word," the "Lord of Hosts," a "Stranger within my gate," and he even has a line that is a prayer to be purged from all

> heresies of thought and speech and pen
> That bid me judge him otherwise than I am judged. Amen! [6]

Nineteenth-century "humanists" such as Kipling do indeed endlessly echo the Bible, yet the more fiercely anti-Christian poets are still more steeped in it. Professor Fairchild, in a discerning aside, writes: "As befits his Methodist ancestry, Kipling is deeply saturated in the Bible; but Swinburne, far more violently and overtly anti-Christian, is even more Biblical in language and matter." [7] Not only is Swinburne; even Shelley, who was expelled from his Oxford college for refusing to disavow his authorship of a pamphlet he had circulated on "The Necessity of Atheism," is not free from vestiges of the ideas and echoes of the language of the inescapable book.

[4] From the *Miserere,* Psalms 51:15-17.
[5] Hoxie Neale Fairchild, *Religious Trends in English Poetry* (New York: Columbia University Press, 1962), V, 131.
[6] *Ibid.,* pp. 129 ff.
[7] *Ibid.,* p. 133.

Of course if a child should be carefully sheltered from exposure to all biblical influence, he could not grow up to reflect it. Such an upbringing, common in many societies on our planet, is possible even for those of the English-speaking heritage; yet within this heritage it would not be easy to have a literary type of education and escape a deep biblical influence, however unconsciously this influence might be imbibed. I venture to suggest that the vitality of the Bible is so prodigious that it has an ineluctable literary force on all who come within even shouting distance of its enchantments. Its effects do not in the least necessarily depend upon any particular exegesis or midrash; they are independent of all doctrinal interpretations and every confessional stance.

Even a self-consciously militant atheism superimposed upon an education so godless as to have been designed to shelter the child from all exposure to religious ideas does not always wholly succeed in destroying the literary influence of the English Bible. I once had a professional acquaintance of such an upbringing and persuasion who taught classical Greek, in which she was a recognized scholar. An unbaptized Gentile, she decided one year that for her beginners' class it might be fun to try the experiment of seeing what they could do with the New Testament. Her reasoning was that though it was indeed a mythology inferior to the classical ones that gave her greatest pleasure, it was written in an easy sort of Greek on which beginners might whet their teeth before proceeding to something worthwhile. The authenticity of her ignorance of Christian practice may be judged from the fact that when the class arrived at the fifth chapter of Matthew and everyone seemed to be translating fluently at sight with no preparation, she could not understand why, nor explain their ill-concealed amusement. I am not even sure that she ever found out. I did only because I had her students as my unsolicited informers. She had been sheltered from the fact that the majority of children of even the most nominal Christian upbringing have a tendency to learn the Beatitudes by heart. The point I wish to make is that even in this rather extreme case there were not infrequent evidences of the literary influence of the Bible. She talked of wolves in sheep's clothing, of casting pearls before swine, of the poor who are always with us, and even occasionally uttered such unoriginal observations as that a soft answer turns away wrath. No doubt she picked up such expressions from others and repeated them without thinking of or even knowing their source, perhaps somewhat in the manner of the man who was taken to see *Hamlet* and, being afterwards asked what he thought of it, replied that it was a fine play though there seemed to be too many quotations in it.

The absurdity of such an extreme ignorance of the Bible is obvious. It is true that the Bible can be used for dogmatic purposes, and as though it were the property of this or that community or church. The claim that the Bible can be *properly* understood only in the context of a specific religious faith or, as many would put it, "in the midst of the Church," ought to command the sort of respect that in our pluralistic society is due to all religious faith and feeling that may not be our own; but in any case the Bible, in its English dress and as the greatest English classic, can be ignored only if we are willing to condemn future generations to incomprehension of a very great deal of the literature of our English tongue. Dr. Cleland Boyd McAfee, alluding to this danger nearly sixty years ago, cited a plea made by Nicholas Murray Butler, then President of Columbia University, speaking as President of the National Educational Association, for the reading and study of the Bible in public schools. The ground of President Butler's plea was not a religious but a literary one. A child cannot acquire the understanding of English and American literature that every English-speaking child should have without some reading and study of the Bible. "Not only the allusions, but the whole tone and bias of many English authors," wrote Dr. McAfee in reporting President Butler's observations on this subject, "will become to one who is ignorant of the Bible most difficult and even impossible of comprehension." Dr. McAfee went on to acknowledge how "monstrous" it would be if the public schools were to become "sectarian or proselytizing"; nevertheless, he insisted, the Bible is not a sectarian book but a book of the "greatest literature." [8]

Strange to most of us today is the picture of New England life depicted by Mrs. Harriet Beecher Stowe in *Old-Town Folks,* where Grandfather, after breakfast, begins the family's day by reading a chapter of the Bible. The Bible, she tells us, "was for the most part read twice a day in every family of any pretensions to respectability, and it was read as a reading book in every common school, in both cases without any attempt at explanation." The Puritans in both England and New England were so nourished on the Bible that an understanding of them is entirely impossible without a considerable knowledge of it. "I think no New Englander brought up under the regime established by the Puritans," writes the same author, "could really estimate how much of himself had actually been formed by this constant face-to-face intimacy with Hebrew literature." All this everyone knows in one way or another; but what it really meant, and the enormous and profound effect it has on literature of the period, is not easy to recapture.

What is increasingly underestimated, however, is the effect of the Bible on our literature during much less obviously "religious" periods in the

---

[8] C. B. McAfee, *The Greatest English Classic* (New York: Harper & Brothers, 1912), pp. 285-86.

history of the English-speaking peoples. In poetry the stream of biblical influence is especially strong and deep. Even in the least "religious" periods and, as we have already seen earlier in the present chapter, in the most unlikely poets, echoes of the Bible are clear. In the great stream of Victorian poetry, in Tennyson, Wordsworth, and the Brownings, for example, the biblical allusions are numerous, important, and inescapable. Sometimes Tennyson's poetry is a very paraphrase of Scripture, for instance, his Enoch Arden's words:

> Is He not yonder in those uttermost
> Parts of the morning? if I flee to these
> Can I go from Him? and the sea is His,
> The sea is His: He made it.

Here verses, one from each of two psalms,[9] coalesce and emerge in a dress so like the one they wear in the English Bible that, far from being new, it can hardly even be said to be refurbished or redesigned.

What would anyone who did not know the Bible make of Tennyson's *Palace of Art?* For example:

> The airy hand confusion wrought,
> Wrote "Mene, mene," and divided quite
> The kingdom of her thought.

The allusion is, of course, to Daniel's vision [10] in which he sees the writing on the wall: MENE, MENE, TEKEL, and PARSIN.[11] Even the current colloquial expression about "seeing the writing on the wall" has its origin in this biblical passage.

Professor Howard Mumford Jones, in his essay entitled "The Bible from a Literary Point of View," [12] remarks upon the difficulty of defining "literature" and "literary," pointing out that "If it be true that literature is the best words in the best order, the telephone directory, clear, succinct, and incomparably organized, is a masterpiece of expository statement." [13] Professor Jones proposes as the chief ingredients of a work of literature the following: "theme, outlook, persons, figure and style. The uses to

[9] Psalms 95:5: "The sea is his, for he made it." Psalms 139:9-10:
> If I take the wings of the morning
> and dwell in the uttermost parts of the sea,
> even there thy hand shall lead me.

[10] Daniel 5:17-31.

[11] Daniel 5:25.

[12] E. R. Goodenough, R. H. Bainton, M. S. Enslin, H. M. Jones, and N. Glueck, *Five Essays on the Bible* (New York: American Council of Learned Societies, 1960).

[13] *Ibid.*, p. 48.

which these components are put and for which they combine we call narrative, drama, lyric, meditation, exposition, persuasion, denunciation and humor." [14] The Bible, he contends, is, judged accordingly, "one of the great primary books in Western literature. The only other members of the class to which it belongs are Homer and the Greek tragic poets." [15] He excludes Plato, whose methods are different and special; he excludes the Norse sagas, the *Niebelungenlied,* and the *Chanson de Roland* because such ethical considerations as are in them are not touched with religion in the same measure or in the incomparable manner of the Bible; and he excludes the other great wisdom books of the West such as the meditations of Marcus Aurelius and Montaigne's essays because they either derive from the Bible, touch life more thinly, or are otherwise clearly inferior.

The literary qualities of the Bible are indubitably striking. The biblical themes of the Bible are vivid and simple. Professor Jones thinks the elemental quality is as primary and often more primitive than that to be found in Homer and the Greek tragic poets.[16] Certainly there is in the Bible none of the endless, labyrinthine type of introspection characteristic of Proust, the subtle intralingual puns of Joyce, the medieval filigree of Dante, or the immaculate fastidiousness of Henry James. Virtues are basic and vices primitive. Men are brave, loyal, faithful, and fearless; they are cunning, cruel, sensual, and hypocritical. Women are heroines and housewives and harlots. They live with the bare elements, the sea, the stars, the desert, the wind, the sun, and the clouds. There is "fighting, farming, a strong sexual urge, and intermittent worship." [17] The men are hunters, shepherds, charioteers, and fishermen. Even wealth is more tangible than it seems on Wall Street. It consists of such things as cattle and asses and fatted fowl, of corn and meal and fine flour. The vigor and realism of the Bible give all these features a simplicity and power that set biblical literature apart from other literatures, even from a purely literary point of view.

In many particulars the Bible is easily outshone by the superior literary merit of other works. The Greeks could portray character with greater artistry and skill, as they could sculpt with an artistry and skill that the Hebrews denied themselves through a religious taboo. The Hebrews were culturally backward compared not only with the Greeks but also with their nearer neighbors, the Egyptians. The biblical writers were not concerned, generally speaking, with chiselling out a fine literary

[14] *Ibid.,* p. 51.
[15] *Ibid.*
[16] *Ibid.,* p. 53.
[17] *Ibid.,* p. 52.

accomplishment. They were not even on the whole much interested in persons in the sense in which, say, a Victorian novelist was. There is no personality cult in the Bible. The New Testament writers focused all their attention, of course, on Jesus, but this is so because the Christian writers invested him with a role that is unique in human history. For Christians the whole Bible is christocentric.

In the Bible, character is not normally exfoliated; it is usually just given without much attempt at literary craftsmanship. The power of the characters lies elsewhere than in their portrayal as characters; it lies in the moral warfare that is presumed to be in progress. The moral grandeur of the Hebrew prophets and the startling proclamation of the Christian apostles and evangelists give the Bible power such as seems to shine through the literary clay, as well as caulking its cracks as a precious ointment might caulk the seams of the rickety boat that had to carry it. St. Paul even suggests a reason why this literary arrangement is suitable to the theme of the Bible. He says, "We have this treasure in earthen vessels, to show that the transcendent power belongs to God and not to us." [18] The work of the biblical authors, whatever be its defects, is anything other than meretricious, studied, or forced. There is certainly no parade of learning, and there is comparatively little exercise of literary skill. It is surely the only literature that comes so close to life without ceasing to be literature, and if generations should arise bereft of the Bible, their plight might well be less literary ignorance than ignorance of life.

[18] II Corinthians 4:7.

INDEX